LEGENDS LIVE at LANCASTER UNIVERSITY
1969–1985

Barry Lucas & Paul Tomlinson

Featuring posters by John Angus
and photos by Geoff Campbell

Paul dedicates this book to his two roadies … Cheryl and Jess.

Barry dedicates this book to his wife Mary, children Moya, Simon and Sergio, and grandchildren Caleb, Santino, Alys and Cara –
see, grandad wasn't always old and grey!

First published in 2017
Second edition 2019
Third edition 2024
by Palatine Books,
Carnegie House,
Chatsworth Road
Lancaster LA1 4SL
www.palatinebooks.com

Copyright © Barry Lucas and Paul Tomlinson

All rights reserved
Unauthorised duplication contravenes existing laws

The right of Barry Lucas and Paul Tomlinson to be identified as the authors of this work has been asserted in accordance with the Copyright, Designs and Patents act 1988

British Library Cataloguing-in-Publication data
A catalogue record for this book is available from the British Library

Paperback ISBN 13: 978-1-910837-49-8

Designed and typeset by Carnegie Book Production
www.carnegiebookproduction.com

Printed and bound by Micropress

The views in this book are those of the authors, and the story is told from their perspective, based on their memories of the events at the time and subsequent research. The publisher cannot be held responsible for the accuracy of the information provided nor give a guarantee that the details are complete and accurate.

Contents

	Introduction by Alan Murray	4
	Foreword by Andy Kershaw	6
ONE	A Moment in Time	8
TWO	Talkin' 'bout my generation	12
THREE	The A–Z	19
FOUR	The Pink Custard Lightshow	325
FIVE	Pushing the Boundaries	330
SIX	Regrets, I've had a few but …	340
SEVEN	The Off Campus Social Centre AKA The Sugar House	348
EIGHT	Lancaster? Where's Lancaster?	356
NINE	Another good night for drunkards	362
	Facts 'n' Stats	387

Introduction by Alan Murray

Lancaster University alumnus.
Former Chief Finance Officer of The Burton Group and Chloride Group.
Former CEO Hanson Group PLC 2002–2007.

Lancaster University opened in 1964 in the middle of a decade that many people regarded as one of the most significant of the twentieth century. In 1961 President Kennedy set the goal of putting a man on the Moon by the end of the decade. The Berlin Wall was constructed in 1961, accelerating tensions in the Cold War. The Vietnam War began in the same year, was to continue through the decade into the 1970s and inspire a younger generation to challenge the reasons for the conflict on a widespread basis. In the field of technology, Concorde made its maiden flight in 1969, and the compact cassette was introduced in 1964. Christian Barnard performed the first heart transplant in 1969, while the contraceptive pill was available from 1960 onwards.

The world of music, and in particular pop music, was not immune to these changes. Going into the 1960s the music scene was a mixture of jazz, skiffle, solo artists and the relatively new rock 'n' roll. The 1960 NME poll winners were Cliff Richard and the Shadows, Elvis Presley, Connie Francis and Gene Vincent. Best single was 'Apache' by the Shadows. There was no mention of LPs, 45s were the medium of choice driven mainly by the demands of radio stations who wanted a three-minute song and no more. By 1970, the NME poll winners had a different look – the Beatles won best LP for 'Let It Be', best single was Mungo Jerry's 'In the Summertime' on the back of their success at the Hollywood (Staffordshire!) Festival, which saw the first UK performance by The Grateful Dead. Richard Branson's Virgin made its appearance that year as a mail order album business. Sales of LPs rocketed in 1970, marking a change in the way artists and the public looked at music. Obviously, LPs allowed bands much more scope to develop their music. Some radio stations and DJ s were key in promoting these changes. In particular, John Peel at Radio 1 was a major influence, ensuring that British and American bands were given the exposure on the airwaves.

With this change in the way artists were recording music came the need to change the way live music was presented. The days of a concert of eight to ten artists on the bill, with no more than twenty minutes for each set, were becoming less common – this was the format of the *NME* poll winners concerts at the Empire Pool, Wembley. Artistes wanted to play music from their albums and it was these same tracks that the fans wanted to hear too. The format of the concert changed to one of two acts (headline and support) with the headline playing for an hour or two. Individual songs could last for the equivalent of the whole side of an album and required much more equipment than in previous years (better PA/instrument amplification and better mixing capabilities). Lighting also became a bigger part of the presentation of the music. A concert became a theatre experience.

In line with the feeling of the time, the 1960s saw more festivals and free concerts. In 1968, the first Isle of Wight festival was held, with T Rex and Fairport Convention headlining. In 1970 the same event saw The Doors, Joan Baez and Jimi Hendrix attract more people than Glastonbury and Live Aid combined. Woodstock was staged in 1969 in New York State and attracted 400,000 people to see the likes of Crosby, Stills, Nash and Young, The Who and Jimi Hendrix. In Hyde Park a series of free concerts were staged: in 1969 Blind Faith played, followed by The Stones; 1970 saw Pink Floyd in the Park playing tracks from *Atom Heart Mother* after their earlier concert there in 1968. The music of the early 1960s had moved on from a three-minute song to longer, more complex music by the end of the decade.

You may ask what all these developments in the music business in the 1960s have got to do with this book and the series of music events that were promoted on the Lancaster campus. Music had become a great part of people's lives, particularly through the second half of the decade. New albums by major artists were eagerly anticipated by the fans. In a pre-internet world, the best way to promote artists and their music was through exposure to a live audience. Record companies almost demanded that bands went on tour and usually with a support band that was on the same label. The number of bands touring in the early 1970s meant that venues had a choice of who to book. Some promoters would handle the whole tour and apart from the municipal venues like the Free Trade Hall in Manchester, Victoria Hall in Stoke-on-Trent and the Empire in Liverpool, they would look to universities and colleges. On the college circuit, Lancaster and Leeds seemed to get the very best bands. Most colleges and universities required that you were signed in by a student if you were to see these bands. By offering open access to students and the public alike, bands knew that they were reaching the most diverse audience with no discrimination. The University itself built a reputation with local people for being open and part of the community which was important at a time when such a small number of people went to university. In the case of Lancaster, being able to see the very best bands on your doorstep was important. If you lived between Preston and Carlisle your choice of music venue was limited without travelling to a major city. In addition, many of the bands liked and requested to play Lancaster which was borne out with multiple appearances by the likes of Eric Clapton and Van Morrison.

This book is a celebration and recollection of the artists and performers at Lancaster between 1969 and 1985, in a period when music seemed to be a much more major part of many people's lives. We hope you enjoy recalling your great nights in the Great Hall at Lancaster University.

Foreword by Andy Kershaw

"Whatever you do, don't book Chuck Berry. He's a bloody nightmare. He turns up with musicians he's never met before, never mind rehearsed with. He plays the absolute minimum. You have to give him cash in his hand before he'll go on stage. And then another bundle of cash, at the side of the stage, before he'll play an encore."

Barry Lucas was giving his advice, over the phone, to a fresh young Entertainments Secretary – me – who had just taken over the job of booking all the bands, and running the concerts at Leeds University. The Refectory at Leeds wasn't just the biggest college venue in the UK but, like Lancaster, a major venue full stop. And I, full of enthusiasm – maybe – had no experience of concert promotion and, at first, little idea of what I was doing. But Leeds University already had a long and proud rock 'n' roll history, and much-admired standards of professionalism, which I was determined to uphold.

So, it was to Barry, over at Lancaster University, to whom I would often turn for guidance. Barry was already something of a legend, a veteran organiser of the Lancaster gigs. And – to my great envy – he'd managed to get himself appointed in that role, a decade earlier, as a full-time employee of the Students' Union. Conversely, and absurd though it was, the Ents Sec. job at Leeds was not even a sabbatical post; I was expected to do my Politics degree at the same time. That was impossible. So, after I became Ents Sec. in March 1980, halfway through my second year, the Politics Department never saw me again.

As venues, Leeds and Lancaster universities had similar capacities – much larger than those of other colleges – so we both had the ability, and the potential ticket sales, to draw the world's biggest bands of the time. Both Leeds and Lancaster also enjoyed a reputation within the live music business for absolute professionalism in the manner in which we ran our concerts. (Even though, in my case – and to visiting bands and road crews – the boss of the Leeds University gigs appeared to be a child of no more than eleven.)

Because of those similarities, many regarded Leeds and Lancaster universities as rivals. I, however, did not. Barry and I would often share our opinions and knowledge about realistic fees for bands, then deploy our combined bargaining muscle and intelligence to bring booking agents to their senses.

There was much else which Leeds and Lancaster shared. You will notice in this book, for example, that the performer who appeared most in the Great Hall at Lancaster during these years was John Martyn. No surprise to me. John was also such a regular with us at Leeds that – as I recall in my autobiography, *No Off Switch* – there was a period in which I began to suspect the dear old thing was living under the Refectory stage. Now, I know the truth: when John wasn't with us, he was – reliably – over in Lancaster.

Barry and I also found ourselves in these dream jobs, at these fabulous venues, in what is now regarded as a golden age for live music – before the era of arena shows, and when even the likes of The Rolling Stones and The Who were still impressed to be playing 2,000 capacity halls.

One only has to skim through the full history here of performers – each and every gig forensically detailed and remembered in this wonderful book – to recognise that Lancaster University hosted, for fifteen years, a definitive "who's who" of rock & roll. (Although, unlike Leeds University, Barry came only close to getting the Stones).

Soon after Barry left the Lancaster job at the end of 1984 and two years after I was obliged to move off into the real world from Leeds, concerts at both great venues became a shadow of their former selves, and would soon fizzle out altogether. There were a number of reasons for this: kids then of college age were not as obsessed with music as we had been; the arrival and domination, from the late 1980s, of digitised and dehumanised Dance music held more appeal for those young people than four or five blokes actually playing music with guitars, drums, bass and keyboards; and the tidy, expanding conspiracy between the legitimised extortionists of the insurance business and the newly flourishing industry of health & safety zealots and killjoys decided that eighteen and nineteen year old kids could not be trusted to run major rock concerts (Oh, yes they could. We did it. And guess what? Nobody died).

Barry Lucas and his Boswell, Paul Tomlinson, have also sprinkled their book with delicious anecdotes about both the delights and horrors of live concert promotion, its characters, its absurdities and implausibility, which give this history – like that of my own at Leeds – the qualities of a mad dream. And although sometimes nudging into nightmare, it's a mad dream that was always, always huge fun, the like of which today's university students will never have the chance to experience, and possibly won't believe.

Simply, you couldn't make it up. And, if you tried to start today what Barry Lucas started at Lancaster and what my predecessors at Leeds started around the same time, the authorities wouldn't let it happen.

Barry and Paul have put together here not just a fascinating account of a rock 'n' roll phenomenon, but a truly important and entertaining cultural and social history.

Now, inspired – and a little shamed by their efforts – I'd better get working on a companion volume about Leeds …

Oh, and I never did book Chuck Berry. Thanks, Barry.

Andy Kershaw

A Moment in Time

ONE

> "The past is a foreign country: they do things differently there."
>
> L. P. Hartley, *The Go-Between*

It was Saturday 25 February 1984 and I was driving down to Manchester Airport to pick up Barry Marshall, one of the top music promoters in the UK. He was flying up to see one of the venues on his tour of Tina Turner – Lancaster University. Barry Marshall was one of the few promoters I hadn't dealt with before, yet here he was, placing one of the hottest acts in the world on a small, north of England college stage. How on earth did that happen? How did a small university of 4,500 students, in a small city of 60,000, nowhere near a major conurbation, become one of the most famous venues in the country? How had the mighty Leeds University been displaced as the major college venue in the UK? Why were artists from all over the world willing to play in a place they had never heard of?

Well it's a story worth telling because, for a moment in time, Lancaster was at the forefront of popular music – it was the stuff of legends.

We need, first, to go back to 1968 when, to much amazement – certainly that of my teachers in Leeds Modern and Cheltenham Grammar schools – I gained a place at the University of Lancaster. "Why choose Lancaster?" I hear you ask. Well, I had been forcibly transported, two years earlier, by my parents, to the savage, uncivilised world known as 'The South'. In the summer of 1966 – notable for many great events such as Henry Cooper versus Cassius Clay, England versus the mighty West Indies (Sobers et al), Sir Donald Campbell's tragic death, and the little matter of an English football team actually winning something – I was exiled against my will from my beloved Yorkshire to the barren wastes of Cheltenham. From Leeds, where I was to have been emancipated from school uniform in the sixth form (you would actually be allowed to wear your own, fashionable clothes), to Cheltenham, where I found out, to my howls of disbelief, that I was expected, nay ordered, to wear a mortar board and gown in the sixth form. And that from ten yards outside your front door, through the centre of town, two buses, to ten yards from the school gates! The S.S., cunningly disguised as school prefects, ensured this with the ultimate deterrent of Saturday morning detention. This was 1966 and the height of the Swinging Sixties, for goodness' sake!

Anyway, I ended up there, and my parents, unbelievably selfishly, would not let a fifteen year old live on his own in Leeds and visit them in the school holidays. Would you believe it? So here was I, applying through UCCA, more in hope than expectation, for a university place. My English teacher said that I should get an 'A' level. My History teacher said, "Lucas, your low animal cunning might get you a pass." But that was it. So I had a go, for a laugh; three years at uni was better than working and a grant (remember them?) was enough to live on, and with a beer-top-up job in the vacations that would give me a three year sabbatical to work out what I wanted to do with the rest of my life. So, six choices of uni to fill in: well, no problem with five northern ones straight away. All had to be 'second class' as I couldn't read English at the old, established universities because I had dropped Latin at thirteen (bored stupid) and you had to have 'O' level Latin to read English at those, but which was to be the sixth? "Anyone know a northern university?" I asked in the sixth form common room. "Lancaster," some joker yelled, to great amusement. So Lancaster it was, sixth and last desperate choice; not Yorkshire but at least it was in the North. The Deputy Headmaster, and Careers Advisor, didn't even know that Lancaster had a university. He thought I was going to St Martin's: "a good teacher training college there," he announced knowingly, although I could see in his eyes the terror that I might be contemplating joining the ranks of his noble profession.

And surprise, surprise (thanks, Cilla), Lancaster was the only one to offer me a place. I like to think it was their foresight. After all it was before the results were out, but, more probably, it was a reflection of their own desperation to fill places, bordering on gratitude. Although to be fair to them I did get two 'A's and a 'B' (yah boo sucks to you Cheltenham Grammar School!).

So there I was, eighteen years old, suitcase, rucksack, falling out onto Lancaster's desolate railway station. It was raining, of course. In Intro Week it always did. Lancaster weather has been nothing if not predictable over forty odd years. "Welcome to Lancaster" – rain! (But "exams are here" – eighty degrees Costa Cauldron.) Well here I was, skinny but suntanned. I had just returned early from our first family holiday abroad. Dad had booked a fortnight in Lloret de Mar as obviously he didn't think I would pass those exams either. But were they going to give up the second week? No! I had to return early and alone – Sir Charles Carter would not agree to postponing Freshers' for a week. I actually asked him, honest – I rang the University admissions to see if I could arrive a week later, but no chance. So one day Spanish sun, chilled sangria, paella, the next Lancashire rain, warm Mitchell's beer and hotpot.

Lancaster station resembled a scene from one of those WW2 evacuation movies. It seemed like hundreds of lost teenagers, suitcases, carrier bags and bewildered faces (all it needed was name tags and gas mask boxes around our necks).

"Lonsdale College – anybody in Lonsdale?" called out two worldly looking second years.

"Yes."

"Off campus?"

"Yes."

"Where?"

"South Road."

"Never heard of it. Bus for campus!"

Never heard of it, where on earth had those unfeeling monsters in University House stuck me? South Road – I could picture it, some desolate track leading to a Cold Comfort Farm, miles towards Preston. "University – what University?" I had no choice but to get a cab, thank heavens he'd heard of it. It was a ten shilling ride via Morecambe, Carnforth, Scafell Pike and Galgate but finally I arrived at South Road (I was later to discover it was a ten-minute walk from the railway station).

The newly opened Central Hall

One of my early experiences seemed to confirm the worries that I had about 'Cold Comfort Farm', or the University of Lancaster as it was known to the outside world. Students were designated a 'moral tutor' to look after their welfare and sort out their personal problems. To show you how ridiculous it was, I became one in the late '70s and had six or seven very nervous first years to give guidance to. Anyway, in 1968, as a rather 'nervous' fresher myself, I was instructed to go and meet my moral tutor, who turned out to be a rather large, African mathematician called Dr O'Doom. I knocked reluctantly on his door and waited for some African Christopher Lee to call, ominously, "Enter". But Freshers' Week was only half way through, the best was yet to come.

My first experience of the pulsating Lancaster University social scene followed and what an unforgettable experience that was! It probably, subconsciously, determined my future career. That first evening was the Lonsdale College Freshers' Disco in the refectory. A bit of bread and cheese, a sausage roll and as many pieces of pork pie as you could eat, or smuggle in your pockets for later. Oh and a glass of revolting, sweet, warm, white wine and – would you believe it – from Spain, where I'd been thirty-six hours before. Now, it was just about drinkable in the balmy, evening heat of the Med., but in the rain-swept wilds of Lancashire? The disco started and from nowhere came hordes of praying mantis disguised as third years. They descended to have the pick of the innocent young freshers. Unfortunately, not a 'cougar' to be seen, the girls were fair game; us boys were, unfortunately, safe. After an hour of peering over, or through, the ranks of enemy storm troopers, I left frustrated and went back to my digs in South Road. Within half an hour all twelve of us had returned from their various college socials with the same disillusioned tale. A last drink in the pub!

On what is now the Pointer roundabout once stood a terrace with the Boundary pub in it. In 1968 it was a typical northern drinking place, long, thin and spartan. After getting twelve pints we all went to sit in the nice front room, or lounge as the southerners amongst us called it. We settled down into armchairs and settees, thinking what a pleasant change it was from the spit and sawdust next door. Twenty minutes later an embarrassed, apologetic landlord stuck his head round the door: "Would you lads mind coming back into the pub now as my wife would like to watch our television?" Twelve rather meek freshers left his front room and returned to the bar. Couldn't wait 'til next year, bring on the freshers!

"Talkin' 'bout my generation"

TWO

In 1968 Lancaster University was somewhat different to the metropolis it is today – they've even had the effrontery to move Lonsdale College to Galgate!

The University started its move from St Leonard's House in Lancaster city centre to the campus at Bailrigg in my first year, 1968. That year it became a split campus; Lonsdale, Bowland and Cartmel colleges were open, and Furness, Fylde and County became operational during the next eighteen months.

The Central Hall, as it was first known, was to open in October 1969 so until then the social events, discos/parties/dances/concerts etc. were mainly held in Bowland and Lonsdale refectories. It was in Bowland, in 1968, that I first became enthralled by live performance – a love which exists to this day. I think I've only occasionally heard a band live when I couldn't say something positive about the show: "The lead guitarist/bass/drummer/singer was good/not bad/promising" etc. Well, one night in Bowland refectory was my epiphany. I was sitting on the floor (most of the beans and chips had been cleared) with my three-quarter full pint of McEwans bitter (I know, I know, but it was the only beer sold on campus in those days) on the wooden stage in front of me. Music/show production was pretty primitive: a small wooden stage about twelve inches high, PA arriving with the band, all crammed into a Ford transit, and the lights were four lamps on a stick either side of the stage. But ...

The band was Aynsley Dunbar Retaliation, an excellent British Blues band, with a terrific first album out, *Dr Dunbar's Prescription*, which I am playing now, as I write this. A four piece, there was Aynsley Dunbar on drums, Victor Brox on organ, Alex Dmochowski on bass and John Moorshead on lead guitar. Sitting at John's feet, listening to him, watching him bend the notes, hearing and feeling the music, I understood what a total experience of sight, sound and feel a live rock show was. And to cap it all, when I reached out to have a slurp, my three quarters of a pint had metamorphosed into a quarter of a pint – the vibrations of the music through the stage had reduced a pint of McEwans bitter to an ice cream cone of froth! I was hooked.

The Great Hall opened in my second year. Fairport Convention played the first concert, and with all those uncomfortable, crested, wooden seats assembled it was very rock 'n' roll – I don't think. This was to provide a foretaste of the University's lack of understanding of popular culture which was to play such an important role in the years to come. Lancaster was, and obviously still is, constructed on a college system. A copy of the Oxbridge college system set, not around a city, but on a hill outside of town – a college campus. In those days the economic, social and political strength of the student body was exercised through the colleges, more specifically the JCRs (Junior Common Room – what

Aynsley Dunbar

a quaint, dated expression). A Students' Union didn't really exist but there was a body, The Student Representative Council, which was really only a meeting place for the JCR Presidents and Treasurers. A strong, successful JCR President was a far more powerful and influential figure than the SRC Chairman. However that was all to change and to some extent it was the Great Hall concerts which led to that evolution.

Each JCR had a social secretary, elected by its college's students – as is no doubt the role today. But then each JCR took it in turns to promote a night in the newly opened Central Hall. A small budget was provided to the social committee but remember – in January 1970 Deep Purple played Lancaster for £350 – those were the days! Well, just after Christmas it leaked out that Bowland College had a budget of £600 to spend on an act, a great deal of money then. Rumours ran wild, who would it be? The 'underground' music scene of those days centred on *New Musical Express* and *Melody Maker*, with little or no coverage on the radio, TV, or in national daily newspapers. The early '60s serious rock artists had now forsaken the Singles Chart for album sales and all the new, 'student' bands followed suit.

Top Of The Pops was ridiculed, except when an act like The Doors appeared to take the piss. Mums and dads had never heard of the acts you would spend your pocket money, grant cheques etc. on. It was almost a secret society passed by word of mouth, "Have you heard the new LP by ...?"

Well, Bowland's Social Secretary spent his money – sorry, his students' money – on The Equals – a top singles band and staple of *TOTPs*, and your mum probably loved them as they played happy disco music! Now The Equals, Eddie Grant et al, probably have more kudos today amongst music fans than they had then. But the booking set in motion a chain of events which was to have a profound effect on Lancaster University and the social lives of several generations within a sixty mile radius …

"Hope I Die Before I Get Old."

So it was that, in a rage of frustration and indignation, Gaz Taylor, a rather eccentric friend of mine, stood against the incumbent Bowland social secretary in the annual election. Gaz, he of the copious hair, wispy beard and outrageous, black, floppy hat, persuaded me to stand in the Lonsdale election. We both won and immediately set our plans in motion. Two budgets are bigger than one. Then we worked our persuasive cunning to get Furness College's social committee to be our 'sleeping partner' – three budgets are even better than two. Suddenly we had over £1,000 to spend on a Great Hall event, but who? Yes, that's right, Who indeed! Gaz knew a small provincial booker just starting out in a traditional entertainment agency in Ferriby, near Hull, coincidently both mine and Gaz' birthplace. Robb Winn, later to join Island Records Agency in London, was told, "Get us The Who!" What an amazing concept today – "Who do you want to book?" "The Who." "OK." Phone call returned an hour later, "It'll cost you £1,000 plus £50 booking fee for me – that's £1,050."

"Done."

Hey, that's a novel idea, I wonder if it'll catch on – want a band, ring their manager, agree a fee, book 'em – couldn't happen today though, could it?

Well, now all hell broke out. £1,000 on a band, it couldn't be done. The Four Horsemen of The Apocalypse would be let loose! The JCRs would be bankrupt – civilisation as we knew it would cease to exist. Lonsdale and Bowland College presidents got together to stop their out-of-control, irresponsible, newly elected lunatics. We signed the contract and just got it in the post box in Alexandra Square as Maurice Hubbard, Lonsdale's President, came racing down the Spine.

But we'd shown 'em – a grand ha! – we laugh in the face of danger and disaster. The politicians were highly critical. So we booked Quintessence for £250 and added a third band, Hammer, for £50; that'll show the politicos! We were convinced – well, after eight bottles of Newcastle Brown in Lonsdale bar we were convinced – that it would be a storming success!

The day arrived, 15 May 1970, a sell-out, proper, professional touts selling tickets (where do they get them from?) along the Spine, queues around the Great Hall. The concert itself was amazing, but what an introduction to the 'business'. The tour manager was called John Wolff, and he was appropriately named; he was a nightmare, and a shaven-headed one at that. Pete Townshend, sensing my terror, said, "Oh, he's OK once you get to know him."

"Mind you," said Roger Daltrey, "He's been with us ten years and we still don't know him!"

The light show was amazing; eight white spots borrowed from the Nuffield Theatre. Eight students in the balcony on them, pull the plug out for off, stick it in for on. Watch the bald demon on the side of the stage for instructions, he'll point at you when he wants it off or on. And don't you dare get it wrong! Sophisticated or what? Several years later the Great Hall was to host one of the first computer-controlled light shows with the Thompson Twins; we were witness to rock growing up.

Daltrey was on stage in his fringed jacket, swinging his mic on a long lead around the stage, threatening to decapitate Moon and Townshend. Here he was, in the same clothes as he wore when he stole the show in Woodstock, but in Lancaster!

After the show the band and entourage retired to their hotel, The Royal Kings Arms – the only hotel in Lancaster at the time – and settled in the bar. 1970 was the height of the anti-Vietnam demonstrations worldwide (remember Kent State University, Ohio, the National Guards murdering student demonstrators?) and the American students had organised an all-night vigil in Market Square. This was a very good place to have an overnight demonstration as the square was also the location of a massive underground toilet. At around two o'clock in the morning, Roger Daltrey and Pete Townshend asked the night porter at the hotel to prepare several trays of sandwiches, teas and coffees. The porter was delighted because, although it was late, he was feeding one of the most famous groups in the world. But no, the two rock superstars loaded up a couple of trolleys and off they trundled to Market Square to feed the demonstrators and sit chatting with them, plotting the revolution until the, even later, early hours. Nice touch – I'd hope they would still do that today, maybe …

Photo possibly Traffic
January 1971
Courtesy of Marion
McClintock.
Photographer
unknown

The Who

15 May 1970　　　　Supports: Quintessence I The Hammer

In January 1970 The Who embarked on a tour in promotion of the rock opera album *Tommy,* released in May 1969. The band started the tour performing the rock opera in Paris, Denmark, Germany and The Netherlands before returning to the UK.

The first UK date on 14 February 1970 was in Leeds University's refectory, where the album *Live At Leeds* was recorded.

Three months later in May, The Who were Barry Lucas' first Great Hall concert booking. They visited Lancaster on one of only twelve university dates on their sixty-eight-date US, European and UK tour schedule.

Band members:
Roger Daltrey – lead vocals, tambourine, harmonica
Pete Townshend – lead guitar, vocals
John Entwistle – bass guitar, vocals
Keith Moon – drums

Unfortunately no definitive setlist for the Lancaster concert exists, but it would probably have included much material from the album *Tommy,* maybe opening the show with the 1965 single 'I Can't Explain'. The set may have ended with either 'Magic Bus' or 'My Generation', with the track 'The Seeker' being sometimes included in the setlist.

Quintessence were a jazz/psychedelic prog. rock band formed in April 1969 in London. The band had an Indian flavour to their sound. The original lineup included Sambhu Babaji (bass guitar), Maha Dev (rhythm guitar), Shiva Shankar Jones (vocals, keyboards, percussion), Jake Milton (drums, percussion), Allan Mostert (lead guitar) and Raja Ram (flute, percussion). They performed at the first two Glastonbury Festivals and released a total of five studio albums. Quintessence played on into the 1980s before breaking up.

First on stage was a Hull band called **The Hammer** who existed for a couple of years in the early seventies. The band had minimal success but were most notable for their keyboard player from Cleethorpes, Rod Temperton. Rod went on in later years to become a renowned songwriter in the USA, penning hits for George Benson and Michael Jackson, including Jackson's massive singles 'Thriller' and 'Rock With You'. Temperton won a Grammy Award in 1991 for his work on 'Birdland', from Quincy Jones's album *Back on the Block.* He passed away at the age of sixty-six in October 2016.

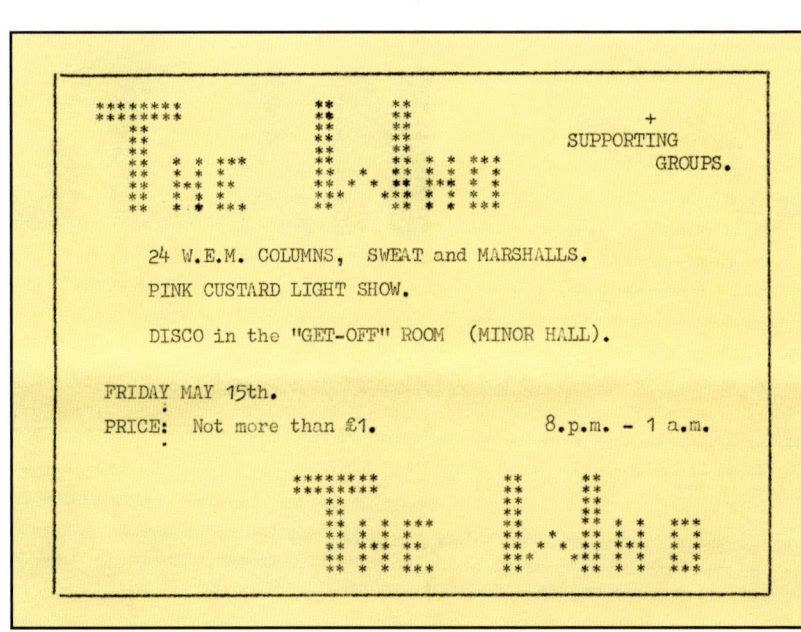

The
A-Z

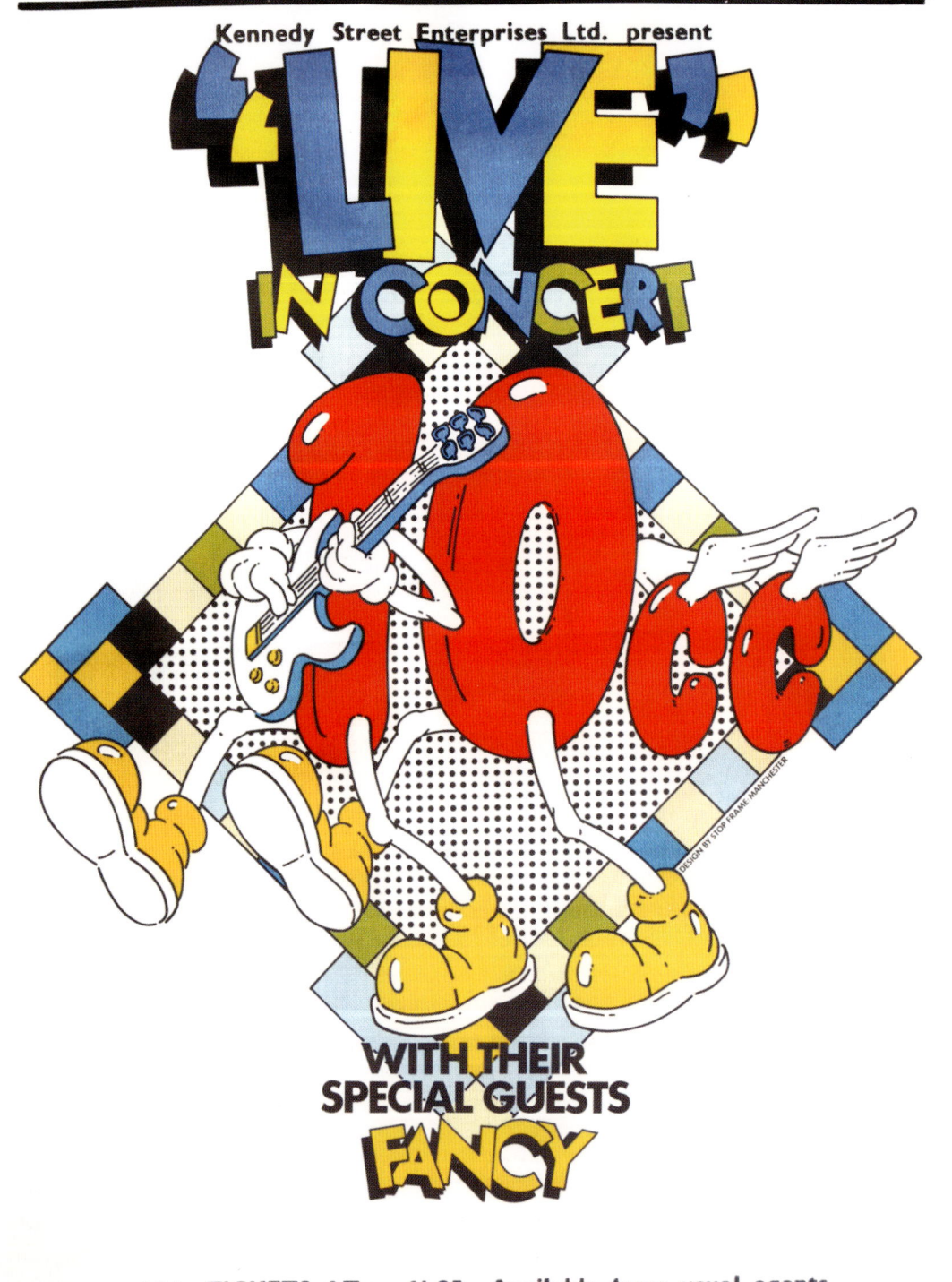

Courtesy of Sir William Taylor

THREE

10cc

2 May 1975 — Support: Fancy

The classic 10cc lineup of Lol Crème, Kevin Godley, Eric Stewart and Graham Gouldman visited Lancaster University three years after their formation. They played the Great Hall in promotion of the release, in March 1975, of their third studio album *The Original Soundtrack*.

The single 'I'm Not In Love' from the album reached the No. 1 slot in the UK Singles Chart of June 1975.

10cc celebrated their fortieth anniversary in 2012 and continue to tour, with Graham Gouldman the only original member.

Band members were seen earlier that evening, before the concert, dining in an Italian restaurant on Church Street in Lancaster.

Support band **Fancy** were the creation of Ray Fenwick and were put together with session musicians he worked with following his short stint with The Spencer Davies Group. The band existed for only a couple of years but during that time had a couple of US hits, one being a cover version of The Troggs 'Wild Thing'.

© David Bradbury

A Flock of Seagulls

2 April 1983   Support unknown

A Flock of Seagulls were formed in Liverpool in 1980 by lead singer Mike Score and his brother, Ali.

According to score the bands names was taken from the song 'Toiler on the Sea' by The Stranglers and the book *Jonathan Livingstone Seagull* by Richard Bach.

In 1982 the group's third single, 'I Ran (So Far Away)', became a worldwide hit, most notably reaching No. 1 in Australia, then reaching the Top 10 in the US and New Zealand, but only No. 43 on the UK Singles Chart. The parent album *A Flock of Seagulls* and another single, 'Space Age Love Song', was also successful for the band in 1982.

They ultimately went on to be best known for their hit 'Wishing (If I Had a Photograph of You)' which reached No. 10 in the UK Singles Chart in late 1982. The song was taken from the album *Listen,* released in May 1983 shortly after their visit to Lancaster.

Band lineup:
Mike Score – vocals
Ali Score – drums
Paul Reynolds – guitars
Frank Maudsley – bass

AC/DC

30 October 1976   **Dirty Deeds Done Dirt Cheap Tour**   Support: Tyla Gang
21 October 1977   **Let There Be Rock Tour**   Support: Suburban Studs

AC/DC came to test the structural integrity of the Great Hall twice in successive years. With Bon Scott up front and the legendary Angus Young belting out the riffs, these were two classic concerts for the lucky few who were there. Their first visit to the university promoted the album *Dirty Deeds Done Dirt Cheap,* released in September 1976.

1976 band lineup:
Angus Young – guitars
Malcolm Young – rhythm guitars
Bon Scott – vocals
Mark Evans – bass guitar
Phil Rudd – drums

Lancaster setlist: 'Live Wire', 'Rock And Roll Singer', 'Jailbreak', 'She's Got Balls', 'The Jack'; 'School Days', 'Rocker', 'TNT', 'It's a Long Way to the Top (If You Wanna Rock 'n' Roll)', 'High Voltage', 'Baby Please Don't Go'.

Almost exactly one year later and AC/DC was back in town, five months after the release of their classic album *Let There Be Rock.*

1977 band lineup:
Angus Young – guitar
Malcolm Young – rhythm guitar
Bon Scott – vocals
Cliff Williams – bass guitar
Phil Rudd – drums

Lancaster setlist: 'Let There Be Rock', 'Problem Child', 'Hell Ain't A Bad Place To Be', 'Whole Lotta Rosie', 'High Voltage', 'The Jack', 'Bad Boy Boogie Rocker', 'TNT'.

Following the sudden death of Bon Scott in February 1980, the remaining members of the band briefly considered quitting. They eventually concluded, however, that Scott would have wanted AC/DC to continue. Auditions were held and AC/DC chose Brian Johnson as Scott's replacement. Johnson was one of the founding members of the rock band Geordie formed in Newcastle in 1971.

More recently Brian Johnson announced his departure from the band due to hearing problems, his replacement being Guns N' Roses frontman Axl Rose, who stepped in to perform as lead singer for the remainder of the band's 2016 Rock or Bust World Tour.

Tyla Gang are a British pub-rock/new wave band formed by Sean Tyla, following his departure and the break-up of the band Ducks Deluxe in 1975. Sean Tyla is an English rock guitarist, keyboardist, vocalist and songwriter, sometimes known as the "Godfather of Boogie," who has also worked with Joan Jett. They released two albums before Tyla dissolved the band in 1979. In 2010 the Tyla Gang re-formed in their original lineup and have since released two albums. Sean Tyla recently celebrated his seventieth birthday.

Suburban Studs were a Birmingham punk band formed in 1976. Their only album, *Slam*, was released in 1977. Maybe an unusual choice of support for AC/DC, as Suburban Studs were more used to backing the Sex Pistols and The Clash for gigs at the 100 Club in London.

John Angus

AC/DC

I was introduced to AC/DC at an early age! They are still one of my favourite bands and I go to see them in arenas to this day. I saw them recently in Manchester with Axl Rose fronting the band. Many years ago now, I was in London at an NUS social secretaries conference and I was meant to be going for a meal that evening with John Glover, one of the directors of Island Artists. However, he phoned me to say that he wasn't feeling well, but he had arranged for me to meet up with Richard Griffiths, a young booker who was a good guy and desperate to meet up with me! OK, free meal, drinks etc. and he worked for a small agency with acts I wouldn't be interested in so there would be no sales pressure to spoil the evening. Why not?

We met up and, after the meal, he said that he was managing a little Aussie band (you know where this is going don't you?) and would I mind going to see them and give him my opinion. They were playing at The Marquee that night. OK, I replied, nothing else going on; if I went back to the conference I would only spend all night in the bar getting berated by drunken social secretaries moaning that they never got the bands Lancaster put on and how unfair it was. So I went to Wardour Street into the legendary Marquee Club. It was my first time and what an amazing disappointment. Here, in this venue, almost every legend of rock music had appeared. But it seemed to be not much bigger than Lonsdale refectory – it looked like a three hundred capacity pub venue! It was just unbelievable.

Then AC/DC hit the stage – running – and about a hundred people in the Marquee were almost literally gob- and ear- smacked. Angus Young was dressed as an eleven year old school boy and Bon Scott was belting out the vocals with Angus on his shoulders, cracking out those unmistakable riffs. I looked around a room full of "The Business" – top agents, managers and promoters (I bet they didn't pay for their tickets either). Richard looked at me, "They're bloody brilliant aren't they?"

"Oh yes, I love 'em!" I enthused.

"I'll never keep hold of them, will I?" The young agent, eyeing a room full of the who's who of the music business royalty, wistfully asked.

"Nope," I agreed sadly.

Now fast forward a couple of years. I had the chance to book AC/DC for the Great Hall. I had already worn their *High Voltage* album virtually smooth and we had been pushing it like crazy at 'Ear 'Ere Records as Nigel (my business partner) was a great rock guitar fanatic. But could I get an audience? NO! About 500 hardy rock souls turned up. We lost money. But WHAT A SHOW! Bon Scott charged round the hall like the maniac he was, with Angus on his shoulders, a radio guitar and microphone used for the first time in the Great Hall. It was truly amazing, although some of my stewards complained to me after the show that it was all taped because there were no microphone or guitar leads trailing around the hall after them!

I have always believed that a promoter promotes music that his punters want to hear. I never believed, as some did, in preaching to, or trying to educate, an audience. Only a couple of times have I tried to convince the Lancaster crowd it was wrong, and that if they trusted me they would be converted to see the light. This was one of those times when, exactly a year later, I booked them again. Surely the word had got around and more people would have heard about the last show and about the rave press the band were receiving. Surely Lancaster will have woken up by now? At least the band thought they were major stars now with their rider containing a few new "silly bollocks" clauses: 200 Marlboro cigarettes, twenty tubes of Smarties with the brown ones taken out – well it gave somebody gainful employment I suppose. But yes, it worked! This time 600 turned up – lost money again! Some people never learn, me included.

Barry Lucas

The Adverts

17 February 1978   Support: Dick Envy

The Adverts were an English punk band who formed in 1976 and broke up in late 1979. The band's lineup included one of the first female punk artists, Gaye Advert, on bass guitar.

They are best remembered for their single 'Gary Gilmore's Eyes' which reached No. 18 in the UK Singles Chart of September 1977.

This was the second appearance in the Great Hall for The Adverts. June of 1977 saw them provide support for their Stiff label mates, The Damned.

Later in their career they went on to support Iggy Pop on tour.

Back up for the evening was supplied by the London-based punk outfit **Dick Envy**, fronted by American punkette Vermillion Sands.

The band were very active on the London punk circuit, mainly as a support to some of the bigger names of the time.

The Alarm

8 February 1984   Support: Orson Family

The Alarm, from Rhyl in North Wales, originally started out in 1977 as a local punk band with the catchy name of The Toilets, before a name change to Seventeen in 1978 and subsequently The Alarm around 1981.

Originally consisting of Mike Peters (vocals, guitar), Dave Sharp (guitar), Eddie Macdonald (bass) and Nigel Twist (drums) 1983 saw The Alarm's best known hit 'Sixty Eight Guns' reach No. 17 in the UK singles chart, with the album *Declaration* which contained the single, climbing to No. 6 in the UK album charts.

Around the same time the band were offered the support slot on U2's War tour in America.

Although The Alarm officially disbanded in 1991 Mike Peters still tours and records with his current version of the band today.

The Orson Family were a short-lived four piece English psychobilly/goth rock band formed around 1982. The band includes Gene Vincent, Eddie Cochran, Lou Reed, The Jam and The Cramps as their influences.

They released two albums, including one live, and a single called 'The Sweetest Embrace'. The Orson Family disbanded in late 1984.

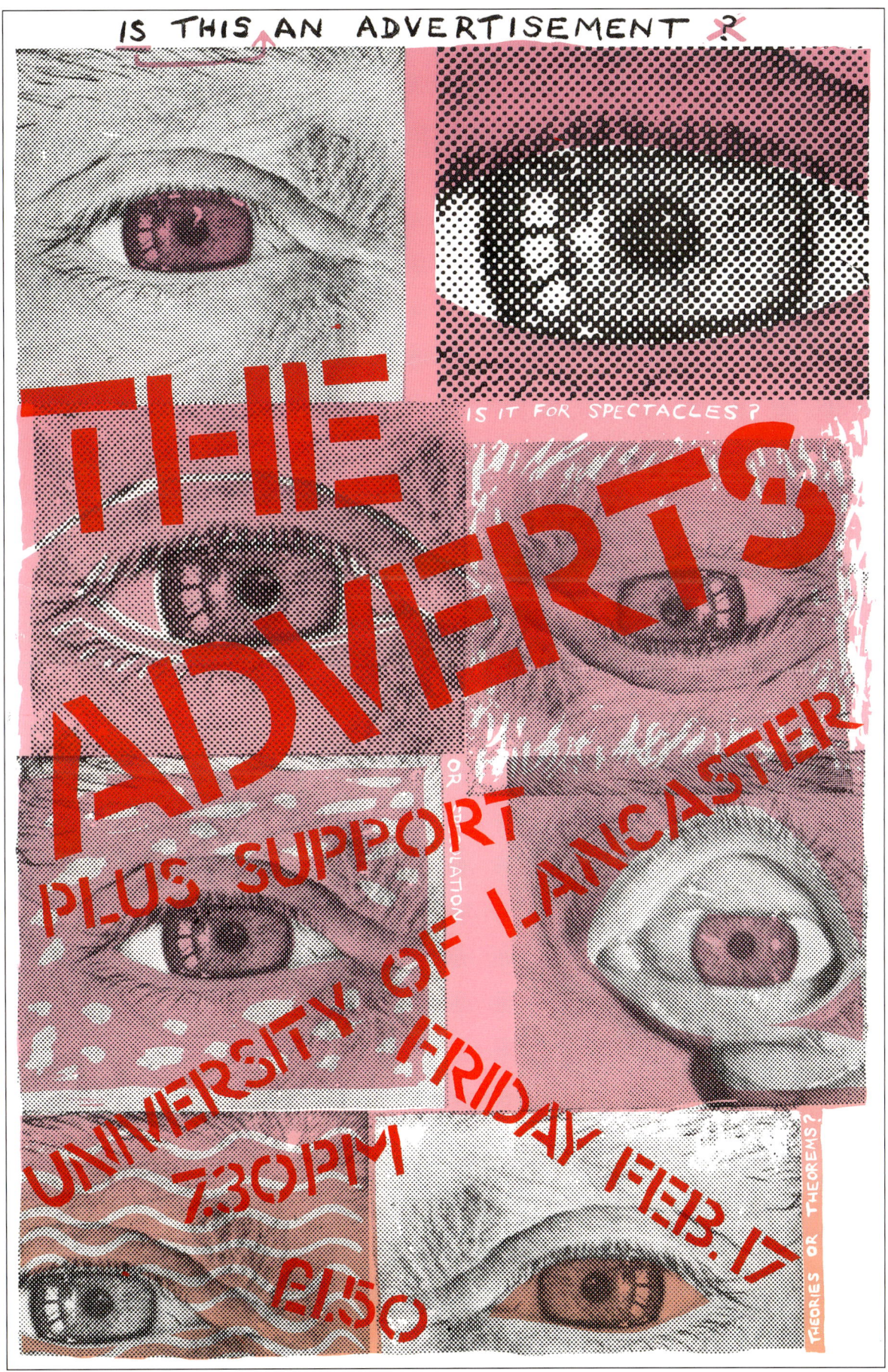

John Angus

Altered Images

11 May 1982   Support: Subway Sect

Altered Images were a Scottish new wave band fronted by Claire Grogan that had six UK Top 40 singles, including 'Happy Birthday' which reached No. 2 in the Singles Chart of October 1981.

A reviewer of the concert in *SCAN* newspaper stated that:

> "Altered Images are, Siouxsie and The Banshees for those who can only eat two shredded wheat. They were very average"

Altered Images disbanded in 1983, with Claire Grogan going on to become a film and television actress, appearing in the film *Gregory's Girl*.

Formed in 1976, **Subway Sect** are a very early punk band led by Vic Goddard. According to *SCAN* newspaper's concert reviewer on the night: "They were tremendous and the crowd demanded an encore"

Vic Goddard and Subway Sect are still active, over forty years after their formation.

Altered Images and Claire Grogan © Geoff Campbell

Alison Moyet

3 November 1984   Support unknown

Prior to finding success as a solo artist, Alison Moyet, from Billericay in Essex, was one half of the British synthpop duo Yazoo, alongside former Depeche Mode member Vince Clarke on keyboards.

In total she achieved nine Top 30 singles and five Top 10 single hits in the UK charts including, 'Is This Love?' reaching No. 3 in 1986 and 'All Cried Out' which peaked at No. 8 in September 1984 shortly prior to this university appearance.

Alison Moyet was a winner of the British Phonographic Industry Award (Brit Awards), for British Female Solo Artist in 1985 and 1988.

Now in her fifties, she continues to perform and in June 2017 released her ninth studio album *Other*.

> There is not really a lot I want to say about this concert except that I like Alison and was a fan from the moment I heard her first recording. She had caused a lot of interest and enthusiastic comments when she broke onto the scene and this was a major tour. However it was also my record loss on a show. In fourteen years and several hundred bands, I had never lost this amount of money. She was paid £4000 and I lost just over £4000. Obviously there are promotion costs on every show but as a reflection of tickets sold that is pretty spectacular. I could not understand it. I still can't …
>
> Barry Lucas

Amazing Blondel

12 November 1971 — Supports: Bronco | John Martyn
10 November 1972 — Support: Stefan Grossman
25 January 1974 — Support: Gasworks

Veterans of five Great Hall appearances, Amazing Blondel are an English acoustic progressive folk band. The band were formed around 1969 by Eddie Baird, John Gladwin and Terry Wincott.

Their music has been compared with that of Gryphon, Pentangle and Jethro Tull. They released a number of LPs for Island Records in the early 1970s and much of the material performed in their two early support appearances would have come from the albums *Fantasia Lindum* and *Evensong*.

Amazing Blondel's first Great Hall concert was providing support for Pentangle in November 1970.

Amazing Blondel returned in January 1971 when they were back again as the support band for Traffic in the 'Elton John no show' concert. Less than a year later, the band returned for the first of these three Lancaster concerts as headliners in their own right.

Amazing Blondel are still active today.

Bronco were an English country-rock band signed to Island & Polydor Records from 1969–1973, previously appearing in the Great Hall as headliners in February 1971.

This was the very first appearance in the Great Hall of **John Martyn**.

Born in Brooklyn, New York, **Stefan Grossman** is an American acoustic fingerstyle guitarist and singer, still performing today.

Gasworks were a folk duo formed in the late 1960s by John Brown and Mike Draper. John and Mike performed an esoteric mix of romantic songs influenced by music hall, played on a multitude of instruments including a phono-fiddle.

This band were friends of/known to Gaz Taylor, my co-promoter in the early days. Originally from the Scunthorpe area, Amazing Blondel were indeed a truly amazing act, performing medieval folk music – an obvious must for rock fans I hear you say. I know, I know, but it worked!

Don't ask me why, but they always went down a storm – and don't get me wrong, I loved 'em, they were brilliant, but to young rock fans?

However, we persevered over the next few years. Supporting, or being supported by, a variety of acts, including John Martyn, Bronco, Stefan Grossman and Roger McGough, among others. Like several good acts I believed in, I stuck with them and eventually they were able to headline nights in the Great Hall and pull a 1000-plus crowd to their shows. Good lads, great music, they really deserved their moments of fame.

Barry Lucas

Amon Düül II

25 May 1973   Support | Zoe

From Munich, Germany, Amon Düül II are a rock band formed within a German art commune, whose members began producing improvisational psychedelic rock music during the late '60s. The group is generally considered to be one of the founders of the German rock music scene and a seminal influence on the development of Krautrock.

Their first album Phallus Dei ('God's Penis'), released in 1969, is considered a milestone in German rock history.

The band visited Lancaster with a probable lineup of:
Chris Karrer – violin, guitars, saxophone and vocals
Peter Leopold – drums
Falk Rogner – keyboards
John Weinzierl – bass, vocals
Renate Knaup – vocals, tambourine
Amon Düül II have released over fifteen studio albums over their fifty year history, and still continue to tour in Europe.

Little information is known about support act **Zoe**.

Argent

20 November 1970   Supports: Barclay James Harvest | Farm | Sam Apple Pie
9 October 1971   Supports: Climax Chicago Blues Band | Duffy Power
May 1972   Support: Hackensack

Argent were an English rock band founded in 1969 by keyboardist Rod Argent, formerly of The Zombies.

Argent's biggest hit was the Rod Argent and Chris White composition 'Hold Your Head Up' which reached No. 5 in the UK single chart of 1972. Their other major chart success was the single 'God Gave Rock and Roll to You', making No. 18 in 1973.

Rod Argent, after many years of writing hits for an array of other artists, is about to set out on his own 2016 tour, playing live for the first time in years.

Prior to headlining twice at Lancaster, in 1971 and 1975, a great second act on the bill was Manchester prog. rock band **Barclay James Harvest**.

The third of three Great Hall support appearances for Aylesbury band **Farm** in 1970. The Great Hall had seen Farm as guests of Deep Purple in January, followed by a concert backing Procol Harum in April 1970.

Sam Apple Pie was a British blues-rock band, of the late 1960s and 1970s, noted for having played at the first Glastonbury Festival in 1970.

Three years after their formation in 1967 **Climax Chicago Blues Band** make their first Great Hall appearance as a support act. They were to return three times as headliners to Lancaster, following the dropping of 'Chicago' in their name in 1972.

The Great Hall had seen **Duffy Power** two years previously as support to Fairport Convention in one of the Great Hall's first concerts.

UK Heavy Metal band **Hackensack** were formed in 1969 by Nicky Moore and existed until 1974. The band released one album on the Polydor label, entitled *Up The Hard Way*.

Band lineup:
Nicky Moore – guitars, keyboards, vocals
Simon Fox – drums
Stu Mills – bass
Ray Majors – vocals, guitars

In 1981 Nicky Moore and his band featured as guests of Wishbone Ash on their *Number The Brave* Tour.

Following the breakup of Hackensack in 1974, drummer Simon Fox joined Bill Nelson's Be-Bop Deluxe.

The Crazy World of Arthur Brown

9 May 1970   Supports: The Henry Lowther Band | The John Dummer Band

The Crazy World of Arthur Brown are an English psychedelic rock band formed by singer Arthur "The God of Hellfire" Brown in 1967. Arthur is originally from Whitby in North Yorkshire. With an alarming stage act and a debut single, 'Devil's Grip', this paved the way for the band's success with their No. 1 hit 'Fire'.

Released in 1968, 'Fire' was one of the one-hit wonders in the United Kingdom and United States in the 1960s. But what a one hit to have! 'Fire' sold over one million copies and was awarded a gold disc.

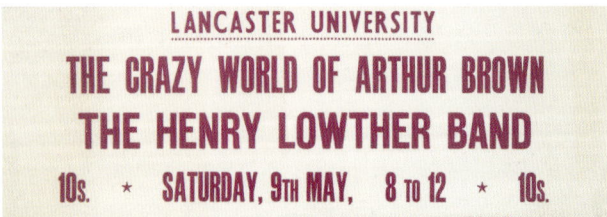

Courtesy of Ray Wilkinson Music Research Archive

In later years, Brown released several solo albums and in 1975 appeared in The Who's rock opera movie *Tommy* as the priest. Arthur Brown presently continues to tour and record.

Henry Lowther is a jazz trumpeter from Leicester who went on to work with numerous notable musicians, including Elton John and Van Morrison. He was also part of the lineup of The Keef Hartley Band, who provided support for Edgar Broughton's 1970 Great Hall concert.

The John Dummer Band, also known as John Dummer's Blues Band, were notable for the inclusion of Tony McPhee in their lineup, who moved on to form The Groundhogs and is rightly regarded as one of the finest blues guitarists to come from this country. The band also played as a support act for Howlin' Wolf and John Lee Hooker on their UK tours. In 1977 Dummer joined the band Darts as their drummer and featured in their 1979 Great Hall concert.

Atomic Rooster

30 October 1970   Supports: Terry Reid | Innocent Child

Atomic Rooster are an English rock band, originally formed by two former members of The Crazy World of Arthur Brown, Vincent Crane, the master of the swirling Hammond organ, and drummer Carl Palmer, who went on to form Emerson, Lake and Palmer. The band initially existed from 1969 to 1975. Throughout their history, Vincent Crane was the only constant member and wrote the majority of their material. By the time of this Lancaster concert, Carl Palmer had left to form ELP and had been replaced by former Farm drummer Paul Hammond.

Atomic Rooster are best known for the hard progressive rock sound of their hit singles 'Tomorrow Night', a UK No. 11 hit, and 'The Devil's Answer', which did better, going to No. 4, both in 1971. Vincent Crane passed away in 1989 at the young age of forty-five.

Lancaster band lineup:
Vincent Crane – organ, piano, bass pedals
John Du Cann – guitar, vocals, bass
Paul Hammond – drums, percussion

In 2016, Atomic Rooster re-formed with permission from Crane's widow, with a new lineup featuring two members from the various 1970s incarnations of the band.

Once produced by Mickey Most, British Hard rock singer 'Super lungs' **Terry Reid** is famous for his powerful soulful voice and equally famous for turning down offers to join Led Zeppelin and Deep Purple. Over his long career he has toured with many high-profile bands such as Jethro Tull and Fleetwood Mac. He also played the 1970 Isle of Wight Festival. He is still active at present.

Little is known about the second support act **Innocent Child**

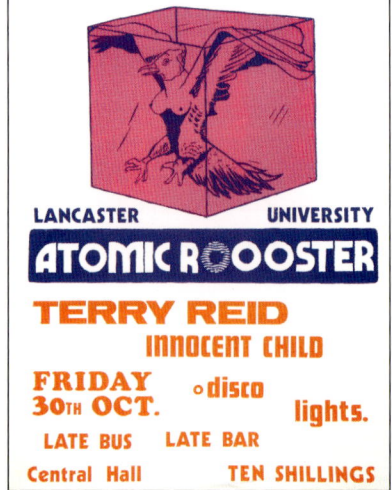

Courtesy of Ray Wilkinson Music Research Archive

Average White Band

2 March 1979   Support: Inner Circle

Formed in 1972 by Alan Gorrie and Malcolm "Molly" Duncan, Average White Band are a Scottish funk and R&B band that had a series of soul and disco hits between 1974 and 1980.

They appeared at the university supporting the release of their seventh album, *Feel No Fret,* with a band lineup of:
Alan Gorrie – bass, vocals
Hamish Stuart – guitars, vocals
Roger Ball – keyboards, alto saxophone
Malcolm Duncan – tenor saxophone
Steve Ferrone – drums
Onnie McIntyre – guitars, vocals

AWB are best known for their 1975 hit single 'Pick up The Pieces' which reached No. 6 in the UK Singles Chart and was a No. 1 hit in the US.

The track was taken from the album *AWB,* also known as *The White Album*, and brought the band major success in America, reaching No. 1 in the US Albums Chart.

'Let's Go Round Again' was another popular disco number for the band in 1980.

Two members of Average White Band, Malcolm Duncan and saxophonist Roger Ball, were previously members of the band Mogul Thrash, who appeared as support band for Johnny Winter's Great Hall gig of 1971, while Onnie McIntyre and founder member the late Robbie McIntosh, were session musicians on Chuck Berry's hit single 'My Ding-a-Ling'.

As of 2017, over forty years after their formation, Average White Band continue to tour and record.

Support came from Jamaican reggae outfit **Inner Circle** who are still active today. The band was formed in 1968 by the brothers Ian and Roger Lewis and are known for their blending of pop and rock with reggae.

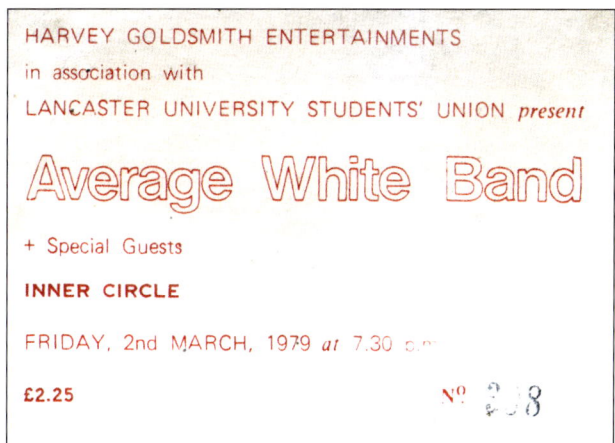

In the mid '70s the soul legend James Brown was so disgusted that a funk band from Scotland was having such acclaim that he created his own version called The Above Average Black Band. It wasn't long though before he acknowledged how good AWB were and disbanded his creation.

Steve Middlesbrough, local DJ legend, went to this gig. Let him tell the story:

> "I had been to several live shows that year, mainly featuring great soul/funk bands. The shows had been breathtaking in their presentation but here was something different. It was the first of many gigs that I attended in the Great Hall and was memorable for the most amazing entrance by a band that I have ever seen. Standing at the back of the hall with some friends, we were eagerly awaiting the band. What would the next few moments hold, explosions, pyro, lights …? Then a few guys wandered onto the stage, one walked up to the mic. 'We were just playing footie out back and thought we ought to come in here and play you a few tunes,' said a broad Scottish voice. It was the greatest opening to an act I've ever seen."

Barry Lucas

Bad Company

7 December 1974
20 March 1979   **The Desolation Angels Tour**

Support: Duster Bennett
No support

Bad Company were formed in Westminster, London, in 1973 by two former Free band members, singer Paul Rodgers and drummer Simon Kirke. Joining them to complete the lineup was ex-King Crimson bassist Boz Burrell, and Mott The Hoople guitarist Mick Ralphs.

1974 saw Bad Company appear in the Great Hall for the first time to promote the release of their debut album *Bad Company*. The album contained the hit single 'Can't Get Enough' and spent twenty-five weeks in the UK Albums Chart, entering at No. 10 and reaching its highest position of No. 3 in its second week.

Possible 1974 Lancaster setlist: 'Little Miss Fortune', 'Rock Steady', 'Ready For Love', 'Don't Let Me Down', 'Easy On My Soul', 'Bad Company', 'Deal with the Preacher', 'Movin' On', 'Can't Get Enough', 'The Stealer', 'Rock Me Baby'.

The band's fifth album, *Desolation Angels*, was released just three days before Bad Company arrived in Lancaster for their second visit in 1979.

Possible 1979 Lancaster setlist: 'Bad Company',' Good Lovin' Gone Bad', 'Gone, Gone, Gone', 'Burnin' Sky', 'Shooting Star', 'Rhythm Machine', 'Ready For Love', 'Simple Man', 'Oh, Atlanta', 'She Brings Me Love', 'Run With The Pack', 'Evil Wind', 'Honey Child', 'Rock 'n' Roll Fantasy', 'Movin' On', 'Live for the Music'.

Encore: 'Feel Like Makin' Love', 'Can't Get Enough'.

Paul Rodgers finally called it a day with the band shortly after the release of *Rough Diamonds*, Bad Company's sixth album, in 1982.

From 2004 to 2009, Paul Rodgers collaborated with Brian May and Roger Taylor of Queen for a number of tours as lead vocalist. It was made clear at the time that Rodgers would not be a replacement for Queen's former lead singer, Freddie Mercury, who died on 24 November 1991, but simply be 'featured with' former Queen members.

Happily, in 2008 Bad Company decided to reform and the band continues to record and tour with Paul Rodgers, Mick Ralphs, and Simon Kirke on drums.

A *SCAN* newspaper concert reviewer said of the March '79 concert:

"Right from the start it had the ingredients of a classic gig. An enormous queue, the air full of expectancy, leather jackets and dirty denims, a stage crammed full of stacks and battery upon battery of lights. For the first time in four years Bad Company were returning to Lancaster. At 8.15 sharp, when the masses had finally pushed, shoved and squeezed their way in, the lights went out, a roar came up – and on they came!"

Anthony "Duster" Bennett was a British blues singer and harmonica player. He was backed on his 1968 debut album, *Smiling Like I'm Happy*, by members of Fleetwood Mac. In 1970 he was a session harmonica player and member of John Mayall & The Bluesbreakers during a US tour. Duster Bennett was tragically killed in a car accident in 1976 at the young age of twenty-nine.

Paul Rodgers of Bad Company 1979 © David Stewart

Bad Company 1979, © David Stewart,
courtesy Colin Sumner

Bad Company 1979, © David Stewart

Bad Company

When my second favourite band of all time packed up (Free were ranked only behind the Doors in my pantheon of all time greats) I was totally devastated. A couple of years later the remnants were re-united as Bad Company – a true super-group of the '70s. They appeared twice, but it was the first date that was really exciting. It was announced that this super-group were only going to do a very, very select tour of six dates, with Mel Bush as their promoter. I got on well with the Mel Bush Organisation but even so I was amazed when he approached me to be one of those six dates. This was much to Leeds University's chagrin as they had desperately begged for a date.

Mel had always put shows, the more middle-of-the-road acts, into Preston Guildhall and so he rewarded them with a date as well. I think it was mainly to thank Alan Baker, who was an outstanding hall manager. It may be hard to imagine now, but Preston was a relatively new venue then without the problems that promoters were later to encounter. I knew that the size and the status of the show would prohibit me from watching any of it but they were my favourite band so I decided to go down to Preston, the night before, to watch. I got myself, Nigel Waller and Alan Murray on the guest list, booked rooms at The Tickled Trout (the band's hotel) and was as excited as any fan.

Unfortunately I was (and still am) of the old school – you can't watch rock 'n' roll sitting down, especially in comfortable, cinema-style seating. It's just not rock 'n' roll! We managed three numbers and retired to the bar, where we were joined by a lonely figure in a floor-length snakeskin coat. We recognised him immediately as the '60s star Dave Berry (with his band, The Cruisers, he had a fantastic hit with the 'The Crying Game') who felt exactly the same way and we spent a couple of hours bemoaning the death of rock 'n' roll. Five years later, Dave Berry was to appear in the Great Hall for a rag ball on the same bill as Darts. As I drank I assured everyone we'd create the atmosphere necessary to watch Bad Company in a proper rock venue, stand-up an' all – Lancaster, the next night.

But we had to get through the rest of that night. We got back to the hotel and continued drinking. Promoters, record company reps, journalists, band, and finally road crew, joined us. At about 1.00 am I found myself in the company of Paul Rodgers. I believe him to be the next best thing to Jim Morrison and therefore, as the latter was dead, in my eyes I was talking to the best rock singer on the planet. He had just started playing guitar on stage – I suppose he wouldn't have dared do it if Kossoff had still been around – and I was sufficiently alcohol-brave to ask him what he was thinking of as he wasn't a guitarist, he was THE SINGER! If I was his manager, I assured him, I would chop his hands off; his voice was his instrument. He didn't argue, just looked pityingly at the drunken, burbling specimen in front of him and left to find some sensible conversation. He was in such a hurry he left his drink – I finished it for him! I finally staggered out of the bar at 3.00 am after mine-sweeping all the unfinished drinks on the empty tables – not an edifying sight. In fact a true disgrace. Not quite as bad as Nigel who spent the rest of the night sat on his expensive hotel toilet, head in the wash basin, emptying his body from both ends at once! Nice!

Lancaster University's gig was, as I knew it would be, brilliant. Just what a rock 'n' roll concert should be: drivin' music, crazy, animated, dancing crowd. It's only rock 'n' roll but I like it.

However, it wasn't so memorable for one musician, the support act, Duster Bennett. The tour was rather hastily put together and it meant that the sound check was somewhat long and drawn out. So much so that, by the time Bad Company had finished, we were past the door opening time. I had things to put in place before we were ready to open, but the schedule was such that Duster was told to go on and begin his set well before I could open the doors. Consequently Duster had to go on stage, pretend there was an audience and play. It took several numbers into the set before I was in a position to open the doors and let the audience in. I can think of several support acts who deserved to play to an empty hall but Duster Bennett wasn't one of them.

The next time Bad Company appeared at Lancaster they were truly world superstars, with several hit singles and albums. When I had got the PA in, sorted the playing and door opening times out with the promoter, Harvey Goldsmith, and the bands had done the necessary sound checks, Alan Murray and I would nip down to Lancaster to grab something to eat, our tea. This was usually in The Blue Anchor but, for some reason that escapes me now, this particular night we chose The Albert. We were just settling down to our braised steak and chips when in walked Bad Company! The whole band had taken up my recommendation and come to The Albert for their tea. Up to the bar to order pints strolled Paul Rodgers, complete with full-length leather coat and scarf, topped off with a very impressive leather cowboy Stetson. Leaning on the bar was an old regular of about seventy or eighty years. He looked Mr Rodgers up and down and asked him what he was doing in his local. Paul replied that he was at the university.

"What ya studying?" he was asked.

"Music," Mr Rodgers replied. The old guy gave him a pitying look as if to say, "You're wasting your time, you won't make a living with that, son."

Barry Lucas

Baker Gurvitz Army

February 1975 — Support unknown, possibly Strife

Former The Gun and Three Man Army members Paul and Adrian Gurvitz joined forces with ex-Cream and Airforce drummer Ginger Baker in 1974 to form Baker Gurvitz Army. Also drafted into the band was former Sharks and Nothineverappens member Mr Snips (aka Steve Parsons) on vocals. This visit was in support of the January '75 release of their album *Elysian Encounter*.

The band released three albums before the death of their manager, which led to the eventual breakup of the band. In the aftermath, Baker briefly led a band called Energy and was also associated with Atomic Rooster and Hawkwind.

Ginger Baker was to return to the Great Hall stage with Hawkwind, drumming for them on their UK 1980 Christmas Tour.

The evening's support slot could possibly have been supplied by the power rock outfit **Strife**, who also appeared as a support band for Budgie in 1978.

Barclay James Harvest

16 April 1971
31 October 1975 — **Time Honoured Ghosts Tour**

Supports: Root and Jenny Jackson | Victor Brox | Gwenyway
Support: Café Society

Oldham progressive rock band Barclay James Harvest were founded in 1966 by Les Holroyd (bass, guitars, keyboards, vocals), Stuart "Woolly" Wolstenholme (vocals, mellotron, keyboards, guitars), John Lees (vocals, guitars) and Mel Pritchard (drums).

They played a total of three concerts in the Great Hall, the first providing support for Argent in 1970. Their second visit to Lancaster saw the band as a headline act, performing tracks from their second album *Once Again*, released in early 1971 and containing probably their best known song 'Mocking Bird'.

Four years later, Barclay James Harvest returned for their third visit, promoting the October 1975 release of the album *Time Honoured Ghosts*.

Lancaster setlist: 'Song For You', 'Crazy City', 'In My Life', 'Sweet Jesus', 'Hymn For The Children', 'Paper Wings', 'Child Of The Universe', 'One Night', 'Moongirl', 'For No One', 'Titles', 'Jonathan', 'Mocking Bird'.

Two versions of the band continue to record and tour: John Lees' Barclay James Harvest, since 1988, and Barclay James Harvest featuring Les Holroyd, who have been touring since 2002.

Root and Jenny Jackson, born in Trinidad, were a brother and sister soul/RnB outfit based in Huddersfield, West Yorkshire. In a similar mould to Ike and Tina Turner the duo were backed by their six piece band, The High Timers.

Victor Brox, from Manchester, is an accomplished musician who has worked with Eric Clapton, Ritchie Blackmore and Ian Gillan of Deep Purple. He has been described by Jimi Hendrix and Tina Turner as their favourite white blues singer. He is still performing as Victor Brox Blues Train.

Café Society were a trio comprising Tom Robinson, Hereward Kaye and Raphael 'Ray' Doyle. They recorded one self-titled album on the Konk record label, produced by Ray Davies of the Kinks. Tom Robinson, who joined Café Society in 1973, went on to have chart success with his own Tom Robinson Band. The band's single '2-4-6-8 Motorway' reached No. 5 in the UK Singles Chart of 1977, and Robinson's solo hit 'War Baby' peaked at No. 6 in 1983.

Active in the early 70s, **Gwenyway** were an acoustic-rock outfit formed by musician Pete Marsh from Cumbria. During the post Beatles era and influenced by the likes of Crosby, Stills, Nash & Young, he assembled the band Gwenyway to perform acoustic covers. During his long career Pete Marsh has worked with the likes of Manfred Mann, 10cc and Vangelis and is still active recording, having released the album *Back To The Beginning* in 2017.

Tom Robinson and Café Society © David Bradbury

Barclay James Harvest 1975 © David Bradbury

Barclay James Harvest 1975 © Neil Yates

Barclay James Harvest

I promoted Barclay James Harvest twice as headliners at Lancaster University, but it was the second date, 31 October 1975, that remains in my memory for a couple of reasons. But before I describe them, I must tell of one of the more bizarre clauses in the band's rider. This stated that the promoter on the night must wear a white suit! Totally ridiculous but it did get me a rather fetching new outfit that I later wore to an NUS conference – see Paul Loasby's memories.

It was a Friday; doors were to open at 7.30 pm with the support band on stage at 8.00 pm, the usual running order by now. We had dropped the 2.00 am, three or four bands programming format by then. I was getting too old, so were the musicians! Now bands on the road were arriving about 2.00 pm, or rather their PA and road crew were. But here we were, 7.00 pm, no band or equipment. It would take at least two hours to set up – what to do? Cancel? Easier to keep the doors shut than have to clear the hall of 1000-plus disgruntled fans – I know it wasn't metal but 'hippies' can get nasty too, you know!

Then, just as I was going to toss the coin to help me make the 'life-changing' or 'life-threatening' decision, a rather harassed, dishevelled roadie turned up. 7.15 pm!

"Traffic," he pleaded.

"Bloody hell, how long before you're ready?"

"Give us some extra humpers and an hour."

"OK. Done."

We very nearly were!

On the bill that night was a support band called Café Society. Now a close friend – agent, promoter, record shop owner and advisor, Mike Lloyd from Hanley, near Stoke – had phoned me up the previous day, saying that he had noticed I had BJH performing on Friday. Well he had had them on the Wednesday (I think it was, forty years is a long time to remember days, too many pints of Mitchell's in the Ring o' Bells) and he had to tell me about the support band. Café Society, he said, was the worst band he had ever had on (a trifle harsh, I thought afterwards). They had left the stage to deathly silence; a lone voice had sarcastically called out "More." The band returned to the stage. "I didn't mean it," cried the voice. Mike said they were so bad he had refused to pay them their measly £50 fee. Again a bit harsh.

Anyway they played Lancaster and, well, at the end of the night I was settling the BJH account with a cheque and had Cafe Society's £50 cash. They never showed up so I presumed that maybe what had happened in Hanley was happening a lot and they had stopped going in search of their petrol/beer/food money. I wasn't about to chase them, so …

It was several years later that the story reached its conclusion. In 1977 a single by a 'new' punk artist reached No. 5 in the national charts, '2-4-6-8 Motorway'. The artist was Tom Robinson – previously in Café Society. Paul Loasby was doing some dates with him and in a conversation I said I really wanted a date, really fancied it. I would even pay £5000! That was a great deal of money for me to guarantee. Unheard of, believe me.

"He won't do it," Paul said.

"Of course he will," I insisted.

"Look, I'll put you on a conference call if you promise to keep quiet."

So I heard, biting my knuckles, that I had cheated him (Tom Robinson) out of £50 and he wouldn't play for me for any amount. I even suggested to Paul that he go back and offer £5050 but same answer – it was a matter of principal.

Well that was almost a first, a matter of principal in the music business. Sort of impressive, wasn't it?

P.S. A further development, or maybe a conclusion, to this story has occurred in the last couple of weeks. On reading this book, as a preface to his writing of the foreword, Andy Kershaw rang me to query my description of Tom Robinson in my *Regrets* section. I explained that the only thing 'monstrous' about him was his fame; he was selling vast numbers of records and tickets. "Oh, that's OK then," Andy responded, "I was just worried because I'd always found him to be a really great bloke. Tom is a good mate of mine that I see fairly regularly."

I outlined the aforementioned story, explaining that I hadn't realised that he had been in Café Society when I was trying to book him. "I tell you what," Andy gleefully promised, "the next time I see Tom I'll give him £50 and explain it's from you and Lancaster University – it's the money you've been owed for years!"

I really hope he remembers to do that and that Tom buys him a couple of pints with it.

Barry Lucas

Bauhaus

30 October 1981   Support: Natural Scientist

Bauhaus were an English rock band, formed in Northampton, England, in 1978. The group consisted of Daniel Ash (guitar, saxophone), Peter Murphy (vocals, occasional instruments), Kevin Haskins (drums) and David J (bass). The band was originally named Bauhaus 1919 in reference to the first operating year of the German art school Bauhaus, although they shortened the name within a year of formation. One of the pioneers of gothic rock, Bauhaus were known for their dark image and gloomy sound. The band though, were probably best known for their first single, the nine minute long 'Bela Lugosi's Dead', released in August 1979.

Bauhaus broke up in 1983, but eventually reunited for a tour in 1998 and then again from 2005–2008 before finally calling it a day.

Bauhaus's support came from Lancaster electro-punk and new wave band, **Natural Scientist**. The band was originally formed around the summer of 1980 by ex-China Street guitarist Martin Pilkington, emerging out of a Lancaster band called Wanda and The Dentists. Over their existence, Natural Scientist went through many personnel changes up until their final disbandment, after two lengthy US tours, in early 1986.

In 1981 they released a 12" EP called Terminal Velocity on their own Dental Records label which reached no 8 in the "Sounds Dance Chart" and was subsequently featured by John Peel on his Radio 1 show, resulting in an invitation to London to record a live session for Peel. This was recorded on the 5th October 1981, the day after the band had stepped in at short notice to play the Great Hall following a last-minute cancellation by Hazel O'Connor. Ultimately the exposure from the Peel session was to result in the offer of a supporting slot to Bauhaus and later Liverpool band The Higsons as well as two nationwide tours of the UK supporting both Shalamar and Rose Royce.

Their first EP was followed up with a 7" single in 1982, A-Side See Through You, B-Side Liar, and another 12" EP in 1984 entitled, Anaesthetic Of Love.

For this Bauhaus gig on 30 October 1981 Natural Scientist lined up as follows:
Martin Pilkington (aka Boris Forrest) – guitar, vocals
Stuart Baldwin – guitar, vocals
Iggy Brockbank – bass, vocals
Mark Carricker – drums
Neil 'Fee' Crossley – keyboards

Courtesy of Gabor Nemeth www.bauhausgigguide.info

I haven't got a great deal to say about this concert except a short story to help give an insight into a promoter's mind. Bauhaus were a very interesting, innovative band, or arty-farty, depending on your point of view. Not to everybody's taste but if you were into them, you were, and enthusiastically so.

Paul Loasby, as PLP, was promoting the show and it hadn't done very well. He was losing a lot of money. So, to cheer him up, drown his sorrows etc., I took him to the ASH bar (Assistant Staff House) opposite the Great Hall entrance. In the middle of his second pint, Paul suddenly said that we had to get back to the hall as the band were on in five minutes and we had to watch them. "Hang on, I don't understand this, you're losing money so why would you want to watch it flowing down the drain?" I asked, bewildered.

"But they're bloody brilliant, got to watch them!" Paul was in the music business as a promoter because he loved the music. It set him apart from most of the other promoters at the time, and it certainly would today. It was also why he had great flair as a promoter and probably explains why he had so many financially disastrous gigs!

Barry Lucas

Be-Bop Deluxe

22 January 1977 — Support: The Steve Gibbons Band

Be-Bop Deluxe were an English progressive rock band who achieved critical acclaim and moderate commercial success during the mid to late '70s. Be-Bop Deluxe were formed by Wakefield-born Bill Nelson in 1972 and went on to achieve success with five studio albums and three live albums. Their single 'Ships in the Night' reached No. 23 in the UK charts of 1976. Bill Nelson was to return to the Great Hall with his band Red Noise in 1979 after Nelson dissolved Be-Bop Deluxe.

Support on the night came from Birmingham rocker **Steve Gibbons**, still doing his stuff today having extensively toured the UK, Europe and Scandinavia since 1986. His band also provided support to Manfred Mann's Earth Band's November 1973 concert.

The Beat

15 May 1981 — Supports: Au Pairs I The Mood Elevators
15 October 1982 — Support: Berlin Wales

British ska band The Beat made two visits to Lancaster University.

They were founded in Birmingham in 1978 and are probably best known for their cover of the classic Motown hit 'Tears of a Clown' which reached No. 6 in the UK charts in 1979, followed by 'Mirror In The Bathroom' which peaked at No. 4 in 1980. 'Mirror In The Bathroom' was the first single released in the UK to have been digitally recorded.

The original lineup of the band broke up in 1983, but after many personnel changes two versions of the band continue to tour today; one under the name of The English Beat, and the other The Beat.

The **Au Pairs** were a post-punk band who were formed in Birmingham in 1979 and were compared in style to The Gang of Four. Fronting the band was vocalist/guitarist Lesley Woods who at the time was described as "one of the most striking women in British rock". They released two albums before disbanding in 1983.

A four-piece band from Birmingham, **The Mood Elevators** were invited to support The Beat on their 1981 tour, after the band saw them perform at a pub gig in 1980.

Little is known about 1982 support act **Berlin Wales.**

Beck, Bogert and Appice

19 January 1974 — Supports: Marie Celeste I Upp

Jeff Beck, Tim Bogert and drummer Carmine Appice formed their hard rock trio in 1972, evolving from The Jeff Beck Group, with Bogert and Appice coming from Vanilla Fudge. Their debut album, *Beck, Bogert and Appice*, was their one and only studio album, followed by *Live in Japan.* This Lancaster concert featured the band performing the song 'Superstition,' originally written for Jeff Beck by Stevie Wonder. The plan was for Beck to release his version of this song first, with his newly formed band. However, due to a combination of the delayed release of Beck, Bogert and Appice's debut album and Motown CEO Berry Gordy's prediction that 'Superstition' would be a huge hit, Wonder ended up releasing the song as the lead single off his album *Talking Book* ahead of Beck's version. It reached No. 1 in the US and peaked at No. 11 in the UK Singles Chart in February 1973. Beck, Bogert and Appice disbanded in 1974.

Marie Celeste were an acoustic five-piece psychedelic/folk band from Wolverhampton, with two female vocalists.

Upp were a 4 piece an English rock/jazz fusion band, active in the 1970s. Jeff Beck met the band UPP in a recording studio and decided to use them as a backing band for a BBC TV programme called 'Guitar Workshop' in 1974. He subsequently played on, and produced their self-titled first album. UPP's second album, *This Way ... Upp* was released on the Epic label in 1976 and featured, amongst many 'friends' guesting, a certain Jeff Beck on guitar.

Bert Jansch

13 November 1974 Support: Decameron
2 March 1978

Following two fabulous Great Hall concerts with Pentangle in the early seventies, Glaswegian folk musician Herbert 'Bert' Jansch returned to Lancaster for two solo concerts post Pentangle break-up. The first visit fell between the release of Jansch's eighth album *Moonshine* and his ninth in 1974 *LA Turnaround*.

Bert Jansch returned five years later for a solo concert in the Nuffield Theatre which fell between the release of his 1977 album *A Rare Conundrum* and his beautiful meditative paean to British birds in the 1979 album *Avocet*.

Bert Jansch made his name, playing alongside his friend and fellow guitarist John Renbourn. Over his career Jansch recorded six albums with Pentangle up to their disbandment in early 1973 and over 20 albums under his own name and several more jointly with Renbourn.

Following a long battle with cancer Bert Jansch passed away in 2011 aged sixty seven; his last appearance was earlier that year for a concert in the Royal Festival Hall in London.

Decameron, formed in Cheltenham were a British folk/prog rock band that existed from 1968–1976. They released a total of four studio albums over their career. One of their first managers was future comedian Jasper Carrot.

This was the fourth appearance by Bert Jansch at Lancaster. In 1970 and 1972 he was on the Great Hall stage as part of the amazing Pentangle, for whom his vocals, and more importantly his guitar work, proved so important in establishing the band at the forefront of British folk music. In 1973 he left to concentrate on his own blend of folk and blues and became an iconic performer, visiting the University early in his career.

I was to use the Nuffield Theatre on many occasions over the years, as it was an excellent venue for those quality acts that couldn't fill the Great Hall but had a substantial, dedicated following. These were mainly folk and blues acts, although there was the truly memorable night when I had Joy Division as a third-on-the-bill act! Being a theatre club, the Nuffield licence did not have a stipulated audience capacity. It didn't make sense to me then and it still doesn't today, but then there have been many aspects of the UK's public entertainments licensing laws that have been beyond my comprehension. With Ken Parrot, the Director of Nuffield, we worked on a capacity of 550 and it created a terrific atmosphere in there.

Bert Jansch provided one such notable evening, when his guitar work was staggeringly good and that raspy voice was so perfect for the blues. He had, by now, been recognised as one of the great British guitarists: "the innovator of the time … so far ahead of what anyone else was doing" (Jimmy Page); "he was one of the most influential and intriguing musicians to have come out of the British music scene" (Johnny Marr). Other artists influenced by him include Donovan, Paul Simon and Neil Young. It was a great night in the Nuffield!

Barry Lucas

John Angus

Big Country

6 October 1984   **Steeltown Tour**   Support: White China

Stuart Adamson, former frontman of The Skids, returned to Lancaster for a concert with his band Big Country, six years after The Skids provided the support to The Stranglers in 1978.

Formed in Dunfermline, they were best known for the single 'Fields Of Fire (400 Miles)' which reached No. 10 in the UK Singles Chart in 1983. After releasing a total of nine studio albums Big Country are still active today.

The band currently features two of the original members: drummer Mark Brzezicki and guitarist Bruce Watson, but sadly without Stuart Adamson, who committed suicide in 2001.

Formed in 1981 **White China** are a five piece band, also from The Skids hometown, Dunfermline.

They disbanded in 1986 then re-formed in 2012 and are still recording and touring.

Bill Bruford's UK

12 May 1978   Support: The Fabulous Poodles

Former drummer with Yes, Genesis and King Crimson, Bill Bruford visited Lancaster University for a second time with his band, UK.

Active from 1977 to 1980 the lineup consisted of:
John Wetton (formerly of Uriah Heep) – bass guitar
Eddie Jobson (from Curved Air) – keyboards, violins
Alan Holdsworth (formerly of Soft Machine) – guitars
Bill Bruford – drums

They produced two studio albums and one live album during their three-year existence.

Bruford had previously appeared as drummer with Yes in the Great Hall in 1970.

Lancaster setlist: 'Alaska', 'Time to Kill', 'The Sahara of Snow', 'Carrying No Cross', 'The Only Thing She Needs', 'Forever Until Sunday', 'Thirty Years In the Dead of Night', 'By the Light of Day', 'Presto Vivace', 'Caesar's Palace Blues'.

Mick Walsh reviewing the concert in *SCAN* newspaper said;

> "UK provided stark contrast to the ribald teen beat love songs provided by support band, The Fabulous Poodles. There was no humour or communication from UK with the audience; just four uncompromising musicians determined to stand or fall on the quality of the music that they produced. I am pleased to report that they stood up quite admirably".

The Fabulous Poodles were a quirky pub rock band formed in 1976, who disbanded in 1980 after releasing two UK albums.

Bill Nelson's Red Noise

16 March 1979　　　　Support: Fingerprintz

After dissolving Be-Bop Deluxe, Bill Nelson formed his new wave band, Red Noise in 1978, along with his brother Ian and one other former member of Be-Bop Deluxe, Andy Clarke. Releasing just the one album, *Sound-on-Sound* in February 1979, and two singles, Red Noise disbanded later that same year.

Lancaster band lineup:
Bill Nelson – guitars
Ian Nelson – saxophone
Andy Clark – keyboards
Rick Ford – bass guitar
Steve Peer – drums

SCAN newspaper reported that, due to adverse weather conditions that afternoon, Bill and his wife Jan did not arrive at the university until 7.45 pm:

> "Without a sound check, Red Noise took to the stage clad in Nelson designed 'Trumpton' soldiers uniforms to a half-filled audience. The opener 'Don't Touch Me (I'm Electric)' set the attack".

Fingerprintz were formed in 1979 by Scottish vocalist Jimmie O'Neill and guitarist Cha Burns. Three albums were released before their disbandment in 1985.

Bill Nelson in the Great Hall © David Stewart

Billy Connolly

1979　　　　**Big Wee Tour**

Billy Connolly was born and raised in Glasgow, Scotland. He left school to work in the shipyards, becoming a welder, and joined the Territorial Army (in the parachute regiment) at around the same time.

He developed an interest in folk music, eventually becoming an accomplished banjo player and a member of the band Humblebums with Gerry Rafferty (later of 'Baker Street' fame). The jokes he told between songs eventually took over his act and he became a full-time comedian. Already a big star in Scotland, he became a household name in the UK after appearing on Parkinson (1971) in the early seventies. Billy has released many recordings and videos of his concert performances over the years and has expanded his repertoire to include acting, appearing in a number of television dramas and films, most recently in the USA. In the '90s he made two documentary series for the BBC, about Scotland and Australia respectively, and in 1997 starred in the award winning film *Mrs Brown*. He is one of the UK's top comedians.

Billy Connolly

"The Big Yin" hit Lancaster on his 'Big Wee Tour'. It was after THE Parkinson interview and THE bike joke. It also marked the very beginning of the era when comedy became the new rock 'n' roll. Promoted like a major music tour, Billy was one of the very first comedians to tour rock venues as opposed to theatres. The show here in the Great Hall was fully seated, so it was limited to 950 tickets, which sold out very quickly.

At this point Billy Connolly was going through his drugs, alcohol and rock 'n' roll period, well documented in Pamela Stephenson's great biography. As she recounted, Billy became very fond indeed of cocaine, finding it a great help to his shows in the early days. I was asked to send someone down to London to pick up an album Mr Connolly urgently required – we weren't told what was being transported back to Lancaster, only that it was a very valuable album and must be guarded accordingly. It wasn't Bing Crosby's 'White Christmas' but maybe it ought to have been!

Billy was a remarkable tour de force and made mincemeat of any hecklers foolish enough to take him on. An outstanding show! I cannot claim that I foresaw the rise of the comedy 'gods' but I did recognise that here was a potentially lucrative market; comedians did indeed provide a good night out.

After the show, Bailrigg Student Television asked if they could have an interview. A TV studio was quickly constructed backstage and Billy gave what turned out to be an hour's performance – it was brilliant but the budding TV producers complained to me afterwards that he was somewhat 'wired' and went on and on when they only wanted a brief ten minutes interview! They had a unique event but I bet they didn't keep it for posterity – what a tragedy.

As a postscript, I heard that Mr Connolly had a great night back at his hotel!

Barry Lucas

Billy Connolly on the Great Hall stage
all © Geoff Campbell

Black Oak Arkansas

14 January 1974   Support: Sassafrass

The legendary influential American southern rock band Black Oak Arkansas were formed in 1963 and took their name simply from their hometown of Black Oak in Arkansas USA.

Led by Jim "Dandy" Mangrum, the band reached the height of its fame in the 1970s with ten charting albums released in that decade, the best known being *High On The Hog,* which reached No. 25 in 1974's Billboard Hot 100 Chart. James Mangrum has continued to record and tour with a series of different Black Oak lineups up to the present day.

Reportedly, Black Oak Arkansas hold the world record for the highest number of successive members of a rock band: sixty-one.

Sassafrass from South Wales were formed in 1970 and were described as a kind of Fleetwood Mac/Eagles hybrid. The use of twin guitar solos was a distinctive feature of their music. In the early 1970s they held the record for highest number of gigs in a single year, with their 332 beating Slade by one!

Black Oak Arkansas

Jim Dandy to the rescue! This is not so much the story of a concert but of a relationship which was so important to the history of rock music at Lancaster University.

College Event, a magazine mentioned elsewhere in this book, was a mini-bible for the music business at one time. It was mandatory reading for college social secretaries, agents, record companies and promoters in the '70s. On a page dedicated to music in the North, it mentioned, as an aside, the red telephone line between Leeds and Lancaster across the Pennines. It largely went unnoticed in the business but it was of huge significance for the future.

Leeds University was for years THE college venue, a reputation and programme which could only be dreamed of by all other college venues in the country. But I was determined to change all that and in the early '70s that process started. Lancaster started to be an irritating thorn in Leeds' side, slowly gaining ground then beginning to get the occasional act that they were unable to sign. Why? I am sure it was a mystery to a succession of social secretaries. I loved it; they were growing to hate it and eventually to fear it. Their social secs were faceless names to me, I never met any of them and that's the way I wanted it to stay – it made it easier to beat them. Of course I knew several of them by name but I had little respect for them as promoters; they were at one of the biggest universities in the UK, sat on the main motorway in the country, in one of the biggest cities in the country, and had no public hall or venue in the city to compete with, so obviously they were always going to be offered the biggest acts. However, I did get to know Andy Kershaw later as he phoned me on his election to the post of social secretary and asked for some advice and guidance. He proved to be a very accomplished promoter and I had to (grudgingly) admire his achievements. The summer after he left Leeds I was backstage at Donnington with Geoff Campbell and several agents and promoters when Andy came up to tell us he had been offered a job with the BBC. He proceeded to regale us all for about thirty minutes with the most entertaining stories and anecdotes. Andy then ended with "Can't think why they've offered me a job." We all looked at each other and thought, "We know why."

A few years earlier at Imperial College, London, NUS Social Secretaries' Conference, on the Saturday lunchtime, young agent Richard Griffiths (mentioned elsewhere as the first AC/DC manager) came up to me: "Hi Barry, do you want to meet the Leeds Social Secretary?"

"No," I abruptly replied, and moved to the bar.

"Oh, well, Barry this is Paul Loasby. Paul this is Barry Lucas from Lancaster. "Not interested", I thought, but then he did offer to buy me a beer, and I'm always a sucker for that. Anyway, one beer progressed to two, to ten. Paul was down at the conference with some of his committee, sleeping in the back of a transit van – very rock 'n' roll, but not very big time. "Erm, he might be OK", I thought.

Paul Loasby was more than that; he became my best mate and without him some of the legendary events detailed in this book simply would not have happened. In today's terminology we bonded; in '70s speak we got pissed together.

We formed a friendship that lasts to this day but in those early days we talked, exchanged ideas, he picked my brain and we set up that 'red phone line' between our offices. One day Paul used that line to tell me he had been offered Black Oak for £1500. They were a biggish American rock band who would do business. I phoned the agent and the conversations that followed were priceless.

"Hey I'm interested in Black Oak but I'm the only professional ents officer, I'm not paying £1500 like that amateur social sec. at Leeds."

"Paul, got it for £1250, your turn."

"Hey, this is Leeds University, the best and the most prestigious university gig in Europe, I'm not paying more than other unis."

"Barry, got it down to £1000."

"Hey I told you, this is my job, my career, I'm not in it for a laugh! I have to make money to justify being the only full time ents officer in Europe. I can't be seen to be paying the same as other unis."

"Paul, got it for £750, over to you again."

We both got Jim Dandy to perform for £750, half the fee other colleges were paying. Get in!

Barry Lucas

Black Sabbath

12 June 1970   **"Black Sabbath" Tour**   Supports: The Pretty Things I Fat Abbots

Pioneers of heavy metal, Black Sabbath were formed in Birmingham in 1968 by guitarist and main songwriter Tony Iommi, bassist and main lyricist Geezer Butler, singer Ozzy Osbourne and drummer Bill Ward.

On 30 August 1969 Black Sabbath played their first ever live gig in Workington, Cumbria.

Their June 1970 concert in the Great Hall was in support of the band's debut album *Black Sabbath*, released in February 1970, which went on to reach No. 8 in the UK album chart.

Probable setlist: 'Paranoid', 'Iron Man', 'N.I.B', 'Black Sabbath', 'Walpurgis', 'Hand of Doom', 'Fairies Wear Boots', 'Guitar Solo', 'Behind the Wall of Sleep', 'Rat Salad'.

Starting in January 2016, Black Sabbath embarked on their final world tour, entitled The End Tour, and, following eighty-one dates, the band played their final concert on 4 February 2017 in their home city of Birmingham.

The Pretty Things are an English rock band from London, formed by Dick Taylor and Phil May in 1963. Their first album, *The Pretty Things*, was released in 1965 and reached No. 6 in the UK Albums Chart. In June 1970 the university saw the band supporting Black Sabbath and performing numbers from their newly released album *Parachute*. This was a landmark album, receiving rave reviews and was a very mature, serious concept recording. In 1972, The Pretty Things returned to Lancaster in a supporting role to Medicine Head.

The **Fat Abbots** were a short-lived Goth rock band from Leicester and were managed by Barry Lucas' sister.

For a short – very short! – time the Fat Abbots were managed by my sister, Carol. We paid them their petrol money to Lancaster and found them a student's floor to sleep on.

In the summer of 1970, Gaz Taylor and I were flushed with the success of The Who and had already booked acts, such as Black Sabbbath and Family, for the autumn term. So we decided to do a little private promoting to supplement our grants. My family had moved to Oadby, near Leicester, and we toured the area until we found a venue in Coalville, a small, former mining town nearby. We called our promoting company 'Tusk Promotions' – Gaz' idea, not mine – and we did two shows, the first with Van der Graff Generator and the other featuring Black Widow.

As you will have no doubt gathered, they weren't wildly successful – we didn't promote any more as there weren't enough tickets sold to bulk up our grants. But Black Widow, a Leicester-born Goth, black magic, heavy rock band, nearly famous for their legendary single 'Come to the Sabbat (Satan's there)', were supported by another Leicester Goth band, the Fat Abbots.

Barry Lucas

Blonde on Blonde

24 October 1969　　　　Support: Eclection

Blonde on Blonde were a guitar-led psychedelic rock group from South Wales and arrived in North Lancashire for one of the first 'Central Hall' concerts.

The band were formed in Newport in 1967 by vocalist and guitarist Ralph Denyer, drummer Les Hicks, bassist Richard Hopkins and guitarist and sitar player Gareth Johnson. The band were named after Bob Dylan's 1966 album of the same name.

They released three studio albums during their four-year existence: *Contrasts* in 1969 was followed by *Rebirth* in 1970 and *Reflections On A Life* in 1971.

Blonde on Blonde appeared at the 1969 Isle of Wight Festival but achieved only modest commercial success. They disbanded in early 1972.

Support band **Eclection** were a short-lived, British-based psychedelic/folk rock band, originally formed in 1967 in London by Norwegian-born Georg Kajanus. They released the one self-titled album on the Elektra label.

Georg Kajanus returned to Lancaster with his band Sailor, the support act for Mott The Hoople in their 1974 Great Hall concert.

Blondie

27 February 1978　　　**Rag Ball Concert**　　　Supports: Advertising | Mungo Jerry

Formed in 1974 and originally called Angel and the Snake, Blondie were one of the first American new wave bands to achieve mainstream success in the United Kingdom and arrived at Lancaster University to promote the February 1978 release of their second album *Plastic Letters*. The album gave the band their first two hit singles, 'Denis', which reached No. 2 in the UK charts, and '(I'm Always Touched by Your) Presence, Dear', going to No. 10.

Later in September 1978, Blondie released the album that would make them international stars, entitled *Parallel Lines*. The album went to No. 1 in the UK Albums Chart and spawned several hit singles, including the No. 1 hits 'Heart Of Glass' and 'Sunday Girl'.

Lancaster band lineup:
Debbie Harry – lead vocals
Chris Stein – guitars
Nigel Harrison – bass
Jimmy Destri – keyboards, backing vocals
Clem Burke – drums

Blondie broke up in 1982 and re-formed in 1997, going on to achieve another No. 1 UK hit with 'Maria' in 1999.

A concert-goer at the time, David Summers remembers seeing Debbie Harry and her entourage prior to the concert eating in the nearby Cartmel College refectory. He told me: "She looked like some sort of beautiful alien creature; a queen bee surrounded by her drones."

Mungo Jerry appeared last on the bill around midnight as late replacements for the initially advertised Alberto y Los Trios Paranoias, the Mancunian comedy rock band.

According to a *SCAN* concert review;

> "Blondie were very ordinary on the night with Mungo Jerry later producing a tremendous set that really livened the evening up; the band performing their classics, 'In The Summertime', 'Lady Rose', 'Long Legged Woman Dressed in Black' and 'Alright, Alright, Alright'."

Little is known about the band **Advertising** but Mick Walsh, writing in *SCAN*, noted:

> "… despite the band finishing with a dry rendition of Petula Clark's 'Downtown' the reception was decidedly lukewarm"

I owe this one solely to 'Ear 'Ere Records.

In this period, Rag Week ended with the Rag Ball. Unfortunately it was organised by the Rag Committee, a group of individuals who were great at zany stunts – throwing flour, eggs and water over OAPs from rag floats in Lancaster city centre etc. Such jolly japes! But these same people had to research, book and organise a rock concert – the Rag Ball – and they were simply not cut out for that. They continually oversaw disasters, as they overpaid and under drew. I offered to incorporate the Ball into my programme, whereby I would book and run the show and they could have all the profits. Al Gordon, later to be a truly great student union president but at that moment Rag Chairman, agreed and gave me free reign.

I was in 'Ear 'Ere one evening when a record company rep. came in with a new 12" single. Picture disc, beautiful blonde, basque, suspenders, stockings torn and ripped – 'Rip Her To Shreds'. I know, very unPC today, but then …

She was American, coming over for a UK tour and record release. I felt immediately that this would not just generate music paper headlines; this would feature in the red-tops, pages of it. It was going to be a sensation, I knew it for certain. But for some unknown reason very few others in the music business did, whatever they may say today.

So it came to pass that I was able to get a date on Blondie's first tour, £500, straight fee, no percentage. It meant that if the show sold as I thought it would we would make a killing. I didn't even attempt to haggle with the agent, a young guy who didn't really know what he had been given, nor, I suspect, did his bosses. It wasn't his fault, although I believe it was to later cost him his job. Al Gordon and "the committee" said that they had never heard of the band and were very nervous. 'Trust me' was all I could say. Well you can guess the rest: a monstrous sell-out. I had stuck a support band on to appease the Rag brigade and help fulfill the criteria of Rag Ball, the good time band, Mungo Jerry.

That evening I was standing at the back of the hall talking to Debbie Harry when the doors were opened. We were almost knocked off our feet by hoards of desperate young lads, crashing into and past us in their eagerness to get to the front of the stage. I said to Debbie: "Do you realise they're barging us over to get to the front to have a better view of you?"

"Yeah, funny, if only they knew," she laughed.

For some bizarre reason Blondie, like several other new, mainstream bands, were labelled as punk. After the show I had to attempt to reassure a confused Debbie Harry, who was towelling off pints of 'gob'.

"Honest, spitting on you means they really like you!"

"Fucking hell, what would they do if they thought I was crap?!"

Barry Lucas

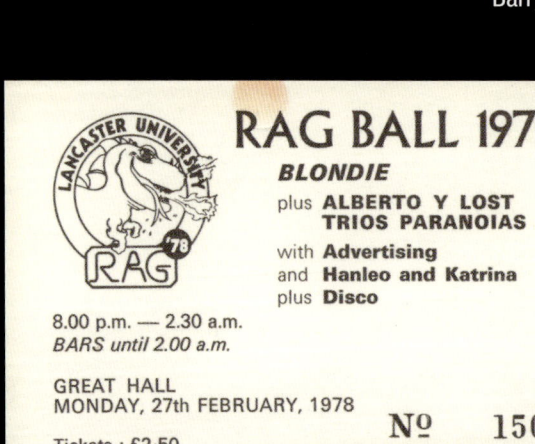

LANCASTER RAG BALL

BLONDIE

BLONDIE - Have been hailed as the American punk band - but to British audiences that can be a very misleading description, British and American punk are poles apart. Their debut album last year "Blondie" featuring the beautiful Debbie Harry tended to the softer pop side of the market. Her vocals were very reminiscent of The Shangrilas but this 2nd album 'Plastic Letters' plays down that side of their music and concentrates on more complex, powerful musical numbers.

Of course the presence of the classical American blonde beauty of Debbie Harry has meant that when they arrived in London a couple of weeks ago every national paper had full page articles especially The Sun, Mirror and Mail, even The Morecambe and Lancaster Guardian managed half a page. Although this has meant many of the inane "Get 'em off" calls from the front rows Debbie Harry has a great line in put downs. Many a budding young male chauvinist has crawled away from many a hall in Britain and America. A 'nice dumb blonde' proves to be anything but.

MUNGO JERRY with their monstrous hits of a few years ago have developed into a great ball band. Their mixture of jug music and rock 'n' roll has resulted in full date sheets at College, Grad, Summer and Rag Balls. It's dancey good-time music nothing more nothing less.

ADVERTISING: are EMI's 'new white hopes' for 1978 bigtime, supporting Blondie on the whole tour.

HANLEO + KATRINA: a real live circus act featuring knife throwing, snakes, fire eating etc.

MR. WIZARD DISCO: one of the most comprehensive, professional outfits in the N. West.

LATE BAR: 2:00 a.m. drinking.

LATE TRANSPORT: Free buses back to Lancaster and Morecambe at 2:30.

TIMES: 8:00 - 2:30 a.m.

TICKETS: £2.00 from SRC Reception or Ear-Ere Records, Lancaster.

selling fast

Blue Jays Justin Hayward and John Lodge

12 December 1975   Support: Trapeze

During the period of The Moody Blue's three-year hiatus, Justin Hayward and John Lodge recorded and released the album *Blue Jays*, in March 1975. The name *Blue Jays* for the album came from being not only, obviously, the name of a bird but also the fact that the album was put together by the Moody Blues members, all of whose first names began with J; the (Moody) Blue Js.

Originally scheduled for 21 November 1975, this concert was cancelled due to Justin Hayward's laryngitis and rearranged to take place on 12 December 1975.

The live recording of the whole of the Lancaster University performance is available as part of an eleven disc Moody Blues compilation album called *Timeless Flight*.

Lancaster setlist: 'Tuesday Afternoon', 'You And Me', 'My Brother', 'Isn't Life Strange', 'Who Are You Now', 'New Horizon', 'Emily's Song', 'I Dreamed Last Night', 'Nights In White Satin', 'I'm just A Singer', 'Blue Guitar', 'When You Wake Up', 'Question'.

Band lineup:
Justin Hayward – guitar, vocals
John Lodge – bass guitar, vocals
Jim Cockey – violin
Tim Tompkins – cello
Tom Tompkins – viola
Kirk Duncan – piano
Graham Deakin – drums

Support on the night was supplied by the Woverhampton hard rock band **Trapeze.** Formed in 1969, the core members of the band were vocalist John Jones, guitarist/keyboardist Terry Rowley, guitarist Mel Galley, singer/bassist Glenn Hughes, and drummer Dave Holland. In 1973, shortly before this Lancaster appearance, Glenn Hughes left to join Deep Purple. Drummer Dave Holland went on to join Judas Priest in 1979. Trapeze had major musical success in the 1970s and 1980s releasing a total of six studio albums along with a successful 1970 single 'Black Cloud' taken from the album *Medusa*, produced by John Lodge. Trapeze finally disbanded in the eary 1990s.

Blue Jays

The Blue Jays' story started with The Moody Blues – of course it did, I hear you cry, but in the case of Lancaster University it has a significant meaning.

When I booked The Moody Blues for a concert in November 1971 – for £1500, the same price as Pink Floyd and more than for The Who – the band were of legendary status. Several hit albums and one of the defining hit singles of the '60s, 'Nights in White Satin', had established them as major artists of the late '60s and '70s. I can still visualise the tour poster. It was a multi-coloured map of the UK detailing their stops and (thrillingly for me then) naming each local promoter, so I had my name up in lights all over the country! Unfortunately I didn't keep a copy of the poster and generally very little memorabilia from the Great Hall concerts; if only I had known then what I know now.

Tickets went on sale and they flew out. People were coming from Scotland, the North East and the Midlands. It was a major music event. On the day of the show I went down into Lancaster to pick up the ticket stubs and money from the local agents. Arriving back at the Students' Union offices in University House at about 3.30 pm, I found Reception slamming the shutters down and the Union's secretaries fleeing the building to cries of, "Well *I'm* not telling him!" Brave Sue remained though, nervously seated behind her typewriter, smiling, sort of. "What's wrong?" I rather hesitantly asked.

"Well," she said, "we've just had a phone call from London. Tonight's show has been cancelled."

"Ha bloody ha, too busy for jokes, I've got a major sell-out on tonight."

"No you haven't, ring this number."

I rang MAM, The Moody Blues agency. The booker was very apologetic: "John Lodge has been taken ill with gasteroenteritis. We have had to cancel a number of dates and the band cannot perform in Lancaster tonight."

"He can't have!"

"He has and we are sending you the Harley Street certificate. Illness, nothing we can do about it. Contract invalid. Sorry."

Bloody hell, he's sorry! Nothing compared to the state I was in. But there really was nothing I could do about it. I couldn't argue with him, just no point. What to do? Lots of people – especially my wife, Mary, who booked and ran The Platform in Morecambe, a local authority arts/music venue – can't stand the hassle, the pressure when things go wrong. I, on the other hand, love it. I really do get a buzz out of thinking on my feet, in a crisis, sorting out a problem. Here was first problem: I can't stop people travelling to Lancaster so I need to refund them when they arrive; banks closed, phone bank manager, get them to re-open and cash me a cheque for 1500 x £1.25p. I went across Alexandra Square with a big holdall – do you know how heavy 1500 x 5p and 3000 x 10p coins are? No? Very heavy, I can assure you! I had to borrow a porters' trolley from University House.

The second problem; people are coming from miles, I felt I couldn't just say sorry and give them their ticket money back, so I decided to give them a 'free' show of a disco and a live band. I quickly rang Mike Lloyd, an agent in Hanley, to ask if he could get me a dancey, rhythm and blues band for three hours time! He could and he did. Right, now to the Great Hall.

After refunding 1500 tickets and explaining 700 times or more the same story, I could relax. The relief band, ironically called Money, had arrived amidst all the chaos and had set up. Go on lads at 8.00 pm. Play two forty-five minute sets, surrounded by a disco. Thanks.

I then went over to the Lonsdale Bar where John Allen sold me a large bottle of coke and a bottle of Three Pipers Scotch. Back to the balcony in the hall. The evening went surprisingly well and most punters seemed to appreciate the effort we had taken to take as much pain away as possible. A quarter of the way through the whisky and coke, the band came on. Money were good lads, semi-pros from Manchester who did cover versions, and I used them again a year or so later for a rag ball where they appeared with The Tremeloes. But nobody had told them why they were here at such short notice. Oh the irony – and I couldn't make this up – when the first number they played was … yes you guessed it, 'Nights in White Satin'! The audience just stood there: were they taking the piss? Then the booing started, then the throwing of plastic glasses. I sent someone on stage to explain the audience's reaction to the band. Big apologies. Then into a Moodie-free set and everybody had as good a time as they could, considering. I finished the bottle of scotch. Absolutely blotto, I invited the band to crash at my flat in Dallas Road. We had to stop twice, crossing the park, for me to be sick in the bushes. I was so ill the next morning, but I had a five-a-side football match in the gym – not a good idea. To this day, if I smell Three Pipers Whisky, I involuntarily retch.

The Blue Jays were a band formed during The Moody Blue's three-year hiatus, by Justin Hayward and John Lodge. But alas it never really had the same kudos in the public's mind. Here we were, four years on from The Moody Blues cancellation, and history was to repeat itself.

The Lancaster date was scheduled for November 1975 and again cancelled at short notice. This time Justin Hayward was suffering from laryngitis. Happily a date was rescheduled for December.

The show did reasonable business but wasn't a total sell-out. However, that night, at about 8.30 pm a limo drew up outside the Great Hall and out got John Conteh, the then world light heavy-weight champion, with several of his brothers. They had just been involved in an investigation into an armed robbery. Unfortunately Jeremy Oppenheim, the sabbatical editor of *SCAN*, didn't know this. Jeremy knew nothing of sport; he was a great guy, a good friend, but if it came to a fight my money would be on the wet paper bag! He said that he didn't care who they were, they were not coming in without tickets and as they didn't want to pay Jeremy was going to stand his ground. I had to pull him away and quietly explain that if he wanted to take them on he would be on his own. They got in!

At the end of a heavy night I arrived home and poured a drink, settling down to watch a movie in bed. Around 1.00 am the phone rang; it was Geoff Campbell from the Great Hall asking if I could get back there ASAP as Jack Nicholson, the senior porter, was fighting with the road crew. Bloody hell, where was John Conteh when you needed him? I arrived back at the hall just in time to see Jack boot a box of Blue Jays programmes out of the porters' lodge, scattering them across the foyer. It wasn't the roadies but the merchandising crew that Jack was after. All his Second World War submariner's skills had come to the fore. He might have been forty years older than them but he'd fought in the war. After half an hour I had calmed him down, reminded him that they were young lads, footloose and fancy free on tour – a bit like him and his mates away in the war. Did they never do anything stupid? Jack conceded and he drank the pint I'd got him from the dressing room. I could now go back to bed but no Sky pause or catch up in those days. I'd missed my film.

Barry Lucas

The Bluebells

4 October 1985 — Support: The Tempest

Following their support slot for Haircut 100 in 1982, Scottish indie band The Bluebells were back in the Great Hall for one of the last university concerts.

The band were active between 1981 and 1985, enjoying three Top 40 UK hits and releasing one studio album, *Sisters*. Their best known hit single was 'Young at Heart' which reached No. 8 in the UK Singles Chart on its original release in 1984.

1993 unexpectedly saw the single achieve the No. 1 slot in the UK Singles Chart following the use of the track in a TV advert for Volkswagen cars.

The Tempest were a 1980s acoustic pop band from Merseyside signed to Magnet Records and were produced by Glenn Tilbrook of Squeeze.

The Blues Band

5 October 1980 — Support unknown

Paul Jones, former lead vocalist and harmonica player with Manfred Mann, formed his own outfit in 1979 along with vocalist and slide guitarist Dave Kelly. Kelly had formerly played with the John Dummer Blues Band, Howlin' Wolf and John Lee Hooker among others. Also in the band's lineup at Lancaster were former Manfred Mann bassist Gary Fletcher, guitarist Tom McGuinness and drummer Hughie Flint, the two having previously been the mainstay of the band, McGuinness Flint.

The band arrived at the university to promote the release of their first album, *The Official Blues Band Bootleg Album*.

More recent albums releases for the band include *Back For More*, *Brassed Up*, *Fat City* and *Thank You Brother Ray*, the last being a set of cover versions of Ray Charles songs, recorded as a tribute.

After a brief break-up in 1983, The Blues Band are now in their thirty-seventh year and still performing across Europe with the same lineup, apart from Rob Townsend, who replaced Hughie Flint on drums in 1982.

Bob Marley and The Wailers

28 April 1973 — Catch a Fire Tour

The legendary Jamaican singer/songwriter, guitarist and activist Bob Marley was the most widely known writer and performer of reggae music and more specifically roots reggae, to emerge from Jamaica.

The Wailers, with Bob Marley, were formed in 1963 and after recording extensively in Jamaica the band were signed to Island Records, which issued its label debut album, *Catch a Fire*, in April 1973, quickly followed by *Burnin'* in October of the same year.

The Wailers arrived in the UK in the spring to embark on a twenty-eight date tour promoting the album, *Catch a Fire*, Lancaster University being the first date following a warm-up gig in Nottingham the night before.

For the sake of accuracy, this was a performance by The Wailers featuring Bob Marley. 'Bob Marley and The Wailers' came into existence in 1974 following the departure of Peter Tosh and Bunny Wailer.

The band appeared very late in the evening following a Great Hall disco and by the time the band took to the stage a large portion of the crowd had drifted away with only a lucky few remaining to unwittingly witness an historic Great Hall concert.

Band lineup:
Bob Marley – vocals, rhythm guitar
Peter Tosh – vocals, lead guitar
Bunny Wailer – vocals, congas and bongoes
Aston 'Family Man' Barrett – bass
Carlton Barrett – drums
Earl 'Wya' Lindo – keyboards

Later that same year The Wailers were to return to the UK for an ill-fated tour and scheduled to include another date at Lancaster University to promote the October 1973 release of the album *Burnin'*.

Barry expands on this in his piece on the next page.

The release of the album *Exodus* in 1977, quickly established Bob Marley's worldwide reputation and he became one of the world's best-selling artists of all time, with sales of more than seventy-five million albums and singles.

Lancaster set list

Chant A
Slave Driver
Duppy Conqueror
Small X
Been Down Low
Kinky Reggae
Concrete Jungle
Stir It Up
Stop That Train
Keep on Movin

No encore

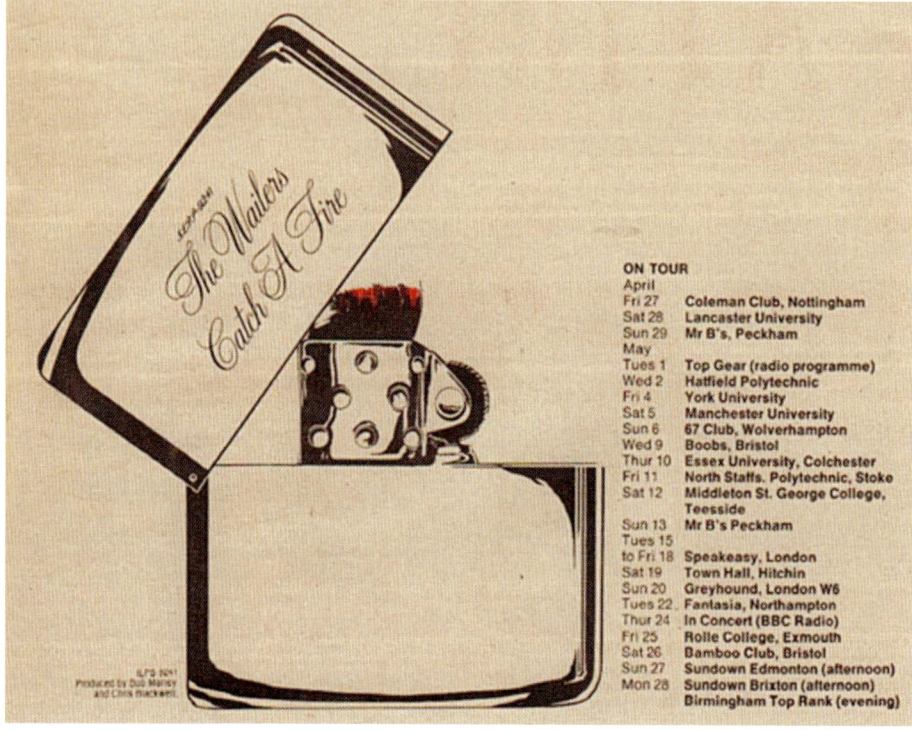

ON TOUR
April
Fri 27 — Coleman Club, Nottingham
Sat 28 — Lancaster University
Sun 29 — Mr B's, Peckham
May
Tues 1 — Top Gear (radio programme)
Wed 2 — Hatfield Polytechnic
Fri 4 — York University
Sat 5 — Manchester University
Sun 6 — 67 Club, Wolverhampton
Wed 9 — Boobs, Bristol
Thur 10 — Essex University, Colchester
Fri 11 — North Staffs. Polytechnic, Stoke
Sat 12 — Middleton St. George College, Teesside
Sun 13 — Mr B's Peckham
Tues 15 to Fri 18 — Speakeasy, London
Sat 19 — Town Hall, Hitchin
Sun 20 — Greyhound, London W6
Tues 22 — Fantasia, Northampton
Thur 24 — In Concert (BBC Radio)
Fri 25 — Rolle College, Exmouth
Sat 26 — Bamboo Club, Bristol
Sun 27 — Sundown Edmonton (afternoon)
Mon 28 — Sundown Brixton (afternoon)
Birmingham Top Rank (evening)

Bob Marley and The Wailers

For a few hundred people this was a special night, a unique moment in rock 'n' roll history and they could say that they were there.

Throughout the '70s I had a good understanding with Island Artists. Robb Winn, who booked The Who for us in 1970, had moved from the small agency in Hull (McCloud Holden) to Island Artists and we had formed a close business relationship, but we also became good friends. Island spent several years trying to persuade me to leave Lancaster and join them. They even left an empty desk in their offices which they said was mine every time I went down to London, but I saw what working in London did to people and I didn't want to become like that. Anyway Robb got me some excellent acts and occasionally I had to do him a favour in return.

This was one of those favours. He phoned me to ask if I would put on one of their new acts. Chris Blackwell, owner of Island Records, had signed this Jamaican reggae band and was certain they would be massive.

"A reggae act? Robb, no one pays to see a reggae act. Sure, they'll dance to the music in a disco, but they wouldn't buy an album or a ticket," I said. Not only were they unheard of, I would have to take the first real date on the tour (although they were playing a warm-up at the Coleman club in Nottingham on the way), so even if they were good, word would not have got out.

Robb said that I wouldn't have to pay a fee, only some petrol and hotel rooms. I explained to Robb that the only way I'd get a crowd would be to put on a disco in the Great Hall and stick the band on after – pay for a disco, 50p, and get a band for free. So that is how Bob Marley and the Wailers came to play Lancaster University.

We managed to get about 1000 to the disco and at midnight I went onto the stage to explain to everybody that there was now a band coming on whom they won't have heard of, but honestly, please stay, as they will be stars some day. I pleaded and about 600 stayed to see the first major date in the UK of Bob Marley.

I had sent a steward to get the band on stage. He had disappeared in a fog of sweet smelling, blue smoke, so I sent another and finally a third, who returned, grinning inanely, with the band and the missing, floating stewards.

"Ladies and Gentlemen, Bob Marley and the Wailers! Thank you!"

A year later Robb phoned me again asking if I would like a date on the next Bob Marley tour – I snapped his hand off – then heard the unbelievable news that the 'support' act would be the American southern rock band, Little Feat – WHAT!

Unfortunately that was the, now legendary, concert that never was. Upon arrival in the UK the tour started chaotically, with Marley's concerts cancelled due to Peter Tosh's food poisoning and further disruption due to heavy snow, which resulted in the early abandonment of the tour in late November '73, including our scheduled date here in Lancaster. A sell-out European Tour as well – Robb had one hell of a time cancelling that one! And Lancaster never did see, what would have been, a truly amazing concert.

Barry Lucas

Bonzo Dog Doo-Dah Band

14 November 1969   Supports: Opel Butterfly I Cleveland Fox

This concert was one of the first in the newly opened 'Central Hall' as it was originally called.

The Bonzo Dog Doo-Dah Band were created in the 1960s by a group of British art students.

The core members of the group for most of the band's career were:
Vivian Stanshall – trumpet, lead vocals
Neil Innes – piano, guitar, lead vocals
Rodney "Rhino" Desborough Slater (saxophone), Roger Ruskin Spear (tenor sax and various contraptions) and Larry "Legs" Smith (drums).

'I'm the Urban Spaceman' produced by Paul McCartney and Gus Dudgeon was a hit for the group in 1968 before they split in 1970 for the first time. Following three splits and subsequent reunions, the Bonzos continue to perform today.

Opal Butterfly were an English psychedelic rock band, from Oxfordshire, active between 1967 and 1970. Interestingly the band featured two future members of Hawkwind, Lemmy and drummer Simon King.

Cleveland Fox were a six-piece band formed in the late 1960s in the Bolton/Atherton area of Lancashire. Described as a soul band, they disbanded in the early 1970s.

Boomtown Rats

18 November 1977		Support: The Bernie Tormé Band
8 December 1978	**Seasonal Turkey Tour Xmas '78**	Support: The Vipers
23 April 1982	**V Deep Tour**	Support: Matt Fretton
8 February 1985	**The Long Grass Tour**	Support: Zerra One

Veterans of four appearances, the Boomtown Rats' 1978 concert holds the record for the largest audience in the Great Hall. They are credited with twelve Top 40 singles and six studio albums.

The members of the original Boomtown Rats lineup were:
Bob Geldof – vocals
Garry Roberts – lead guitar
Johnnie Fingers – keyboards
Pete Briquette – bass
Gerry Cott – rhythm guitar
Simon Crowe – drums

All six members originated from Dún Laoghaire, Ireland. The Boomtown Rats broke up in 1986, but re-formed in 2013, without Johnnie Fingers or Gerry Cott, and continue to tour.

The Bernie Tormé Band were a punk band formed in 1976 and led by the singer, songwriter and rock guitarist from Dublin, Bernie Tormé. Tormé revealed that he secured the supporting band slot with the Boomtown Rats by agreeing to go around London putting up posters advertising the tour. Later in his career, Bernie went on to play lead guitar in Ian Gillan's band, Gillan, and most likely appeared on stage with him for his 1980 Lancaster concert.

The Vipers were an Irish new wave band active in the late 1970s who also toured with The Jam and The Clash. Not to be confused with The Jam's support act for their 1979 appearance, who were The Vapors, of 'Turning Japanese' fame.

Support for The V Deep Tour 1982 may possibly have been **Matt Fretton,** who was probably best known for being a support act for Depeche Mode in the Early 1980s. He had a hit in May 1983 with 'It's So High', which reached No. 50 in the UK Singles Chart, and was performed on Top of the Pops.

Zerra One are another Irish outfit, active between 1982 and 1987. The band were also utilised as openers for U2 and The Cure on various tours.

A Lancaster University alumnus remembers the 1978 concert:

> "The Great Hall was where my musical baptism took place. In the late '70s it attracted many great bands. I remember a packed gig when The Boomtown Rats played. I guess it must have been 1978 shortly after they'd become global superstars on the back of 'Like Clockwork' and 'Rat Trap'. Even Bob Geldof seemed surprised at the huge turnout. It was so packed I couldn't get on to the Great Hall floor and ended up watching them from the balcony. Who would have thought they are still playing almost forty years later?"

Alan Milburn, Chancellor, Lancaster University 2015 to present, and former Labour MP.

Hello Paul,

I read with interest the recent article about Barry Lucas and the Lancaster University concerts. My late brother, John Allan, was the Bar Steward of Lonsdale Bar from about 1967 until 2006. He was a friend of Barry's and was very involved in helping with the events that were held there – often organising the bar. He had many tales to tell of the early days. I was fortunate to be able to attend many events – i.e. Paul McCartney and Wings and saw behind the scenes as John was setting up the bar. I remember going to meet John when he was preparing the bar for the Boomtown Rats concert. They were doing a sound check and had pushed all the sliders on the console to maximum. The volume of sound from the towers of amplifiers was so great it could be physically felt – and it caused one of the porters to have an asthma attack!

Regards

Fiona Allan

Hi Paul,

I remember the Boomtown rats in 1982 or 1983, I think. Sir Bob did all the parts of 'Do They Know its Christmas' and then went for a drink in County Bar after the show. I was a Bowland College boy, but the County Bar had Fosters on and I saw him in there. I can safely say that's the first time I have thought about the Fosters at County for thirty years!

Best wishes,

Nick.

Great Hall 1977 © David Stewart

> The 1978 show was quite simply the biggest in the history of the Great Hall; maybe not in stature, nature or quality but just in size. The show had the greatest number of punters in the venue of all the shows ever staged in the Great Hall.
>
> Barry Lucas

Johnny Fingers 1982 © Andy Docherty

Bow Wow Wow

13 November 1981   Support: No Flowers

1980s band Bow Wow Wow, fronted by Annabella Lwin, were created by Malcolm McClaren and were best known for their 1982 Top 10 hits 'Go Wild in The Country' and 'I Want Candy'. Their music is described as having an "African-derived drum sound".

The group released three full-length albums before disbanding in 1983 with Lwin quitting to pursue a solo career.

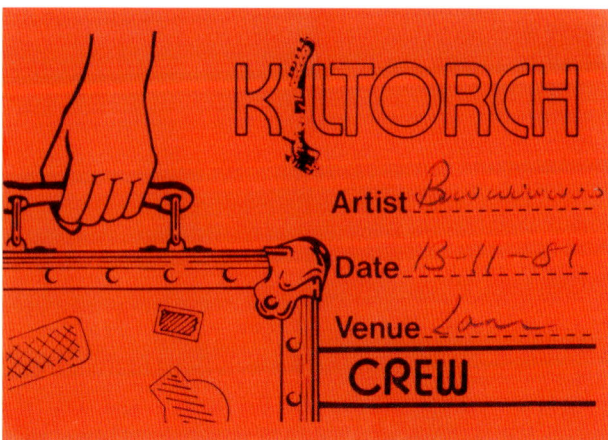

Bow Wow Wow's best-selling US EP, *The Last of the Mohicans*, created some controversy at the time of its release in 1982. The cover featured a nude photograph of a fifteen year old Annabella Lwin, depicting her as the woman in Manet's painting, *Le Déjeuner sur l'herbe*.

Support on the evening was provided by local Lancaster band **No Flowers**, comprised:
Mike Dodd – vocals, guitar
Paul Breuer (vocals, guitar) Jon Carricker (bass) and Mark Carricker (drums).

No Flowers went on to be known as Cottonmouth, releasing a couple of singles and an album, *Overload of Love*, on the Atlantic label.

Brian Augers Oblivion Express

19 March 1971   Support: Clouds

Brian Auger is a jazz keyboard player who specialised in the Hammond organ.

In 1965 Auger formed a band called The Steampacket along with Long John Baldry and Rod Stewart. The outfit was short-lived and broke up following Rod Stewart's departure in 1966.

The band released a number of albums but it was with his next band, Trinity, that Brian hit the heights of success with the addition of the stunningly beautiful Julie Driscoll. A single, 'This Wheel's on Fire' (the reworking of the Bob Dylan song) peaked at No. 5 in the UK Singles Chart of 1968 and came to represent the psychedelic era in Britain. Of course many will know the song as the theme tune to the hit TV show *Absolutely Fabulous*.

His Oblivion Express were formed in 1970 and included future Average White Band drummer Robbie MacIntosh and guitarist Jim Mullen.

Throughout the 1970s, Oblivion Express released a series of albums fusing rock with jazz, blues and soul and were particularly well received in the USA where they consistently charted, leading to Brian moving to California in 1975. This university concert would have seen Alex Ligertwood on stage with Brian Auger. Alex went on to be best known as lead vocalist with Santana and currently tours with Brian to the present day.

Clouds were a Scottish rock band formed in the 1960s with members including:
Ian Ellis – bass guitar and lead vocals
Harry Hughes – drums
Billy Ritchie – keyboards

The band broke up shortly after this concert in October 1971. Billy Ritchie is notable as one of the first keyboard players to take a leading role in a rock band, providing a model for the likes of Keith Emerson and Rick Wakeman.

Bronco

5 February 1971 — Support: Barbed Wire Soup

Bronco were an English rock/country band formed by Jess Roden in 1969 following his departure from The Alan Brown Set and were signed to the Island Records label. The band released three studio albums, *Country Home* (1970), *Ace of Sunlight* (1971) and *Smoking Mixture* (1973), before disbanding in late 1973. Bronco also appeared at the university for a concert in 1972, along with John Martyn, providing support to The Sutherland Brothers.

Barbed Wire Soup started in 1963 and were originally called The Jaguars. Hailing from the Preston area the original lineup was Jon Worsley, Jon Shaw and Bill Breakall on guitars and John Flynn on drums. They were later joined by Dave Newsham providing vocals.

Budgie

7 May 1976 — Support: Hobo
20 October 1978 — Support: Strife

Budgie have been covered by Metallica and are one of Wales' greatest rock bands. The band have influenced many heavy metal bands over the years and were fronted by bassist/vocalist Burke Shelley, with Tony Bourge on guitar and vocals and Ray Phillips on drums.

Budgie's music is often described as a cross between the progressive textures of Rush and the heaviness of Black Sabbath. In their early career Burke Shelley's voice was compared in timbre and style to that of Shirley Bassey. Coincidentally both Burke and Shirley were born in Tiger Bay, Cardiff.

Having eleven studio and four live albums under their belt, Budgie went through a number of splits and reunions over the years. At present, due to Burke Shelley's ill health, the band are on hiatus.

Croatian band **Hobo** were formed by keyboardist Mato Dosen in Zagreb in 1972. They once played support to Deep Purple in a 1975 concert.

A serial support band, **Strife** were a tremendous high energy rock band and by all accounts had a reputation for blowing main acts off the stage. *Rush* was a classic album released in early 1975 on the Chrysalis label. Strife may have been support to The Baker Gurvitz Army in February 1975.

Buzzcocks

16 March 1978   Supports: The Slits I F Church

A concert with its problems on the night.

Buzzcocks were formed in Bolton in 1976 and were led by Pete Shelley alongside singer/songwriter Howard Devoto.

The band were a major influence on the Manchester music scene with their best known single 'Ever Fallen in Love (With Someone You Shouldn't've)' peaking at No. 12 in the UK charts of September 1978.

Following the departure of Devoto from the Buzzcocks in February 1977, he appeared again in November 1978 for a concert in the Great Hall with his new band Magazine.

Continuing fights and disturbances during the support acts resulted in the Buzzcocks playing the gig with house lights turned on. Barry Lucas has written more about this gig in his 'Punk' chapter.

The Slits were a female British punk rock/post-punk/reggae band, formed in London in 1976 and were originally an all-female outfit led by Arianna Forster (aka Ari Up). The lineup also featured Viv Albertine (guitars), Tessa Pollit (bass) and Palmolive (drums). Prior to arriving in Lancaster for this gig the band had backed-up The Clash on their 'White Riot' tour in 1977 along with The Buzzcocks. The Slits released a total of four studio albums with the best known probably being their debut album *Cut*, on the Island label. Since the band's first split in 1982, The Slits have had many different lineups but finally dissolved following Aris' death in 2010.

Local Lancaster band, **F Church** were first up on stage that night. F Church had evolved out of The Kassels; Lancaster's first true punk band and were fronted by my old mate from art school, Neil Thompson on vocals. The band on the night also featured China Street bassist Adam Williams on drums with John Elles (guitars), Alan Greenwood (bass) and Steve Normanton (keyboards) completing the lineup. Some month's later F Church's Adam Williams and Steve Normanton moved on, with the band adding Oscar (Chris) Heywood (guitars) and Baz on electric violin and becoming known as The Permanents with John Elles taking up the full time drumming role.

Buzzcocks Great Hall 1978 © S. Earnshaw

Camel

25 October 1975   Support: Wally

Camel are an English progressive rock band formed in 1971 and for this concert were fronted by the former keyboard player of Van Morrison's Them, Peter Bardens. Completing the lineup were founder members Andy Latimer, Doug Ferguson and Andy Ward.

The concert featured Camel performing their epic masterpiece *The Snow Goose*.

Supporting act **Wally** are a progressive rock band which originated in Harrogate in the early 1970s. They have been described as having a sound somewhere between Dire Straits and Pink Floyd.

Wally were led by singer-songwriter and founder Roy Webber and in 1973, after playing the northern UK pub rock circuit, the group entered a new act competition organised by the music paper *Melody Maker*. The band made it to the finals held at London's Roundhouse Theatre, but did not win. They did however catch the eye of one of the judges, "Whispering" Bob Harris, legendary DJ of The Old Grey Whistle Test. The runners-up prize was the opportunity to record a session for Harris's BBC radio show *The Monday Program*. Taking Wally under his wing, Harris secured a recording contract with Atlantic Records. "I really liked them," recalls Bob Harris. "I liked the swirling sound they made … acoustic guitar, electric guitar, fiddle, Fender Rhodes piano and pedal steel guitar. I liked their harmonies, the way their voices matched. I liked their influences … David Crosby, Jackson Browne and Neil Young. But most of all I liked Roy Webber's songs."

Many a concert hall in the 1970s echoed to random shouts from the audience of "Wally" during the wait for the bands to appear on stage. The shouting on this evening was particularly loud and frequent!

A couple of stories exist about the origins of the shouting of "Wally" at concerts. One being that it started at the Reading Festival in 1972 with a guy looking for his lost dog and shouting his name with the crowd joining in; the other that it originated from the 1970 Isle of Wight Festival with someone shouting trying to locate his lost mate in the crowd.

In 2009, the surviving members of Wally's original lineup (Roy Webber, Paul Middleton, Pete Sage, Roger Narraway and Nick Glennie-Smith, augmented by Frank Mizen on pedal steel and Will Jackson on guitar) reunited and performed to a sell-out crowd in their hometown of Harrogate.

Wally continue to tour and record.

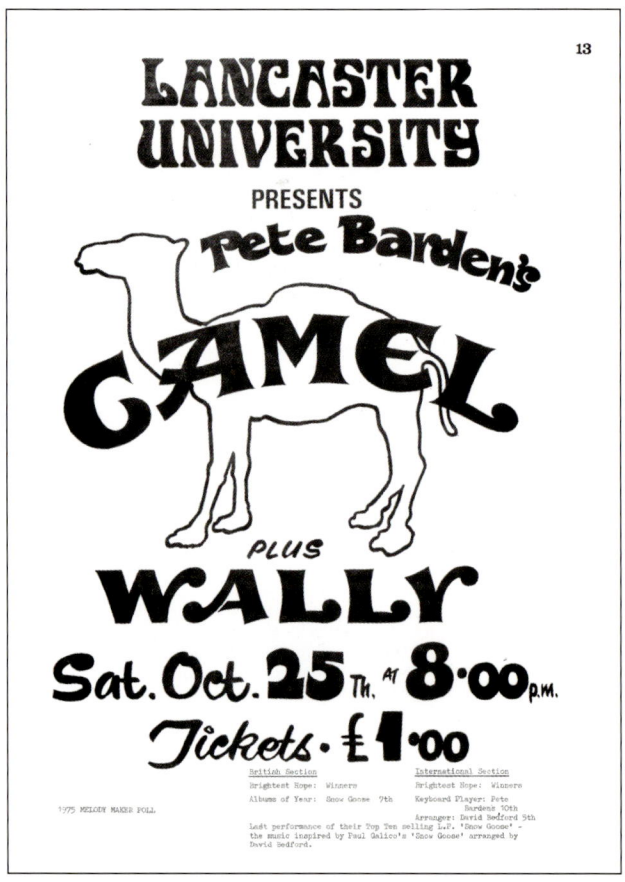

Top: Camel, bottom: Wally, both © David Bradbury

Caravan

23 April 1976   Support: Stars

Caravan are a psychedelic jazz rock fusion outfit formed in 1968 in Canterbury, Kent, and were an important band on the Canterbury scene alongside other bands such as Soft Machine, Gong, and Hatfield and The North.

Caravan are veterans of fourteen studio albums, the most critically acclaimed being *In The Land of Grey and Pink*, released in 1971. Their seventh album, *Blind Dog at St Dunstan's*, was released on the day of this Great Hall concert.

Caravan remain active on the live scene still fronted by the original founder member Pye Hastings.

During a concert in 1969 at The Marquee Club, London, Pye Hastings was dramatically electrocuted on stage, although thankfully he went on to make a full recovery.

Stars were an Australian country and rock band from Adelaide that were active between 1975 and 1979.

The Chieftains

18 November 1978   Support unknown
16 November 1982   Support unknown

The Chieftains, formed in 1962, have been around for over fifty years, entertaining audiences with their mainly instrumental Irish sounds. The group released a string of successful records throughout the 1970s and 1980s and their work with Van Morrison in 1988 resulted in the critically acclaimed album *Irish Heartbeat*.

Still at the helm is founder Paddy Moloney, the uillean piper from Dublin. Two tracks by The Chieftains feature on the Martin Scorsese film *Gangs of New York*.

Chuck Berry

22 March 1972   Support: The Roy Young Band

The legend and pioneer of rock music that is Chuck Berry visited Lancaster on one of only five UK dates as his famous hit 'My Ding-a-Ling' was on its way to the No. 1 slot in the UK Singles Chart of 1972. Originally written in 1952 by David Bartholomew, it was Chuck Berry's only No. 1, both in the UK and the US.

Berry penned classic hits such as, 'Roll Over Beethoven', 'Sweet Little Sixteen' and 'Johnny B Goode'. Berry also wrote the hit 'You Never Can Tell' which featured in the movie Pulp Fiction, with John Travolta and Uma Thurman dancing to the song at Jack Rabbit Slims restaurant.

Despite his advancing years, he continued playing one-night concerts and embarked on a European tour in 2008 at the age of 82.

John Lennon famously said "If you tried to give rock and roll another name, you might call it Chuck Berry."

Chuck berry died in March 2017 aged 90.

Roy Young is a British rock and roll singer and keyboard player who recorded with David Bowie on his *Young Americans* and *Low* albums. Active since 1958 he has toured with the likes of Cliff Richard and The Shadows, Ian Hunter and Mick Ronson. He formed The Roy Young Band in 1969 and in 2006 released an album entitled *Still Young*.

Chuck Berry

Over the years Lancaster played host to several legends of the music business, names that have gone down in history, but arguably none as big as Chuck Berry. He had just had his only British chart success with the appalling, 'My Ding-a-Ling' (just compare it to his back catalogue) and he was coming to the UK to play just five dates – one of which was to be at Lancaster. Historic – definitely one to say you were there, one to say I saw that man live to your grandchildren. A sell-out then? No! Inexplicably Lancaster again had one of those nights, about nine hundred and fifty people with less than half the tickets sold. Why? Don't ask me, I've no idea. Suggestions on a postcard please.

Ripped off by record companies and promoters, even gaoled by a racist American Southern State legal system, Chuck Berry's history was such that he was never going to trust anybody again at his age. A hit record meant that he could cash in at last, even in his advanced years. At £1500, the fee was high enough in those days, but I had to lodge £750 before he would leave the shores of the USA and agree to give him the balance, in cash in his hand, before he went on stage. Even if I hadn't understood the reasons (which I did) I would have agreed. If you can't get Elvis you get, arguably, the next most influential figure in modern pop music, don't you?

Unfortunately, the tour was just that, a chance to earn some swift bucks. We had the first date so when he landed at Heathrow he was driven in luxury straight up to Lancaster. The backing musicians were just a cheap rock 'n' roll band of young lads from London. One minute they are playing in London pubs, the next they are preparing to play with one of the legends of rock music. They stood nervously in the dressing room awaiting the arrival of what must have been their hero, a rock 'n' roll god. He got out of his limo at the back of the Great Hall, walked up the corridor, took the cash off me and went into the dressing room, saying "Hi, let's go!"

"But what's the set order?" they asked.

"You know my songs, I'll start, you follow, now let's go."

The guys slowly followed him out of the dressing room. I must say, I felt so sorry for them. Their big moment, their moment in the sun – how would it go now? Well you can probably guess. Maybe the missing audience already knew something I didn't, but at least I can tell my grandchildren I saw that guitarist live at Lancaster.

Barry Lucas

The Clash

23 January 1980   **16 Tons Tour Europe**   Supports: **Mikey Dread | Interference**

The Clash released the album *London Calling* in December 1979 and played the Great Hall in January 1980 in support of the album with the classic lineup:
Joe Strummer – lead vocals, rhythm guitar
Mick Jones – lead guitar, lead vocals
Paul Simonon – bass guitar, vocals
Nicky 'Topper' Headon – drums

London calling was awarded *Rolling Stone* magazine's best album of the eighties and peaked at No. 9 in the UK Albums Chart.

The Clash were formed in 1976 and originally included Keith Levene on guitars, who was fired soon after their formation and went on to form Public Image Ltd with John Lydon in 1978. After releasing six studio albums, The Clash disbanded in early 1986. Johnny Green, The Clash's long time road manager, is a Lancaster University alumnus.

Lancaster Setlist: 'Clash City Rockers', 'Brand New Cadillac', 'Safe European Home', 'Jimmy Jazz', 'London Calling', 'The Guns of Brixton', 'Train in Vain', 'Protex Blue', 'Koka Kola', 'I Fought the Law', '(White Man) In Hammersmith Palais', 'Bankrobber', 'Clampdown', 'Wrong 'em Boyo', 'Stay Free', 'Police and Thieves', 'Capital Radio', 'Janie Jones', 'Complete Control', 'Armagideon Time', 'English Civil War', 'Garageland', 'Tommy Gun', 'London's Burning'.

Michael George Campbell aka **'Mikey Dread'** was a Jamaican singer, producer and broadcaster who became great friends with The Clash and was involved in producing the band's single 'Bankrobber'. Mikey also performed on a number of tracks on the Clash's 1980 album, *Sandinista!*

First up on stage that night were local Lancaster four piece punk outfit **Interference**. The band were active from 1977-1980 and generally consisted of:

Ged Heggerty – vocals
Les Palmer – drums
John Palmer – lead guitar
Iggy Brockbank – bass guitar

The band also played as support to The Fall during their career and provided a soundtrack for a Granada TV documentary about borstals in the UK.

Joe Strummer
© Doug Price

Clash sound check © Geoff Campbell   below all © Geoff Campbell

Cliff Richard

Early 1972   Support unknown

An eventful concert for Cliff Richard, 'The Peter Pan of Pop', at Lancaster University, resulting in disruption due to protests by gay rights demonstrators.

Cliff Richard is the most successful British male solo artist of all time. He also has the distinction of being the only artist to have achieved UK No. 1 singles throughout five consecutive decades, in the 1950s, 1960s, 1970s, 1980s and 1990s.

He was made an OBE in 1980 and was knighted in 1995.

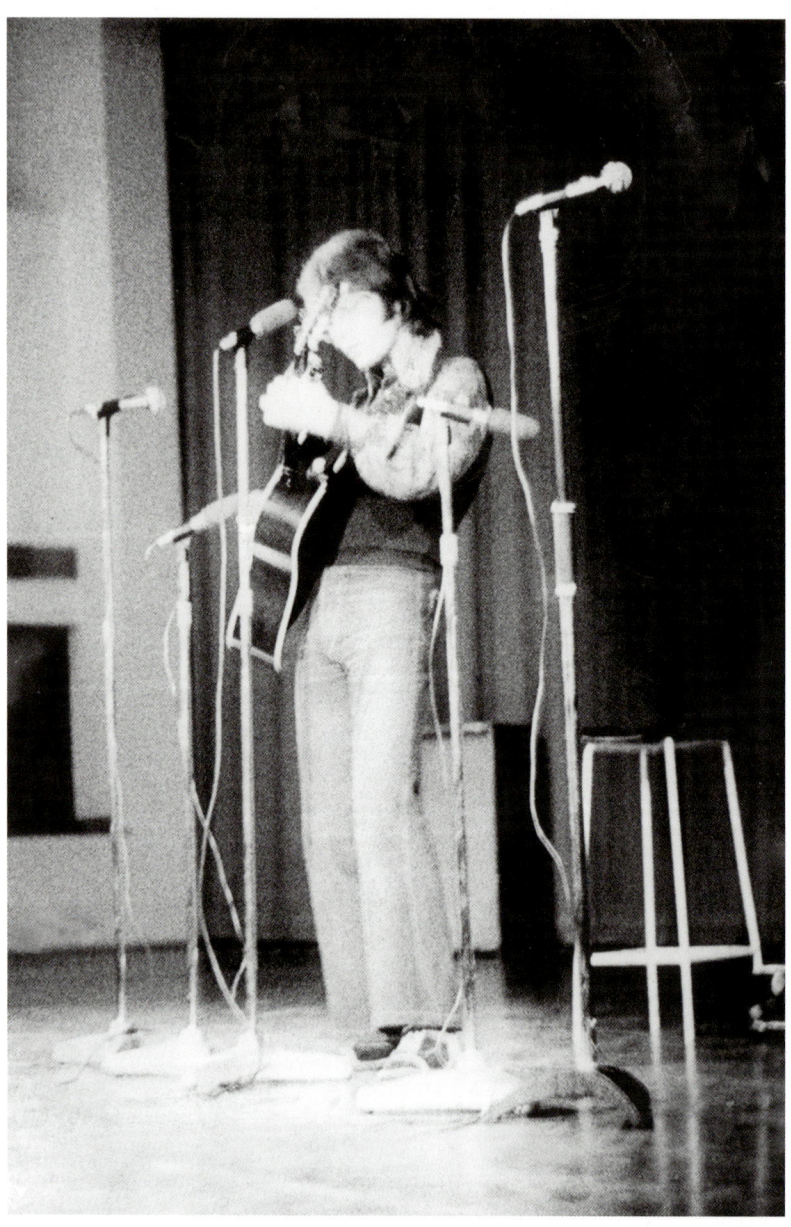

Cliff Richard on the Great Hall stage photographer unknown

Cliff Richard

1970s, Cliff at Lancaster University, the home of rock 'n' roll in North West England – doesn't sound quite right does it? But it happened, and how …

Of course even I would not have been brave enough to book Cliff into Lancaster University in the 1970s. The booking was arranged by an organisation called Nationwide Festival of Light, a Christian movement which was campaigning against the Permissive Society. As the date drew closer, the University authorities advised the organisers to contact me and use the Students' Union's expertise to help stage the show. I readily agreed; after all Cliff was (is), whatever you think of him artistically, a legend.

The show date approached and I became aware of a problem: the Gay Liberation Front was planning to organise a major demonstration during Cliff's performance. They had obtained a block of tickets and were to attend the actual show in force. I doubled my stewards but I knew we were going to have problems. The concert was to be an acoustic set, with a talk element, it couldn't drown out a section of the audience determined to disrupt like an amplified, band-driven set, could.

The concert was a seated sell-out, obviously, but artistically it was a disaster. The GLF came in full drag to demand that Cliff 'came out'. It destroyed the show, without a battle which would devastate the evening; I couldn't control that element of the audience.

At the end of the show I had a meeting in the dressing room with Cliff. At this point in the story I must say that he is one of the nicest, most genuine, people I have ever met in the music business. I still think there is a painting in the attic though – he looked like a teenager! He was clearly upset about the destruction of the evening which was about his Christian beliefs and how they governed his life. He said that he would like to meet the leading figures in the GLF, but not now, just after the show, as it was too raw. He asked me to ask them if they would come back next week to meet him to discuss their issues. I was impressed.

They agreed and the following week Cliff arrived, in a very flash sports car, at The Chaplaincy Centre and met with the representatives of the GLF. What was discussed is confidential and I have to respect that. All I can say is that Cliff Richard is a very impressive human being and when I am asked about who were the nicest stars I ever met, he is among the first I mention.

Barry Lucas

Climax Blues Band

15 October 1976 — Support: Jo Anne Kelly
5 May 1978 — Support: Dire Straits
30 January 1982 — Support: The Look

Climax Blues Band are a British band formed in Stafford in 1967 and were originally called Climax Chicago Blues Band. In 1972, due to name confusion with an American band called Chicago Transit Authority, the group dropped the Chicago tag.

With seventeen studio albums to their name and a 1976 No. 10 UK chart hit with 'Couldn't Get It Right', they were a popular draw for the Great Hall. The band continues to tour.

Jo Anne Kelly was an English blues guitarist and singer and described as "the queen of British country blues singers". During her career she worked extensively with Tony McPhee of The Groundhogs and appeared on two albums by The John Dummer Band. Following a trip to perform in the USA she was invited, but turned down, offers to join Canned Heat and Johnny Winters band. 1973 had seen her on stage in the Great Hall as support to Andy Fraser's Sharks. Jo Anne Kelly died in 1990 aged forty-six.

Dire Straits were a treat for anyone lucky enough to have emerged from the bar area and get their money's worth on the night. The set would have featured tracks from their debut album *Dire Straits*, released in October 1978. The album produced the hit single 'Sultans of Swing', which reached No. 8 on the UK Singles Chart.

Writing his concert review in *SCAN* newspaper, Mick Walsh pointed out that *Melody Maker* had tipped Dire Straits as one to watch in '78, "So don't be surprised if they turn up on the rock 'n' roll scrapheap in a couple of years, alongside previous *MM* favourites such as Deaf School, Staa Max etc".

The Look are a UK pop band who had a No. 6 hit single in the UK Singles Chart in 1981 with 'I Am The Beat'. The band are still performing and touring.

Climax Blues Band October 1976 © Neil Yates

Climax Blues Band

It may come as a surprise to some readers but Climax were a big band around this time. They had had a little success in the UK as Climax Chicago Blues Band when they went to the States, getting rave reviews there and Canada, and enjoying chart success when their single 'Couldn't Get It Right' reached No. 3 in *Billboard*. This Great Hall show had an audience of approximately 1500 but those that had tickets will still be kicking themselves if they arrived late or stayed in the bar and missed the £50 support act – Dire Straits.

However, there are a couple of other stories about Climax and Lancaster. This was their second appearance. Previously they had headlined the Freshers' Ball. Don't ask me why but for some reason I hadn't been able to use the Great Hall that particular Freshers' Week, so the end of the week extravaganza was held in the Lower Ashton Hall Lancaster. Climax were headlining, along with two or three other bands whose names escape me now, and Bernard Manning – I know, but it seemed like a good idea for a Ball (?) at the time!

In those days bands arrived around six o'clock in a transit van with a couple of roadies, got the gear in, set up the PA, sound checked and were ready to play by 7.30 pm. I hold my hand up. I didn't read the contract properly where the rider did say 12.00 noon get in and three humpers for the gear. I was living in Dallas Road at the time and wandered casually down at 6.00 pm. I was met by an irate band. I hadn't bothered to ask the Beadle to unlock the Town Hall or to arrange for any humpers. "Where's the fucking social sec.?" the band demanded, ranting about being stood around for six hours.

Quickly thinking on my feet I said, "Oh, he's a well known prat. Totally disorganised and couldn't organise a piss-up in a brewery. Look, I'm not doing anything, I'll get the hall opened and help you with the gear down those steps."

"Thanks mate, that's great of you, but how can we get our hands on that jerk of a social sec.?"

"Don't know. Would you believe he has been known not to turn up at some gigs and left the treasurer to pay the band?"

"Unfucking believable. What an arse."

"Yes, I agree – I'll get the Beadle sorted out with the keys."

"Thanks mate, there's a beer waiting for you."

"Great, be back soon." Phew. Drank on the band that night. Great show though. But Bernard went down so badly, heckled so mercilessly that he wouldn't play another college gig for ten years.

Now fast forward twenty years. I had a club in Morecambe, The Gardens, and promoted a lot of rock. Climax were on at the 350-capacity venue and I had sold about 150. There was only one member of the original band left, the rest were eager young blues musicians. In the bar at the end of the night we were having a post-gig beer and chat when I asked if he could remember the last time he was playing in this area at the Great Hall. He said he did vaguely. "Do you remember your support act?"

"No, who were they?"

"Dire Straits."

It was priceless to see the looks on his young band members' faces – a 'where did it all go wrong?' moment!

Barry Lucas

Cockney Rebel

19 October 1974 Support: Life

Fronted by the horse-racing pundit Steve Harley, his band Cockney Rebel played the Great Hall shortly before his best-known hit, 'Make Me Smile (Come Up and See Me)', charted at No. 1 in the UK Singles Chart of 1975.

One of Cockney Rebel's first ever gigs was as a support act to The Jeff Beck Group in a concert in London in 1972. Steve Harley and Cockney Rebel are still actively touring, with original band members violinist Barry Wickens and drummer Stuart Elliot.

Not much is known about support act **Life**.

> Steve Harley was at the height of his fame but I can safely say that I certainly would not 'come up and see' him and neither could I ever ever envisage me 'making him smile'. When I get those questions —you know, "Who were the nicest artists?", and "Who were the most unpleasant?" – Mr Harley springs instantly to mind as an answer. Can you guess to which question?
>
> Barry Lucas

Colosseum

27 November 1970 Supports: Brian Davison's Every Which Way | Anno Domini

Colosseum were founded in 1968 by legendary drummer Jon Hiseman, along with sax player Dick Heckstall-Smith and bass player Tony Reeves. Soon they were joined by Dave Greenslade.

They released three studio albums, including the highly acclaimed double album, *Colosseum Live* in late 1971. Colosseum's lineup for this 1970 concert in the Great Hall included Chris Farlowe (later a member of Atomic Rooster) on vocals and Dave "Clem" Clempson (later of Humble Pie) replacing a founder member James Litherland on guitars.

Soon after the release of *Colosseum Live* the band separated, with Dave Greenslade going on to form his band Greenslade.

Brian "Blinky" Davison was a British drummer and former member of The Nice, who, after their breakup, formed his band **Every Which Way**. The band were short-lived, releasing just the one album. Blinky Davison returned to perform in Lancaster in 1973 with the band Refugee.

Anno Domini were a Northern Irish band who toured Germany with Rory Gallagher and Taste.

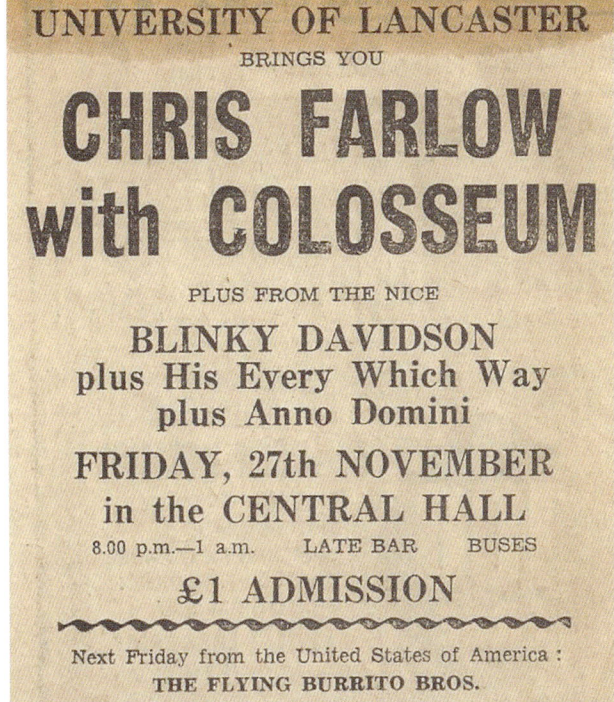

Country Joe and the Fish

5 May 1972   Supports: JSD Band I Smith Perkins and Smith

Country Joe and the Fish were an American psychedelic rock band formed in California in1965. The band was fronted by "Country" Joe McDonald and Barry "The Fish" Melton and were best known for their rendition of the song 'Don't Bogart Me'. The band Little Feat also covered the song, the original being written by sixties psychedelic country rockers Fraternity of Man.

Joe's is also well remembered for his song "The "Fish" Cheer/I-Feel-Like-I'm-Fixin'-to-Die Rag", a dark comedy novelty song about the Vietnam War, whose familiar chorus was ("One, two, three, what are we fighting for?"). The track was written in about 20 minutes for an anti-Vietnam War play and performed at the Woodstock festival on the Saturday and the Sunday in August 1969.

The JSD Band were a Scottish-based Celtic and folk rock band, active from 1969–1974.

Brothers Steve and Tim Smith, along with Wayne Perkins, came together in the early 1970s to form **Smith, Perkins and Smith**. They recorded just the one album and toured in England on the same bill with Free, Family, and Vinegar Joe with Robert Palmer. They were to appear later that same year in the Great Hall, as support act to Free. Later in their careers Steve Smith worked alongside Robert Palmer, with brother Tim, going on to work with Lynyrd Skynyrd.

I was a student of the '68 generation. I came to the university in the autumn of that year, the year of student revolts around the world; demonstrations in London, Paris, Mexico, Berlin, Rome, Prague, Brazil, Spain, Poland, China, Havana, Boston, Canada, Carolina, LA, New York, Chicago and Sweden. Many were violent, with a youth movement seemingly dedicated to changing society. As Jim Morrison sang, "They've got the guns but we've got the numbers. Come on we're taking over. We want the world and we want it now!"

One band could, and indeed does, claim to be the one that ended the Vietnam War: Country Joe and the Fish. Their 'Vietnam Song' became the anthem of the anti-war movement:
And it's one, two, three,
What are we fighting for?
Don't ask me, I don't give a damn,
Next stop is Vietnam;
And it's five, six, seven,
Open up the pearly gates,
Well there ain't no time to reason why,
Whoopee! We're all gonna die.

How could I, a revolting student of 1968, not take a date on Country Joe and the Fish when it was offered? However, there is another aspect to this concert's story which was significant. The support act was an American band, 'Smith, Perkins and Smith', who were later to support Free at Lancaster. They were a nice country rock band, featuring two brothers. Good time music, terrific guys.

I had a phone call from the USA asking me to get one of the brothers to call home because it was urgent. When the band had finished their set I relayed the message. In order to phone the States and to give him some privacy I took him to my office in Alexandra Square, where he tragically discovered that his wife had suddenly died.

Sometimes you realise that the music isn't the be all and end all.

Barry Lucas

The Cure

15 November 1980   Support: Tarzan 5

The Cure played the university following the release of their second album, *Seventeen Seconds,* in April 1980.

Formed in Crawley, West Sussex, in 1976, the band was fronted by guitarist, vocalist and principal songwriter, Robert Smith. The Cure were one of the first alternative bands to have chart and commercial success in an era before alternative rock had broken into the mainstream. In 1979 The Cure played as a support band for a UK tour with Siouxsie and The Banshees. Partway through the tour, The Banshees lost their lead guitarist and Smith was invited to stand in for the rest of the tour, playing in both bands on the night.

The Cure are still active, with the band enjoying a European tour in 2016 which ended in three dates at London's Wembley Arena and more recently an appearance headlining the main stage at Glastonbury 2019.

Lancaster band lineup:
Robert Smith – vocals, guitar, keyboard
Lol Tolhurst – drums
Simon Gallup – bass
Matthieu Hartley – keyboards

Tarzan 5 were an eighties indie dance band.

Simon Gallup of The Cure

Curved Air

29 January 1972   Support: Sunshine
6 December 1975   Support: possibly Banco or Halfbreed

Curved Air, the highly acclaimed progressive folk rock band visited the university twice with the charismatic Sonja Kristina on lead vocals. Curved Air were one of the first rock groups to use an electric violin, played by Darryl Way.

They released eight studio albums and their single 'Back Street Luv' peaked at No. 4 in the UK Singles Chart of 1971.

In 1974 Curved Air recruited Stewart Copeland as their road manager. Eventually he moved on to drumming for the band in 1975, subsequently leaving to join up with The Police in early 1977.

In 2008 Curved Air were re-formed and continue to record and perform internationally.

Little is known about **Sunshine**, other than that they may have been a folk rock band from Belfast.

Possible support act Banco del Mutuo Soccorso, or **Banco** for short, are an Italian progressive rock band formed in the 1970s in Rome, inspired by the likes of Gentle Giant and Jethro Tull. They are still currently active.

There may also have been a support slot by a band called **Halfbreed**, of which little is known.

Curved Air: The classical prog-rockers are just launching into their party-piece (Summer from Vivaldi's Four Seasons), when their violinist slips and falls flat on his back bringing Summer to an end. The audience with commendable maturity are restrained; the rest of the band thinks it's hilarious.

Maurice Hubbard (Pink Custard Light Show)

A terrific show, with the one and only Sonja Kristina belting out those songs, accompanied by Darryl Way's violin in such a unique style. Towards the end of the set, her furious solos were performed with one stockinged leg braced on the front of stage monitors while eager fans ran their hands up and down.

In the dressing room after the show, the band had done their scheduled encores and were looking forward to relaxing back at the hotel. In came Sonja:

"Let's go back out!"

"No!" was the chorus.

"But lads, I'm having sooo much fun," she smirked.

Barry Lucas

The Damned

27 June 1977   Support: The Adverts

The Damned are an English punk band formed in London in 1976 by lead vocalist Dave Vanian, guitarist Brian James, bassist Captain Sensible and drummer Rat Scabies. Along with the Sex Pistols and The Clash, they helped to spearhead the punk movement in the United Kingdom.

The band appeared for a date at the university between the release of their February 1977 debut album *Damned Damned Damned* and the November 1977 album *Music For Pleasure*.

Punk band **The Adverts** provided the evening's support, returning to Lancaster as headliners in February 1978.

The Damned on the Great Hall Stage © David Stewart

Punk by Barry Lucas

This period of the Great Hall concerts deserves dealing with as a whole rather than as a series of events. The list of punk bands that played the Great Hall is impressive. Punk truly shook up the rather complacent music world in the mid '70s. It was a movement that was sorely needed. The pretentiousness of the major established artists and their failure to tour around the country had made a mockery of rock 'n' roll as the music of working class youth. Tours of twenty to thirty dates, to all corners of the UK, were a thing of the past. Bands ensconced themselves in one of four or five big cities, camping down in an arena and saying to the fans, "If you want to see us, we're here." Fans had to buy ever more expensive tickets, then catch trains, coaches or cars, adding even more expense to the privilege of seeing their favourite artists. These artists were in that position because those very fans, who they now treated with disdain, had bought the tickets for previous shows, together with albums, shirts, merchandise, programmes etc. They had put the bands in their positions of wealth and power and how were they rewarded? With ever increasing indifference by the bands, which often flew in from tax exile or country estates to play live once every year or two.

However, I do have to confess that I wasn't instantly a disciple of punk. Of course I liked and could see the quality of bands like Costello, Blondie, Rats, Stranglers etc., but some of the younger, angrier bands … One evening, after work, I drove down to meet the staff of 'Ear 'Ere Records in the Slip Inn, conveniently next door to the shop. As we all consumed the Mitchells (or for the more discerning, any lager that was available) sat around 'The Barrel', we started discussing the relative merits of this new wave of music, punk. There was Nigel, Roger, Malcolm, Eric, Kevin, myself and a couple of others.

The critique followed this course:

"They can't play their instruments."

"You can't make out the lyrics."

"It's just a wall of noise."

"It'll never last."

Then I suddenly stopped the conversation.

"Do you know, that's exactly what my mum and dad said about The Beatles and The Stones? When did we become our parents, we're only in our twenties!" Everybody laughed and agreed, little knowing at the time how wrong we were. Except Malcolm, I think he knew exactly what was going on; after all he was the youngest there. A little while later he was to write to Patti Smith via 'Ear 'Ere, suggesting she release the track 'Because The Night' as a single. It became a hit and she had the good grace to write back to 'Ear 'Ere thanking the staff, and Malcolm in particular, for the advice.

Lancaster had, by the end, a good punk pedigree: Stranglers, Damned, Costello, Hazel O'Connor, Ian Dury, The Jam, Siouxsie and the Banshees, Adverts, Buzzcocks, The Clash, The Slits, Boomtown Rats, two Stiff Records tours, Pretenders, Public Image Ltd, Ramones, Ultravox, Undertones, Rezillos, Stiff Little Fingers, Skids, Toyah, Magazine, and who could forget the legendary Dick Envy!

Not a bad list but there is a conspicuous omission. Anybody spot the deliberate mistake? Ask anyone about Punk, even those not born when it happened, and the one band they will all come up with, is missing: The Sex Pistols. Why didn't they ever play the premier college venue in the country? Well, they didn't actually play many live gigs but that's not the story. For the first time I will explain the real reason, or rather I will *confess* the real reason.

University House had decided, in their wisdom, that punk had to be banned from Lancaster University. Paula Richardson, the hall booker and a close friend, had to tell me the news. She was embarrassed, to say the least, but explained that when I completed a hall booking form I had to state the act and describe what type of music they would perform. The information would be sent through to Arthur Gray, a lovely ex-policeman, but sixty-odd years old and a real old-fashioned gentleman. He was to decide on the musical merits of the acts I had booked. It lead to some brilliant moments: I persuaded him that The Stranglers were a country and western band and The Undertones were an Irish folk act etc. You really couldn't make it up, the incompetence of University House was unbelievable.

The Pistols were booked into Lancaster, but as the date approached I was getting increasingly concerned about the growing violence surrounding punk shows in the Great Hall. With the smaller bands went smaller crowds and I still felt able to control the shows, but The Pistols would be taking things to a whole new level. Audiences of eight hundred to a thousand were all the punk bands were generally pulling. I knew The Pistols would sell out and draw many more, I anticipated 2500 plus, many of whom would not just say, "Sold-out, I haven't got a ticket, I'll go home, fifty or sixty miles or so. Thanks, good night!" Increasingly Pistols' shows were degenerating into violence, the stage show orchestrated it and I didn't feel

Lancaster needed any help to descend into a riot. Punk shows had become an excuse for football gangs from Barrow, Preston, Blackpool and Lancaster to meet and have a ruck in the Great Hall. Bloody stupid, I know, but the music was an irrelevance where it could be used as an excuse, a background, for a ritualistic battle.

But I didn't want to be the one to call a halt on one of the most important bands, in the most important movement in music, since Elvis. Morally, intellectually, I didn't want the image or the legacy of a censor. I went to see Maggie Gallagher, who was the first female Students' Union President. She was a Trotskyist but we got on extremely well and I liked and respected her. I showed her the press cuttings of whips, leather, bondage, the 'defilement' of women etc., plus the threat – or as I put it, the promise – of violence at a Students' Union gig. She thought that we shouldn't be seen to be supporting this kind of event. I 'reluctantly' agreed.

"Cancel it," she said.

"If you're sure," I said.

If you are reading this, sorry Maggie, I conned you, but for the best of reasons.

The Buzzcocks were a band I loved. I had travelled to Blackpool to watch them in a small club/bar – I was a real fan. But at Lancaster the concert became problematic. The violence, the mayhem, it was totally out of control during the support acts. The Buzzcocks got on stage but I had to put on the house lights midway through their first number, with the remainder of their set played in full illumination. Let me show you how silly and dangerous, it got. One of my stewards, from the left hand stage fire doors, dragged a young lad into the porters' lodge. He was antagonised and holding a steel bar, "This prat was laying into people with this and tried to belt me."

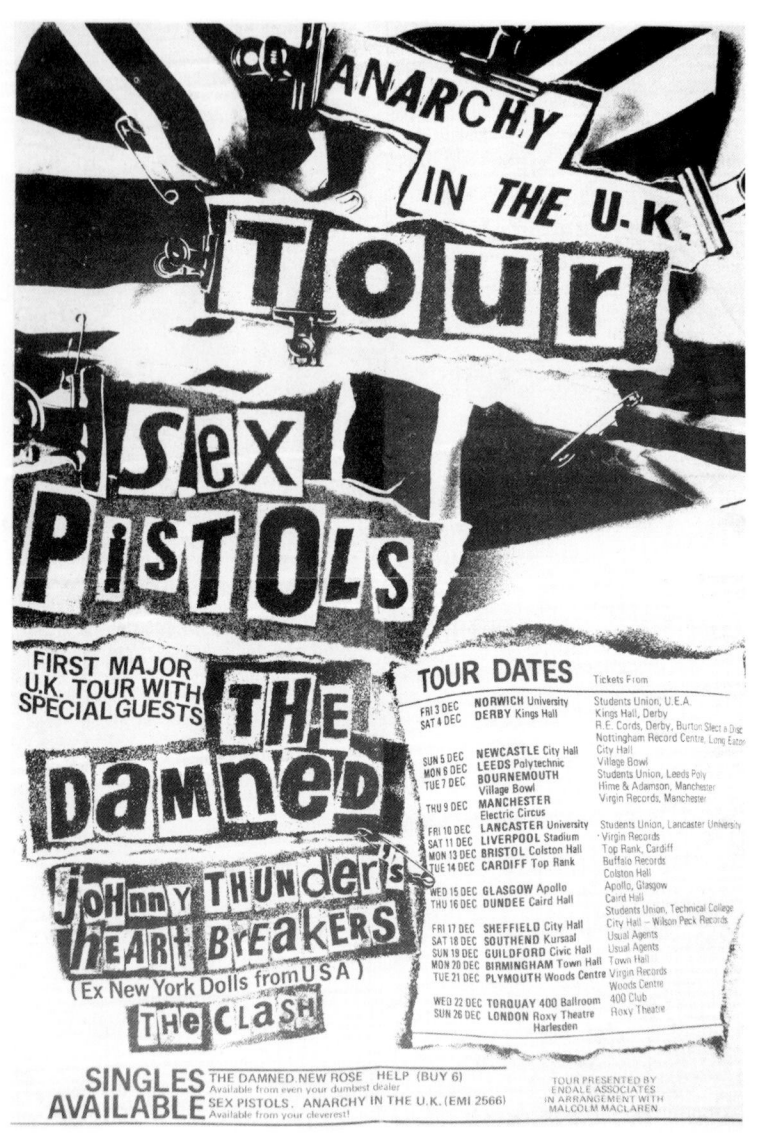

I told the lad that I was going to call his mother to come and get him. He just broke down sobbing, "Don't tell my mum, she'll kill me." I missed my calling. I should have been an interrogator at Guantanamo Bay.

Seriously though, the Buzzcocks was the end. I would not put on any more punk shows, it was too dangerous.

I knew that the next weekend Preston Polytechnic had The Vibrators on. Out of professional courtesy I phoned the Entertainments Manager (I had been on the interviewing panel, creating that particular professional post at Preston Polytechnic in the past). I explained what had happened at Lancaster over several months and my decision to cancel all future shows. I advised her to cancel her show next weekend. She told me that she felt she could handle it. I said that that is what I thought, but it was getting too dangerous. However, she felt confident in her, and her staff's ability, to handle any situation. I was sadly, so tragically, proved right. The concert resulted in the death of one person and serious injuries to three others, being reported in the press the next day with the headline 'RIOT AT PRESTON GIG'.

Darts

26 February 1979   **Rag Ball Concert**   Supports: Dave Berry and The Cruisers I The Late Show
20 February 1982   Support: Weapon of Peace

Doo-wap revival band Darts are a nine piece band assembled by lead singer Den Hegarty in 1976. They had a string of chart successes in the late '70s and early '80s, the best known being 'The Boy From New York City' and 'Duke of Earl'.

In 1981, Hegarty became a television presenter, including being part of the team fronting the children's programme *Tiswas*.

The band re-formed in 2006 for occasional appearances which consistently sell out.

Dave Berry from Sheffield is a 1960s pop singer who was popular in Belgium and The Netherlands. Berry was noted for writing the song 'The Crying Game', which was covered by Boy George and was the soundtrack of the film of the same name.

Little is known about **The Late Show**.

Weapon of Peace, the reggae band from Wolverhampton, were the unusual undercard to Darts in 1982.

This turned out to be a nightmare of a show. I had forgotten all about this particular evening – I think that I had somehow wiped it from my memory for self-preservation. But unfortunately Maurice Hubbard, of Pink Custard Light Show fame, reminded me all about the evening and so it all came flooding back. I'm shuddering as I write this even now, 38 years later.

The event was a Rag Ball, which meant that the Rag Committee wanted a variety of acts and more importantly, a late bar. Darts were a very successful, popular band at the time and were on a conventional, city hall type, tour. They did not want to be going on to half-pissed students at 12.30 at night, playing a set and leaving the venue around 2.00 am. Their road crew certainly were not looking forward to a get-out at that time, meaning that they wouldn't be hitting the road until something like 4.00 am. So obviously they refused to go on as the headline act, that is, closing the show. They insisted on taking the stage at around 9.00 pm and not only that but they also required that their crew took their equipment off stage immediately after they finished their set.

Quite simply, a nightmare. I knew what would happen but actually it was even worse than I could have foreseen. The band finished a great set, left the stage after an encore or two and then their roadies took over to a deafeningly silent Great Hall. Dave Berry was to follow but his only big hit was 'The Crying Game' way back in 1964. I think Maurice describes it best, "They finish their set and the audience watch for nearly an hour, in silence, as their gear is broken down and removed. The road-crew become the main attraction. Dave Berry has to follow this, playing to people, most of whom had probably never heard of him."

You know when people say that they wanted the ground to swallow them up? Well …

Barry Lucas

Dead or Alive

12 May 1984 — Support unknown

Liverpool dance group Dead or Alive, fronted by Pete Burns, achieved the first ever No. 1 hit for the production trio of Stock Aitken Waterman in March 1985, with the single 'You Spin Me Round (Like a Record)'.

Following Pete Burns' appearance in 2006 Celebrity Big Brother, the hit from the 1985 *Youthquake* album was re-released and once more reached the top five in the UK Singles Chart. Having got twenty-eight singles and seven studio albums under their belt they completely disbanded in 2011.

Pete Burns died following a sudden cardiac arrest on 23 October 2016 at the age of fifty-seven.

Deaf School

4 December 1976 — Support: The Count Bishops

Deaf School assembled their lineup at Liverpool Art School in 1973 and had some interestingly named members:
Bette Bright – vocals
Enrico Cadillac – vocals
Cliff Hanger – guitars
Eric Shark – vocals
Max Ripple – keyboards
Steve "Average" Lindsey – bass guitar
Tim Whittaker – drums

Between 1976 and 1978 the band recorded three albums for the Warner Brothers label, in an art rock style that had its roots in cabaret, moving towards a harder punk rock sound.

Following splits and reunions over the years Deaf School are currently still active, having released the album *Launderette* in 2015.

Pub rockers **The Count Bishops** were formed in 1975 and existed up to 1980, along the way releasing four studio albums and being described as a grimier version of Dr Feelgood.

1977 saw the band playing support to Motorhead on their first tour.

Deep Purple

23 January 1970   **European Tour**   Supports: Farm I Urbane Gorilla

Another early concert in the 'Central Hall' featuring Deep Purple with the classic lineup of:
Ian Gillan – vocals
Ritchie Blackmore – guitars
Jon Lord – keyboards
Roger Glover – bass guitar
Ian Paice – drums

The band performed tracks from the upcoming *In Rock* album.

Possible Lancaster setlist: 'And the Address', 'Kneel and Pray', 'Into the Fire', 'Kentucky Woman', 'Child in Time', 'Mandrake Root', 'Wring That Neck (aka Hard Road)', 'Ritchie's Blues', 'Paint It Black, instrumental', drum solo.

Richard 'Dick' Dixon, currently a County College porter at the university, recalls being unable to gain entry to the concert on the night due to its being a total sell out. "Basically we stayed and listened to the gig outside the Great Hall. It was loud enough to enjoy out there"

In 1972 Deep Purple were recognised in *The Guinness Book of World Records* as the loudest band in the world. A gig at London's Rainbow Theatre registered 117 decibels and rendered three members of the audience unconscious.

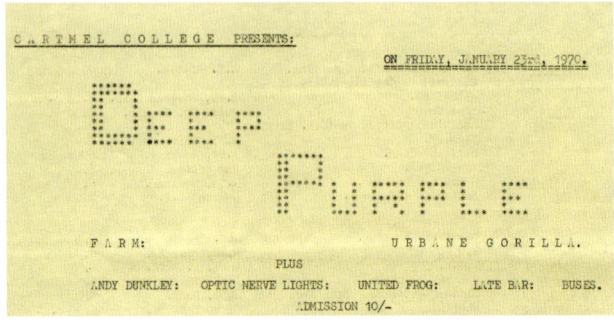

Warming up for Deep Purple, from Aylesbury in Buckinghamshire, the rock band **Farm** made their first of three 1970 appearances in The Great Hall.

Farm consisted of Bill Stallwood (vocals), Malcolm Graham (bass), Dave Janes (guitar), Mick Barnard (guitar), Paul Hammond (drums) and Pete Tyson (sax and flute).

Shortly following this concert, bassist Malcolm Graham left the band and was replaced by Nigel Harrison, who later went on to join Blondie in 1977. Harrison became Blondie's long serving bass player, appearing with the band for their 1978 Great Hall concert.

Mick Barnard, for a brief time, was the guitarist of the band Genesis, following the departure of founding member Anthony Phillips. Barnard was eventually replaced by Steve Hackett.

Another Farm member of note was drummer Paul Hammond, who went on to join Atomic Rooster.

Farm returned to Lancaster in April 1970 as guests of Procol Harum and in November 1970 as support for Argent.

Originally called Urban Gorilla, this was a Lancaster band that went through various singers and guitarists but were essentially built around steel guitarist Henry Ayrton, sax player Julian Holt and bass player Jeff Dade. Henry was a student at Lancaster University and under the influence of Captain Beefheart, the seed of the band was planted around 1967. At some point later, the band changed their name to **Urbane Gorilla** before disbanding in 1971. Billed as Urban Gorilla the band also made a Great Hall appearance providing support to Family for their October 1970 Great Hall date.

Farm photo courtesy of Malcolm Graham. Standing L to R: Dave Janes and Mick Barnard

Sitting on Gate L to R: Malcolm Graham, Bill Stallwood, Pete Tyson and Paul Hammond.

Dire Straits

12 December 1980   **The On Location Tour**   Support unknown, possibly no support act

Following their 1978 appearance in a support slot for Climax Blues Band, the band revisited Lancaster University for a date on their On Location tour to promote the October 1980 release of the album *Making Movies*.

Band lineup:
Mark Knopfler – guitar, vocals
John Illsley – bass
Pick Withers – drums
Alan Clark – keyboards
Hal Lindes – guitar

Lancaster setlist: 'Once Upon a Time in the West', 'Expresso Love', 'Down to the Waterline', 'Lions', 'Skateaway', 'Romeo and Juliet', 'In the Gallery', 'News', 'Sultans of Swing', 'Les Boys', 'Portobello Belle', 'Angel of Mercy', 'Tunnel of Love', 'Wild West End', 'Where Do You Think You're Going'.

It was during the recording of *Making Movies* that musical differences between the Knopfler brothers surfaced, resulting in the departure of David prior to the tour.

Dire Straits finally broke up in 1995, after releasing a total of six studio albums.

Like many of the bands who appeared in the '70s and early '80s, many colleges could say that they had them on as support acts, as up and coming acts, as breaking headliners. But NO colleges had a list of acts that played there as major international arena and festival headliners. No college, that is, except Lancaster.

Dire Straits had played Lancaster as a £50 support act. But here they were – post 'Sultans of Swing' – world superstars playing a smallish college; something that was unique to Lancaster and which would never be repeated anywhere in the world on the regular basis, it occurred in North West England.

Barry Lucas

© Geoff Campbell

Dr Feelgood

10 October 1975   Support: GT Moore and The Reggae Guitars
10 December 1979   Support: Phil Rambow Band

British pub rock band Dr Feelgood were formed in Canvey Island, Essex, by the late Lee Brilleaux, Wilko Johnson, John B. Sparks on bass guitar and John Martin, aka "The Big Figure", on drums.

Dr Feelgood were known primarily for their high energy live performances and both of these uni gigs were no letdown on the night. The set of the 1975 concert would have featured songs from the album *Down by The Jetty*, released in 1974, and the 1975 classic Feelgood album *Malpractice*. Their 1976 album *Stupidity* reached No. 1 in the UK Albums Charts. Shortly afterwards, in March 1977, due to conflicts with Lee Brilleaux, Wilko Johnson was to leave the band and did not appear on stage at their 1979 gig being replaced by Gypie Mayo. 1979 also saw the band hit the Top 10 of the UK charts with the single 'Milk and Alcohol'.

A version of the band (featuring none of the original members) continues to tour and record to this day.

GT Moore and The Reggae Guitars were the incarnation of Englishman Gerald Thomas Moore with his band sometimes featuring two drummers along with congas and a three-piece brass section. They were considered to be one of the first white reggae bands and also featured ex-Gentle Giant drummer Malcolm Mortimore. GT and his band released two studio albums, *G.T. Moore & The Reggae Guitars* in 1974 and *Reggae Blue* 1975. During his career, GT Moore performed and recorded with such illustrious artists as Joan Baez, Johnny Nash and Lee 'Scratch' Perry. Gerald Moore died in 2011 aged fifty-eight.

Canadian-born pub rocker **Phil Rambow** emigrated to England in 1973 and immediately formed an outfit called The Winkies, playing as backing band to Brian Eno on his first and only solo tour in early 1974. The Winkies were to disband in 1975, after which Phil Rambow assembled his own Phil Rambow Band. He performed at the tribute concert in 2002 to the late Kirsty MacColl following her accidental death.

Lee Brilleaux 1979 © Geoff Campbell

Gypie Mayo 1979 © Doug Price

John Angus

Echo & The Bunnymen

1 May 1981
21 October 1984 **Ocean Rain Tour**

Support: Blue Orchids
Support: The Triffids

Formed in 1978, the original lineup of Liverpool band Echo & The Bunnymen was frontman and vocalist Ian McCulloch, Will Sergeant on guitar and Les Pattinson on bass guitar. The Bunnymen did not feature a drummer but instead used a drum machine. By 1980 the drum machine had been replaced by real-life drummer Pete de Freitas.

Their first Great Hall concert featured songs from the band's second album release, *Heaven Up Here*, which reached No. 10 in the UK Albums Chart.

1984 saw The Bunnymen return for a second concert, this time with four studio albums and ten singles to their name, including 'The Killing Moon' and 'The Back of Love'.

Following a complete split of the band in 1993, McCulloch and Sergeant regrouped with Pattinson in 1997 and returned as Echo & the Bunnymen, having a UK Top 10 hit with 'Nothing Lasts Forever'.

But maybe some things do, as Echo & The Bunnymen are still active today.

Manchester post-punk band **Blue Orchids** were formed by ex-Fall guitarist Martin Bramah in 1979 and are still active today.

The Triffids were an Australian band active from 1978 to 1989 and have been described as Australia's best-loved post-punk group.

© Geoff Campbell

Echo & The Bunnymen 1984 © Geoff Campbell

John Angus

Eddie and The Hot Rods

15 October 1977   Support: No Dice

Hailing from the same neck of the woods as Dr Feelgood, Eddie and The Hotrods were formed in 1975 in Canvey Island, Essex, and were initially called The Rods.

They are best known for their Top 10 hit of 1977 'Do Anything You Wanna Do'.

Still touring and recording today, they originally split up in 1981, but have re-formed several times since, with lead singer Barrie Masters the only constant member.

The Hotrods on this evening featured ex-Kursaal Flyers lead guitarist Graeme Douglas.

January 1976 had previously seen The Hotrods in the Great Hall as guests of The Kursaal Flyers.

No Dice were a four-piece band from North London who released two albums, *No Dice* and *2 Faced.* They toured extensively from 1976 until the early '80s.

© David Stewart

Edgar Broughton Band

6 November 1970   Supports: The Keef Hartley Band | Stoneground

The Edgar Broughton Band, formed in 1968 in Warwick, were a psychedelic rock band. Edgar's voice was compared to that of Captain Beefheart, and his screeching guitar playing was likened to that of a cat sliding down a blackboard. Edgar's brother Steve was the band's drummer.

Only a month earlier, Edgar and his band had appeared as guests of Jack Bruce in the Great Hall.

After over forty years and with eight studio albums and six singles under their belt, Edgar called it a day and dissolved the band in 2010.

The Keef Hartley Band were formed in 1969 and mixed elements of jazz, blues and rock 'n' roll. The band made an appearance at the Woodstock Festival of 1969.

Keith "Keef" Hartley was a local lad born in Preston, Lancashire, beginning his career as the replacement for Ringo Starr on drums for Rory Storm and the Hurricanes, a Liverpool-based band.

Keith Hartley passed away in Preston Hospital in November 2011.

Stoneground were a rock band formed in 1970 in Concord, California. Originally a trio, Stoneground expanded to become a ten-piece band by the time of their 1971 debut album *Stoneground*. The album featured seven different lead vocalists. Stoneground continued as an act through to 1984, disbanded and re-formed again in 2003, finally calling it a day in 2005.(NB Not to be confused with the band Stonefeather, who appeared as support to Mott The Hoople in 1970.)

Elvis Costello and The Attractions

13 March 1981   **A Tour To Trust**   Support: Dave and The Mistakes
2 October 1982   No Support
27 October 1984   **Bedrooms of Britain Tour** Support: The Pogues

Elvis Costello OBE was born Declan Patrick MacManus on 25 August 1954 in Paddington, London.

A four-time visitor to the university, Costello very much liked playing the Great Hall, and by all accounts his appearances were all sell-outs. Costello is probably best known for his 1979 single 'Oliver's Army' which spent four weeks at No. 2 in the UK Singles Chart of 1979. The song was written by Elvis Costello and produced by Nick Lowe. Notably, on his 1977 Stiff Tour appearance, the Great Hall witnessed the first known live performance of Costello's 1978 hit single 'Pump It Up'. Over his career he has released more than 25 albums from *My Aim is True* in 1977 to *Look Now* in 2018.

Suggested partial Lancaster setlist for the 1981 concert: 'Accidents Will Happen', '(I Don't Want To Go To) Chelsea', 'Possession', 'Clowntime is Over', 'Alison', 'Mystery Dance', 'Watching The Detectives', 'I Can't Stand Up For Falling Down'.

Openers for the 1981 show were Swedish band **Dave and The Mistakes**, led by Dave Nerge. They released just the one album, in 1980.

Celtic punk outfit **The Pogues**, fronted by the dentally challenged Shane MacGowan, were the great support act on the night of the 1984 concert. Their 1985 album *Rum Sodomy and The Lash* is one of my all time favourite album titles.

© Geoff Campbell

The Equals

6 February 1970   Supports: Sky I Penny Arcade

The Equals were a five-piece band formed in 1965 by Eddy Grant, writer of their million-selling chart hit 'Baby, Come Back', which reached No. 1 in 1968 and subsequently stayed in the UK charts Top 75 for eighteen weeks.

The Equals disbanded in 1979, with Eddy going on to pursue his solo career and eventually release singles such as 'Electric Avenue' and 'I Don't Wanna Dance', a No. 1 UK hit for him in 1982.

Sky were an American rock band from Detroit, active in the early 1970s and disbanding in 1973. Over their three-year existence they also played as openers for bands such as The Who, Traffic and Jethro Tull.

Not much is known about **Penny Arcade** other than the possibility that the band's proper name may have been The Impact. The Impact sometimes played under the name Penny Arcade and eventually evolved into chart-topping pop outfit Black Lace around 1973.

> This is the show that, arguably, started it all – the reason I stood for the position of Lonsdale College Social Secretary in April 1970. At this time why would any social secretary spend a king's ransom on a teenie-bopper *TOTPs* act?
>
> Barry Lucas

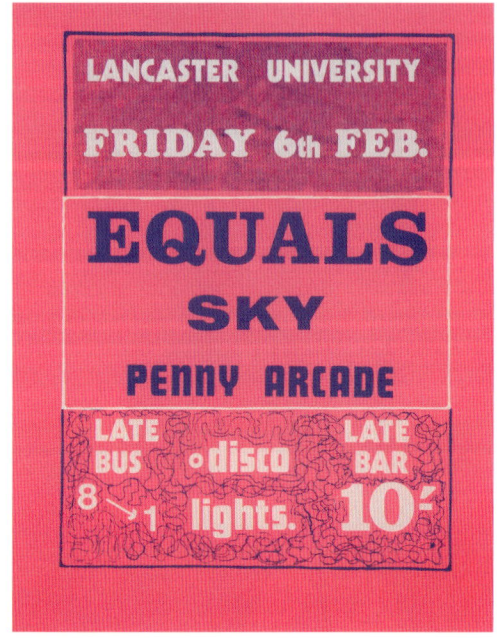

Courtesy of Ray Wilkinson Music Research Archive

Eric Clapton

7 August 1976   Support: Mr Pugh's Puppet Theatre
6 May 1980   Support: Chas and Dave

Before going solo, Clapton was a member of several bands, including the Yardbirds, Cream, Blind Faith, and Derek and the Dominos in the mid-'60s to early '70s.

Brian May said of Eric Clapton: "His fingers are directly wired to his soul".

This 1976 tour featured venues that all had a view of the sea; of course the view from the top of the university's Bowland Tower qualified Lancaster for a first visit from Eric and his band, to promote the album *No Reason To Cry*. Eric's two female backing singers on the night included Yvonne Elliman, who found fame and chart success in 1978 with the single written by the Gibb brothers

'If I Can't Have You' from the film *Saturday Night Fever*.

His second backing vocalist, the American Marcy Levy, wrote Eric's hit single 'Lay Down Sally' and went on to be a member of the '80s pop outfit Shakespears Sister.

7 August 1976 — No Reason To Cry – UK Tour

Band lineup:
Eric Clapton – guitar, vocals
George Terry – guitar
Dicks Sims – keyboards
Carl Radle – Bass
Jamie Oldaker – drums

Sergio Pastora Rodriguez – percussion
Yvonne Elliman – backing vocals
Marcy Levy – backing vocals

Possible Lancaster setlist: 'Introduction', 'Hello Old Friend', 'All Our Past Times', 'Tell the Truth', 'I Shot the Sheriff', 'Double Trouble', 'Blues Power', 'Going Down Slow', 'Stormy Monday', 'Layla', 'Further On Up The Road'.

6 May 1980 — Just One Night – UK Tour

Eric played only 14 dates on this short UK tour with Albert Lee taking the leading guitar role on this night as a result of Eric being the worse for wear through drink.

Albert Lee, along with Chas Hodges of Chas and Dave, were former members of the band Heads Hands & Feet who provided support to Wishbone Ash's first Great Hall gig in 1971.

Gary Brooker, founder member and lead singer of Procol Harum, also featured, on keyboards.

Band lineup:
Eric Clapton – guitar, vocals
Albert Lee – guitar, vocals

Chris Stainton – keyboards
Gary Brooker – keyboards, vocals
Dave Markee – bass
Henry Spinetti – drums

Possible Lancaster setlist: 'Tulsa Time', 'Early In The Morning', 'Lay Down Sally', 'Wonderful Tonight', 'Country Boy' (featuring Albert Lee), 'Thunder And Lightning', 'Blues Power', 'All Our Pastimes', 'Setting Me Up' (featuring Albert Lee), 'Leave The Candle' (featuring Gary Brooker), 'If I Don't Be There By Morning', 'Ramblin' On My Mind', 'Mean Old World', 'Have You Ever Loved A Woman', 'Home Lovin' (featuring Gary Brooker), 'After Midnight', 'Cocaine', 'Further On Up The Road'.

Created by Ted Milton, **Mr Pugh's Puppet** Theatre provided Eric's early evening entertainment for his 1976 visit.

Travelling Europe and Britain, poet, puppeteer and musician Ted Milton, would present surreal puppet plays like "Pere Ubu" by pre-dadaist playwright Alfred Jarry, as well as his own creations like "Operation Wordworth". He also released a self-financed 7" inch single entitled, 'Confessions of an Aeroplane Farter'. With a B side of, I Don't Want To Go Poo-Poo! It was housed in a 12" picture cover with a free air sickness bag inside.

In 1976, film director Terry Gilliam invited Ted to perform the role of the puppeteer in his movie Jabberwocky.

He also toured as support to Ian Dury and The Blockheads with a witness to one of his shows writing,

'I first saw Ted Milton supporting Ian Dury and The Blockheads in 1978. He did this awful punk performance art Punch and Judy puppet show, puerile stuff like one of the puppets drinking snot from the others nose!'

Ted Milton continues to perform with the band he created in the mid-70s called Blurt, and have released a number of studio albums over the years.

Chas & Dave (often billed as Chas 'n' Dave) were an English Cockney pop rock duo, formed in 1972 in London by Chas Hodges and Dave Peacock.

Over 45 years of performing, the band accumulated an impressive list of hits and albums including the chart singles, 'Gertcha' and 'The Sideboard Song' in 1979 and 'Aint No Pleasing You' reaching number two in the UK Charts of 1982.

In 1983, Chas & Dave also presented their own TV variety show set in an East End pub called, Chas and Dave's Knees Up, and broadcast on ITV.

This was a third time on the Great Hall stage for Chas Hodges, having appeared twice in the early 70s with Heads Hands and Feet.

Sadly in September 2018, the death was announced of Chas Hodges aged 72.

Eric Clapton

EC was here. Yes, "Old Slow Hand" actually played a university date as a world superstar, not once, but twice. By now even Leeds could only sit back and wonder, why? How?

Well, in the summer of 1976 Paul Loasby, ironically an ex-Leeds Social Secretary, who was now running Harvey Goldsmith's office, phoned to ask if I could see the sea from Lancaster University. I explained that if you went to the top of Bowland Tower you could. "That'll do," he said. "Do you want Eric Clapton in August? He's doing a traditional seaside resorts tour so I'll tell him Lancaster is a seaside town." I thought, "well it is sort of, but do I want Clapton?" Is the Pope a Catholic? I would have some explaining to do to the returning students — "Er, by the way while you were at home one of the greatest rock stars in the world was here, shame you missed him". But I'd live with that.

I'd had to help Paul with some crew and security for his date in Blackpool, a small seaside resort rivalling Lancaster! Consequently I was well prepared for the staging requirements of the show. Eric Clapton had managed to rid himself of the terrible heroin problem he'd had, but by this time he had replaced it with Courvoisier brandy. It didn't prevent an outstanding show though. In the afternoon he had placed a bet on a horse and I had to send somebody down to the bookies pick up his winnings of £500. He was ecstatic — it was amazing, all that fame and fortune he enjoys and he was over the moon about that £500.

We managed to do another gig with him, this time in term time, luckily for the student population … and me.

However this had an other story. Although Paul Loasby had put several dates from Harvey Goldsmith tours into Lancaster by now, this date was the first that the great man himself, Harvey Goldsmith, had ventured up to the wilds of Lancaster. It was vitally important to me (and Paul) that he was impressed with the show and with the organisation of the venue, so we were both walking on eggshells all night. Sat in the porters' lodge in the Great Hall foyer, Harvey, behind Jack Nicholson's desk (head porter), said how great the show was and then suggested to Paul that they put a night at Lancaster on all their tours. "Great idea, Harvey, I never thought of that," agreed Paul sycophantically. Everything brilliant. Then … In stormed the tour manager, screaming, "The bloody bouncers have nicked Eric's bottle of Southern Comfort!" I just prayed for the ground to swallow me up. My regular three dressing room stewards were a bit, well, you could say they were 'characters', you know, local lads, salt of the earth — that kind of crap. But surely they wouldn't, surely not that … Oh yes. I went theatrically nuts but what would Harvey say? Just, "Sack 'em!" The gig was such a success and Harvey made so much money though, that a little thing like a bottle of whisky was not going to alter his opinion. Phew, close one though.

I didn't sack them and lived to regret it — see Tina Turner.

Then worse(?) was to follow. Geoff Campbell came to see me in the foyer: the humpers wanted a pay rise or they were not going to do the get out. They knew I was vulnerable, Harvey Goldsmith himself being there, and it was a massively important gig, arguably the biggest we had ever staged and it was 11.00 pm. I couldn't find other humpers, the majority of the stewards had left and the road crew wanted to get the gear out and get back to the hotel bar. I was furious but fairly helpless. I pointed out to them that they had done bigger get outs without any complaints, but they were leaving me with no alternative but to give in. "Right," I told them, "I will pay you more, but you will never work a show here again." They had obviously gone away triumphant, but then talked. Geoff returned to say they would do the get out at the usual rates. Once again, phew, I desperately did not want Harvey, back in the hotel, talking about breweries and piss-ups.

Barry Lucas

Hi Paul,

I was interested to read about your book being written about the Lancaster University concerts, a great place for a gig and I saw quite a few there. My name is Mark Thornley.

I worked at a record shop in Blackpool called Music Mania in 1978 for a couple of years when I was seventeen. We were also ticket agents for the concerts and also used to get some stock from 'Ear 'Ere Records in Lancaster and if I remember correctly, Barry Lucas had something to do with them.

I remember meeting him a few times when I used to go with the guy who used to pick up the records.

They would keep promotional stuff for me relating to Eric Clapton as I was a big fan and I still am. One of the best gigs I saw was Clapton in 1980 on the Just One Night tour. I was desperate to meet him after the gig and managed to get myself right outside the door of the dressing room, but could not get in. Maybe Eric was busy with his brandy at the time. But I did speak to him during the gig though!

I was right at the front and having smoked something exotic before the gig was in a fine mood, at a quiet moment I shouted "play Blues Power Eric," to which he replied "already played it mate," and then somebody else shouted back "well play it again then". Great gig and Eric was on top form and looking liked he was having a great time. He inspired me to start playing the guitar when I was fifteen. I also remember having a pint with Phil Mogg of UFO when I saw them just after their sound check. I was in early because I knew the guys on the door and asked him if being the singer in a rock band was all it was cracked up to be, "oh yes" was the answer. It would be wouldn't it!

I also remember Bad Company was a particularly good gig in 1979.

Anyway, hope you don't mind me dropping you a line. Happy memories from those days and I am still playing myself, being fortunate enough to have played some good gigs over the years. Notably supporting Peter Green with his first incarnation of the Splinter Group including the late great Cozy Powell on drums, when I was in a band called The Healers.

All the best

Regards,

Mark.

Eric Clapton and Marcy Levy in 1976

1980 © Geoff Campbell

Eric Clapton and Albert Lee 1980 © Doug Price

The Europeans

10 October 1983 — Support: Annabel Lamb

From London, The Europeans were a British new wave group formed in 1981 and disbanded in 1985. They released three albums, two studio and one live, none of which achieved much in terms of chart position. In 1989, their former keyboard player and lead vocalist from Kendal, Cumbria, Steve Hogarth, also known as "h", joined Marillion as their lead vocalist.

Annabel Lamb is an English singer and songwriter. She had a British Top 30 hit in 1983 with her cover version of The Doors song, 'Riders On The Storm', her only hit in the UK Singles Chart. She has released eight albums and is still active, having worked with, in the past, Kiki Dee.

Fairport Convention

4 October 1969 — Supports: Indo-Jazz Fusions | Brett Marvin and The Thunderbolts | Duffy Power
10 March 1973 — Support: Claire Hamill
20 November 1974 — Support: Bryn Haworth
14 October 1975 — Support: David Lewis
9 December 1976 — Support: Arbre

Veterans of five Great Hall appearances Fairport Convention were formed in April 1967 by a group of folk musicians, Richard Thompson (guitarist), Ian Matthews (singer) and Ashley Hutchings (bassist), in Muswell Hill, London.

Fairport Convention are regarded as one of the most important groups of the folk rock movement.

By the time the band made their first appearance at Lancaster, to play what was the first concert in the newly opened Central Hall, they already had three albums under their belt.

Their first album was *Fairport Convention*, a mixture of original songs and covers from American folk singers. In 1968, following suggestions from their producer Joe Boyd, the band recruited singer Sandy Denny. 1969 then saw the addition of highly regarded songwriter and violinist Dave Swarbrick who emerged, alongside Denny, as one of Fairport's leading figures until their disbandment in 1979. Dave Swarbrick passed away in 2016 at the age of seventy-five.

With the band now stretching to over five decades in the music business and having gone through numerous lineup changes, the Fairports are undoubtedly the greatest British folk group of all time. Since the band's reformation in 1985, they have hosted the Cropredy Festival in Oxfordshire, which is the largest annual folk event in England.

Individually and collectively the members of Fairport Convention have received numerous awards recognising their contribution to music and culture and, as of 2017, they continue to record and tour.

In what was probably the first "big gig" in the newly opened Central Hall, folk-rockers Fairport Convention were bizarrely supported by the eccentric British pub blues band, **Brett Marvin and the Thunderbolts.**

Formed in 1968, curiously the band did not and never have featured a Brett Marvin amongst the lineup but on the night did feature Jona Lewie, famous for his 1980 hit single 'You'll Always Find Me in the Kitchen at Parties' and the perennial Christmas number, 'Stop the Cavalry'. Jona returned to the Great Hall, almost ten years later, as part of the Be Stiff Tour in 1978.

The Indo-Jazz Fusions were a British-based outfit formed in the mid-sixties that fused jazz and Indian sounds. The band was the creation of classically trained Indian composer John Mayer and the Jamaican-born jazz saxophonist Joe Harriott.

The Joe Harriott-John Mayer partnership composed the distinctive theme tune, 'Acka Raga', for the early episodes of the BBC quiz show *Ask the Family*, which was broadcast between 1967 and 1984. The theme featured Mayer on sitar.

Duffy Power was a British pop star turned R&B vocalist who in 1963 teamed up with Graham Bond, Jack Bruce, Ginger Baker and John McLaughlin to record 'I Saw Her Standing There', one of the first cover versions of a Beatles song. He passed away in 2014 at the age of seventy-two.

Claire Hamill from County Durham in northern England is a British singer-songwriter. This was the first of her three appearances at the university. She played support for the Sutherland Brothers in 1972 and in 1981 appeared on stage as guitarist with Wishbone Ash on their *Number the Brave* Tour.

Bryn Haworth is a British Christian singer-songwriter, guitarist and pioneer of Jesus music in mainstream rock. Born in Blackburn, Lancashire, he has released some twenty-two albums and several singles since the 1970s, as well as guesting as guitarist on many other albums by rock and folk artists.

1975 support act **David Lewis** was most probably the Belfast singer, songwriter and guitarist who was a former member of a band called Andwella's Dream.

Andwella's Dream recorded three studio albums between 1969 and 1971, the last two under the band name Andwella.

Following the band's split David pursued a solo career, releasing two albums on the Polydor label in 1976 and 1978.

David also wrote many songs for other artists, including 'Happy To Be On An Island In The Sun' for legendary Greek crooner Demis Roussos.

Arbre were a rock band from Wallsend, Tyne and Wear. Active in the '70s, they re-formed as The Caffreys in 1999 and continue to perform.

Sandy Denny on stage in 1975 © David Bradbury

David Lewis
© David Bradbury

Courtesy of Ray Wilkinson Music Research Archive

The Fall

9 November 1985 — Support unknown

Originally formed in Manchester, England in 1976, post punk band The Fall went on to have over forty years of recording and performing with their founder and sole constant leader Mark E Smith. Readers should note here that Mark E Smith, the Vice Chancellor of Lancaster University from 2012–2019, was not one and the same!

With numerous personnel changes over the bands 42 year existence, The Fall released over 31 studio albums, 32 live recordings and 23 John Peel sessions. The Fall's last album in 2017 was entitled *New Facts Emerge*.

Shortly following the first release of *When Rock Went to College* in October 2017, The Falls' Mark E Smith died on 24 January 2018 after a long illness.

Reports of the concert are scarce but a setlist of the time would maybe have been: 'Cruiser's Creek', 'Clear Off', 'Rollin' Danny', 'The Man Whose Head Expanded', 'Couldn't Get Ahead', 'Barmy', 'Draygo's Guilt', 'Stephen Song', '2x4', 'Gut Of The Quantifier', 'What You Need', 'I Feel Voxish', Spoilt Victorian Child', 'My New House', 'God Box', 'LA.', 'No Bulbs'.

Family

16 October 1970 — Supports: Nothineverappens | Urban Gorilla

The earliest and most well-known of the Leicester rooted prog bands, Family assembled in 1967, mixing beat with psychedelic, classical, folk and experimental music. They were adept at both chart hits and being weird in their early days. Fronted by the gruff, gargly voice of Roger Chapman, the rest of the band comprised Charlie Whitney (guitar), Rick Grech (bass, violin), Jim King (woodwinds) and Rob Townsend (drums). Their debut album *Music In A Dolls House* came out in 1968 and is an oddball mixture of pop hits, prog and eccentric stuff and went some way to hinting at their finest, 1969's *Family Entertainment,* where they pulled out all the creative stops and really went for it. Of course it wasn't until they pretty much left Leicester for good that they became internationally famous, getting into the charts with singles like 'The Weavers Answer' and 'Burlesque'. The band didn't exist long beyond 1973 though, with Chapman & Whitney forming Streetwalkers, who later changed into Roger Chapman & The Shortlist. Rick Grech is, however, the most prolific member, having been involved in the super group Blind Faith and a wealth of other bands.

Yorkshire's finest ever psychedelic rock/folk rock band from Kingston upon Hull, **Nothineverappens** were formed in the late 1960s and disbanded in 1972.

Billed here as **Urban Gorilla** the local Lancaster band were onstage again having previously backed Deep Purple earlier that year.

Family were a great band, doing some amazing stuff and, in Roger Chapman, they had one of the most unforgettable rock voices, although I remember the show mainly for one thing; a personal nightmare. It was the first and only time I went on stage unprepared to make an announcement. You must never, ever, ever not know what you want to say, word for word. There had been some technical problems with the PA, the mixer in particular, and a delay had ensued. The band's manager had asked me if I would go on stage, explain, apologise and say it wouldn't be much longer before the show started. No problem!

I went on stage. "Ladies and Gentlemen er, er ..." The "ers" echoed around the hall through the PA. More stuttering, "Erm" – "Erm" came back at me like the ponderings of The Almighty (and not the band either). "There's been a mix-up with the mixer and the ... er ... mix-up should be sorted soon and the mixer sorted so the mix-up is fixed," I babbled. Oh no, so many sonorous 'mix-ups' – if only the stage had had one of those old fashioned trap doors I could have disappeared down. I swore, as I crept shamefully off the stage, that I would never again walk onto a stage without a script.

Barry Lucas

UNIVERSITY OF LANCASTER

presents

FAMILY

and

NOTHIN'EVER'APPENS

and

URBAN GORILLA

Friday, 16 October • Central Hall

8 p.m. to 1 a.m.   Late Beer, Birds and Buses

★ ADVANCE TICKETS 15/- ★

from SIMMONS, Common Garden Street; or GAS TAYLOR,
c/o Bowland College, University

AT THE DOOR . £1

John B. Barber & Son, Ltd., New Street, Lancaster.

Courtesy of Music Research Archive

Fanny

18 May 1973   Supports: Heads Hands & Feet I Fumble

Formed in 1969 by guitarist June Millington and her sister, bassist Jean, Fanny was an American rock band, notable for being one of the first all-female rock groups to be signed to a major label (Reprise Records), and enjoy commercial success. Fanny have influenced bands from Joan Jett and The Blackhearts to Courtney Love. They released a total of five studio albums and achieved two UK Top 40 hits with two US Billboard Hot 100 top 40 singles.

Fanny did enjoy greater commercial success in the UK than the USA, as a result of touring the UK in support of Jethro Tull and Humble Pie. They were also banned from performing at the London Palladium on the grounds they were "too sexy."

The band that visited Lancaster consisted of June Millington (guitar), Jean Millington (bass), Alice de Buhr (drums) and Nicky Barclay (keyboards). The tour was in promotion of their fourth studio album, *Mothers Pride* and was produced by Todd Rundgren.

By 1974 the lineup had changed to include Patti Quattro (sister of Suzi) as a replacement for June Millington. Although Fanny were to break up in 1975, 2018 saw the Millington sisters re-unite to form a band called, Fanny Walked The Earth and in March 2018 released a studio album of the same name.

> "One of the most important female bands in American rock has been buried without a trace. And that is Fanny. They were one of the finest … rock bands of their time, in about 1973. They were extraordinary … they're as important as anybody else who's ever been, ever; it just wasn't their time. Revivify Fanny. And I will feel that my work is done."
>
> —David Bowie (1947–2016)

Heads Hands & Feet were a country-influenced six-piece band featuring the legendary Albert Lee on guitars and Chas Hodges on keyboards. Heads Hands & Feet became a popular live band in the UK, making appearances on The Old Grey Whistle Test and also in Europe, where they appeared on the German music programme Beat-Club. They disbanded in 1973.

Albert Lee was to play alongside Eric Clapton at his 1980 Great Hall appearance, when Chas Hodges and Dave Peacock provided Eric Clapton's support act on the night.

From Weston-super-Mare, **Fumble** were originally formed in 1967 by Des Henly (guitars and vocals), Mario Ferrari (bass), Barry Pike (drums) and the late Sean Mayes on piano. Originally known as The Baloons (sic) they became Fumble in 1972 and specialized in covering rock 'n' roll classics, releasing two studio albums over their career. Their debut *Fumble* in 1972, was followed-up with *Poetry in Lotion* in 1974. Fumble arrived in Lancaster fresh from a tour supporting David Bowie on the US leg of his Ziggy Stardust tour.

They were one of the first, probably the first, all-girl rock bands. I still don't really believe it but, by the time they reached Lancaster, our American friends hadn't been made aware of the difference in meaning of the band's name on both sides of the Atlantic. It made for a fun discussion!

Also on the bill that night were Heads Hands & Feet, featuring one of my favourite guitarists, Albert Lee. His mastery of country rock is just wonderful and over the years I have seen him in many great venues. Later that same year, I was lucky to be given a complimentary box at The Royal Albert Hall by Island Records to see Albert Lee again with Heads Hands and Feet, in a concert that included Mott The Hoople, on the condition, that my party and I launch a couple of hundred Frisbees into the audience!

Later in 1976 and then 1980 came the Great Hall Clapton gigs. Then, about eight years ago he appeared in concert at the Carlton in Morecambe, where only about sixty people (including complementary tickets) were there to hear a remarkable twenty minute version of his iconic song 'Country Boy'. Do you know, sometimes, I just don't understand. Only sixty people for a legend and yet many bemoan the fact that venues don't promote live music anymore. Thanks Mike O'Brien for a great night.

Barry Lucas

The Flying Burrito Brothers

4 December 1970   Supports: Hard Meat I The Greatest Show on Earth

In 1968, ex-members of The Byrds, Chris Hillman and Gram Parsons, formed in Los Angeles, what some people considered to be the greatest country rock band of all time: The Flying Burrito Brothers. Completing the original lineup were Sneaky Pete Kleinow on pedal steel guitar and Chris Ethridge on bass with the Burritos initially utilising a variety of session drummers. The band sounded like nothing else around at the time and also looked like nothing else. Regular stage attire was smart country and western style suits, with Parson's suit being decorated with marijuana leaves and naked women on the lapels. The Burritos played the infamous Altamont Free Concert headlined by The Rolling Stones in 1969. For this Great Hall appearance, shortly following the departure of Parsons in June 1970, the band lined up as follows; Rick Roberts (replacing Parsons) Chris Hillman, Sneaky Pete, Bernie Leadon on guitars and former Byrds drummer Michael Clarke. The band performed tracks from their seminal 1969 album *The Gilded Palace of Sin* and their 1970 release, *Burrito Deluxe*. Gram Parsons tragically died in 1973 at the age of 26 as the result of an overdose of morphine and alcohol. His death at a motel in The Joshua Tree National Park in California was followed by incredible events including the theft of his body from Los Angeles International Airport by friends and their subsequent cremation of Parsons in the desert, according to Parsons' wish. The Burritos eventually disbanded in 1972 following Chris Hillman's departure from the band with Kleinow and Ethridge instigating a reformation of the band in 1975 which continued through to 1984. The band was reformed once again in 1985 and were disbanded for a final time in 2001.

Hard Meat were a UK psychedelic progressive rock band consisting of:
Mick Dolan – electric Guitar, acoustic guitar, lead vocals
Steve Dolan – electric bass, string bass, vocals
Mick Carless – drums, congas, percussion, assorted loud noises

The band made two albums released by Warner Bros in 1970: *Hard Meat* and *Through a Window*.

The Greatest Show on Earth were a UK progressive rock band active from 1968 to 1971. They recorded two albums on Harvest Records in 1970: *Horizons* and *The Going's Easy*. The band was also notable for its album covers, designed by the artist group Hipgnosis.

> This band were quite simply the greatest country rock acts, and they played the Great Hall on a very early tour. For me it was memorable for the best forged tickets I came across – unfortunately well after the concert!
>
> Barry Lucas

Forged ticket

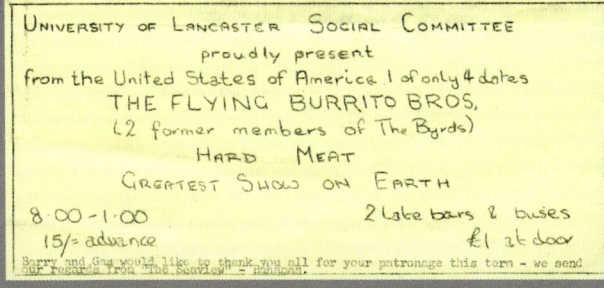

Focus

28 February 1976 Support: Charlie

Focus are a Dutch progressive rock band formed in Amsterdam in 1969 by Thijs van Leer.

Based around the technical mastery of van Leer on keyboards, flute and vocals, and Jan Akkerman on guitars, Focus were on the whole an instrumental group. The band achieved their popularity following the huge success of their 1971 album *Focus II,* which contained the hit single 'Hocus Pocus'.

On the night Jan Akkerman failed to appear on stage following his sacking from the band in early 1976 by Thijs Van Leer, and much to the disappointment of fans, Akkerman had been replaced on the night by Belgian guitarist Philip Catherine.

Jan Akkerman returned to the Great Hall a year later with his own band.

Focus continue to record and tour, with Thijs Van Leer and drummer Pierre van der Linden in the lineup. In 2014, Focus released their eleventh studio album *Golden Oldies*, a collection of newly re-recorded versions of some of their most popular songs, including 'Sylvia', 'House of the King' and 'Hocus Pocus'.

Charlie were a British rock band that were formed in 1971 by singer-songwriter Terry Thomas, and included former Argent guitarist John Verity. Although success in the UK eluded Charlie, they had luck with four minor hit singles in the US.

John Angus

Frankie Miller Band

23 November 1977   Support: Meal Ticket

Born in 1949 in Glasgow Frankie Miller was once described by Rod Stewart as "… the best white soul singer in the world"

In 1975 Miller formed The Frankie Miller Band with Henry McCullogh (guitar), Stu Perry (drums), Chrissie Stewart (bass) and Mick Weaver (guitars). They recorded the album *The Rock* in 1975, which was greeted quite positively by the critics but sold only moderately. June 1977 saw the release of Frankie's fourth album, *Full House*, and Frankie visted Lancaster in support of its release. 'Be Good to Yourself', a composition by Andy Fraser of Free, was issued as a single from the album *Full House* and reached No. 27 in the UK Singles Chart, becoming Miller's first chart hit.

Henry McCullogh had previously been on stage in the Great Hall as guitarist in Paul McCartney's new band Wings for their 1972 concert.

Meal Ticket were a country rock band that played the London pub circuit in the 1970s. Reviewing the concert in *SCAN* newspaper, Paul Johnson wrote: "Meal Ticket were by far the better act on the night".

A great bill – Meal Ticket were an excellent band – that saw the only appearance at Lancaster of one of the best R&B singers in history. If you haven't heard Frankie Miller I beg you to find some back catalogue and give it a go – he is really special.

The concert was fantastic – oh it made a loss, only about 500 people, if I remember rightly, and I sat in the balcony feeling a tremendous kinship with those discerning souls down in the hall enjoying truly great music. In my mind I was composing a rant for *SCAN*, lecturing all those Philistines who didn't attend. Never sent the letter though – their loss, I decided, not mine. But actually on ticket sales, it was mine also!

Barry Lucas

Free

9 October 1970   Support: Wishbone Ash
6 October 1972   Support: Smith Perkins and Smith

Legendary rock band Free were formed in London in 1968 by Paul Rodgers, Andy Fraser, Paul Kossoff and Simon Kirke. The remarkable fact about this group of lads was their ages at the time: Rogers and Kirke were eighteen, Kossoff was seventeen and Andy Fraser was fifteen! The band were best known for their signature hit single 'All Right Now', which spent a total of five weeks at No. 2 in the UK Singles Chart of summer 1970. Their first appearance in the Great Hall featured the classic lineup of Free, including Paul Kossoff, with support provided by a fledgling Wishbone Ash, who by all accounts produced a fantastic performance, almost blowing Free off the stage. In October 1972 Free returned to Lancaster but with a changed lineup. During a period of chaos for the band in mid-1972, mainly due to Paul Kossoff's unreliability and drug addiction, Andy Fraser had left Free, to be replaced by Tetsu Yamauchi on bass and John 'Rabbit' Bundrick had been added as keyboard player.

Free finally disbanded in 1973 with lead singer Paul Rodgers going on to become the frontman of Bad Company, together with Simon Kirke on drums, and bassist Andy Fraser assembling his band Sharks. Lead guitarist Paul Kossoff went on to form Back Street Crawler but tragically died from a drug-induced heart attack at the age of twenty-five, in 1976.

Exactly a year after their formation, **Wishbone Ash** took to the Great Hall stage as a support band to Free, performing tracks from their debut album, *Wishbone Ash,* released in December 1970.

Smith Perkins Smith, the American country-rock band of the early 1970s who included guitarist and singer Wayne Perkins, together with Tim Smith and Steve Smith, were back again following their May 1972 support slot for Country Joe and The Fish.

Free

After The Doors, this band is my favourite. A collection of fifteen, sixteen and seventeen year olds put together an album, 'Tons of Sobs', which I still play, and can sing along to, to this day. It truly is a class album.

So in 1970 I had booked Free to perform. They had just been hailed as one of the great acts at the Isle of Wight Festival that summer, playing in front of an estimated 600,000 people. They had released one of the great rock anthems – featured to this day on virtually every classic rock collection – 'All Right Now'. Despite all our memories it only reached No. 2 – I wonder if you can remember what kept it off the No. 1 spot? Look it up!

The support act that day was a little-known band: Wishbone Ash. They had a sponsorship deal with a PA company (Orange) and on the 60ft-wide stage were a handful of small orange (the colour, not the contents) boxes. They looked almost laughable, as by now PAs were becoming macho big, but what sound they produced – wonderful. Unfortunately you sort of knew they wouldn't catch on, because for the rock gods of the '70s size really did matter! And what a set the band produced, the battling guitars just blew me away. I didn't think it possible but I didn't want it to end, even if that meant Free not walking onto stage to replace them. It wasn't only me either, the whole audience went crazy.

Free followed, did their set, leaving 'All Right Now', the massive current hit single, as their anthem encore. I stood with them in the corridor at the side of the stage. It was strangely quiet, no applause, no stomping, nothing. Paul Rodgers and I slowly opened the doors to find that the audience had left. Free could not follow their support act that night.

The next time I had Free on was a nightmare from start to finish (almost). Don't get me wrong, this time Free were brilliant, the show fantastic, truly memorable, only … I had booked the band for the Freshers' Ball, in those days the first concert of Freshers' Week, the first weekend in October. Word obviously got out and I released tickets to the nine agencies covering the NW, plus obviously mail requests. Don't ask me how, I don't know to this day, but demand was such that it sold out in a week. What was I thinking about – as in, Freshers' Ball 1972 sold out before the first years had even arrived? Talk about cock-up, that must rank as the daddy of them all. So good news freshers: your introductory week is climaxed by one of the biggest bands in the UK. Bad news: it's already a sell-out. I suppose it didn't do my advance ticket sales for future shows any harm, as first years quickly appreciated that if you wanted to see an act in the Great Hall you had better get your ticket early – even if that was two weeks before you knew it was on!

The second part of my personal nightmare was the middle support act – a circus knife thrower. Mick Cater (later to become UB40's manager) was the booker at Island Artists. The company had finally employed Mick in exasperation, fed up of waiting for me to take up their job offer. Mick and I got on really well and had many escapades. We were to become close friends, although perhaps never as close as that night.

He had, earlier that year, booked a tour for Mott the Hoople's Rock 'n' Roll Circus. The evening featured bands plus two unlikely supports, the legendary old-time comic genius Max Wall, and a certain circus knife thrower. Mick asked me to look after their date in Carlisle Market Hall. Now, that could be a chapter in itself. I had to bring up some of the Great Hall's stewards and humpers, for the venue was not used to this sort of event and couldn't cope. If you want to know what it's like doing a show there, read George Melly's autobiography where there is a brilliant description which was as valid for Mott as it was when it was written several years before – nothing had changed, I promise you. Anyway Mick now informed me that he had booked the same knife thrower for the Free bill – again, I've no idea why but it was the kind of crazy thing done occasionally in the '70s. They were called La Vivas and, after this night I can't imagine why I booked them again but by this time they had changed their name to Hanleo and Katrina. I think I know why!

Now, the knife thrower was a legendary drinker and when I arrived at the hall at 5.00 pm for the sound checks he was already on his second pint in the ASH house. I said hello and asked him where his wife was, as she was his usual partner on stage. He said that she was in hospital as he had had rather too many at the last show and put a 8" Bowie knife through her thigh. Unbeknown to me, the climax of his act was when he "arranged" for the promoter of the show to be his on stage "victim". So after he had finished with his audience participation bit, a signal to the in-the-know stewards saw Mick and me frog marched to the small stage which had been set up in the middle of the hall. We had to remove our shirts and then stand back to back. It was all a bit of a laugh until he leant forward to me and whispered, hand over mic, that I had to put my arm behind my body and pull my stomach in – bloody cheek! Suddenly an 8" knife was vibrating 3" from my stomach. And I knew how long he had been in the ASH bar. Gulp. Then came a real gasp from the audience. Mick uttered a funny squeak and I turned around to see a similar instrument of death quivering AGAINST Mick's groin. The rest of the act was conducted with Mick's – and my – eyes firmly shut and our bodies squeezed as close as we could possibly get.

Barry Lucas

Genesis

23 February 1973   **Foxtrot Tour**   Support: String Driven Thing

Genesis were formed at Charterhouse School, Godalming, Surrey, in 1967 and were one of the most successful rock acts of the 1970s, 1980s and 1990s.

Genesis' first album, *From Genesis to Revelation*, was released in March 1969, followed by *Trespass* (1970) and *Nursery Cryme* (1971).

In February 1973 the classic Genesis lineup of Peter Gabriel, Tony Banks, Mike Rutherford, Steve Hackett and Phil Collins (on drums) visited Lancaster in support of the October 1972 release of their fourth studio album, *Foxtrot*.

Over the years, Genesis have enjoyed a longevity exceeded only by the likes of the Rolling Stones and the Kinks, and in the process provided a launch pad for the superstardom of Peter Gabriel and Phil Collins.

The band's first live album, *Genesis Live*, was released later the same year in August of 1973 and is formed from the recordings of shows straight after the Lancaster appearance, at The Free Trade Hall, Manchester, on 24 February and De Montfort Hall, Leicester, on 25 February 1973.

Possible Lancaster setlist: 'Watcher Of The Skies', 'Happy The Man', 'Fountain Of Salmacis', 'Get'em Out By Friday', 'The Musical Box', 'The Return Of The Giant Hogweed', 'Supper's Ready', 'The Knife', 'Harold The Barrel'

Peter Gabriel returned to Lancaster University in 1978 to perform as a solo act.

String Driven Thing are a folk rock band formed in 1967 in Glasgow and were part of the famed Charisma stable, alongside Genesis, Lindisfarne and Van Der Graaf Generator.

Led by husband and wife Chris and Pauline Adams, they featured the electric violin of Graham Smith. In April 2009, String Driven Thing re-formed with Chris, Pauline and Graham playing gigs in 2012 to coincide with the fortieth anniversary of their *Foxtrot* tour, with Genesis.

Gentle Giant

17 March 1972   Support: T2

Gentle Giant were a British progressive rock band active between 1970 and 1980. The band were known for the complexity and sophistication of their music and for the varied musical skills of its members.

Gentle Giant were considered to be one of the most experimental rock bands of the 1970s and all of the band members, except Malcolm Mortimore, were multi-instrumentalists. Although not commercially successful, they did achieve a cult following.

Shortly prior to this concert, drummer Malcolm Mortimore was seriously injured in a motorcycle accident and was replaced by John Weathers.

Lancaster lineup:
Gary Green – guitar, mandolin, vocals, recorder, bass, drums, xylophone
Kerry Minnear – keyboards, lead vocals (on recordings only), cello, vibraphone, xylophone, recorder, guitar, bass, drums
Derek Shulman – lead vocals, saxophone, recorder, keyboards, bass, drums, percussion
Phil Shulman – lead vocals, saxophone, trumpet, clarinet, recorder, percussion
Ray Shulman – bass, trumpet, violin, vocals, viola, drums, percussion, recorder, guitar
John "Pugwash" Weathers – drums, percussion, vibraphone, xylophone, vocals, guitar

London band **T2** returned to Lancaster a year after their appearance with The Groundhogs.

First up on stage was the former Bonzo Dog Doo-Dah Band multi-instrumentalist **Roger Ruskin Spear and his Giant Kinetic Wardrobe Show** (a.k.a Giant Orchestral Wardrobe). Roger's repertoire of instruments included saxophones, clarinet, piano, guitars and percussion.

A feature of his one-man show was a female tailor's dummy fitted with proximity switches, which produced increasingly high-pitched screams when a hand neared her chest (or 'sensitive zone').

Gilbert O' Sullivan

11 May 1977   No support act

Gilbert O'Sullivan, real name Ray O'Sullivan, is an Irish singer-songwriter, best known for his early 1970s hits 'Alone Again (Naturally)', 'Clair' and 'Get Down'. The music magazine *Record Mirror* voted him the No. 1 UK male singer of 1972. That same year saw Gilbert charting at No. 8 in the UK with the single 'Ooh-Wakka-Doo-Wakka-Day'.

Worldwide he has achieved sixteen Top 40 records, including six No. 1 songs, two of them in the UK.

Gilbert O' Sullivan, now in his seventieth year, recently performed at the BBC proms in the park in September 2017.

The concert that evening was unusually all seated.

Gillan

1 November 1981   Supports: Budgie I Nightwing

This fabulous value for money, triple bill Great Hall gig is well remembered by many North West rock fans.

Following his resignation from Deep Purple in 1973, the former lead singer and lyricist took a break from the music business to pursue other business ventures. Ian Gillan then formed his jazz fusion outfit, The Ian Gillan Band, in 1975.

With the band's jazz fusion direction unappealing to pop and rock fans alike, he dissolved The Ian Gillan Band and formed Gillan in 1978.

Gillan were one of the hard rock bands to make a significant impact during their existence, achieving commercial success in the United Kingdom during the early 1980s, with five albums in the Top 20 UK Albums Chart.

In 1982, much to the disappointment of fans, Ian Gillan announced that the band would fold, as he needed to rest his damaged vocal cords.

First on stage that night were **Nightwing**, a British heavy metal band originally formed in 1978 as 'Gordon and Friends' by bassist Gordon Rowley (formerly of Strife), keyboardist Kenny Newton and guitarist Eric Bert Percival. Nightwing disbanded in 1987 after the release of six albums, including *Something in the Air* in 1981.

Second up were Welsh rockers **Budgie**, fronted by Burke Shelly, and they would have provided a tremendous undercard performance prior to Gillan's appearance. Budgie had previously paid two visits to Lancaster University as headliners.

© Geoff Campbell

Gillan

When I left the Students' Union at the end of 1984, one of the first projects I became involved with was the world tour of the newly re-formed Deep Purple. The only date they were to perform in the UK was Knebworth. That was, if Knebworth could get its entertainments licence back that it had lost as the result of a few operational problems when it staged The Rolling Stones some years earlier. Paul Loasby was able to achieve that and so Deep Purple at Knebworth in 1985 actually happened.

I was primarily responsible for the dressing room areas and the backstage 'ambience', as the American production company called it. Yes, I hadn't the faintest idea what they were talking about either at that first meeting. Anyway, it transpired that I had to create a 'medieval fayre' for all the guests, record companies and general music business dignitaries – you know, all those people who were getting in without paying. But, more importantly, I was specifically responsible for the dressing room area. A nightmare. The backstage area set aside for artists' dressing rooms was a fairly large, fenced-off field but when I received Deep Purple's rider it had to be dramatically expanded. They wanted a separate area for them, away from the other bands, not a usual requirement I must say. Each band – and there were about seven – had one or two Portakabins to act as dressing rooms. However, although Deep Purple had just re-formed, there was obviously no love lost between the band members. I had to provide each member with their own dressing room, each desperate to be away from the others and individually fenced off. Indeed, Ritchie Blackmore insisted that every window in his particular room be covered in kitchen foil so that none of the other band members could see him. I wonder why they got back together – couldn't have been the money, could it?

A year or so later, I opened The Gardens in Morecambe. It was formally a 350-capacity nightclub/disco, The Blue Rhapsody, which I, in partnership with Jean Yates, turned into a rock music venue. Although, to be fair, we featured a really wide range of live music, not just rock. My old contacts enabled us to 'punch above our weight' and we featured many artists who should not have been playing in a three hundred and fifty capacity, seaside venue: Jools Holland, Humphrey Lyttleton, Ronnie Scott, Ted Hawkins, Shakespears Sister, Napalm Death, Terence Trent D'arby, and Joe Louis Walker. And Ian Gillan. Paul Darwin (of Great Hall flying points fame – see Ultravox) rang me one day to ask if I wanted Ian Gillan in my rock club. Well, arguably one of the greatest rock singers in the world, leader of arguably one of the greatest rock bands in the world – of course I didn't! But there was a caveat – and it was a beauty. Ian was going out with some very old friends from his youth – proper mates, not rock 'n' roll legends – and he was not doing dates in order to play the superstar. Very commendable I hear you say but …

The band were to perform under the name of, Garth Rocket and The Moonlighters. A name so catchy I could not remember it and have had to look it up for this piece. The words 'Ian Gillan' and 'Deep Purple' etc. were not to appear in any publicity, posters, flyers or ads. Once again I see you nodding in agreement; what a nice chap. As a fan I can agree, but as a promoter it was a nightmare. I pleaded with Paul, "How can I sell tickets to see an act nobody has ever heard of? I can sell it on Gillan's name but a load of unknown lads in a pub, rock band (£5 a ticket I think it was) – no chance. Paul, give me a break."

Paul was very sympathetic, he understood but he was adamant – any mention of the star, or his pedigree, and the gig wouldn't happen, even if that was as the doors were opening.

As I said, a dilemma! What would you have done? After all, it was my actual cash involved now. So, yes you've guessed it, the area was covered in posters reading "From Deep Purple – the legendary singer Ian Gillan in … at The Gardens, Morecambe."

On the morning of the gig, Paul rang me to ask how it was doing. I told him that it had been sold out for several weeks. "Bloody great! Hang on, how did you manage that? Nobody else is selling out." I knew Paul well enough to be honest. I read him out a poster. "Struth, Barry, it'll never happen. I told you and I wasn't joking."

"Ok Paul, how are you coming into Morecambe?"

"From the north, off the motorway at the Carnforth junction and then down the coast road." Paul had tour-managed many acts into Lancaster University and he was from the NW. "Ok, leave it with me," I reassured him. Quick phone call to two of my club bouncers, Hughie and J.C., one bucket, one sponge, one scraper and all the posters from Carnforth to The Gardens on Morecambe seafront were carefully removed. Nobody was any the wiser.

Ian Gillan actually congratulated me on getting a sell-out, he thought that I must be a brilliant promoter.

Sweaty, steamy rock club, 350 (or so) bodies crammed in – rock 'n' roll as it was meant to be, courtesy of Ian Gillan on a night of making Morecambe rock.

Barry Lucas

Gong

12 March 1976 Support: Wigwam

A psychedelic rock band formed by Australian Daevid Allen, formerly of Soft Machine and Gilli Smyth in France in 1969. Gong became pioneers of a new brand of psychedelia/space-rock/trip-rock with a conceptual ethos involving aliens and alternative realities and are probably best known for their 1971 album *Camembert Electrique* and 1973's *Flying Teapot*. As a truly international outfit, Gong became increasingly linked to other bands of the Canterbury scene at the time and many musicians came and went.

Following the departure of founder Daevid Allen in 1975, the band continued on with Steve Hillage as leader for a short while before morphing into the more jazz-rock styled Pierre Moerlen's Gong around 1978. There have been many other versions of Gong over the years and no other band has such immediate word association with 'hippies' as Gong. The band visited Lancaster on the first date of their 1976 tour and featured Gong's long serving French percussionist Pierre Moerlen and saxophonist Didier Malherbe in a new Gong lineup, following the release a month earlier, of the band's sixth studio album *Shamal*; the first to be recorded without Allen. A version of Gong are still active today with the album *Rejoice! I'm Dead!* released in September 2016.

Support act **Wigwam** are a Finnish progressive rock band formed in 1968 and presently still touring and recording. In Finland they have a loyal and lasting (although limited) following and their influence on Finnish rock music is still widely recognised.

Graham Parker and The Rumour

11 November 1977 Support: Clover
10 March 1979 Support: Sports

Graham Parker and The Rumour were formed in London in 1975 with a sound bridging new wave with the earlier pub-rock scene.

The band built a reputation as incendiary live performers and these two university appearances were, according to reports, no exception. The Rumour were recording artists in their own right and released three albums before teaming up with Parker in 1976 as his backing band. The Rumour's bass player Andrew Bodnar went on to join The Thompson Twins and was seen on stage with them for their two Lancaster concerts. They recorded five albums together until they split in 1980. In early 2011, Parker reunited with all five original members of The Rumour to record a new album entitled *Three Chords Good*, which was released in November 2012 with a further album, *Mystery Glue* following in 2015.

Grahams Parker's 1977 visit to Lancaster was a memorable one for him. Not for the great reception the Great Hall audience gave him, but for the great storm that raged during the night as they stayed in their Morecambe seafront hotel. The huge tide that night washed into the hotel and also destroyed one of Morecambe's piers.

Huey Lewis and his band **Clover** appear for the third time in the Great Hall in a supporting role.

Support for the 1979 concert were the Australian band **Sports**, hailing from Melbourne. They were invited over to the UK after being spotted by Graham Parker during a tour of Australia.

John Angus

Graham Parker 1977 © David Stewart

Graham Parker and The Rumour

A concert at Lancaster University which was an incredible, unforgettable night for Morecambe. And it was all recorded in the national press.

Graham Parker was another artist who, for some unfathomable reason, was labelled as punk. It was a good show, with the excellent Clover (later to become Huey Lewis and the News) as support, although having a steward with a mop and bucket at the side of the stage to rush on and clean up the audience's spit, was slightly disconcerting for Huey! It wasn't easy explaining to him, as he was towelling off pints of spittle in the dressing room, that this was a sign that the fans really liked him.

But the evening was also memorable for another outstanding event: the destruction of Morecambe! It was a Friday night and the bands were staying at The Strathmore Hotel on the sea front in the town. On tour with the bands was a journalist from *Sounds* – one of the big three weekly music newspapers – and what a story he had to file about a night of mayhem on the road with a rock'n'roll band. It was the night that Morecambe was hit by one of the fiercest storms in living memory, and it was combined with a massive high tide. One pier was completely destroyed, and the promenade was battered and flooded, as indeed was a major part of the town. The Strathmore and all the hotels and shops on the promenade were flooded. The band and crew had to decamp to the first floor to drink and watch the ensuing mayhem. The next morning the town looked like a battle scene as children scavenged on the beach to collect coins that had spilt out of the wrecked one-armed bandits lying on the sands. But what a great story for the travelling journalist. Under the banner headline the next week, 'Graham Parker Hits Town, £500,000 Worth of Damage Done', were pictures of Morecambe's mass destruction. The Stones could only destroy hotel bedrooms, Graham Parker could destroy towns!

Barry Lucas

Graham Parker 1979 © Geoff Campbell

Brinsley Schwarz, Graham Parker & Andrew Bodnar 1979
© Geoff Campbell

The Groundhogs

22 January 1971 — Support: T2
25 February 1972 — Supports: CCS l Johnny Johnson and the Bandwagon

Active now for over fifty years, The Groundhogs, fronted by Tony McPhee on guitar and vocals, are a top progressive blues rock group. Emerging in the early sixties as a blues band and noted for backing visiting American blues artists such as John Lee Hooker, the band evolved in the latter part of the sixties into a heavy rock group, scoring a hit with their fourth and possibly most popular album *Split*. Through the '70s the band continued to record and play live as a trio, albeit with changing band members, and towards the end of the seventies they were recording as a four-piece with the addition of a second guitar. The band disbanded in the late seventies, to reform once again a year or so later as a trio but with new members. The Groundhogs continued through the '80s, with many personnel changes through to 2004 when Tony McPhee laid the band to rest.

In 2007 Tony McPhee once again put The Groundhogs together for live concerts. To date the band is still working, still fronted by Tony despite his having suffered a stroke. Tony "T.S." McPhee is regarded as one of the very best blues guitarists to come from these shores.

From London, **T2** were a British progressive rock band, best known for their 1970 album *It'll All Work Out in Boomland*. They were a spin-off from a band called Please. T2 returned to Lancaster a year later as the support act for Gentle Giant.

Alexis Korner was a British blues musician and radio broadcaster who has sometimes been referred to as "a founding father of British blues". A major influence on the sound of the British music scene in the 1960s, Korner was instrumental in bringing together various English blues musicians, including Peter Thorup, a Danish guitarist, singer, composer and record producer. Peter joined up with Alexis for this concert and they would have been known at the time as Collective Consciousness Society, aka **CCS**.

CCS are best known for their instrumental version of Led Zeppelin's 1969 track 'Whole Lotta Love', which got into the UK Singles Chart in 1970 and was used as the theme music for the BBC pop programme *Top of the Pops* for most of the 1970s. CCS also found UK chart success with the single 'Tap Turns On The Water' reaching No. 5 in September 1971.

First up on stage were **Johnny Johnson and the Bandwagon**. They were an American vocal soul group formed in 1967 and were originally known simply as The Bandwagon. They featured Artie Fullilove, Billy Bradley, Terry Lewis and lead singer Johnny Johnson.

Gypsy

16 January 1970 — Support: Mighty Baby

An early concert in the Great Hall, Gypsy were a British band from Leicester influenced by late '60s Californian folk-psychedelic rock. They made two LPs and issued a few singles. Their debut album *Gypsy* came out in 1971.

Band lineup:
John Knapp – guitar, keyboards, vocals
David McCarthy – bass, vocals
Robin Pizer – guitar, vocals
Rod Read – guitar, vocals
Moth Smith – drums

After United Artists cancelled their contract in 1973 the band, in dismay, split up.

Psychedelic rock outfit **Mighty Baby** were formed in 1968 from the ashes of a band called The Action. They released two albums, *Mighty Baby* in December 1969 and *Jug Of Love* in October 1971.

Mighty Baby performed on the first day of the 1970 Isle of Wight Festival.

Haircut One Hundred

6 March 1982 — Support: The Bluebells

Haircut One Hundred are a British new wave group formed in 1980 by frontman Nick Heyward. The band had four UK Top 10 hit singles between 1981 and 1982, including 'Favourite Shirts', 'Love Plus One' and 'Fantastic Day'.

They released two studio albums and continue to tour with Nick Heyward still at the helm.

Scottish indie band and 1985 Great Hall headliners **The Bluebells** had three Top 40 hit singles in the UK, all written by guitarist and founder member Bobby Bluebell (real name Robert Hodgens): 'I'm Falling', 'Cath', and their biggest success, 'Young at Heart'.

I have got to be brutally honest here; I cannot really remember anything about the show. To be fair to the band I probably spent most of the evening in the ASH bar. Phil McIntyre (ex-Preston Polytechnic Social Secretary mentioned elsewhere in the book) was promoting the tour. Phil was, and still is, a brilliant promoter, but that evening he had his brother, Nigel, and his right hand man, Paul Roberts, on the show. So Phil, who in those days liked a beer, was not needed in the hall and therefore dragged me, kicking and screaming, to the bar as soon as the band walked on stage.

At the end of the night, Phil wanted the settlement, ninety per cent of the net ticket sales, paid to him in cash. I think he needed to pay the band something and have 'on-the-road' cash available. So after the invoices etc. were agreed, Phil took the cash balance and stuffed it into his lumberjack shirt, announcing, "Let's go and get something to eat. Where's open at this time?" Well, 'this time' was about 11.00 pm. I used to always recommend The Steak and Kebab but it had changed hands and then closed, re-opened and closed again etc. etc. So there was only really Pizza Margherita in Lancaster at that time in the area. Nigel was told to stay and oversee the 'get-out' and the rest of us, about six or seven, went to have the meal. As pizza restaurants go it's all right, but they gave us funny looks arriving at 11.15 pm. Phil splashed the cash and, surprise surprise, we were treated really well, but poor old Nigel arrived at about 11.55 pm looking a bit harassed after getting the band away from their fans and supervising as the gear was loaded onto the trucks. He was starving (Nigel likes his scran). But the manager of the restaurant said no food could be ordered after 11.30 pm. We couldn't believe it, we had only just started our meals so a quick pizza wasn't going to hold the staff up for any longer. The manager was insistent, 'rules is rules, we can make no exceptions'. We all pleaded on Nigel's behalf to no effect. Phil, who remember was paying the bill, started to get really annoyed but nothing would change their minds. It was very like an experience I had had at The Steak and Kebab with John Martyn, and that lost them hundreds of pounds in future business as well.

Accepting defeat, we shared our food with Nigel, but Phil turned to me, patting his bulging stomach, and said "I wouldn't mind but I've probably got enough money to buy the bloody place stuffed inside me shirt!".

Barry Lucas

Hawkwind

17 November 1972	**Space Ritual Tour**	Support: Magic Muscle
8 February 1974	**The Ridiculous Roadshow Tour**	Support: Alberto y Los Trios Paranoias
31 January 1975	**A Dead Singer Tour**	Supports: Liquid Len & The Lensmen I Andy Dunkley
14 October 1977	**Spirit of The Age Tour**	Support: Bethnal
17 November 1978	**Hawklords Tour**	No support
16 December 1980	**UK Christmas Tour**	Support: Vardis

From London and formed in November 1969 by guitarist and singer Dave Brock, guitarist Mick Slattery and saxophonist/flautist/singer Nik Turner, Hawkwind have gone through many incarnations and styles of music over the years. Dozens of musicians, dancers and writers have worked with the group since their inception.

Even though essentially an underground/festival band, they had major commercial success with their 1972 hit 'Silver Machine'. The single spent a total of twenty-two weeks in the UK charts in 1972 and reached No. 3.

Over the decades the band has been variously known as Hawkwind Zoo, Hawkwind, Hawklords and then, again, Hawkwind. The 1980 university Christmas concert featured Ginger Baker on drums and ex-Comus and future Toyah drummer Keith Hale on keyboards.

In February of 2014, Hawkwind performed *Space Ritual* at a benefit concert entitled Rock 4 Rescue. English actor Brian Blessed performed on the track 'Sonic Attack' and a studio recording was subsequently released as a single. The concert was eventually released as a CD/DVD set called *Space Ritual Live* in March of 2015.

Veterans of six appearances in the hall, many concert goers have great memories of the gigs, although some have none at all!

At the time of writing, Dave Brock is still at the helm of Hawkwind and busy recording and touring.

Magic Muscle were a psychedelic space/rock group from Bristol, formed around 1969. Following their support slot for Hawkwind on the Space Ritual Tour they earned themselves the nickname "Bastard Sons of Hawkwind".

Master of Ceremonies for the evening was DJ Andy "The Living Jukebox" Dunkley. Hawkwind's lengthy Space Ritual show also included contributions from a naked dancer with a 52" bust named Stacia Blake, the poet Robert Calvert, and the sci-fi writer Michael Moorcock.

Alberto y Lost Trios Paranoias were formed in Manchester in 1972 and were a comedy rock band, in the same vein as the Bonzo Dog Doo-Dah Band. During the period of the band's existence up to 1982 they achieved success in their own right, moving on to being a headline act and being supported by up and coming bands of the time, such as The Police, The Stranglers and Blondie.

Liquid Len & The Lensmen provided the lightshow for many Hawkwind gigs of the early years. Len also worked with Traffic, Free, Mott The Hoople and Black Sabbath.

Andy Dunkley was once again MC for the evening.

For the 1977 Spirit Of The Age Tour Hawkwind employed the support act services of **Bethnal**, who were a British proto-punk/rock band formed in 1972. In 1978 they released two albums on Vertigo Records.

Hawkwind's 1980 Christmas tour saw **Vardis,** an influential three-piece hard rock band from Wakefield, West Yorkshire, as guests. Vardis enjoyed hits between 1978 and 1986. Their second album, released in April 1981 and called *The World's Insane*, featured a cover version of Hawkwind's 'Silver Machine'.

Silver Machine – there, said it all. No, that's not fair. Hawkwind are a really hard working, honest, rock band, who I had on many occasions in many guises. At times they boasted the unforgettable 6ft plus Amazonian stripper/exotic dancer Stacia, and then with Michael Moorcock, the acclaimed sci-fi writer who walked onto stage in a long flasher-type raincoat and who I had to save from bouncers who wanted to forcefully remove "This weird bloke from the audience who had wandered on stage", and finally the legendary rock drummer, Ginger Baker. Hawkwind were also responsible for one of the more outlandish rider demands – that their dressing room be painted totally green. I refused to do that one and it was never mentioned on the night but I wonder how many venues had had to call in the decorators.

Hawkwind wanted to play their final date in the Christmas holidays. I knew there would be very few students about but I also knew that the band had a strong local following. I said that out of term time I couldn't justify risking students' money on a concert, so the band agreed to play on a straight percentage. I was therefore in no danger of losing money, so why not?

On the evening, the tour manager asked if I had planned to open the balcony. I said that, as I had only sold 800 tickets, I probably wouldn't in order to help create a good atmosphere. "Oh good," he said. I asked why? "Well, drink and drugs have taken their toll on Ginger and he frequently needs the toilet during the set, so we have a bucket by the bass drum. Probably not the best sight from the balcony."

I agreed, no viewing from the gods that night.

Barry Lucas

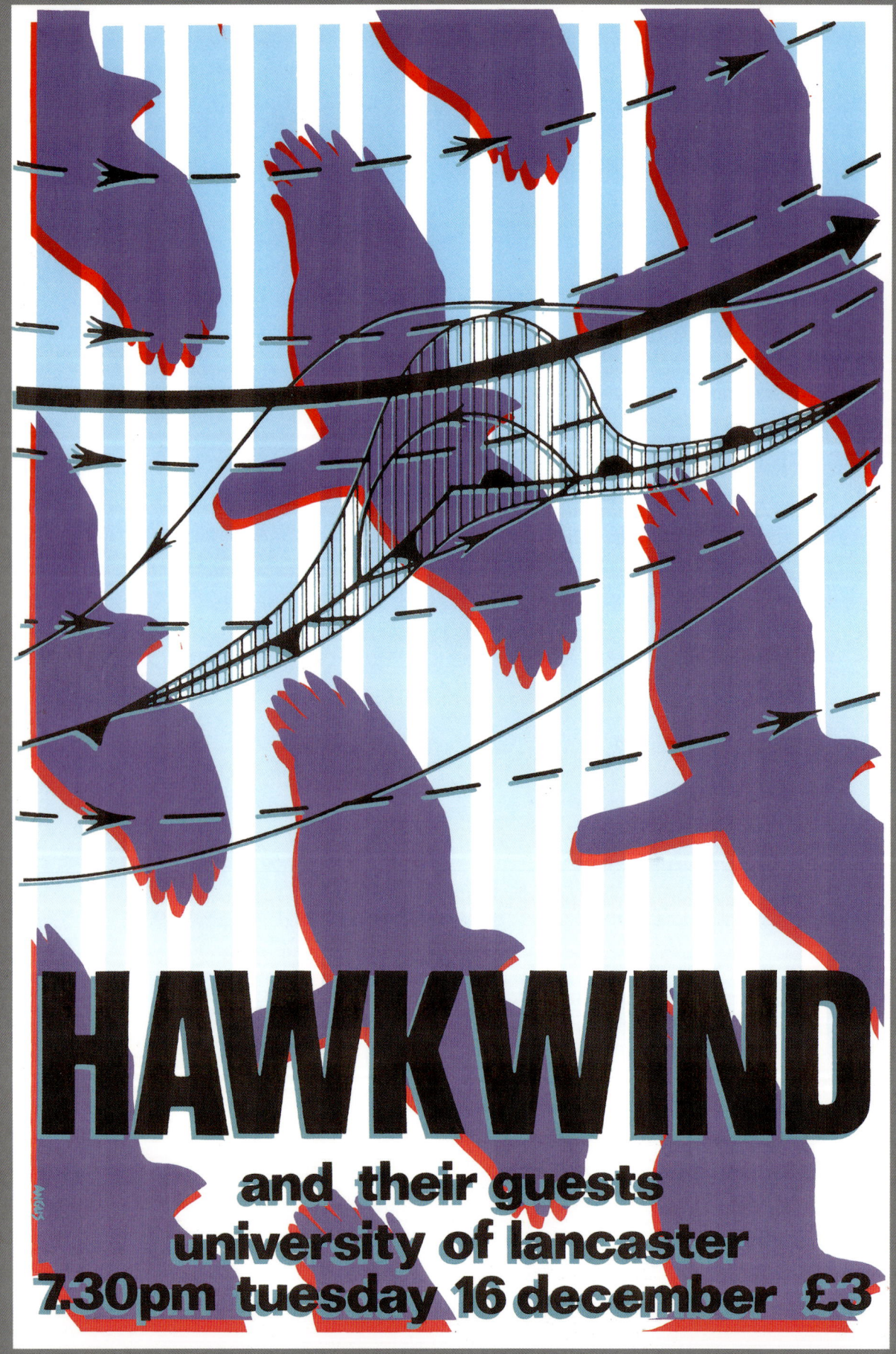

John Angus

John Angus

Hazel O'Connor

22 November 1980 Support: Duran Duran

English singer-songwriter and actress Hazel O'Connor became famous in the early 1980s with her hit singles 'Eighth Day', 'D-Days' and 'Will You', and was also to become prominent as an actress when she played the role of Kate in the critically acclaimed 1980 film *Breaking Glass*.

Hazel O'Connor, with her backing band Megahype, visited Lancaster for a date on her UK tour in support of her UK No. 5 album *Breaking Glass*. For the tour she selected as her opening act a then-unknown group called Duran Duran; it was the band's first opportunity to play to large audiences in the UK and gave them the exposure they needed to secure a recording contract, although they were a support act that concert goers may have missed whilst in the Great Hall bar!

Hazel O'Connor continues to record and tour and released her twentieth album *See You Again* in 2017.

Originating in Birmingham UK, **Duran Duran** was created in 1978 by Nick Rhodes and John Taylor with the later addition of Roger Taylor, Andy Taylor and Simon Le Bon; none of the Taylors are related. Guitarist Warren Cuccurullo was also a member of the band from 1989 to 2001, and drummer Sterling Campbell was a member from 1989 to 1991. The band took their name from villain *Dr Durand Durand* in the cult science-fiction film *Barbarella*, starring Jane Fonda.

Since the 1980s, Duran Duran have had fourteen hits in the Top 10 of the UK Singles Chart and have released fourteen studio albums, including their only UK number one album *Seven and the Ragged Tiger*. Their best known singles are, 'Is There Something I Should Know' a number UK number one hit in 1983 and 'The Reflex' another UK number one from 1984.

Lancaster band lineup:
Simon Le Bon – vocals
John Taylor – bass
Andy Taylor – guitar
Nick Rhodes – keyboard
Roger Taylor – drums

Horslips

10 May 1974 Support: Bees Make Honey

Horslips, founded in Dublin in 1970, are generally regarded as the founding fathers of Celtic rock and were one of Ireland's leading rock groups of their era.

Often compared to early Fairport Convention, Horslips drew on their distinctly Irish roots and were capable of playing straight folk material when the moment called for it, but weren't afraid to turn it up loud and hard on the right songs, in the best art-rock style.

They released nine studios albums and one live one before disbanding in 1980.

2004 saw some of the members re-forming Horslips and they still perform intermittently today.

1973 had seen Horslips in the Great Hall as guests of Steeleye Span.

Irish band **Bees Make Honey** were one of the original pub rock groups of the early '70s. The band included Bob Siebenberg, who was later to become Supertramp's long-serving drummer. They disbanded in 1974 after recording two albums on the EMI label.

John Angus

Hot Chocolate

7 November 1975 — Support: D'Dancer
3 March 1978 — Support: Smiling Hard

Hot Chocolate were a pop and soul band originally from Brixton, London, who were most popular during the '70s and '80s. Formed by frontman Errol Brown, who passed away in 2015, the act had at least one hit every year between 1970 and 1984, with their iconic song 'You Sexy Thing' becoming the only track to make the British Top 10 in the 1970s, 1980s and 1990s.

In 1997 'You Sexy Thing' reached the No. 1 slot in the UK charts after it was featured in the movie *The Full Monty*.

An article in *SCAN* newspaper about the upcoming 1975 gig described support band **D'Dancer** as "… a superb funky rock outfit discovered by Chris Squire of the band Yes". They had an English vocalist, backed by a Latin American, a West Indian and a bassist from Los Angeles.

Smiling Hard were a five piece disco/soul band from Portsmouth.

Mike Igoe, *SCAN* Review 25.4.78: "The support band was Smiling Hard who were lifted from the lowest rung of the musical ladder by their interesting use of saxophones and flutes".

At a recent reunion Mark Lane, my head of stewards (see Stiff Tour), told me the full details of a back stage incident this night.

For a period of a couple of years I had quite a few problems with Lancaster's "Satan's Slaves". These were the city's very own Hell's Angels but not quite the impressive Californian breed. They had obviously seen the film of The Altamont Festival and decided that they too would provide 'security' at local concerts. The only problem was that, unlike the promoters and bands at Altamont, I wasn't going to employ them – I'd seen the film as well! However, it didn't stop them attending and causing quite a few problems and feelings of unease and intimidation amongst my audiences. Little did the other concert goers realise, but these Angels couldn't afford a bike between them. They caught the bus up and the last bus back, sitting upstairs in the front seats, making engine noises and pretending to drive the bus home. I don't know whether they made the bus do imaginary wheelies but I wouldn't be at all surprised.

Their leader was called "Edge" – he gave himself the nickname to indicate his preference for knives in fights. At this concert, for some reason that nobody could fathom, he decided that he was going to kill Errol Brown, Hot Chocolate's lead singer. Mark saw him marching down the Great Hall corridor towards the dressing rooms, knife in hand. He and a couple of others grabbed Edge and Mark held his knife hand above his head. The police were called and arrived about fifteen minutes later. All this time Mark had held Edge's arm up above his head, knife and all. Edge was frog marched out of the hall and I almost felt sorry for him. He looked terrified as he was thrown into the back of a police van. I only hope Edge was a dog lover, although he didn't look like one as he saw he would have two companions on the journey back to Lancaster. It would be nice to think that he was able to claim a refund on his return bus ticket.

Mark had to appear in court as the prosecution's main witness. He said that he was ever so slightly nervous as he had to push through hoards of angry Angels milling around outside the court. Luckily, Mark wasn't called as Edge pleaded guilty and received a custodial sentence.

Barry Lucas

The Human League

22 November 1981   Support: Debonair

The Human League are an English electronic new wave band formed in Sheffield in 1977. The band arrived at Lancaster for a concert in support of the October 1981 release of *Dare*, the band's most popular album.

Dare yielded the single 'Don't You Want Me' which was the band's best-known and most commercially successful recording, and was the 1981 Christmas No. 1 in the UK. In total it has sold over a million copies.

The only constant Human League member since 1977 has been vocalist and songwriter Philip Oakey. Joining the band in 1980 were The Human League's two female vocalists, Joanne Catherall and Susan Ann Sulley, who along with Phil Oakey continue to tour today.

Since 1978, The Human League have released nine studio albums, four EPs, thirty singles and several compilation albums. They have had five albums and eight singles in the UK Top 10 and have sold more than twenty million records.

SCAN newspaper reviewer Mike Gould reported that: "throughout the concert images from feature films such as *Nosferatu*, *The Texas Chainsaw Massacre* and *Psycho* were projected onto three black screens behind the band".

Another interesting happening was the apparent disappearance of Phil Oakey prior to the concert. Following a disagreement about the stage setup with his manager, he threw his toys out of the pram and stormed out.

SCAN newspaper reported: "Search parties were dispatched and the man with the Veronica Lake hairdo was eventually found in Garstang, a town eight miles south of the university".

Little is known about support act **Debonair**.

© Geoff Campbell

This was a band who were to describe themselves, only a year later, as bigger than The Beatles. Well I'm not one to argue with superstars but …

On this tour they were certainly a huge draw, selling out very quickly. I had been asked, in advance, for the stage and roof clearance sizes. Lancaster's stage was certainly a large frontage at 60ft, but was only about 30ft deep, although we could, and frequently did, enlarge it with an in-house stage extension. The height of the hall's roof above the stage was massive, again 60ft I think. I relayed this information to the band but forgot to tell them about the sloping roof. It was a slope that meant at the very back of the stage there was only 15ft clearance. However, this had never been a problem in fourteen years.

Well it was this time. The band had brought along a mate who was to provide projected images onto a backdrop and needed to do this from behind said backdrop. Thinking of our stage dimensions I could see their problem; not enough clearance at the rear of the stage. An impasse ensued as it was going to be impossible to achieve this setup. The only solution would be to maybe use front projection. Later that afternoon the bands manager strode into the hall to announce that the gig was off as back projection was an integral part of the whole show. I said to him that actually the band and the music was the show and not some static images but he just stormed off. Then later at around 6.00 pm he phoned me from his hotel in Garstang, some eight miles south of Lancaster. He wanted me to drive there and grovelingly apologise to himself and Phil Oakey and if I did the band would then perform.

Alan Murray said, "You're not doing that, tell them to get stuffed." But we had a sell-out show, people had travelled miles, I really didn't have an option. So Alan drove me down to Garstang, though I made him stay in the car while I did the dirty deed – I could see the scouser in him surfacing and him flattening somebody! The band really made it uncomfortable for me but the concert went ahead and none of the audience had any idea how close it had been to disaster. So, in the end, front projection it was. And do you know, I bet nobody walked out of the hall saying, "If only the images had been projected from behind the backdrop it would have been a fantastic show".

Barry Lucas

Incredible String Band

23 October 1970   Support: Trees

The Incredible String Band were a psychedelic folk band formed in Scotland in 1966 by three folk musicians, Robin Williamson, Mike Heron and Clive Palmer.

The band built a considerable following, especially within the British counterculture, before splitting up in 1974. The group's members were musical pioneers in psychedelic folk, integrating a wide variety of traditional musical forms and instruments. The Incredible String Band re-formed in 1999 and continued to perform with changing lineups until finally disbanding in 2006.

They have twelve studio albums under their belt, the best known being *The Hangman's Beautiful Daughter*, released in 1968 and reaching No. 10 in the UK Albums Chart. The band featured at Woodstock in 1969.

Influenced by Fairport Convention, but with a heavier and more psychedelic edge, **Trees** were an English folk rock band that existed between 1970 and 1973.

Iron Butterfly

15 January 1971   Supports: Yes I Dada

Iron Butterfly are an American psychedelic rock band from San Diego, California, originally formed in 1966. They are probably best known for their 1968 hit 'In-A-Gadda-Da-Vida', from the album of the same name. It went on to sell over thirty million copies worldwide and was the first album to be awarded platinum status when the Recording Industry Association of America (RIAA) began the certification in 1976. August 1970 saw the release of *Metamorphosis*, their fourth album, with the band arriving in Lancaster six months later for a date on The Age of Atlantic Tour. All three featured bands were on the Atlantic Record label. Iron Butterfly had their own PA shipped over from America for the tour, and Maurice Hubbard of Pink Custard recalls that, "Iron Butterfly were memorable for the huge PA cabinets they arrived with, occupying over half the stage. They opened up with a recording of Strauss's 'Dawn' from *Also Sprach Zarasthustra*, known at the time as the soundtrack to the film, *2001: A Space Odyssey*. To be fair it did sound pretty good, but what were the band going to do after such a dramatic introduction? 'Follow That Man' boomed out from the stage after the echo of the final organ chord had died away. And sadly they couldn't".

Following the tour, the outsized PA was sold to Yes, thus avoiding the cost of return shipping to the US.

Iron Butterfly's heyday was the in late '60s and, albeit reincarnated several times over the years, Iron Butterfly continue to record and perform today.

In my first full year of promoting we used to have the shows going on until 1.00 am and still a student, I had to live up to the image.

Iron Butterfly were a major American band, with an anthem for the age 'In-A-Gadda-Da-Vida'. Yes were to become a major British band and Dada were an extraordinarily large band featuring two musicians who were to become legends, Elkie Brooks and Robert Palmer. The show climaxed in a finale at 1.00 am where all three bands came on stage in a gigantic jam session involving something like thirty musicians! It went on and on and on … finally finishing around 2 am.

Like many of these concerts it couldn't happen today, with restrictions on licensing hours etc. But more to the point, the artists and promoters are too old now; we would be away to our beds by 11.00 pm!

Barry Lucas

Second on the bill that night were **Yes**, the English rock band formed in 1968 by bassist Chris Squire and singer Jon Anderson. Yes are distinguished by their use of mystical and cosmic lyrics, fabulous live stage sets and lengthy compositions, often with complex instrumental and vocal arrangements.

They are best known for their 1971 singles 'I've Seen All Good People', the 1972 nine-minute long US Top 20 hit 'Roundabout', and their 1983 No. 1 hit 'Owner of a Lonely Heart'. Nine of their twenty-one studio albums have reached the Top 10 in either the UK or US, with two reaching No. 1 in the UK Albums Chart.

Despite many lineup changes, occasional splits and the influence of the many changes in popular music, the band has endured for forty years and still retains a strong international following.

Possible Lancaster setlist: 'Astral Traveller', 'Yours Is No Disgrace', 'Clap', 'America'.

Band members:
Jon Anderson – vocals
Steve Howe – guitar and vocals
Chris Squire – bass and vocals
Tony Kaye – piano, Moog synthesizer
Bill Bruford – drums

Dada were a twelve-piece jazz fusion band from London that featured Yorkshireman guitarist Robert Palmer and Salford born singer Elkie Brooks. Dada released the one self-titled album *Dada* in 1970 on Atco Records (a subsidiary of Atlantic) and existed for only a short period before morphing into the R&B band Vinegar Joe in late 1971. They played as a headlining band for a Great Hall concert in March 1973.

Iron Maiden

20 February 1981   **Killer World Tour**   Support: Trust

Iron Maiden are an English heavy metal band formed in Leyton, East London, in 1975 by bassist and primary songwriter Steve Harris. Named after a medieval torture device, the band's discography has grown to thirty-eight albums, including sixteen studio albums and twelve live. This Lancaster concert promoted the release of the *Killers* album and featured lead singer Paul Di'Anno, who was eventually to be replaced by the charismatic ex Samson lead singer Bruce Dickinson in September 1981.

Dickinson, the airline pilot, broadcaster and brewer still leads the band along with founder member Steve Harris.

Trust were a French heavy metal band founded in 1977 and popular in Europe in the first half of the '80s.

An interesting Lancaster University/Iron Maiden connection is provided by "Shack". David Shackleton was at school in Leeds when he applied to Lancaster University. He admits that, like the majority of others at that time, he wanted to come to Lancaster because of the concerts – some confession, coming as he did from Leeds. Unfortunately, he arrived in the Autumn of 1985, just a few months after I had left, so he found a 'live' music desert. However, he spent his time travelling to shows in the North and began a career as a music journalist for Kerrang. I hope he visited The Gardens, my rock venue in Morecambe from 1986 to 1994, as at that time Kerrang was my main advertising tool, and in fact did a three-page story about the club. On graduating, Shack went to London and eventually became a member of staff at the magazine. He got a job in 1990 at BMG Records, and many other jobs followed until he ended up at Sony, where he eventually became Vice President of International for Sony UK. He left in 2013 to pursue other activities. He married Pop Idol judge Nicki Chapman and became MD of Phantom Music, Iron Maiden's management company. Having read about his fondness for a beer I have little doubt that he has taken a serious interest in the launch of the band's own brew, Trooper.

Barry Lucas

Jack Bruce

2 October 1970 Supports: Matthews' Southern Comfort I Edgar Broughton Band
8 March 1977 Support: Hunter

The legendary Scottish ex-Cream bassist Jack Bruce graced the Great Hall twice in the 1970s.

It was in July 1966 that Jack Bruce, Eric Clapton and Ginger Baker formed the three-piece British super group Cream. Cream combined Clapton's blues guitar playing with the powerful voice and intense bass lines of Jack Bruce and the manic drumming of Ginger Baker at the rear. Bruce wrote and sang most of Cream's songs, including 'Sunshine of Your Love' and 'White Room'. When Cream broke up in 1968 after a successful two-year run, he released albums and collaborated with other musicians, launching a solo career that lasted more than forty years.

Jack's first visit to Lancaster was with drummer Tony Williams, guitarist John McLaughlin (Mahavishnu Orchestra) and organist Larry Young, together forming the band Tony William's Lifetime. The group recorded two albums, with Bruce joining on the second album, *Turn It Over*. However, Lifetime did not receive much critical or commercial acclaim at the time and the band broke up in 1971.

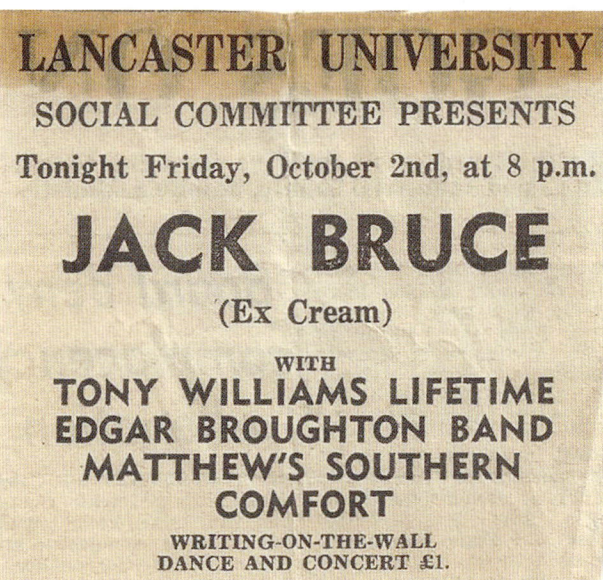

Almost seven years later in 1977, Jack Bruce returned to Lancaster University with his new band, consisting of drummer Simon Phillips and keyboardist Tony Hymas. Then Phillips returned to Lancaster as drummer for Toyah in 1982 and later moved on to become the full-time drummer for American band Toto. Classically trained keyboardist Tony Hymas went on to work extensively with Jeff Beck. The group recorded Jack Bruce's fifth studio album, called *How's Tricks*, which was released in March 1977 to coincide with the tour.

Five months after their headlining gig, folk rock band **Matthews' Southern Comfort** were back again to provide the support for Jack Bruce.

Completing a fabulous value-for-money triple bill was **Edgar Broughton Band.** Edgar and his brother Steve, on drums, returned a month later for their own headlining concert.

Jack's support for his 1977 visit was provided by his mate Steve Hunter, the American session musician from Illinois.

Over the years, **Hunter** has enjoyed an illustrious career having worked with, Peter Gabriel, Dave Lee Roth, Alice Cooper and Lou Reed. His first solo album release in 1977 was the critically acclaimed *Swept Away*. Steve Hunter is still recording and performing live.

Jackie Lomax's Heavy Jelly

13 March 1970   Supports: Jodie Grind I Spring

Jackie Lomax was an English guitarist and singer songwriter from the Wirral UK.

In 1970 Jackie Lomax joined Heavy Jelly following on from his spell in the late '60s as the first ever signing as a solo artist with Apple Records and being championed by The Beatles. Heavy Jelly consisted of former Aynsley Dunbar members and drummer Barry Jenkins from The Animals. In 1970 the band recorded their debut album titled *Heavy Jelly*.

British progressive rock band **Jody Grind** issued two obscure albums combining hard rock, jazz, blues and classical influences, with lineups emphasizing Hammond organ, guitar and drums. Prone to long instrumental riffing and rather ponderous, stern original material, they were similar to other very early organ-oriented UK progressive rock acts.

Spring were a Leicester-based British progressive rock band that represented the early 1970s progressive rock movement. A one-shot band, it recorded only one album in its career, a self-titled LP released in 1971. Spring's music is notable for the use of the mellotron, with three of its five members credited with playing the instrument on the album.

Courtesy of Ray Wilkinson Music Research Archive

The Jags

28 September 1980 — Support: Cardiac Arrest

The Jags were a short lived British rock band formed in North Yorkshire in 1978, composed of Nick Watkinson (vocals), John Alder (guitar/backing vocals), Steve Prudence (bass), firstly Neil Whittaker and then Alex Baird (drums), Michael Cotton (bass/backing vocals) and Patrick O'Toole (piano/keyboard). This free admission concert was arranged by 'Ear 'Ere as a thank you to loyal customers. They signed a deal with Island Records in July 1978, and in September 1979 released their first 7" single "Back of My Hand" written by Watkinson and reaching number 17 in the UK singles chart. The single was included on their debut album *Evening Standards*, which was released the following year. 1981 saw the release of their second, and what proved to be, final album, *No Tie Like a Present*. The Jags disbanded in 1982.

The Jags support for the evening was provided by Lancaster power-pop punk outfit **Cardiac Arrest**. The band featured future Natural Scientist members, Stuart Baldwin and Neil Crossley on lead guitars and bass respectively. Completing the lineup were, Howard Clark (drums) and Michael Byrd (vocals and guitars). 1979 saw the band release a 7" single entitled 'Running in the Street' on the Another Records label, produced by Martin Pilkington.

Jags

When Paul was doing his amazingly detailed research he did miss a couple of concerts which are now corrected in this new edition. Tut, tut, Paul, shameful. But no blame or criticism could be apportioned for missing this one and if I hadn't found this ticket in an 'Ear 'Ere bag in my attic it would have remained a hazy memory for a few of our loyal, local audience. The year was 1979 and Nigel Waller and I decided that, rather than give the tax man some more money, we would throw a party. Our clever accountant, Gary, found a way of calling it a legitimate business expense, so …

For many years 'Ear 'Ere Records would use the last Saturday before Christmas as an excuse for a day-long celebration of music and alcohol. I realise now that it was a truly irresponsible, quite disgusting, idea but it was Nigel's idea and combined the two great loves of his life, rock 'n' roll and booze. Who are we to criticise? So for that Saturday, the customers who came into 'Ear 'Ere to buy records, and even those who came just to listen on the headphones, were supplied with free alcoholic beverages – I can't remember whether Nigel offered a soft drink alternative but I really doubt it.

Anyway to return to the concert. I know we decided to do it to reward our loyal customers, free bands, free(ish) bar etc and also to celebrate something, some significant anniversary. I can't for the life of me remember what it was, so I recently rang Roger Moorhouse, our long suffering manager but he couldn't remember either. Well, 'Ear 'Ere opened in December 1971 so it wasn't the 10 year anniversary – a celebration of 8 years? Not really, perhaps it was just what it was, a good night!

Now out of the proverbial blue I've been contacted, over the last year, by many a friend that I haven't spoken to for ten, twenty even thirty years and one of them was Stuart Baldwin. He now works in Shanghai but still returns to Lancaster regularly for business (he owns a building company here) and pleasure – he likes a British pint. He was in a band called Natural Scientist, which is mentioned a couple of times in the book and he wanted to say he remembered being in the Great Hall to support The Jags. However the band he was in at the time was called Cardiac Arrest – what a brilliant name, should have been a success for that alone.

The Jags were formed in North Yorkshire in 1978 and had a hit with "Back of my hand" (he'd written her address not belted her!) which reached number 17 in the singles chart. An EP and then album on Island Records followed, with the track on it.

A long-forgotten addition to the evening was remembered by Roger, complete with photo, Sam Armistead came on stage to give a fantastic rendition of 'Albert and the Lion'.

Barry Lucas

The Jam

14 December 1977
30 November 1979

Modern World Tour

Supports: New Hearts I China Street
Support: The Vapors

The Jam were a punk/mod revival group formed in Woking, Surrey, in 1972, consisting of Paul Weller (vocals, guitar), Bruce Foxton (bass, vocals) and Rick Buckler (drums). They released six albums and had eighteen consecutive Top 40 hits in the United Kingdom between 1977 and 1982, including four No. 1 singles: 'Going Underground', 'Start!', 'Town Called Malice' and 'Beat Surrender'. Their singles 'That's Entertainment' and 'Just Who Is The Five O'clock Hero' are the best-selling import singles in UK history. The band drew upon a variety of stylistic influences over the course of their career, including 1960s beat music, soul, rhythm and blues, and psychedelic rock, as well as 1970s punk and new wave. The trio was known for its melodic pop songs, its distinctly English flavour and its mod image. The band launched the career of Paul Weller, who went on to form The Style Council and later had a successful solo career. Weller wrote and sang most of The Jam's original compositions and he played lead guitar using a Rickenbacker. Bruce Foxton provided backing vocals and prominent bass lines, which were the foundation of many of the band's songs, including the hits 'Down in the Tube Station At Midnight' and 'The Eton Rifles'. The 1977 tour saw The Jam play the Great Hall in support of the November release of their album *This Is the Modern World*. They visited Lancaster again in 1979, this time in support of the album *Setting Sons.* In October 1982 Paul Weller announced that he was to disband The Jam. The decision was solely Weller's, stating that he considered the band had achieved all they wanted or needed, both commercially and artistically.

New Hearts were a British new wave band from London, active 1977–78. They released two singles. In 2009 Cherry Red Records released a retrospective album called *A Secret Affair*.

Lancaster's very own **China Street** were veterans of four support appearances in the Great Hall, mainly in 1977–1978, for bands including Steel Pulse and Sad Café.

The Vapors are an English new wave/power pop band from Guilford that existed between 1979 and 1982. They had a hit with the song 'Turning Japanese' in 1980, which reached No. 3 in the UK Singles Chart. They were discovered and managed by John Weller, father of Paul. More than thirty years after the band called it a day in 1982, The Vapors reunited in late 2016 and announced tour dates.

The Jam 1979 © Doug Price

The Jam 1977 © David Stewart

The Jam

Another of the truly great bands thrown up by the punk revolution. Like several others, The Jam would have always broken through and established themselves as major stars, punk just made it quicker and easier for them.

They were touring extensively and I had a date on the 1977 tour, which was a great show. I was talking to Paul Weller's Dad, John, who was their manager, all afternoon and evening. He was a tremendous guy; I don't know if he actually was from a market trader background but he could easily have been a memorable character from *Only Fools and Horses* or *Minder*. He obviously wasn't sure how long this fame and accompanying fortune would last, but he was going to look after his lads and make it as profitable as possible for them. He was a "diamond geezer", terrific bloke and we got on well.

In 1979 I noticed that the band were doing some dates. All were to be major venues and noticeably, for the first time, no university dates were in the schedule. I phoned their agent to request a date, only to be told, "Sorry but the band are too big to play universities now. They wouldn't even consider a gig at Lancaster". So I asked him to phone John Weller and to say that Barry Lucas at Lancaster University wants a date, he'll pay you cash on the night. The agent rather snootily replied, "I don't know what you're talking about. Waste of time. They won't play universities – too big. I'm not going to waste my time, it's too valuable". But I was convinced I knew what would appeal to John Weller.

"Just make the call," I insisted. I knew he would have to put the offer in front of the band's manager because if he didn't and John was to find out, then he would most probably lose the band and at that stage of their career that was not something he, or his bosses, would want to contemplate.

About an hour later (instantaneous in music business terms) the agent called me back. "I just don't understand it. We all agreed they wouldn't do any more colleges, they're too big, it would be a backward step and it could damage their careers … We had all agreed."

"So what did he say?" I asked.

"He told me to ring you and fix the date. I just don't understand it …"

I do remember smiling … I understood and so would Del Boy.

P.S. The agent never forgave me for, in his eyes, making him look foolish and he tried for years to get his revenge, avoiding offering me bands, but by that time Lancaster was too important to need any agent's goodwill.

Barry Lucas

Bruce Foxton 1979 © Doug Price

Paul Weller 1979 © Doug Price

Jan Akkerman and Kaz Lux

4 March 1977   Support: Kayak

Jan Akkerman, along with Thijs Van Leer, was an original member of the Dutch progressive rock band Focus, from 1969–1976.

Following his sacking and the disappointment of his non-appearance in the Great Hall for Focus' 1976 concert, the Dutch jazz fusion guitarist visited Lancaster with his newly formed band.

A musician of near legendary prowess, Jan Akkerman for a time eclipsed Eric Clapton, Jimmy Page and Jeff Beck in the music press readers' polls in England for top guitarist in the world. *Melody Maker* readers voted him best guitarist in the world in a 1973 poll.

After his departure from Focus, Akkerman teamed up with Dutch vocalist Kaz Lux to create a concept album named *Eli*, which was released in 1976 on Atlantic records.

The concert was a real treat for all fans of Dutch jazz fusion music, featuring former Focus drummer Pierre van der Linden, classically trained concert pianist Joachim Kühn and bass player Cees van der Laarse.

Now in his seventieth year, Akkerman continues to tour and released his latest album, *North Sea Jazz*, in 2013.

Kayak are a Dutch progressive rock band, still active today, formed in 1972 in the city of Hilversum by Ton Scherpenzeel and Pim Koopman.

A month after Queen's Great Hall concert of November 1974, Queen invited Kayak to be their support act for a concert in The Hague, Netherlands, on 8 December 1974.

Japan

11 December 1981
6 November 1982

Visions of China Tour

Support: Blancmange
Support: Sandii & The Sunsetz

Fronted by the androgynous David Sylvian, Japan played the Great Hall twice, with guests Blancmange in 1981 and Sandii and The Sunsetz in 1982.

Japan's bass guitarist, David Rhodes, later went on to join Blancmange. Japan were formed in 1974 and achieved nine UK Top 40 hits, two of which reached the Top 10. Personal and creative differences resulted in their last ever performance on 16 December 1982.

Lancaster setlist 1982: 'Canton', 'Swing', 'Gentlemen Take Polaroids', 'Alien', 'Talking Drum', 'Visions Of China', 'Quiet Life', 'My New Career', 'Ghosts', 'Cantonese Boy', 'Methods Of Dance', 'Still Life In Mobile Homes', 'European Son', 'The Art Of Parties', 'Life In Tokyo', 'Fall In Love With Me', 'Canton' (finale).

Blancmange, formed in Harrow, Middlesex, in 1979 by singer Neil Arthur, are an English synthpop band who came to prominence with a string of hits in the early to mid '80s and are still active today. The band are best known for their 1982 single 'Living on the Ceiling', which reached No. 7 on the UK Singles Chart.

Sandii & The Sunsetz were originally formed in the '70s after changing names several times ("Sandy and the Sunsetz" etc.). The band consisted of guitarist Makoto Kubota, guitarist Kenichi Inoue, bassist King Champ Onzo and percussionist Hideo Inoura, and were fronted by founder and lead singer Sandii, born Sandra O'Neale (of Japanese/Spanish/American heritage). They issued a string of albums with the band, finding moderate success throughout the '80s.

© Geoff Campbell

December 1981 © Geoff Campbell

David Sylvian 1981 © Dean Weston

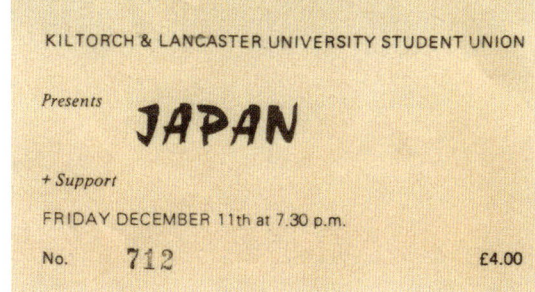

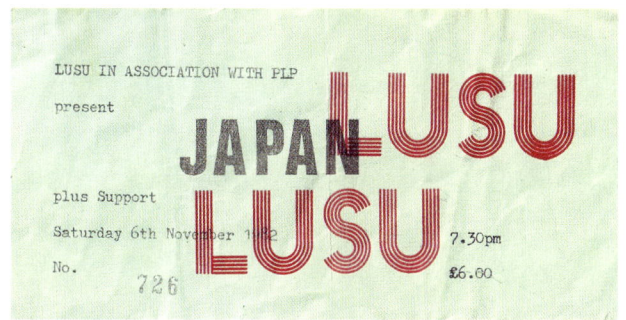

The Jeff Beck Group

10 March 1972   Support: Heaven

Two-time visitor to Lancaster University Geoffrey Arnold "Jeff" Beck is an English rock guitarist. Jeff Beck was one of the three noted guitarists, the others being Eric Clapton and Jimmy Page, to have played with The Yardbirds. Beck was ranked fifth in *Rolling Stone* magazine's list of the 100 Greatest Guitarists of All Time.

The concert featured tracks from the October 1971 album *Rough and Ready* and also tracks from his soon to be released *Jeff Beck Group* album. This album became to be known as the 'orange album'.

Beck is best known generally for his hit single 'Hi Ho Silver Lining' which was originally released in 1967, reaching No. 14 in the UK Singles Chart.

At the time of this first appearance for Beck at Lancaster, the single had been re-released and went on to reach No. 17 in the UK charts and no doubt would have been performed on the night in the Great Hall.

Along with Beck on guitars, the lineup on the night was:
Alex Ligertwood – vocals
Max Middleton – keyboards
Cozy Powell – drums
Clive Chaman – bass

In 1974 Jeff Beck returned to Lancaster with his band Beck, Bogert and Appice.

Sometimes compared to the bands Chicago, and Blood, Sweat & Tears, **Heaven** were a British jazz-influenced rock band from Portsmouth who appeared at the Isle of Wight Festivals of 1969 and 1970.

The band released one album in 1971, *Brass Rock 1*, a double album with a lavish gatefold sleeve, before splitting up. *Brass Rock 1* was reissued on CD by Cherry Red Records in 2008.

I had Jeff Beck on in a couple of bands, The Jeff Beck Group and the world super-group Beck, Bogert and Appice.

My business partner in 'Ear 'Ere Records was Nigel Waller, who sadly died a few years ago. Despite a falling-out which resulted in us not speaking for the last few years, he had been my friend and business partner for many years after we had got to know one another during his period as head of stewards for the Great Hall shows, so I wouldn't miss his funeral. Unfortunately there was a misunderstanding over the date. I attended the crematorium a week early and sat through a service describing a life I didn't recognise, surrounded by mourners I had never clapped eyes on before – but that's another story for another book.

I mention Nigel because he introduced me to Jeff Beck. Of course I knew of The Yardbirds and Beck's disco classic 'Hi Ho Silver Lining', but Nigel had literally every bit of vinyl Jeff had ever recorded anywhere in the world, including numerous bootlegs. He convinced me of his genius and I still believe he is one of the most gifted, most imaginative, unique guitarists the UK has produced.

As I said earlier, we had Jeff Beck on a couple of times, the second being in 1974 as the leader of Beck, Bogert and Appice, a true world super-group. They were toured by Ricky Farr, who had just promoted the highly successful Isle of Wight Festival and was now managing them.

In 1972 I had the Jeff Beck Group at Lancaster. Nigel, forever the optimist as far as Jeff was concerned, had just ordered 100 copies of the band's new album for 'Ear 'Ere Records, an unheard of number for a small, regional record shop and the record company rep. must have thought all his Christmases had come together. Nigel asked me to introduce him to his hero. I asked him if he was sure, I hated meeting my heroes as it was always such a disappointment. No, Nigel insisted.

"Jeff, this is Nigel, your biggest fan."

"Hi, Nigel."

"I wonder if you'd mind signing your new album, just out today?"

Jeff was clearly impressed with such dedication, "Yes, certainly." Nigel then left the dressing room and returned with five boxes, 100 albums, to sign!

Jeff Beck seemed too gobsmacked to object and signed the lot.

The next day in 'Ear 'Ere Records, The Jeff Beck Group's new album, signed cover an' all, was on proud display in the window … and everywhere else. However, the best bit of the story was when a customer came back in with the album he'd just bought and asked if he could have a new record as somebody had scribbled all over the cover of this one. Nigel went apoplectic, grabbed the record and threw him out. The staff were rolling on the floor in hysterical laughter.

Barry Lucas

John Angus

Joan Armatrading

22 June 1980 — Support: Richard Digance
5 December 1981 — Support unknown
17 April 1983 — Support unknown

Joan Anita Barbara Armatrading, MBE, is a British singer and songwriter who made her first appearance in the Great Hall in 1975 providing support to Supertramp, her first major date as a support act.

Armatrading followed up this gig with three headlining visits in quick succession during the early eighties and was a favourite of the Great Hall audiences.

Over her career she has had several British hit singles, the biggest of which were 'Love & Affection', 'Me Myself I' and 'Drop the Pilot'.

In May 2015 Armatrading appeared on BBC Two's *Later … with Jools Holland*, singing 'Me Myself I'.

Richard Digance is a comedian and folk singer from Essex. He found his first solo success with his 1975 album, *How the West Was Lost*. Featuring such tongue-in-cheek tunes as "Working Class Millionaire" and "Drag Queen Blues," the album was named Folk Album of the Year by *Melody Maker*. He later went on to find further success with a TV career that included shows such as *A Dabble With Digance*, and *Stop the World*, for the BBC in the 1980s.

© Geoff Campbell

© Geoff Campbell

Joan Armatrading

I had Joan Armatrading on several times and she was a major star at the time, always drawing sell-out crowds.

But what exactly was a Lancaster sell-out? At this point I will take some time to explain what it meant to sell out Lancaster University's Great Hall. The official capacity of the Great Hall for a stand-up concert was 1050, plus 300 for the Minor Hall which was always used for a disco or chill-out room. During numerous meetings with the licensing officers at Lancashire County Council they explained to me that the capacity was established by using a formula based on the floor space for dancing and the width of fire escapes for a total evacuation in two minutes. At the time I was holding off campus socials on the Central Pier in Morecambe. The ballroom at the end of the pier had a floor area the same as the Great Hall's but it had a licensed capacity of 1500, a third bigger. This confused me as the ballroom was at the end of an old Victorian pier and when the tide was in, effectively had only one fire exit. If that was out of action it was a disaster waiting to happen.

So I had a further meeting with the licensing officers and they agreed it was a ridiculous position but explained that the Pier licence was an old one with "grandfather rights" and therefore could not be altered. I know, it was beyond my comprehension too – how would you explain that one to grieving relatives in the event of a disaster? They also agreed that, because the Great Hall was a new building made of concrete and hard woods, it was unlikely to be quickly engulfed in a fire and the dancing calculation used was for a ballroom dancing scenario, not a stand-up rock concert crush. Add another exit down the left-hand side of the hall (which has since been done) and they could see no objection to a stand-up capacity of 1700 to 1800.

I knew we ran a highly responsible, organised team who produced safe concerts, so I worked on that figure of 1800 as a capacity. I understood it to be legally wrong but I thought I could justify it as correct. All the major entertainment disasters had occurred when somebody had acted illegally and/or stupidly: locking fire escapes to save on stewarding costs, filling the hall with combustible materials, furnishing venues with lethal smoke-producing seating, etc. We, obviously, had never resorted to any of these things.

However, the day before a sell-out Joan Armatrading concert I had a phone call from University House informing me that the local fire brigade was going to do an in-performance inspection. The show was sold out so I couldn't do anything about the 500 people who shouldn't be there. The University authorities were ecstatic. They had me at last and it wouldn't be them who would stop the shows, as that would have been politically very difficult. Result. Checkmate, mate!

I phoned the senior fire officer who was to do the inspection and he said that he wanted to come up in the afternoon to reconnoitre the hall and see all the equipment being used, in situ. When he arrived he said that he and his wife were big Joan Armatrading fans. Brilliant! I suggested that for this evening's visit he come slightly earlier and I would introduce him to Ms Armatrading (I also provided T-shirts, albums, posters, autographs etc.). He came, he saw, she conquered.

During the show I took him up to the balcony, stage right, and showed him that the fans, crushing close to the stage, had still left enough room at the back to have a five-a-side football game. "No problems here," he assured me, "great show, wasn't it?"

"Certainly was a great night," I answered. I was going to love telling University House. Game, set and match I think.

But Jack, the hall porter, informed me that John Halstead, a senior figure in the university administration and responsible for the Great Hall, had taken the bags of collected tickets and left the hall. The porters had a home phone number for him, so I called, sounding in a panic (which I was, but for a different reason), and I explained that the artist was on a percentage and needed to count the tickets before we could finalise the payment settlement. He had to return with the tickets. I assured him he could have them back later.

He – a trifle sheepishly, I thought – returned to the hall and handed over the two bin liners full of tickets. I gave them to Alan Murray and instructed him, with a rather knowing look, to give them to the artist's manager. He went straight to the boot of his car and emptied a few hundred tickets in, waited a sensible time and then returned them to John.

On the Monday morning I was summoned to University House, to John Halstead's office. I really liked John but thought he had a very difficult job trying to control the Great Hall shows. He was there with the university beadle and the senior security officer. In front of them, in piles of fifty, were set out the concert tickets. "I have 1375 tickets here," he announced.

"Yes, sorry, I went over by twenty-five because there were some people hanging about and I thought we were better able to control them inside the hall than out," I replied, using the usual well-rehearsed response.

"That's not the problem. Before your phone call to my house I had already counted 1500 and still had half a bin liner to count," he retorted.

What the hell could I say? He was grinning because he thought he had me. "Fair cop guv," was what I should have said, but I knew he would have counted them on his own, at home, at 11.30 at night. So I just came back with the only thing I could think of:

"I don't believe you."

"What! What do you mean?"

"I don't believe you counted that many, you couldn't have; we didn't sell more than 1375."

He was totally flummoxed. Thankfully, just then Al Gordon, the Students' Union President, barged in. He had heard I was in trouble and, like the US cavalry, arrived just in time. "Barry, go back to our offices. Mr Halstead, if you want to talk to one of my staff could you please have the courtesy to ask my permission first? Thank you, gentlemen." And we left, never to hear anything more about it.

Phew, close shave that show was, on every front.

Barry Lucas

Joan Jett and The Blackhearts

22 October 1982   **I Love Rock and Roll Tour**   Support: The Smart

Born Joan Larkin on 22 September 1958, in Philadelphia, Pennsylvania, Joan Jett entered the music business at the age of fifteen with the punk-pop band The Runaways.

One of the top women in rock, Joan Jett had a string of hits during the 1980s and 1990s.

Joan Jett and The Blackhearts were formed in 1981. Soon after the success of her Billboard Hot 100 No. 1 hit 'I Love Rock and Roll' Joan and her Blackhearts played a fabulous gig in the Great Hall. 'I Love Rock and Roll' is Billboard's No. 56 song of all time.

Joan, now aged fifty-eight, continues to perform and has also had a career in film and television.

The Smart were a UK rock band formed in Chelsea, London, that existed from 1980 to 1984. They released one single in 1981, titled 'Mr Right'.

John Cale

24 November 1975   **Slow Dazzle Tour**   Support: Nasty Pop

John Davies Cale, OBE, is a Welsh musician, composer, singer-songwriter and record producer who was a founding member of the American experimental rock band the Velvet Underground. John Cale played the university on his Slow Dazzle Tour to support his 1975 album of the same name.

Cale's band featured Chris Spedding on guitar, who in 1973 had appeared at the university with Andy Fraser's band, Sharks.

Spedding had a Top 20 solo hit single in the UK with 'Motor Bikin' in 1975.

Liverpool band **Nasty Pop** existed from 1975–1978 and were notable for member Keith Wilkinson, who was to become bassist for Squeeze from 1985–1997.

John Cooper Clarke

19 June 1979   **Supports: Joy Division I Fàshiön Music**

The "Bard of Salford" Dr John Cooper Clarke, arrived at the university for a second visit, this time in a headlining role for a concert in The Nuffield Theatre alongside, Fashion and Joy Division. He had previously performed in the Great Hall, on the same bill as Third World for a Rock Against Racism concert in November 1978. John Cooper Clarke became famous as a "punk poet" during the punk rock era of the late 1970s, with his best known work being the classic 1980 album *Snap Crackle and Bop*, spawning tracks such as 'Beasley Street' and 'Evidently Chickentown'.

In July 2013, Clarke was awarded an honorary doctorate of arts by the University of Salford as "acknowledgement of a career which has spanned five decades, bringing poetry to non-traditional audiences and influencing musicians and comedians" Upon receipt, Clarke commented: "Now I'm a doctor, finally my dream of opening a cosmetic surgery business can become a reality".

He released several albums in the late 1970s and early 1980s and continues to perform regularly. In 2016, in a collaboration with ex-Strangler, Hugh Cornwell, the pair released the album, *This Time It's Personal*.

Fàshiön Music were a British new wave band consisting of Dee Harris, Al "Luke Sky" James, Alan Darby, John Mulligan, Marlon Recchi and Dik Davis. The band released the album *Product Perfect* in 1979, and between 1978 and 1980 they played shows with many bands such as Toyah Willcox, UB40, Hazel O'Connor and Billy Idol. The band also were used as openers for the B-52s on their UK tour. Being re-formed in 2008, Fashion, as they are now known, are still active.

Joy Division were an English post-punk band formed in 1976 in Salford, Greater Manchester. Originally named Warsaw, the band consisted of singer Ian Curtis, guitarist and keyboardist Bernard Sumner, bassist Peter Hook and drummer Stephen Morris. Joy Division is considered to be the pioneering band of the post-punk movement of the late 1970s and the early 1980s.

The band released two studio albums but is best remembered for their single 'Love Will Tear Us Apart'. The song was first released as a single in June 1980 and became the band's first chart hit, reaching No. 13 in the UK Singles Chart.

The band dissolved in May 1980 after Ian Curtis' suicide. The remaining members re-formed as New Order and went on to achieve much critical and commercial success, with a Great Hall concert in March 1985.

Joy Division never played in the Great Hall but they did appear as part of a triple bill in the Nuffield Theatre on 19 June 1979. As the Nuffield is part of the Great Hall complex I feel justified in mentioning this show in this book. I used the theatre several times for acts that would benefit from a more intimate atmosphere, such as Sonny Terry and Brownie McGee, Al Stewart, and a terrific series of lectures on film by Philip Jenkinson (the BBC's film critic and presenter of the very successful *Film Night*).

But here I used it because I realised that the show would not command a large audience, as only people who were sufficiently "in the know" about the developing Manchester music scene would be there.

Joy Division are seen now as one of the most influential bands of the late '70s.

It is hard to believe today but they were third on the bill! Below Fàshiön Music and under headliner, poet John Cooper Clarke. They made for a memorable night. Well, the 300 who attended had a night to remember. It was less than a year later that Ian Curtis, their charismatic lead singer, would commit suicide.

The re-incarnation of the band as New Order would prove impossible for me to pin down to a date, despite a couple of years trying. Well, they were for me; Geoff Campbell, my successor for six months before he headed south to Exeter University and a very successful promoting career, managed it in 1985. A real triumph!

Barry Lucas

The Bard Of Salford in The Great Hall Third World concert 1978

John Martyn

9 May 1973	Support: John Renbourne and Jackie McShee
8 March 1974	Support: David Elliot
8 January 1975	Support: Brown's Home Brew or Lucas & McCulloch
30 April 1976	Support: Brian Robertson Band (with Herbie Flowers)
29 November 1977	Support: Prelude
22 November 1978	Support unknown
1979	Exact date or support unknown
1980	Exact date or support unknown
27 October 1981	Support unknown
6 October 1982	Support unknown

Iain David McGeachy (aka John Martyn, OBE) was a Scottish singer-songwriter and guitarist whose music reflected influences of jazz, blues and rock.

John Martyn was the first white solo act to be signed by Island Records, who released his debut album *London Conversation* in 1968 and started a career that spanned four decades. He went on to release a total of twenty-one studio albums working alongside artists such as Eric Clapton, David Gilmour and Phil Collins.

Martyn was described by *The Times* newspaper as "an electrifying guitarist and singer whose music blurred the boundaries between folk, jazz, rock and blues". He sadly passed away in Kilkenny, Eire, in 2009.

Five months after the January 1973 split of Pentangle, former members **John Renbourne** and **Jackie McShee** teamed up and provided John's support on the night.

David Elliott is a folk rock singer-songwriter who had two solo albums released in the UK on Atlantic Records in the '70s, *David Elliott* and *Solid Ground*.

1975 support may have come from either Joe Brown's **Home Brew** or **Robin Lucas & Drew McCulloch**, who were a Scottish songwriting duo originally from Ayrshire, Scotland. They were signed to British Lion Music, writing songs and touring with a number of acts, including John Martyn and The Pretty Things, often playing at The Marquee Club in Wardour Street, Soho, London.

Brian Alexander Robertson is a Scottish musician, actor, composer and songwriter, from Glasgow, better known as **B. A. Robertson**.

He had a string of hits in the late 1970s and early 1980s, characterised by catchy pop tunes and jaunty, humorous lyrics, most notably his 1979 single 'Bang Bang', which spent twelve weeks in the UK Singles Chart and peaked at No. 2. He also penned hits for Cliff Richard, including 'Carrie' and 'Wired for Sound'.

Renowned bassist Herbie Flowers featured in Brian's band on the night. During the mid '70s Herbie had worked in a writing and production partnership with Brian Robertson. Flowers was a founder member of the successful UK pop group Blue Mink, a member of CCS and also responsible for penning Clive Dunn's UK number 1 hit 'Grandad'.

John's guests for his 1977 concert were **Prelude** who had previously appeared with Ralph McTell in March 1976.

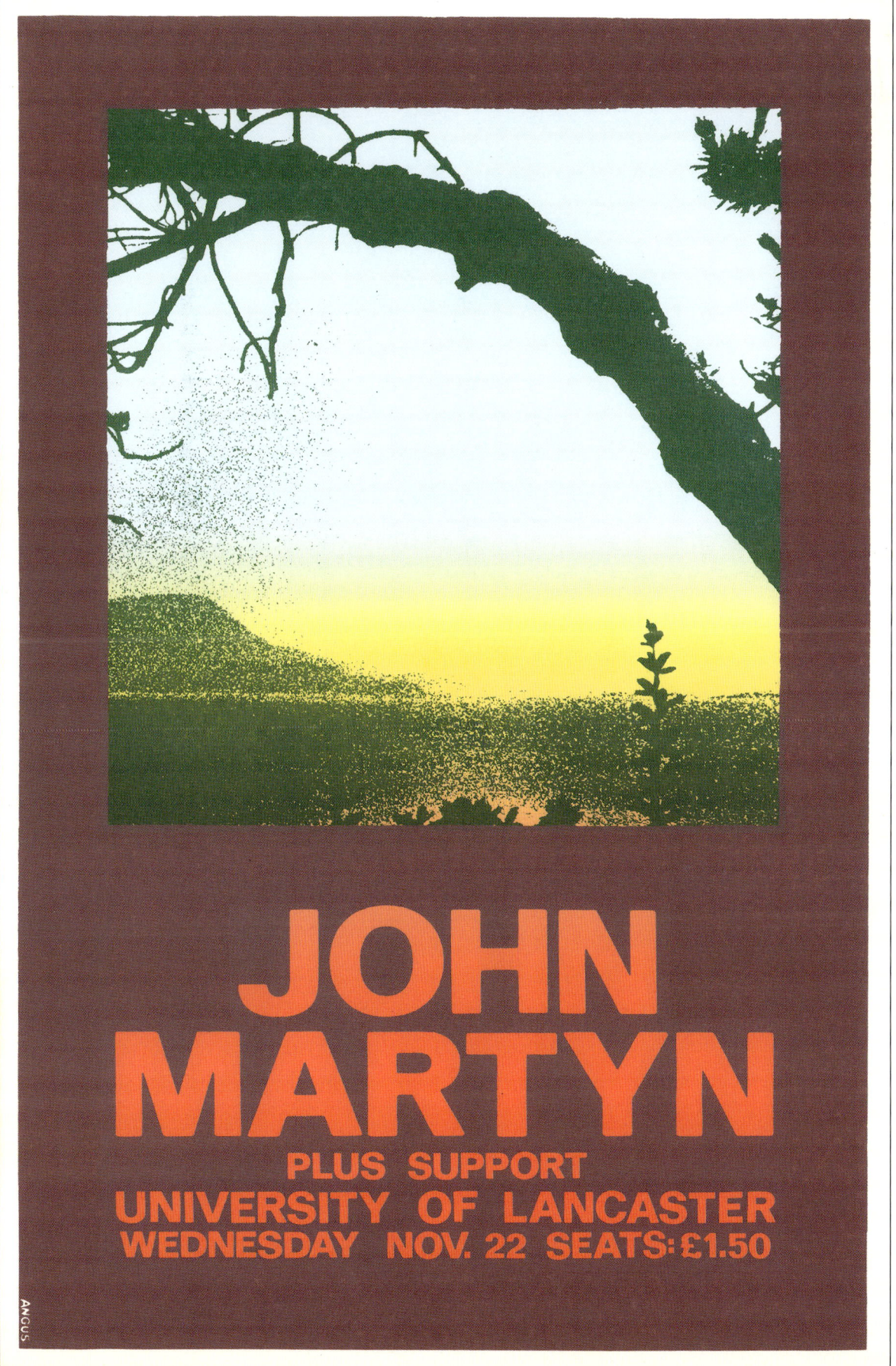

John Angus

John Martyn

That the album *John Martyn Live* was made at Leeds University, was probably one of the biggest mistakes ever made when it came to live albums. It would, on the other hand, have made a truly historic and memorable recording had the unique rapport between artist and audience that was a John Martyn concert been captured at Lancaster University.

John, who sadly died in 2009, had a magical relationship with Lancaster. It had been built up over several years while John graduated from interesting support act to major star, at Lancaster. Latterly, his shows would sell 1500 tickets and it is simply impossible, in words, to describe the unique atmosphere he created. I don't really remember how it first happened but John, sat on his own, on a single chair, on the vast, empty stage, looked and felt lonely. Onto the stage came his audience, soon to become his friends. Joints were rolled and passed around from audience member to audience member, from audience member to John and from John to audience. The shows were remarkable as nobody, especially John, wanted them to end. And end they didn't. His shows would last two to three hours and beyond. John just enjoyed creating those incredible guitar sounds, a one-man Pink Floyd, and he loved sharing the experience with all his friends.

I was close friends with his manager, Robb Winn. Yep, the same provincial agent who had booked The Who for us all those years ago, small world isn't it? Robb now worked at Island Artists. I was staying with Robb for a few days at his place in Cookham whilst I was in London sorting out a few deals. We had been out for a meal at a beautiful restaurant on the Thames and had had a few – quite a few – vodka and fresh oranges. This was a music business tipple of the moment, as people fooled themselves into believing the fresh orange made it healthy; worked for me! Back at the house the phone rang. It was 2.00 am, who would be ringing at that hour? "Oh it'll be John," said Robb, "he always phones, no matter what time it is, when he has an idea." It was. "He's a bloody genius," said Robb, "but bloody hard work to manage."

I could imagine. I said to Robb that John's shows at Lancaster were brilliant and always did the business, but them going on so long was getting counter productive. You could almost see the audience, sat around at his feet, looking at their watches. They wanted to go home but would not dream of offending a friend. You all know the old music hall adage, leave them wanting more. Robb could see my point but …

At the next John Martyn show at Lancaster I was in the foyer, putting up posters, when I heard this booming Scottish voice: "Hey you!" Now John Martyn was a bit of a scary legend, a great drinker, a bit of a battler, a fiery Scot and unpredictable. Not a great combination. What the hell was wrong? "What the fuck have you been saying to my manager about my shows here?" Obviously Robb had helpfully passed on my thoughts and observations. Thanks Robb, my old pal, bet you're in your local Cookham hostelry right now.

"Well John, I just said that maybe you could cut the act a bit …" I just got it out when John said "What the fuck's it got to do with you? I'm who they are paying to hear."

No arguing with that so I demurely agreed. After all he was right, they loved him, he was the star and … he was scary.

Anyway it still should have been 'John Martyn Live at Lancaster' – big mistake, Island.

Barry Lucas

John Mayall

29 April 1972   Supports: Eggs Over Easy I Matching Mole

John Mayall OBE, is a blues singer, guitarist, organist and songwriter from Macclesfield, Cheshire, whose musical career spans over fifty years. In the 1960s, he was the founder of John Mayall & the Bluesbreakers, a band which has counted among its members some of the most famous blues and rock musicians. Past members of John's band include: Eric Clapton and Jack Bruce of Cream, Peter Green, John McVie, Mick Fleetwood and Mick Taylor (who went on to have a five-year stint with the Stones.) The studio album recorded with Clapton, entitled *John Mayall & The Bluesbreakers*, was recorded in 1966 and is widely considered on both sides of the Atlantic to be one of the great classic blues albums.

At the start of the 1970s Mayall relocated to the USA, where he spent most of the next fifteen years, recording with local musicians for various labels. Here he assembled a band and recorded a live album, *Jazz Blues Fusion*, which was released in early 1972, with Mayall on harmonica, guitar and piano, Blue Mitchell on trumpet, Clifford Solomon and Ernie Watts on saxophones, Larry Taylor on bass, Ron Selico on drums and Freddy Robinson on guitar. This was John's lineup for his visit to Lancaster.

John Mayall continues to record and tour in his eighties.

Eggs over Easy were an American country rock band of the early 1970s who, after visiting London, decided to stay, record an album and become the resident band in a North London public house called The Tally Ho, starting what was to become known as pub rock. The album that started it all for Eggs Over Easy was *Good 'N' Cheap*, released in 1972. The band existed from 1969 to 1981 and featured ex-Animals drummer John Steel.

Matching Mole were an English progressive rock band associated with the Canterbury scene, formed by Robert Wyatt in October 1971 following his departure from Soft Machine. With Wyatt providing vocals and drums he was joined by David Sinclair, of Caravan, on organ and piano, Phil Miller on guitar and Bill MacCormick, formerly of Quiet Sun, on bass. Matching Mole disbanded in late September 1972.

The Lancaster story contains many momentous events, but it also includes many missed opportunities. Moments when readers of this book will say, "Wow, really?!" or "Bloody hell I remember that, why didn't I go?" or, "OMG, I didn't realise that they had played there!" Or some such thing.

Well in 1972 John Mayall played his only college date in Europe, at Lancaster. Talk to any R&B, rock, or blues musician from the middle '60s to the late '70s about John Mayall and they will have either played with him (if they were good enough), or been massively influenced by him. Every British musician was in awe of John Mayall.

Not the Lancaster audience though. It is almost impossible to believe now but only about 600 people turned up. I could not believe it at the time and find it even more confusing today, that, even if they didn't have his records, more did not come just to say they had seen a legend. Bet there's many more today regretting the missed opportunity.

Barry Lucas

John Miles

10 March 1978 — Support: Johnny Cougar
30 April 1979 — Support: Bandit

John Miles, from Jarrow, Tyne and Wear, is an English rock music vocalist, songwriter, guitarist and keyboard player, best known for his 1976 Top 3 UK hit single 'Music'. John made two visits to Lancaster for headlining concerts having previously appeared in March 1976 as support to Procol Harum.

Throughout the late '80s and into the '90s John Miles was musical director to Tina Turner on her various tours, as well as playing on several of her albums. He also played Hammond organ on Joe Cocker's 1992 album *Night Calls*. Today he is still making music, which he famously refers to as his "first love".

2002 saw him issue the DVD *John Miles – Live In Concert*.

John Miles brought along **Johnny Cougar** to provide support for his 1978 Lancaster show. Johnny's first record was released under the stage name of "Johnny Cougar" at the behest of Tony DeFries, his first manager. A few years later in 1982, he made his breakthrough with the album *American Fool*, which included the hit singles 'Hurts So Good' and 'Jack and Diane' under the stage name John Cougar.

With 1983's *Uh-Huh* album, he added back his real last name to become known as John Cougar Mellencamp. By the time 1987's *The Lonesome Jubilee* album had appeared he had dropped the Cougar moniker altogether and has been known since as John Mellencamp.

John Miles Great Hall 1979 © David Stewart

Bandit were a British rock band that existed from 1976 to 1979. Bandit included future AC/DC bassist Cliff Williams, former founder and guitarist of Colosseum, James Litherland, and drummer Graham Broad, now of Roger Waters' band. The band released two albums on Arista records with two different lineups. Interestingly, the only member of Bandit to appear on both of these albums was Danny McIntosh who is now guitarist for, and husband of, Kate Bush. 1977 saw Bandit also provide support at Lancaster to The Sensational Alex Harvey Band.

Johnny Winter Band

12 February 1971 — Support: Mogul Thrash

John Dawson Winter III, known as Johnny Winter, was an American musician, singer, songwriter, multi-instrumentalist and producer. He was born cross-eyed and albino and disregarded Mother Nature's unkindness to fashion himself a career as one of the few great white blues-rockers.

Johnny Winter was something of a musical child prodigy, growing up in Beaumont, Texas, on a diet of blues and rock 'n' roll. His first instruments were the clarinet and the ukulele, eventually settling on the guitar by the age of eleven. Over his career he released a total of nineteen studio albums and seventeen live albums, including the March 1971 release of his album *Live Johnny Winter And,* shortly following his Great Hall concert.

The album was recorded live during the autumn of 1970 at the Fillmore East in New York City and at Pirate's World in Dania, Florida, and as Barry describes was basically the Lancaster University set.

Lancaster band lineup:
Johnny Winter – vocals, guitar
Rick Derringer – vocals, guitar
Randy Jo Hobbs – vocals, bass
Bobby Caldwell – drums, percussion

Brother of rocker Edgar Winter, Johnny sadly passed away in 2014, aged seventy, whilst on tour in Switzerland.

Mogul Thrash were a UK progressive rock band active in the early 1970s. The band consisted of former Colosseum guitarist James Litherland, plus future Average White Band members Michael Rosen and the so-called "Dundee Horns", aka saxophonists Roger Ball and Malcolm Duncan. Mogul Thrash also included future King Crimson and Uriah Heep bass guitarist John Wetton.

Following the demise of Mogul Thrash in 1971, Wetton immediately joined Roger Chapman's Family for a year. The band released just the one album, the eponymous *Mogul Thrash* in 1971. It was produced by Hammond organ maestro, Brian Auger, who contributed piano on one of the tracks.

Johnny Winter on stage in the Great Hall

Over the last forty-seven years one question has been asked of me more than any other: "OK, so what was your favourite concert?" Probably impossible to answer, I hear you say – memorable, unique, momentous, exciting, innovative, unusual, history making – what definition to use?

But every time over those forty-seven years I have answered instinctively with this show. If you were not there and you want to know what I am talking about, listen to *Johnny Winter Live And*; it is the Lancaster set and captures, as well as any recording can, the feel of a live show.

It was an early booking of mine and made through the John and Tony Smith Agency. To me, Winter was a legendary figure; not many albino rock/blues guitarists around and I didn't need a hard sell. The agency had a young booker there at the time called Harvey Goldsmith (you'll hear more of him at other points in the book) who was a bit reluctant to put the date in as he had the band in Redcar the day before and he wanted to be assured there would be no audience clash. I suggested he consulted a map of the UK – the last bus to Lancaster from Redcar probably left in 1935, and not at twenty-five to eight!

If you were there it will have been a show you will never forget. It was so exciting people were stood on the balcony rails, dancing (health and safety, where were you when you were needed?), though nobody died! Two duelling guitarists, Johnny Winter and Rick Derringer (already a great in his own right, he was in The McCoys – 'Hang On Sloopy' – and then played with Steely Dan and Alice Cooper) trying to outdo each other. Then Johnny Winter split the audience down the middle and we had a panto-style singing competition, his half against Rick's, with "A Whole Lotta Shakin' Going On". Can't remember who won it, but WHAT A NIGHT!

Barry Lucas

Judas Priest

27 January 1978
4 November 1978   **Killing Machine Tour**

Support: English Assassin
Support: Lea Hart

Leathery and loud, Judas Priest were another band that tried to undermine the structure of the Great Hall. They enjoyed playing Lancaster so much that they came back for more, eleven months later in 1978.

Led by Rob Halford, decked out in leather and chains, the band fused the gothic doom of Black Sabbath with the riffs and speed of Led Zeppelin, as well as adding a vicious two-lead guitar attack; in doing so, they set the pace for much popular heavy metal from 1975 until 1985. Judas Priest have released seventeen studio albums, six live albums and thirty-three singles, their best known being 'Living After Midnight' which reached No. 12 in 1980.

English Assassin were a short-lived rock band that featured Nigel Benjamin, previously a singer and guitarist with Mott The Hoople from 1974–1976. They recorded an album for Arista but it was never released.

Lea Hart Band were a heavy metal band led by frontman Lea Hart. Hart featured on many top name rock albums as a backing vocalist or guitarist, including Joan Jett's *Bad Reputation* album.

Judy Tzuke

28 April 1982   **The Shoot The Moon Tour**

Support: Danceclass

Judie Tzuke is an English singer-songwriter. She is best known for her 1979 hit 'Stay With Me Till Dawn', which reached No. 16 on the UK Singles Chart. In 2010, Tzuke released a thirty-year celebratory double album entitled *Moon On a Mirrorball* and continues to record and tour.

Danceclass were a UK power pop quartet from the North East of England, and the band featured Dave Taggart on vocals, Tony McAnaney on bass, Ali Reay on guitar and Trevor Brewis on drums. Danceclass were signed to A&M Records in 1981 and their self-titled album, produced by Mike Chapman, was recorded and released in 1982.

© Andy Docherty

Juicy Lucy

20 February 1970   Support: California Purple

Juicy Lucy were a British blues/rock band formed in 1969, following the demise of a band called The Misunderstood. Vocalist Ray Owen, steel guitarist Glenn Ross Campbell and saxophone player Chris Mercer later recruited another guitarist in Neil Hubbard, along with bassist Keith Ellis and a drummer, Pete Dobson, to form Juicy Lucy. The band are best known for their UK Top 20 hit, a cover version of the Bo Diddley composition 'Who Do You Love?' which reached No. 14 in 1970.

In August 1971, Juicy Lucy appeared on the bill at the Weeley Festival near Clacton-on-Sea, Essex.

Information is scant regarding the support band **California Purple.**

> I didn't book this as it was before my election but I did attend. It was an incredible show and if anybody reading this book has not listened to the album *Juicy Lucy* I suggest they do so as soon as possible. The slide guitar (which I must confess I am a sucker for) of Glenn Ross Campbell is fantastic. Listen to the album and then envisage 700 people sitting crosslegged on the Great Hall floor, shakin' their heads. Yes, that's what we were all doing back then – out of control head shakin'. Wild or what?
>
> Barry Lucas

Kevin Coyne Band

9 May 1975   Support: Starry Eyed and Laughing

Kevin Coyne from Derby was a musician, singer, composer, film-maker and a writer of lyrics, stories and poems.

Coyne was notable for his unorthodox style of blues-influenced guitar composition and the intense quality of his vocal delivery.

Kevin worked from 1965 to 1968 as a social therapist and psychiatric nurse at Whittingham Hospital near Preston in Lancashire before going on to work for *The Soho Project* in London as a drugs counsellor. During this period of working with the mentally ill he performed regularly. His writing also reflected the injustice of the treatment of the mentally ill. Subsequently, his musical aspirations took precedence and he signed a record deal in 1969.

Notably, in Coyne's band was lead guitarist Andy Summers, before later joining The Police.

Championed by John Peel, Kevin Coyne released numerous albums and singles and was widely admired amongst his contemporaries, including Sting and John Lydon, but sadly Kevin did not achieve any real chart success in his career.

Kevin passed away in 2004.

Starry Eyed and Laughing were a British Rock band of the 1970s. Formed in London in 1973, they released two albums on the CBS label, recorded three Peel Sessions and undertook a US tour, before dropping the 'Laughing' and evolving into Starry Eyed. The band finally dissolved in 1976.

Kid Creole and The Coconuts

9 October 1982   Support: Musical Youth

Kid Creole and the Coconuts are an American band created and led by August Darnell. Their music incorporates a number of styles, including big band jazz, disco and in particular Caribbean and Latin American salsa. The Coconuts are Kid Creole's glamorous trio of female backing vocalists.

The band achieved three UK Top 10 singles during 1982. 'I'm a Wonderful Thing, Baby' reached No. 4, 'Stool Pigeon' No. 7, and 'Annie, I'm Not Your Daddy' went to No. 2 in the UK Singles Chart. The band also has fourteen studio albums under their belt to date.

A tremendous live act, Kid Creole and The Coconuts continue to tour stateside. August Darnell currently has a home in Sweden and one in Hawaii, where he runs a Martini bar.

Musical Youth are a British reggae band from Handsworth, Birmingham, formed in 1979. They are best remembered for their successful 1982 single 'Pass the Dutchie', which became a No. 1 hit around the world and remained at No. 1 in the UK Singles Chart for three weeks, selling over five million copies worldwide.

The band recorded two studio albums and released a number of successful singles throughout 1982 and 1983, including a collaboration with Donna Summer.

Musical Youth earned a Grammy Award nomination before disbanding in 1985 after a series of personal problems. The band returned in 2001 as a duo and continues to tour and record, with an album due for release in 2017.

> Like many bands, Kid Creole's crew had major difficulties with the physical structure of the Great Hall. While it was designed to be acoustically perfect for classical music concerts, it was not ideal, by any means, for rock'n'roll. The sound did have a tendency to bounce from the back wall. But Kid Creole, on being informed of the difficulties his crew was having doing the pre-sound check, just responded like a true pro. "No problem. I've played so many college sports halls in the States, same construction. Just stick some blankets or sheets up on the back wall. It'll be OK, man. Let's do it."
>
> Barry Lucas

The Kid and his Coconuts in the Great Hall © Geoff Campbell

© Geoff Campbell

King Crimson

8 October 1971 Supports: Ashton Gardner and Dyke | The Reason Why

British art rockers King Crimson were formed in early 1969, emerging out of an outfit called Giles, Giles and Fripp (aka drummer/singer Mike Giles, bassist/singer Peter Giles and guitarist Robert Fripp). Later the band added bassist Greg Lake and lyricist Peter Sinfield.

The lineup of King Crimson has varied drastically from album to album. Original lead singer and bassist Greg Lake left the group after a year – as did lyricist Peter Sinfield – and went on to fame with Emerson, Lake & Palmer in 1970, replaced by Gordon Haskell, Boz Burrell and, briefly, Jon Anderson of Yes. Also from Yes came drummer Bill Bruford, who joined King Crimson in 1972 and became one of the more enduring members. For the next three years, Bruford and Fripp were joined by future Asia frontman, John Wetton.

Robert Fripp has been the sole consistent member throughout the group's history and continues to front the current incarnation of King Crimson that are still active today.

King Crimson 1971 Lancaster band lineup:
Robert Fripp – guitars
Ian Wallace – drums
Boz Burrell – bass guitar
Mel Collins – sax, flutes
Peter Sinfield – keyboards, synthesizers

This was the first King Crimson tour since 1969, with the band performing tracks from the the album *Islands*, which was released in December 1971 and reached No. 30 in the UK and No. 76 in the US album charts.

Ashton, Gardner and Dyke were a rock trio, most popular in the early 1970s. They are best remembered for their 1971 hit 'Resurrection Shuffle' which got to No. 3 in the UK Singles Chart. The song was their only hit record, earning them the designation 'one-hit wonder'. The song has since been covered by a number of artists, including Tom Jones.

The Reason Why completed the night's triple bill but little is known about the band.

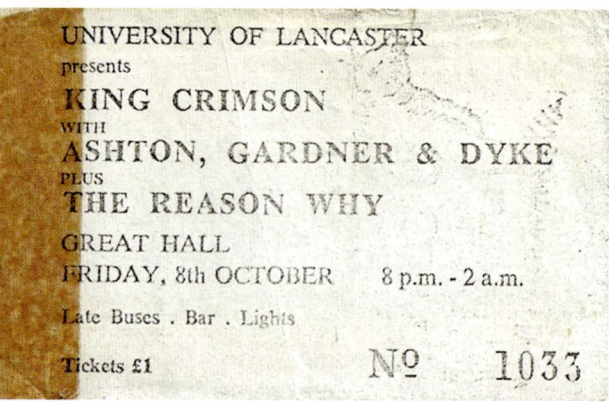

The Kinks

26 February 1971   **Rag Ball**   Supports: Quintessence I Shakin' Stevens and The Sunsets
15 March 1974   Support: Snafu
12 March 1976   Support unknown

The Kinks were an English rock band formed in Muswell Hill, North London, in 1963 by brothers Dave and Ray Davies with bass player Pete Quaife, later joined by drummer Mick Avory. During the early to mid 1970s, The Kinks visited the university on three occassions. The band rose to fame during the mid 1960s with singles such as 'You Really Got Me', a No. 1 hit in the UK and reaching No. 7 in the US in 1964. 'All Day and All of the Night' in 1965 was followed up by the single 'Dedicated Follower of Fashion' in 1966. The Kinks were active for more than thirty years between 1963 and 1996, releasing twenty-eight regular albums in the UK (twenty-four studio and four live), along with seventeen Top 20 singles. Ray Davies was recognised in the 2016 New Year's honours list with a knighthood for services to the arts.

Support for this 1971 Rag Ball event was provided by the jazz/psychedelic outfit **Quintessence**, who appeared with The Who in their 1970 Great Hall concert.

Shakin' Stevens put the university's Bechstein grand piano through its paces!

Snafu's first Great Hall support slot prior to returning a year later with Status Quo.

> **The Kinks**: I have lots of affection for the chroniclers of 60s Britain and glorious songcraft. Ray Davies is in a white flared suit. The set ends and they leave the stage to a rapturous response. House lights stay down but the stage remains empty and there is no encore. A deflated audience wanders off into the night.
>
> Maurice Hubbard (Pink Custard Light Show)

The only thing I can remember about this show – a Rag Ball I think it was, I was booking them by then – was the fact that an artist of Shakin' Stevens' calibre was demanding a grand piano, tuned to concert pitch on the day. It was the day that convinced me – or rather the Director of the University's Music Department – that we should purchase one. I had persuaded him to let me borrow the department's Bechstein grand. It took a lot of doing; after all, would a pop star off *TOTPs* treat a concert grand with the respect it deserves? Of course he would, I assured the good doctor.

I sat in the balcony as Shakin' Stevens jumped up on the piano then sat and played the song by banging the keys with his heels – enough said!

Barry Lucas

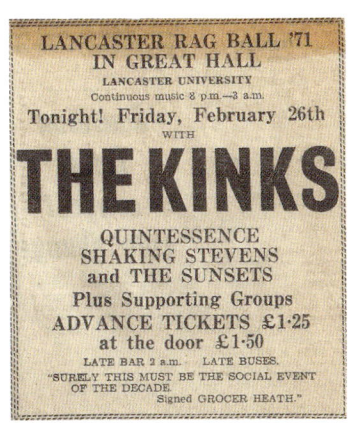

Kursaal Flyers

30 January 1976   Support: Eddie and The Hot Rods

The Kursaal Flyers were a British band formed in Southend-On-Sea, Essex, in 1973 and had a solid reputation on the London pub rock scene. They are most famous for their November 1976 single 'Little Does She Know', which reached No. 14 in the UK Singles Chart; their one and only hit.

Soon after the success of The Kursaal's single, the lead guitarist Graeme Douglas became concerned about the over-commercialisation and general direction of the group's music and left to join their support act on the night, Eddie and the Hot Rods.

Eddie and The Hot Rods' first visit to the Great Hall was as support to the Kursaal Flyers, soon after making a name for themselves on the London pub circuit.

Later in 1976, Eddie and The Hotrods headlined at The Marquee club in London.

Their opening act was a young band named the Sex Pistols, playing their first London gig, which descended into chaos with the Pistols smashing the Hot Rods' gear. October 1977 saw the Hot Rods back at the university as headliners.

This was THE concert poster, the one that began a long and very fruitful relationship between myself and John Angus. There is some disagreement between us as to how it all began. I think that John's wife, Mary, came to see me to say that she had got a teaching post at the University and her partner was coming up from Birmingham to join her. She explained that he was an artist/screen-printer and asked if I would be interested in giving him work producing my concert posters. They tell the story differently, that it was John and not Mary who came to see me. Well, it *was* over forty years ago!

Whatever the beginning, it was a very opportune moment to meet John. Most of my 'artistic' posters were produced in Yorkshire by an old friend of Gaz Taylor. He had been doing them since 1970 and had created some great ones, but the distance did have its problems. I frequently required a poster at a few days notice and BR's Red Star Service was in constant use. It was fairly efficient but it naturally added a couple of days to each turnaround. Having somebody based in Lancaster seemed a godsend so I gave John 'Kursaal Flyers' to see how things went. Now, John doesn't particularly like this poster, but to me it is so important. As soon as I saw it I knew that I had, fortuitously, stumbled on a winner.

About three shows in Mike Lloyd came up to see me to discuss that year's Graduation Ball's artists. I always booked the acts through Mike, who owned a couple of record shops, a small provincial booking agency and was also a promoter at Hanley Victoria Hall, Stoke-on-Trent. He was a good sounding board in the early days and taught me a great deal. He was also able to recommend the big bands, jazz groups, comics etc. that I had started to use on the, now formal, balls. Before we went to lunch I had to show him John's posters. I was so excited by my discovery of this new talent that I couldn't wait to show it off. I spread out three posters for different shows. "Aren't they great?" I enthused. Mike was not as excited, indeed he was most underwhelmed.

"They're OK, but can you see them at night, on a billboard, in the rain, on the top deck of a number seven bus in Stoke-on-Trent? Dayglo, that's your answer, black letters on orange background. That's a poster, that'll do the job for you."

Well, he had a point, but John's posters were works of art, real collectors' pieces. Many a time I had been sticking posters up on the Spine's noticeboards, only to find on the return journey to my office that they had been carefully peeled off and removed to some student's bedroom to dry out.

To me this book has four key, unique elements: Paul Tomlinson's meticulous research and collecting of memorabilia, memories and photos; Geoff Campbell's great photographs; my narrative and reminiscences of the period; and John Angus' iconic posters. No single element is more important than any other but without any one of these elements the book would be significantly diminished.

In total, John produced gig posters for around seventy-five concerts and everybody has their favourite – I personally loved the Stiff Little Fingers poster – but the John Angus style is instantly recognisable and memorable. John kindly agreed to allows us to reproduce over forty of them in this book.

Barry Lucas

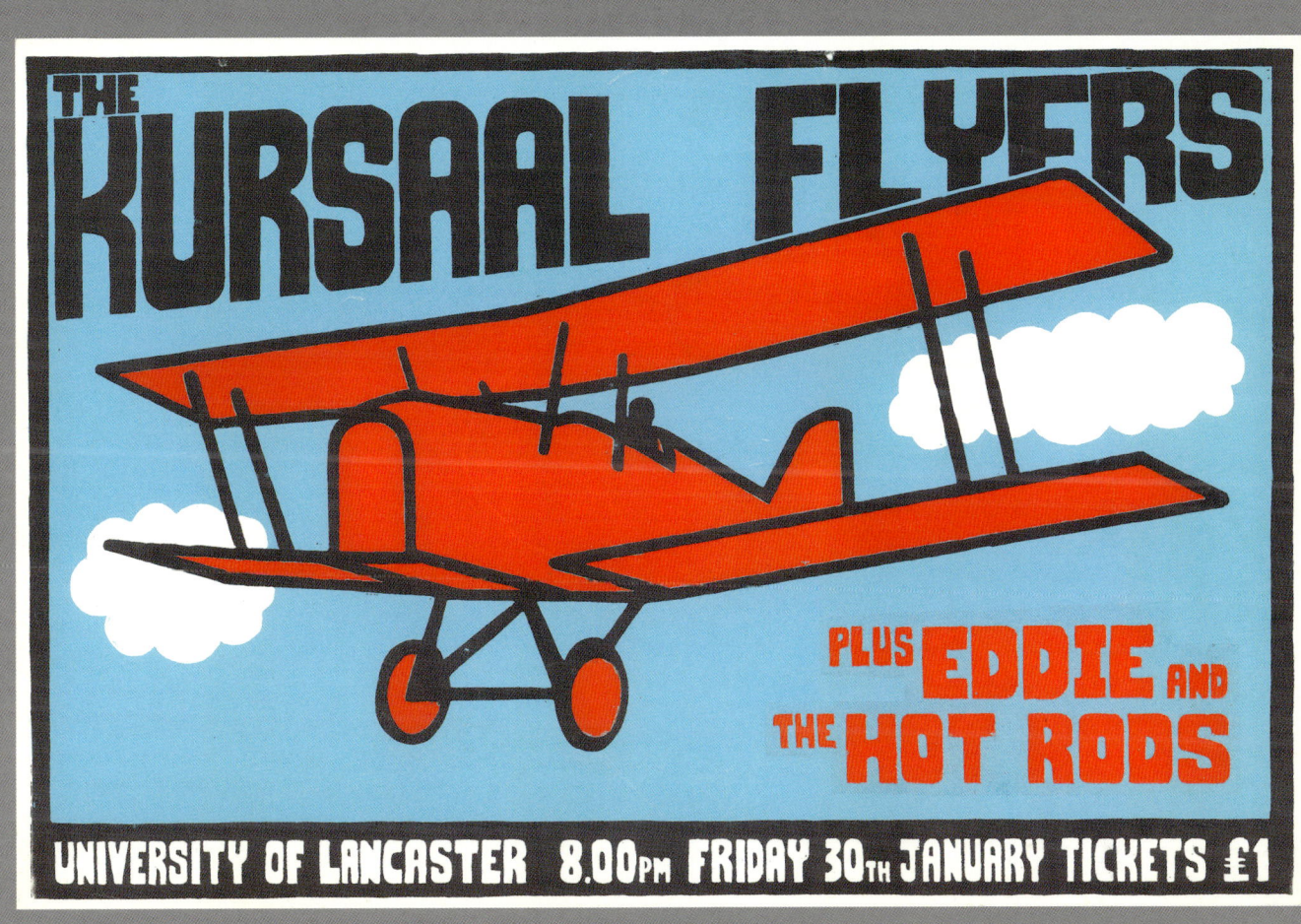

John Angus

Lancaster University Gig Posters 1976–1981
by John Angus

In 1975, I was based at Birmingham Arts Lab, designing and screen-printing posters for various arts and music events and organising exhibitions. I had decided not to pursue an academic career in genetics and had learnt screen-printing from two friends. I had no plan and I hadn't been at the Arts Lab for long, but it was a great place to be. Then my partner, Mary, got a job as a lecturer at Lancaster University, so I had to decide whether to move too. My friends thought it was crazy: "It's a tiny place with nothing going on and there won't be any demand for posters". I had grown up in big cities, so I shared these misgivings, but decided to give it a go.

Looking around, the most interesting events happening in Lancaster were the rock concerts up at the university. In fact the programme was surprisingly good for such a small place, and they didn't seem to have any posters. This seemed like an opportunity! I found out that Barry Lucas was the man to speak to, so I took some of my work along to show him. He asked me to do a poster for the next concert, a band called Kursaal Flyers. I didn't know anything about them, but a bold drawing of a bi-plane seemed appropriate. Barry was presumably satisfied with the result as he asked me to do some more, and a fruitful regular working relationship began, which helped me to settle in Lancaster.

Mary and I had been able to buy a four-storey Victorian terrace house, as they were fairly cheap here at that time. There was lots of space and for the first few years, I was printing posters in a room on the top floor. I made the printing table and the screens myself. At first I didn't have a drying rack, but spread the wet prints out on the floor of the adjoining room. I set up a darkroom in the cellar and the screens were cleaned in the bathroom. Later, I found a huge space above two shops in the centre of town and that became my workshop, allowing our house to become more domesticated.

I produced posters for about seventy-five of these concerts between 1976 and 1981. For each poster, I screen-printed one hundred plus copies by hand, using two to four hand-painted and photographic stencils. I often used more than one colour of ink when printing from a single stencil to produce a graded or blended effect, so getting more colours for the effort and price. This effect is easy to achieve on a computer now, but it was a skilled technique then, especially to maintain consistency over many prints.

All these posters were produced quickly. I would get a phone call from Barry, with the name of the band, the gig date and ticket price. The finished posters were usually needed within a week, so there was not much time for thought. I would search around for appropriate images, in the library, the record shop and elsewhere, or would draw something. There was no internet.

I didn't know anything about most of the bands. For me, producing posters was about creating artworks which had a purpose. Barry was an ideal commissioner. As long as the name of the band was clear and all the other information legible, he didn't mind what was on the poster. He never asked to see a design and anyway, there was no time for that. So I had freedom to play, which was great. I was creating bold, brightly coloured images, with the intention that these images would attract attention to the information which the poster was intended to communicate.

Occasionally I used an image of the band, if I could find one, but that was rare – The Damned, Hazel O'Connor – and sometimes I did drawings based on photos of the performer, including Joan Armatrading, Graham Parker, John Cooper Clarke and AC/DC.

Sometimes I visually punned on the name. For a band called MAN, the letters of the name suggested to me the shape of a moulded jelly/blancmange. It seemed a bit contrary to any macho image, especially in pink, but no-one seemed to mind. I continued with Thin Lizzy as an elephant, Focus a pair of spectacles and Deaf School one of men with their fingers in their ears.

I used photographs I had taken, such as an old Citroen I saw somewhere in France (Jack Bruce), a billboard 100 yards from our house (Peter Gabriel), shop window mannequins (Wishbone Ash), a landscape (John Martyn), a closed cafe in Morecambe (Sad Cafe), the gasometer behind our house (Hot Chocolate), some gargoyles (Climax Blues Band).

I also used B&W photos I noticed in the newspapers which I used when cleaning the screens – The Undertones, Hawkwind, The Rezillos, and Judas Priest.

I made collages from these and other images – a band photo and other stuff (The Jam), eyes (The Adverts), various newspaper clippings (Third World). Sometimes it was a combination of my photos and found ones – a young woman in Birmingham and a newspaper clipping (Steel Pulse).

Producing these posters was a very satisfying activity. I was designing and making things by hand, delivering them and getting paid in cash. As posters, they had a function and were displayed in public. But they would not be around for long, so they were not precious and I felt I could experiment. This was my personal training ground and I tried to learn something about technique, colour or design with every poster.

An extra source of income was to print a few more than the 100 posters required and to sell these extras in the foyer at the concerts. We would get in early and set up stall. When the doors opened there was a rush and some kids would head straight for the posters. This sometimes seemed a bit scary as they were punks in black leather, torn T-shirts, chains and spiky dyed hair. They would even argue about the price (50p!). But when we got chatting, they were all perfectly friendly and harmless.

Bands didn't do much merchandising in those days, so they generally didn't care about me selling posters. On a few occasions the band or their staff would come for a look and to comment. The Jam complained that I'd made them look like a punk band, which I thought they were. Lindisfarne were the only ones who would not let me sell. Someone with Stiff Records asked me to work for them, but required me to move to London and to set up there.

The posters I was producing for these gigs at Lancaster University began to attract attention and other venues started asking me for posters. I went on to design posters for arts events across the North West and all around the UK, for the next twenty-five years.

I had exhibitions of posters, including at the Royal Northern College of Music in Manchester, which was reviewed in *The Guardian*, and an Arts Council tour of venues in North West. These exhibitions included some of the Lancaster gig posters. In 2012, the Peter Scott Gallery at Lancaster University hosted an exhibition entitled "Was I there?" which included about twenty of these posters and reflected on people's memories of these concerts.

These gig posters were only intended to last for a week, or two at most, so there was no thought of them being around over forty years later. Over the past few years, various collectors, including one living in Venice, have contacted me and purchased some of the posters I have kept. Some posters have appeared in books, such as *The Art of Punk* and someone sent me a photo of a framed Stiff Little Fingers poster which they had rescued from a nearby skip in Los Angeles, now on display by their swimming pool. You never know what will happen to things that you make, but I'm delighted that these ones still have a life.

John Angus 2016

Leo Sayer

15 January 1975   Support: Sundance

On the back of three UK Top 10 singles, Leo Sayer, real name Gerald Hugh Sayer, played the Great Hall to promote his 1975 album release *Another Year*.

There was a poor audience on the night according to accounts.

Leo Sayer first came to attention with his 1973 hit record 'The Show Must Go On', performing it dressed and made up as a Pierrot clown. His first seven hit singles in the United Kingdom all reached the Top 10; a feat previously achieved by his first manager, Adam Faith.

Shortly prior to this Lancaster appearance, October 1974 saw the release of his album *Just a Boy*, which reached No. 4 in the UK Albums Chart and featured hits such as 'One Man Band' and 'Long Tall Glasses'. The album also featured the single 'Giving It All Away' written by Sayer for Roger Daltrey's debut solo album *Daltrey*.

In October 1977 Leo Sayer released the album *Thunder in My Heart*, with the single of the same name reaching No. 22 in the UK Singles Chart that year. The track once again became a hit single in the UK when a remix by Meck (titled 'Thunder in My Heart Again') reached No. 1 in 2006 and stayed there for two weeks.

Sayer's career has spanned four decades and he now lives in Australia. He continues to record and tour, appearing in 2015 at The Grand Theatre, Lancaster.

A *SCAN* newspaper concert reviewer noted: "On the basis of Wednesday's performance he'll probably be around for a long time. If not at Lancaster then probably Las Vegas"

Not much is known about **Sundance** other than they were a Swedish jazz rock band that released one album in 1976.

Leo Sayer © Neil Yates

Level 42

19 November 1982   Support unknown

Level 42 are an English pop rock and jazz-funk band, who had a number of worldwide and UK hits during the 1980s and 1990s.

Their most successful single in the UK was 'Lessons in Love', which reached No. 3 in the UK Singles Chart and No. 12 on the US Billboard Hot 100 Chart, upon its release in 1986. The earlier single, 'Something About You', was their most successful single in the United States, reaching No. 7 on the Billboard Hot 100 Chart.

After much success as a live and studio band in the 1980s, Level 42's commercial profile diminished during the early 1990s following a series of personnel changes and musical shifts. After disbanding in 1994, the band re-formed in 2001 and continue to tour and record.

Lindisfarne

6 October 1973 — Supports: Darien Spirit I Capability Brown
11 November 1978 — Supports: Chris Rea I Mike Elliot
7 October 1979 — Support: Mike Elliot
11 October 1981 — Support unknown

During the 1970s Lindisfarne were one of the hottest folk rock bands. Established in 1968 and originally called 'Brethren' they were led by singer/guitarist Alan Hull. The band also featured Simon Cowe on guitars, Ray Jackson on mandolin, bass player Rod Clements and drummer Ray Laidlaw. All were from the Newcastle upon Tyne area.

Lindisfarne were best known for their No. 1 single 'Fog on The Tyne', taken from their 1971 album of the same name which went on to become the UK best selling album of 1972. They also had major chart successes with songs such as 'Meet Me On The Corner', 'Lady Eleanor', 'Run For Home' and 'We Can Swing Together'.

Darien Spirit, the English folk/soft rock band consisted of Jack McAllister (guitar, vocals), Harry MacDonald (guitar, keyboards, vocals), Dennis Cowan (bass, vocals), Alan Waterson (drums). The band had previously visited Lancaster, providing support for Refugee in February 1973.

Capability Brown were a six piece multi-instrumental progressive rock band featuring terrific vocal harmonies with all six members contributing. The lineup consisted of Tony Ferguson (guitar, bass), Dave Nevin (keyboards, guitar, bass), Kenny Rowe (bass, percussion), Grahame White (guitar, lute, balalaika, keyboards), Joe Williams (percussion) and Roger Willis (drums, keyboards). They produced two studio albums, the best known being *Voice* from 1973, before disbanding in 1974.

Chris Rea is an English singer-songwriter and guitarist, recognisable for his distinctive, husky voice and slide guitar playing. Hailing from Middlesbrough his most well-known success was his 1989 UK No. 1 album *The Road to Hell*. With twenty-three studio albums and thirty-three UK hit singles under his belt, Rea is as busy as ever recording and touring.

Mike Elliot, also known as "Mike the Mouth", was a stand-up comedian, actor, television presenter and radio personality from Sunderland. Elliott had a number of acting roles, including George Watson in *Billy Elliot* and various roles in television drama series, including *Crocodile Shoes*, *Byker Grove*, *Spender*, *Harry* and *New Voices*.

This Lindisfarne story has nothing to do with their concert at Lancaster but everything to do with them as a band.

When I left Lancaster University, one of the ventures I became involved with was a company called Mayday. With fellow directors John Marsh and Steve Powell, we were involved in many fundraising activities for causes on the political left in the UK. These in included, among others, The African National Congress, Anti-Apartheid, and The Anti-Racist Alliance, and we were bi-annually committed to a fundraising event at The Labour Party Conference and the Trades Union Congress on behalf of *The Morning Star*.

The *Star* events had proved very successful as socials in raising much-needed funds for the newspaper. We had had bands such as Dr Feelgood, Climax Blues Band, Shane McGowan and Dick Gaughan etc., but for that year's Glasgow conference we were struggling. Obviously, *The Star* was the most left wing of the UK's national daily newspapers, with many past and current associations with the Communist Party, and this was a fundraising event, so a) the band couldn't mind the political connotations, and b) would play for a reduced fee. My two business partners and myself were scratching our heads. Steve suggested just sending a round robin letter to loads of bands. John and I shook our heads at such naïvety – we were worldly wise in the music business. "That will never work," we told him. A couple of days later, Steve rang to say that he had ignored our cynicism and sent the faxes anyway. By return, Lindisfarne had agreed to do it. That was brilliant but I was intrigued to know why. So, on the day, in Glasgow, I asked the band why they had so readily agreed to do it. One of the band pulled out a faded press cutting from his wallet. "When we were starting out *The Star* gave us our first national review. It raved about us. We always carry it around to remind us of the start and we like to repay a debt." Really says it all about this band.

Barry Lucas

Loudon Wainwright III

30 October 1980   Support: Beverley Martyn

Loudon Snowden Wainwright III is a Grammy Award-winning American songwriter, folk singer, humorist and actor who started his career in the late '60s, singing humorous and autobiographical songs.

He is the father of musicians Rufus Wainwright, Martha Wainwright and Lucy Wainwright Roche, and is the former husband of the late folk singer Kate McGarrigle. Loudon is probably best known for his song 'Dead Skunk' and continues to put out new albums and to tour.

To date, Wainwright has released twenty-six studio albums.

Beverley Martyn is an English folk rock singer, songwriter and guitarist. In 1969 she met John Martyn, whom she later married. As a duo they issued two albums, *Stormbringer!* and *The Road to Ruin,* both of which were released on the Island Records label. They couple were divorced in 1980. Beverley Martyn had previously appeared in the Great Hall as a support act to Sparks in 1974. Martyn released a new album in 2014 entitled *The Phoenix and The Turtle*.

Love

16 May 1974   Support: Casablanca

Love, founded by Arthur Lee in Los Angeles, are one of the seminal garage/folk/psychedelic bands of the 1960s, recording three albums on the Elektra label including *Forever Changes*, an album that is regarded as one the greatest rock albums of all time.

Signed to Elektra records, along with the Doors (who were influenced by them in their early days), Love were the kings of the Los Angeles psychedelic rock scene during the late sixties.

Arthur Lee continued to make music under the name Love after the original lineup split in early 1968, as well as working on his solo material.

The original theme tune for the BBC's *Holiday* programme in the early 1970s was Love's 'The Castle'. Gordon Giltrap's 'Heartsong' was used as the theme tune from 1978 until the end of the 1985 series.

Written by Arthur Lee's fellow songwriter Bryan MacLean, the song 'Alone Again Or' was a single released by The Damned in 1987 on the MCA label. They recorded it as an acknowledgement to one of their influences, the band Love.

Arthur Lee spent his last years touring the *Forever Changes* album with a new backing band following his release from prison in 2001, and performed the entire *Forever Changes* album in a concert in the Royal Albert Hall in 2003.

Arthur Lee died in Memphis in 2006, aged sixty-one.

A version of the band called Love Revisited is still active, featuring original guitarist and co-founder Johnny Echols.

Support on the night came from an eight-piece band called **Casablanca** who were fronted by singer-songwriter Aliki Ashman, known for her previous role with Ginger Baker's Air Force around 1970. Also in the lineup was former Dada and Vinegar Joe bassist Steve York.

Lynyrd Skynyrd

12 February 1977   **The Street Survivors Tour**   Support: Clover

The Street Survivors Tour was the sixth major concert tour by American Southern Rock band Lynyrd Skynyrd. It was one of their last ever UK concerts and was a fabulous gig at Lancaster University.

Band members:
Ronnie Van Zant – vocals
Allen Collins – guitars
Gary Rossington – guitars
Steve Gaines – guitars
Billy Powell – keyboards
Leon Wilkeson – bass
Artimus Pyle – drums

Setlist on the night: 'Workin' For MCA', 'I Ain't The One', 'Saturday Night Special', 'Whiskey Rock-A-Roller', 'That Smell', 'Travelin' Man', 'Ain't No Good Life', 'Gimme Three Steps', 'Call Me The Breeze', 'T For Texas', 'Sweet Home Alabama', 'Free Bird'.

The tour took place in North America, Europe, and for the first time Asia. It was also the final tour of the original band, as a number of the band members were tragically killed in a plane crash on 20 October 1977 following the final show of the tour. The hired plane carrying the band ran out of fuel and crashed in Gillsburg, Mississippi, near to the end of its flight from Greenville, South Carolina, to Baton Rouge, Louisiana. Lead singer Ronnie Van Zant, guitarist/vocalist Steve Gaines, backing vocalist Cassie Gaines (Steve's older sister), assistant road manager Dean Kilpatrick, pilot Walter McCreary and co-pilot William Gray all died as a result of the crash. Twenty others survived.

Lynyrd Skynyrd were the definitive Southern rock band with a hard rebellious Southern image, playing hard-driving Southern rock and roll. For those who don't know and for those who are curious, the band's name was a mocking tribute to a physical education teacher at Ronnie Van Zant's High School, Leonard Skinner. Mr Skinner was notorious for strictly enforcing the school's policy against boys having long hair.

Over Lynyrd Skynyrd's career they released a total of fouteen studio and six live albums.

Following the air tragedy, survivors Gary Rossington and Allen Collins teamed up to form The Rossington Collins Band in 1980 and were scheduled to appear at Lancaster University that same year, but cancelled due to the sudden death of Allen Collin's wife.

Clover were an American country rock band formed in San Francisco in 1967. They are best known as the backing band for Elvis Costello's 1977 debut album, *My Aim Is True*. Notable members of the band included lead singer Hugh Anthony Cregg, better known as Huey Lewis, who joined the band in 1972 and performed with them until their split in 1978. Providing pedal steel guitar was John McFee, who went on to join The Doobie Brothers in 1979. The band had previously appeared at the university as guests of Thin Lizzy in November 1976 and would return again to support Graham Parker in November 1977.

Ronnie Van Zant © Gina Thistlethwaite

Gary Rossington © Gina Thistlethwaite

Allen Collins © Gina Thistlethwaite

Lynyrd Skynyrd

Huey Lewis and Clover providing support to Lynyrd Skynyrd © Gina Thistlethwaite

I can't say a great deal about Lynyrd Skynyrd's performance except that it was monumentally important for all the wrong reasons. Put into Lancaster by Paul Loasby at Harvey Goldsmith's, the only university date in the UK. It was also one of their final dates in the UK. Sadly, later in October that same year three band members along with others would die in a plane crash in the United States.

Also on the bill that night were a support band called Clover. A superb band. I had them on three times as a support act. Graham Parker and the Rumour and Thin Lizzy were other headliners involved. *College Event* – a magazine for the college circuit in particular and the business in general – asked ten major figures on the music scene, one Christmas, for their predictions as to who would make it big in the coming year. I was one of those asked but I was very disappointed that every other contributor picked a band that had almost made it already, not an up and coming unknown. I picked Clover and had to endure months of ridicule from within the business. Later that year they changed their name ... to become Huey Lewis and the News. I rest my case!

Barry Lucas

Magazine

30 November 1978   Support: Neo

Magazine were an English post-punk band formed in Manchester by Howard Devoto shortly after he left Buzzcocks in 1977. The band were active from 1977 to 1981, then again from 2009–2011. This Great Hall appearance was included in the band's UK tour to promote the release in June 1978 of the acclaimed album *Real Life*, which went on to reach No. 29 in the UK Albums Chart. In total they produced five studio and four live albums, along with ten singles.

Magazine's music continues to be an influence today. Radiohead in particular draw on the lyrical style of the group and have performed the single 'Shot By Both Sides' from *Real Life* in their live sets.

Neo were an early new wave band formed in London. The group were formed by the American-born singer/bassist Ian North, who was the frontman and the only continuous member from the band's formation in 1977 to their split in 1979. Neo guitarist Robert Simon left the band in late '78 to join Ultravox, only to leave them in 1980 and join up with Magazine.

Howard Devoto in the Great Hall © Geoff Campbell

Man

26 January 1973 — Supports: Badger I Brush
4 October 1974 — Supports: Badfinger I Brown's Home Brew
13 February 1976 — Support unknown

Welsh rockers Man, led by Deke Leonard visited the university for three concerts in the 1970s. Formed in 1968 in Merthyr Tydfil, the band has gone through numerous personnel changes over the years. Famous for their long jamming sessions, Man's style is a mixture of West Coast psychedelia, progressive rock, blues and pub rock. Soon after the band's 1976 concert at Lancaster the band dissolved, being reformed in 1983 and continuing to record and tour to the present day.

Man's latest album *Reanimated Memories* was released in February 2015.

The band's February 1976 Lancaster concert was a warm-up gig, prior to their tour proper, to coincide with the release of the album *The Welsh Connection* in April of that year.

Badger were a rock band co-founded in 1973 by former Yes keyboard player Tony Kaye and David Foster. The lineup also included former Ashton Gardner and Dyke drummer, Roy Dyke. They disbanded in 1974.

Brush were a short-lived band created by Irish guitarist Brush Shiels who was best known for his role as the frontman of Gary Moore's first band, Skid Row. The band also featured on guitar Adrian Fisher, who was to go on to perform with Sparks.

Badfinger were a pop-rock band that originated in Swansea, Wales, signed to the Apple label. Adopting the name Badfinger in 1969, the band were touted as the heir apparent to The Beatles, in part because of their close working relationship with the Fab Four.

Badfinger's meteoric rise and demise (marked by the suicides of founder-member and leader Peter Ham on 24 April 1975, and later of band member Tom Evans on 19 November 1983) remains a cautionary tale for the rock music industry. They're probably best remembered for the Ham/Evans-penned Badfinger song 'Without You', which became an international hit for Harry Nilsson in 1971 and later a hit for Mariah Carey in 1994. Other popular singles included 'Baby Blue', 'Come And Get It' and 'No Matter What'.

Joseph Roger "Joe" Brown, MBE, is an English entertainer. He has worked as a rock and roll singer and guitarist for more than five decades. He was a stage and television performer in the late 1950s and a UK recording star in the early 1960s and is highly regarded in the business as a musician's musician. He has had numerous chart hits throughout his career, including in 1962 'A Picture Of You', reaching No. 2, and 'It Only Took A Minute' which went to No. 6 in the UK charts. In 1972 he formed **Brown's Home Brew**, playing rock 'n' roll, country and gospel music and featuring his wife Vicki. Joe's daughter Sam frequently sings with Jools Holland's Orchestra. Soon after this concert Joe's band played Lancaster again, this time as guests of John Martyn in January 1975.

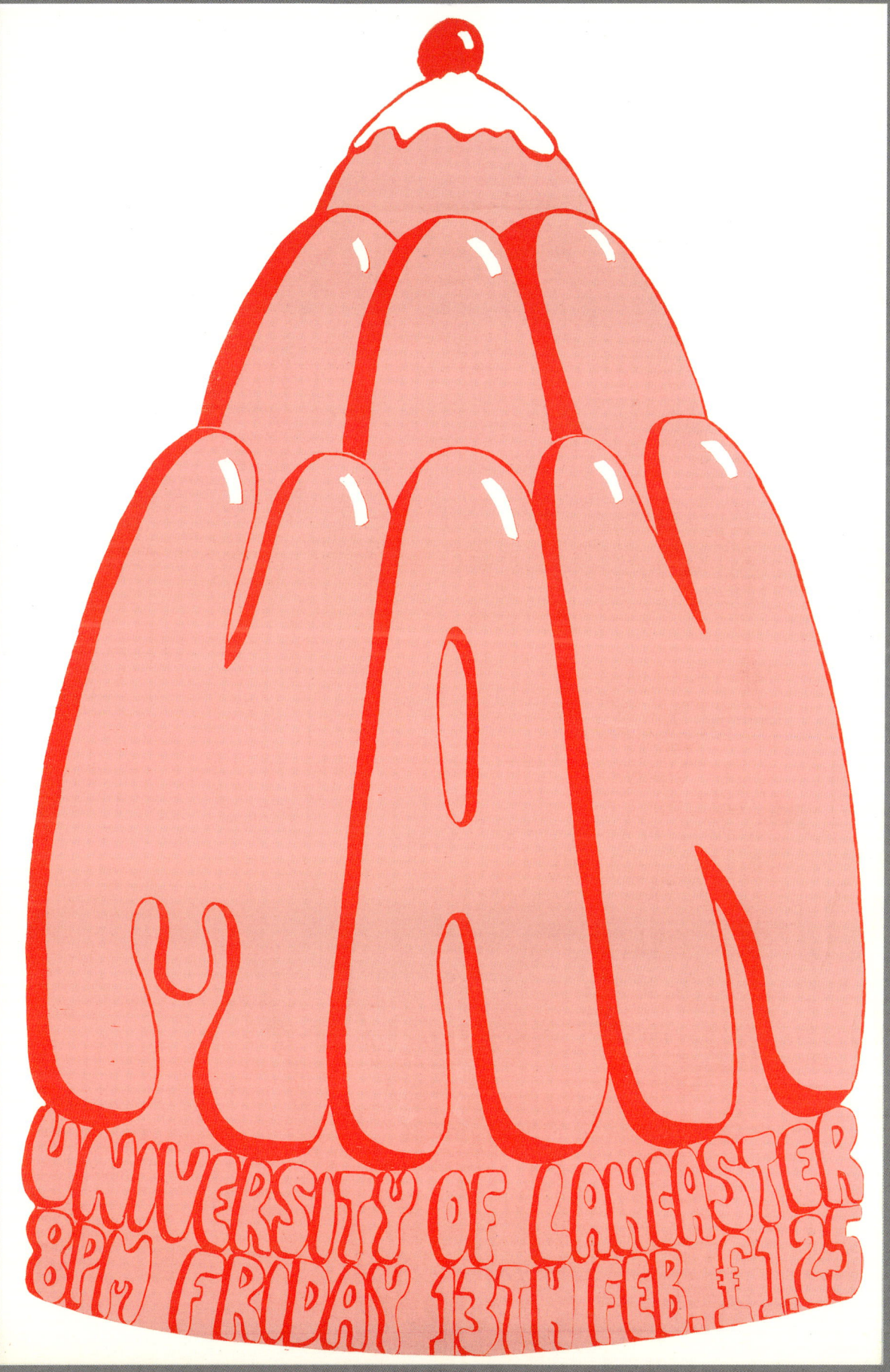

John Angus

Manfred Mann's Earth Band

9 November 1973   Support: Steve Gibbons

Manfred Mann's Earth Band are an English rock band formed by South African musician Manfred Mann. The band's hits include covers of Bruce Springsteen's 'Blinded by the Light' in 1976 and 'Spirit In The Night'. After forming in 1971 and despite a short hiatus in the late 1980s/early 1990s, the Earth Band has continued to perform and tour through to the present.

Mann started in the 1960s with the self-titled British invasion band that had such hits as 'Do Wah Diddy Diddy' and 'The Mighty Quinn', and then moved on to jazz fusion-inspired Manfred Mann Chapter Three, before forming the Earth Band in 1971.

Manfred Mann's Earth Band have been releasing albums and singles since 1971 and to date have released seventeen studio albums, three live albums and seven compilation albums. The band are also well known for their 1978 single 'Davy's on the Road Again'.

Steve Gibbons from Harborne, Birmingham, is an English rock vocalist and guitarist.

1971 saw Steve Gibbons form his new band and begin to work the pub and club circuits until 1975 when they were spotted by Peter Meaden, the former manager of The Who. This led to The Steve Gibbons Band joining The Who's management stable and recording their first Polydor album *Any Road Up* in 1975 (with John Entwistle of The Who playing on a few tracks). This was followed in 1976 by a tour with The Who in the UK, Europe and the United States.

Their next album *Rollin' On*, included their biggest hit single 'Tulane', a covered Chuck Berry song.

Playing large concert arenas, the band shared stages with the likes of Lynyrd Skynyrd, Little Feat, The Electric Light Orchestra and Be Bop Deluxe for their visit to Lancaster in 1977.

With many more albums under his belt over the years Steve Gibbons continues to record and tour.

January 1977 saw Steve Gibbons back in the Great Hall for a concert as guests of Bill Nelson's Be-Bop Deluxe.

Marc Almond

1 November 1985   Support unknown

Probably one of the worst attended concerts I came across during my research, former member of Soft Cell, Marc Almond, attracted an audience of just over 200 souls according to the concert review in *SCAN* newspaper.

A concert-goer remembered Marc Almond announcing to the audience: "At this point I normally introduce the band to you, but I think it would be quicker if you introduced yourselves to us."

Soft Cell are an English synth-pop duo who came to prominence in the early 1980s, consisting of vocalist Almond and instrumentalist David Ball. The pair are best known for their 1981 hit version of 'Tainted Love'.

'Tainted Love' is a song composed by Ed Cobb, formerly of American group The Four Preps, and was originally recorded by Marc Bolan's girlfriend, Gloria Jones, in 1964.

By 1983, fame and near-constant drug use were having a bad effect on Soft Cell and led to the duo splitting, with Almond pursuing a solo career. He achieved Top 10 UK single chart successes with 'Something's Gotten Hold of My Heart' (featuring Gene Pitney) in 1989 and 'The Days of Pearly Spencer' in 1992.

In 2011 Soft Cell re-formed and the band periodically still tour.

Marillion

9 May 1982 — **Saliva Tears Tour** — Support unknown
12 February 1984 — **The Fugazi Tour** — Support: Rage

Marillion were formed in 1979 as Silmarillion, after J.R.R. Tolkien's book *The Silmarillion*, by drummer Mick Pointer and guitarist Steve Rothery.

Derek William Dick, better known as "Fish", joined Marillion in 1981 and came to the public's attention as the band gained popularity over the next couple of years, leading to the release of their Top 10 debut album, *Script for a Jester's Tear,* in 1983. The band achieved further chart success in the UK, attaining Top 10 hit singles in 1985 with 'Kayleigh' and 'Lavender', and again in 1987 with 'Incommunicado'.

Fish has sometimes been compared to Peter Gabriel, lead singer of Genesis in the early 1970s, and his voice has even been described as "uncannily close" to Gabriel's.

Fish left Marillion in 1988 to pursue his solo career.

In 1999, DJ Simon Mayo commented on BBC Radio 1: "Marillion … where are they now? And who cares anyway?" Fans objecting to the comment brought the station's computer system to a standstill with thousands of emails of complaint.

Marillion continue to record and tour.

Formed in 1984 under the name Avenger, **Rage** are a German heavy metal band, founded by Peter "Peavy" Wagner, who are still active today.

> I was asked to take a date on Marillion in about 1983 but unfortunately the period they wanted was in the Easter vacation. Now, I had promoted some acts when the students were on holiday but these were considerably bigger draws than Marillion: Clapton, Peter Gabriel, Hawkwind (with Ginger Baker), Steve Winwood and Souixie and the Banshees, for example. As the audience would all be locals, and as the Students' Union would get the bar take, I offered them The Sugar House. They, somewhat reluctantly, agreed and we did the date. The audience was about four hundred and fifty, so approximately what I had expected. However, Fish was not amused with the gig, the stage and the dressing room etc. In fact he wrote with indelible marker all across the dressing room walls, "This is the worst shit'ole I have ever played". You must remember he was a major star then! I wonder if that statement is still true today? The graffiti lasted considerably longer than their "stardom".
>
> Barry Lucas

Mark-Almond

21 November 1971 — Support Unknown

Formed in 1970 by two musicians, Jon Mark and Johnny Almond, this jazz influenced pop group were sometimes also known as The Mark-Almond Band. The pair met whilst performing in John Mayall's Bluesbreakers band in 1969, subsequently leaving to form Mark-Almond in 1970.

Jon Mark had previously worked with Marianne Faithfull, with Johnny Almond being better known for work as saxophonist with The Alan Price Set and on Fleetwood Mac's 1968 album *Mr Wonderful*.

The band split in 1981 having released a number of albums.

Marmalade

6 March 1970   **Rag Ball concert**   Supports: Colonel Bagshots Incredible Bucket Band I New York Public Library I The Bermudans Steel Band

Marmalade are a Scottish pop rock group from the east end of Glasgow, originally formed in 1961 as the Gaylords and then later billed as Dean Ford and the Gaylords. In 1966 they changed the group name to The Marmalade. The most successful period for the band in terms of UK chart success was between 1968 and 1972. From the early 1970s, after the original players began to drift away, the band evolved with many further changes and still exists to this day touring the nostalgia circuit. With the departure of Graham Knight in September 2010, there are now no original Marmalade members remaining in the band.

Marmalade is probably best known for the single 'Ob-La-Di, Ob-La-Da', a song by the Beatles from their 1968 album *The Beatles* (often called The White Album). Although credited to Lennon and McCartney, the song was written solely by Paul McCartney.

Marmalade released their rendition of 'Ob-La-Di, Ob-La-Da' in 1968. Their version reached No. 1 in the UK Singles Chart in January 1969, making them the first Scottish group to ever top that chart. Their cover sold around half a million in the UK and a million copies globally by April 1969. They appeared on *Top of the Pops* to perform the track in kilts.

Marmalade still exists to this day touring the nostalgia circuit.

Colonel Bagshot's Incredible Bucket Band were a British psychedelic folk rock band formed in late '60s in Liverpool, comprising Brian Farrell, Terry McCusker, Dave Dover and Kenny Parry. They had several record deals, toured Europe and played gigs like the Reading Festival. A record by the band from that period, 'Six Day War', was remixed by DJ Shadow and also featured in the 2002 hit film *Phonebooth* which starred Colin Farrell.

New York Public Library are a UK rock 'n' roll band originally called The Cherokees. The band originate from Leeds and have been in existence as NYPL since 1966. They are still performing today.

Details of **The Bermudans Steel Band** are scant.

> Most people reading this won't have any recollection of The Bermudans but they were a brilliant steel band. Don't know if they are still playing but if they are anywhere near you, check them out. From this appearance I was so impressed that I booked them nearly every year to appear at the Graduation/Summer Ball. If you remember eating your Grad Ball dinner in Cartmel Refectory to the sweet sounds of a Caribbean steel band, it was them – good, weren't they?
>
> Barry Lucas

Matthews' Southern Comfort

1 May 1970   Support: Steamhammer

Matthews' Southern Comfort were a British folk rock band led by Iain Matthews.

From 1967 to 1969 he was a vocalist with Fairport Convention, later forming his own band, Matthews' Southern Comfort, which had a UK No. 1 hit in 1970 with a cover of Joni Mitchell's 'Woodstock'. Later the same year Iain was to return to Lancaster with Matthews' Southern Comfort, providing support to The Jack Bruce Band.

In December 2011 Matthews performed at the Great British Folk Festival at Butlins, Skegness, and performed a set of both his old and new songs.

Steamhammer were a five-piece blues-rock band from Worthing, West Sussex, that were active from 1968 to 1973. The band was founded in 1968 by Martin Quittenton (guitar) and Kieran White (vocals, guitar, harmonica). They produced four studio albums, the best known entitled *Mountains*.

Medicine Head

22 January 1972 Support: The Pretty Things

Medicine Head were a British rock-blues duo from Stafford consisting of John Fiddler (vocalist, guitarist, pianist and drummer) and Peter Hope-Evans (harmonica, Jew's harp and mouth bow player).

At various times the lineup also included Tony Ashton, formerly of Ashton, Gardner and Dyke, and Keith Relf, the former Yardbirds vocalist. Their biggest single success was in 1973, with 'One and One Is One', a No. 3 hit on the UK Singles Chart. Other notable chart successes were 'Rising Sun' which made No. 11 in 1973, and 'Slip and Slide', reaching No. 22 in 1974. The group also recorded six studio albums.

June 1970 had seen **The Pretty Things** at Lancaster on the same bill as Black Sabbath. Returning to Lancaster in 1972 The Pretty Things would most probably have performed tracks from their upcoming album *Freeway Madness,* to be released in December of that year. *Freeway Madness* was the sixth album by The Pretty Things and was the second album without founding member Dick Taylor and the first without bassist Wally Waller as a full member, who had been with the band since the band's 1967 album *Emotions*. Interestingly, following the release of The Pretty Things' fourth album, *S.F. Sorrow*, Dick Taylor took some time out from the band to produce Hawkwind's 1970 self-titled debut album on which he also played guitars.

Mike Harding

4 February 1976 No support
24 November 1976 No support
9 November 1978 No support

Former road digger, dustbin man, schoolteacher, steel erector, bus conductor, boiler scaler and chemical factory worker Mike Harding brought his popular one man show to the university three times in quick succession.

Singer, songwriter, author, poet and broadcaster, Harding began performing as a folk singer and as a member of several local Manchester bands in the 1960s and developed his show

> Mike Harding was one of the artists I booked to change the concept of student ents. He was a folk artiste who had a witty banter between the songs, which grew into hilarious observational routines until music was virtually abandoned and comedy took over. I reasoned it would have wide local support. It did: a rapid 950 sell-out.
> Barry Lucas

telling jokes between songs and eventually extending them into longer humorous anecdotes which became the main focus of his act. Mike Harding is best remembered for his release in 1975 of the single 'The Rochdale Cowboy', which reached No. 22 in the UK Singles Chart, bringing him national recognition. Harding is a dedicated hill walker and a former president, and now life vice-president, of the Ramblers' Association.

Mike Oldfield

12 April 1980 No support

Mike Oldfield is an English musician and composer. His work blends progressive rock with folk, classical, electronic, ambient and new age music. He is best known for his 1973 album *Tubular Bells*, which launched Virgin Records and became a hit after its opening was used as the theme for the film *The Exorcist*. The album was groundbreaking, with Oldfield playing more than twenty different instruments in the multi-layered recording. *Tubular Bells* stayed in the UK Albums Chart for a total of 279 weeks. It climbed the charts slowly but steadily for over a year, not reaching No. 1 until 1974.

Oldfield also achieved further chart success with his 1983 hit single 'Moonlight Shadow' and again with his rendition of the Christmas piece 'In Dulci Jubilo', a UK No. 4 single in 1975. Over his career Oldfield has released more than 20 albums with the most recent being a sequel to his 1975 album *Ommadawn* titled, *Return to Ommadawn*. It was released in January 2017. According to a review in *SCAN* newspaper, Oldfield had passed the peak of his success and the Great Hall was only half full on the night.

Motorhead

17 November 1979   **Bomber Tour**   Support: Saxon

Motorhead were a British heavy metal band formed in London in 1975 by bassist, singer and songwriter Ian Fraser Kilmister, better known by his stage name of Lemmy.

Although Motorhead are typically classified as heavy metal their fusion of punk rock into the genre helped to pioneer speed and thrash metal. Lemmy disliked such labels, preferring to describe the band's music simply as "rock 'n' roll", and usually opening live their shows with the line "We are Motorhead. We play rock and roll".

Prior to forming Motorhead, Lemmy was bassist for Hawkwind, joining them in 1971. In 1975 Lemmy was arrested at the Canada/US border in Windsor, Ontario, on drug possession charges; he spent five days in jail, causing Hawkwind to cancel some of their North America tour dates, but was released without charge. Nonetheless he was fired from Hawkwind. He immediately set about forming a new band which he called Bastard. When his manager informed him that a band of that name would never get a slot on *Top of the Pops*, Lemmy changed the band's name to 'Motorhead' – the title of the last song he had written for Hawkwind. Motorhead's discography includes twenty-two studio albums and nine live albums. Lemmy and Motorhead visited Lancaster to support the release of the album *Bomber* in October 1979. The album reached No. 12 in the UK Albums Chart. Lemmy died on 28 December 2015 from prostate cancer and heart failure. After his death, drummer Mikkey Dee and guitarist Phil Campbell both confirmed that Motörhead would not continue as a band.

Support on the evening was provided by South Yorkshire heavy metal band **Saxon**. Established in 1976 Saxon were one of the early leaders of the so called, new wave of British heavy metal. Fronted by Biff Byford they were originally called Son of a Bitch, eventually changing their name to Saxon in 1978. The concert featured tracks from their self-titled debut album, *Saxon* and from their UK No. 5 and platinum selling album, *Wheels of Steel*, released in May 1980. The band still tours regularly and has sold more than fifteen million albums worldwide to date.

This concert was memorable for two reasons. Firstly, the mind-blowing stage set, obviously inspired by the name of the album and tour, *Bomber*. The audience walked through those heavy, wooden Great Hall doors to be greeted by a replica of a Second World War bomber which dominated the whole stage. As the band took to the stage the hall was filled with the sound of engines firing up and then the propellers were created by several bright, sheer white spotlights. They slowly revolved, speeding up as the roar of the 'engines' got louder and louder, until, in a blur of spinning light and screaming, deafening engines, the band sprang onto the stage. Tremendous.

I understood that Motorhead had a biker following in those days but I must admit we were not prepared for the sight of three Hells Angels chapters arriving at the doors of the Great Hall. However, they all paid their entrance money without any complaint and we had no problems whatsoever. But these were proper Angels, not the local gang who couldn't afford a bike between them and used to arrive on the bus. Our lot frequently caused trouble, trying desperately to ape the Angels at Altamont, although they didn't quite live up to their scary name – Satan's Slaves – as they always had to leave a fight early to catch the last bus back to Lancaster! At about 8.00 pm another group of bikers approached. They were enormous, and one turned to speak to the others as they arrived at the main door. On his back it just stated 'Hells Angels – President', and on the next one, 'Hells Angels – Treasurer'. These were the real deal. I suggested to the door staff that they were on the band's guest list – I had no idea if that was true and I wasn't about to stop them to find out!

In 1985 I went to work with/for Paul Loasby, initially on The Return of the Knebworth Fayre with Deep Purple, Meatloaf, Scorpions, et al., and then out of Paul's offices in London. One of the tours we did that autumn was with Saxon, and at Hammersmith Odeon they broke the decibel record for that venue. Talk about bleeding ear drums!

Barry Lucas

Motorhead on the Great Hall stage 1979 © Doug Price

Saxon on the Great Hall stage 1979 © Doug Price

WANTED

MOTT the HOOPLE

QUEEN

MEL BUSH PRESENTS

NOV. 12 Leeds Town Hall
NOV. 13 Blackburn King George's Hall
NOV. 15 Worcester Gaumont
NOV. 16 Lancaster University
NOV. 17 Liverpool Stadium
NOV. 18 Hanley Victoria
NOV. 19 Wolverhampton Civic
NOV. 20 Oxford New Theatre
NOV. 21 Preston Guildhall
NOV. 22 Newcastle City Hall
NOV. 23 Glasgow Apollo
NOV. 25 Edinburgh Caley Cinema
NOV. 26 Manchester Opera House
NOV. 27 Birmingham Town Hall
NOV. 28 Swansea Brangwyn Hall
NOV. 29 Bristol Colston Hall
NOV. 30 Bournemouth Winter Gardens
DEC. 1 Southend Kursall
DEC. 2 Chatham Central Hall
DEC. 14 Hammersmith Odeon

REWARD

75mins of the best Rock & Roll music in the land

Poster courtesy of Flon… he was there!

Mott The Hoople

3 October 1970 — Support: Stonefeather
15 October 1971 — Supports: Graphite I Inner Sound
16 November 1973 — Support: Queen
30 November 1974 — Support: Sailor

Mott The Hoople were a glam rock group that was formed in 1968 in Herefordshire, led by lead vocalist Ian Hunter, until his departure in 1974. The band itself eventually broke up in 1976. The group are best known for their 1972 international hit single 'All the Young Dudes', written by David Bowie.

Mott The Hoople also found chart success with the hit singles 'Honaloochie Boogie' and 'All the Way from Memphis', both featuring Andy Mackay of Roxy Music on saxophone.

Lancaster saw the first appearance of Mott The Hoople in 1970 following the September release of their album *Mad Shadows*, with a lineup of Ian Hunter, Mick Ralphs, Verden Allen, Pete "Overend" Watts and Dale "Buffin" Griffin.

Almost exactly a year later the band returned with the same lineup, along with two support acts, to promote the upcoming release of the band's fourth album *Brain Capers*.

Two years on, in November 1973, with Aerial Bender replacing the departed guitarist Mick Ralphs (who left to join Bad Company), a legendary Great Hall concert takes place, remembered not for the performance of Mott The Hoople, but for the unknown support act: Queen.

Almost everybody who was there on the night will remember Queen blowing Mott The Hoople off the stage with a short but explosive set. Those who don't remember must have been in the bar area, waiting for the main event of the evening.

Eventually a visibly annoyed Ian Hunter took to the stage with his band to try to follow Queen, with shouts of "we want Queen!" ringing around the hall.

As the tour progressed it was suggested that Mott The Hoople cut down the duration of Queen's set, to minimise collateral damage as it were.

1974 and Mott The Hoople are back in Lancaster, this time featuring ex-David Bowie guitarist Mick Ronson. The tour promoted the release of the band's seventh album, *The Hoople*, and included charting singles such as 'The Golden Age Of Rock and Roll' and 'Roll Away The Stone', the latter a UK No. 8 single, and the album reaching No. 11 in the UK.

Stonefeather started life in 1967 as a band called Sweet Feelings. After releasing only three singles, Sweet Feelings then evolved into the psychedelic rock outfit, Rupert's People. Rupert's People continued playing live up until the late '60s, by which time they were being handled by future Police manager and music mogul, Miles Copeland III. At the beginning of the 1970s, they changed their name to Stonefeather, and featured Miles' brother, and future Police drummer Stewart Copeland on drums. Stewart Copeland was to return to the Great Hall in 1975 on drums, performing with Curved Air.

Graphite were a rock band from the early 1970s formed at Reading University. They gigged professionally on the rock circuit from 1970 to 1973, supporting many big names of that era, such as Pink Floyd, Arthur Brown's Kingdom Come, Mott The Hoople and T-Rex. Graphite returned a year later to Lancaster as back up for Roxy Music. Amazingly, Graphite got a billing above Queen at a festival in Truro, Cornwall, in 1971.

Inner Sound were a Scottish rock band from the Gourock area.

As history tells us, **Queen** turned out not to be the best choice of support band for Mott to have to follow onto stage. Over forty years ago in July of 1973 Queen released their first album, *Queen*, sometimes known as *Queen I*.

Freddie Mercury – lead vocals, piano, tambourine
Brian May – guitars, backing vocals
Roger Taylor – drums, backing vocals
John Deacon – bass guitar

Typical setlist from the 1973 tour: 'Procession', 'Father To Son', 'Son And Daughter', 'Ogre Battle', 'Hangman', 'Keep Yourself Alive', 'Liar'.

And a medley including: 'Jailhouse Rock', 'Shake Rattle And Roll', 'Stupid Cupid', 'Be Bop A Lula', 'Big Spender', 'Bama Lama Bama Loo'.

During research for this book I came across this appeal posted on a Queen fan site (thanks to www.queenconcerts.com for permission to reproduce this letter of appeal):

> "I am trying to find a photograph of Queen from their performance at Lancaster University in England on 16 November 1973. I have a jacket that Freddie borrowed from me that he wore during the concert and I'm interested in obtaining a photo, any ideas?
>
> I lived in Wigan at the time; my friend and I were drinking and talking with Freddie in the Students' Union bar before the show (the whole band were there). Freddie asked me for my coat (a vintage top coat w/tails) and I said he couldn't have it but I would trade with him. So I swopped him my coat for his leather jacket. At the end of the show he wanted his jacket back and I got mine back. The coat is black, with a striped silk lining."

Ian Edwards.

Sailor are a British pop group best known in the 1970s for the song 'A Glass of Champagne', which was a massive hit throughout the world in 1975 and a UK No. 2 single, followed by 'Girls Girls Girls' in 1976, peaking at No. 7. Interestingly, Sailors frontman was one Georg Kajanus (born Prince Georg Johan Tchegodaieff, on 9 June 1946 in Trondheim, Norway). Apart from lead vocals his on-stage repertoire also included twelve-string guitars, acoustic guitars, charango, Veracruzana harp, harmonium, synthesizers and "Klockwork machinery". Georg had previously made an appearance in the Great Hall with his band Eclection in October 1969, providing support for the Welsh band Blonde on Blonde. Sailor are still very much active today and celebrated their fortieth anniversary in 2014.

In 1973 I was to have the third of my Mott dates, but this was by far the most memorable. At the time Mott were a massive band sponsored by David Bowie with a string of hit albums and singles. They were at the forefront of glam rock and their stage show received rave reviews. The tour was a major one with about twenty gigs announced, but ours was the only university date; not even Leeds featured on this one.

However, it wasn't Mott that interested me but the £40 support act. Nigel, my business partner at 'Ear 'Ere Records, had insisted that I listen to a new album that had come in called 'Queen'. What an album, what a sound, and this little-known band were supporting Mott. I couldn't claim any kudos for that; they were just the bog-standard tour support. But I couldn't wait.

By the night of the gig, the fourth night of the tour, Queen's set had been reduced from an hour down to about twenty-five minutes. Mott's management were finding it almost impossible for their band to follow them on stage and Queen certainly exploded in the Great Hall that night. I stood at the back of the hall with Nigel and we just looked at each other. This was the real deal. If we had wanted to be rock 'n' roll stars this would be how we would have done it! And this isn't with the help of hindsight. Those who were there that night knew they were in the presence of greatness and will never forget it.

Barry Lucas

Mungo Jerry

26 November 1971   Supports: John Lee Hooker I Eroll Dixon

Mungo Jerry came to prominence soon after their formation in 1970, following an appearance at the Hollywood Festival in Newcastle under Lyme, Staffordshire. The reception they got from the crowd resulted in the organisers asking them to play again on the second day. The band grabbed all the headlines in the UK music press as they stole the limelight from the festival headliners, Black Sabbath, Traffic, Ginger Baker's Airforce and Grateful Dead.

Led by Ray Dorset, the first band's first and best known single, released in 1970, was 'In The Summertime', and it reached No. 1 in charts around the world, including seven weeks in the UK Singles Chart. According to Ray Dorset, the lead singer, the song took ten minutes to compose on his second-hand Fender Stratocaster. In total they achieved nine charting singles in the UK, including two No. 1s and five Top 20 hits in South Africa.

Mungo Jerry took their name from a poem by T.S. Elliot, 'Mungojerrie and Rumpelteazer', from the book *Old Possum's Book of Practical Cats*. Seven years later, Ray and his band returned to Lancaster as guests of Blondie for a Rag Ball concert, where they did the same thing to Blondie, as well as to the giants of the time headlining at the Hollywood Festival, completely stealing the show.

Mungo Jerry, still led by Ray Dorset, continue to tour and record.

The legendary American blues singer, songwriter and guitarist **John Lee Hooker** was the second billing on the night. Born in Mississippi, he came to prominence performing an electric guitar-style adaptation of the Delta blues. Some of his best-known songs include 'Boogie Chillen' (1948) and 'Crawling King Snake' (1949). Hooker recorded over a hundred albums during his career. He appeared and sang in the 1980 film *The Blues Brothers*.

Errol Dixon is a singer and ultra fast boogie woogie/blues pianist from Jamaica. He later moved to the United Kingdom, where he started his music career and had a No. 1 hit with his 1960 debut single 'Midnight Train'. In 1965 he was a member of the Ram Jam Band before Geno Washington joined. During his career he has released more than fifteen albums and thirty singles, and his resumé includes collaborations with B.B. King and Muddy Waters.

New Order

14 March 1985   Support unknown

New Order were formed in 1980 by the three remaining members of Joy Division, Bernard Sumner, Peter Hook and Stephen Morris, after the lead singer Ian Curtis committed suicide. Pioneers of dance music, New Order's members hailed from Salford and Macclesfield and became one of the most critically acclaimed and influential bands of the 1980s. The 1983 single 'Blue Monday' is arguably their most famous song and the biggest-selling 12" single of all time. New Order continue to tour and record, without founder member Peter Hook.

Lancaster setlist: 'Sooner Than You Think', 'This Time Of Night', 'Confusion', 'Blue Monday', 'Face Up', 'Thieves Like Us', 'Love Vigilantes', 'Sunrise', 'Age Of Consent', 'The Perfect Kiss'.

Both photos © Geoff Campbell

Nils Lofgren

15 May 1976 — Support: Unicorn
9 May 1977 — Support: Tom Petty & The Heartbreakers

Nils Lofgren is an American rock guitarist, songwriter and multi-instrumentalist. Along with his work as a solo artist he has marked over twenty-five years as a member of Bruce Springsteen's The E Street Band.

In 1968 at the tender age of seventeen Lofgren joined Neil Young's Crazy Horse, playing piano on the album *After the Gold Rush*. Following his gig with Neil Young, Lofgren went on to join the band Grin from 1971–1974, but they failed to hit the big time and were eventually released by their record company. In 1975 Lofgren released his self-titled solo album featuring songs that went on to become staples of his solo performances: 'Keith Don't Go' and 'Back It Up'.

In 1984, Bruce Springsteen asked Lofgren to join the E Street Band for his *Born in the USA* tour. Lofgren was an instant hit with Springsteen fans for his instrument playing and vibrant on-stage persona with Lofgren remaining a stalwart of the E Street Band to the present day.

Nils visited Lancaster twice in the mid '70s, on dates almost exactly a year apart. The first concert was well received by the Great Hall crowd, but the second was a standout concert, helped on by a fabulous support band, Tom Petty and The Heartbreakers.

A band once compared to The Byrds and The Eagles in style, **Unicorn** from the UK played their own brand of country-rock and broke up in 1977. During his career David Gilmour of Pink Floyd took several artists and bands under his wing by supporting them with production and recording. Unicorn were probably the first of those protégés. Several of the band's albums were produced by and featured David Gilmour of Pink Floyd.

Thomas Earl Petty is an American musician, singer and songwriter, multi-instrumentalist and record producer. He is best known as the lead singer of **Tom Petty and The Heartbreakers**, but is also known as a member and a co-founder of the late 1980s super-group the Traveling Wilburys. Tom Petty first found success in Europe with his well-received 1976 debut album *Tom Petty & The Heartbreakers*. The album sold well in Germany and France, reaching No. 20 in the UK Albums Chart, but not charting in the USA until a year later. Impressed by their European success, they headed over to tour and give performances that earned them the title of "worthy successors to The Byrds".

Nils Lofgren

I've had many of the world's greatest guitarists on the stage at Lancaster University but I don't think I've had any better than Nils Lofgren. However, as I own three of his solo albums, I would say that, wouldn't I?

After the first couple of years I rarely watched any whole performances, but I always tried to watch the intro, the first number, the last number and the encore. The feeling of anticipation and, at the end, the roar of appreciation, followed by that legendary Lancaster stomp, was what it was all about for me; the fan, not the businessman.

Well, Nils Lofgren produced the greatest final number ever. Across the front of the stage every week were the wedges, black boxes acting as sound monitors for the artists to hear themselves. Nils Lofgren had one monitor disguised – it was actually a mini trampoline. As he hit the final notes he raced across the stage, jumped into the 'monitor' and somersaulted backwards, still playing and just before he landed the lights cut out. There was no way he could follow that with another encore. We knew that was definitely the end – safely on with the house lights.

Barry Lucas

Just one of those, 'Wow what a bill!', 'Did it really happen?' nights. Throughout this book you will come across some amazing support acts, bands/artistes that are now superstars in their own right but I don't think you'll find two acts as good as this on the same Great Hall night – well in my highly subjective opinion. Tom Petty was a brilliant artist and his band gave outstanding concerts. He was a fabulous musician, much respected by all in the music business. He continued producing fantastic albums right up to his sad death in 2017 – do yourselves a favour, check out one of his last ones, 'Mojo'.

Both photos Nils Lofgren 1976 © Neil Yates

John Angus

Nothineverappens

5 February 1972

A giant disco in the Great Hall featuring the Yorkshire band Nothineverappens. Nothineverappens were a psychedelic rock/folk rock band from Kingston upon Hull.

Formed in the late 1960s and eventually disbanding in 1972, they were described as "Yorkshire's premier psychedelic band".

Nothineverappens were fronted by singer Mr Snips (aka Steve Parsons) who later went on to join Ginger Baker and his Baker Gurvitz Army, and also Sharks, with Andy Fraser and Chris Spedding. Nothineverappens also featured the keyboard player, Keith Hale, who later went on to play with the band Comus, subsequently joining Hawkwind as a replacement for Tim Blake, who had left during Hawkwind's *Levitation* tour of 1980. Together with drummer Ginger Baker, Hale left Hawkwind after a well-documented band bust up in 1981. Soon after leaving Hawkwind, Hale began to collaborate with Toyah Willcox, co-writing and co-producing her first album *Sheep Farming in Barnet*.

Her version of Hale's song 'It's a Mystery' reached No. 4 in the UK Singles Chart. Nothineverappens were previously brought along to Lancaster by Family to provide their support act in October 1970.

Orchestral Manoeuvres in the Dark

7 November 1981   **Architecture and Morality Tour**   Support: Random Hold

OMD, formed in 1978 by Andy McCluskey and Paul Humphries from the Wirral, are a synthpop group that had a brilliant knack of creating catchy singles.

Their visit to Lancaster was in support of the release of OMD's third album, *Architecture and Morality*, which is widely regarded as one of the greatest electronic albums of the 1980s. In addition to twelve studio albums, OMD had seven Top 10 singles in the UK charts, featuring hits such as 'Enola Gay', 'Electricity' and 'Locomotion'.

By the mid 90s, however, synthpop had become unfashionable and McCluskey dissolved the band in 1996, months after their last successful single, 'Walking on the Milky Way'.

In 1998 McCluskey formed and served as a principal songwriter for the band Atomic Kitten featuring Kerry Katona.

OMD were re-formed in 2006 by McCluskey, along with his original partner Paul Humphries, and featuring Martin Cooper on keyboards and saxophone. They continue to record and tour.

Random Hold were a five-piece British rock band active between 1977 and 1980 and signed to the Polydor label in 1979.

Andy McCluskey of OMD © Geoff Campbell

Paul McCartney and Wings

14 February 1972   No Support

It was on 10 April 1970 that The Beatles announced their split to the world.

Following his second solo album *Ram* in 1971, ex-Beatle Paul McCartney and his wife Linda formed Wings, which was intended to be a fully-fledged recording and touring band. Denny Laine, a former guitarist for the Moody Blues, and drummer Denny Seiwell joined the lineup, with Wings releasing their first album, *Wild Life*, in December 1971.

McCartney and Wings, which now featured former Grease Band guitarist Henry McCullough, spent 1972 as a working band, releasing three singles: the protest tune 'Give Ireland Back to the Irish', the reggae-fied 'Mary Had a Little Lamb' and the hard-rocking 'Hi Hi Hi'.

February 1972 saw Paul, Linda, the band and their three daughters set off from London for an impromptu tour of ten universities. Following visits to Nottingham, York, Hull, and Newcastle the band arrived in Lancaster for a Valentine's Day gig in the Great Hall.

Setlist (this is from Nottingham University five days earlier on 9 February 1972, but it would have been similar for the Great Hall gig): 'Lucille', 'Blue Moon of Kentucky', 'Seaside Woman', 'Some People Never Know', 'The Mess', 'Bip Bop', 'Say, Darling', 'Smile Away', 'My Love', 'Henry's Blues', 'Wild Life', 'Give Ireland Back to the Irish', 'Long Tall Sally'.

Great Hall 1972 © Sheryl Walmsley

Great Hall 1972 © Sheryl Walmsley

Macca on the Great Hall stage;
Photographer unknown

Around Christmas 1971 I was reading a three week series of articles in the *NME* about The Beatles. One of the main parts of the third week was an account of the problems the band faced, later in their career, playing live. After Shea Stadium it soon became obvious that The Beatles were simply too big to play live in any venue, in any town in the world. New York, the biggest city in the world (I know, not in terms of population but arguably in terms of stature) had had to shut down when The Beatles landed at their airport. Imagine that today, London, New York, Paris, Rome etc. CLOSING because a pop group was arriving! It's unimaginable to people under fifty reading that today but The Fab Four were just that important, that big, that the authorities could not control the media attention and the fans. That is why today, when I hear people saying a band are "the new Beatles", I just shake my head and smile.

Well, the article talked about an idea, a suggestion, by Paul that the band should just arrive at a small village hall, with just a few posters advertising them – e.g. 'Bert and the Beers' for a Saturday night dance. 50p (ten shillings) to get in. But those that chanced it would find themselves facing The Beatles. Ringo was up for it but John and George weren't. I thought it was a brilliant idea.

I had formed a great relationship with June Whyton over the previous few months. She was an agent of the old school and we got on really well, chatting about the state of the music business and indeed the world. She had booked John Mayall into Lancaster, and she understood, and had contacts with, those legendary acts from the '60s. I asked her if she knew – or more importantly could 'get to' – Paul McCartney.
I had an idea …

In a couple of months I had a Rag Week, culminating in a Rag Ball. What if Paul McCartney and the new band he had just put together, Wings, were to put in an unannounced appearance? I would make up a name, stick them third on the bill and the audience that turned up would see a Beatle and his new superstar band. June thought the idea was a runner and promised she would get it to Paul – that was great, you can never be certain in the music business that any idea or concept will ever find its way through the innumerable layers of management and representation that surround artists today. Here was a chance.

I heard nothing for several weeks, then on the Monday morning of Rag Week June phoned me just to say, "It's on!" This was almost impossible to grasp. I had started with The Who, and now The Beatles (well almost, you know what I mean).

I went to see Paula Richardson, who was in charge of Great Hall bookings. I'm not sure why, probably just to make certain nothing could stop Friday's Rag Ball happening. When I returned to my office Alan Murray was sitting with two strangers, long hair, jeans etc., you know the usual looking blokes in 1972. Alan announced, "Hey Barry, these guys say they're Paul McCartney's roadies and they're playing here tonight!"

Now, I had naturally assumed from June's message that 'the' date was, as I suggested, Friday's Rag Ball. But this was Monday. Wait a minute, this is Rag Week – jolly japes etc.

"Hang on, if you're the crew where are the band?"

"On some grass, near the hall," came the answer.

"Ok, let's see," I said, still unsure.

We all went over to the Great Hall. On the grass, by the Barbara Hepworth statue, was a group of people. A lady, cradling a baby, and some guys playing football. Suddenly, I could see Paul McCartney, Henry McCulloch and Denny Laine. Bloody hell, it's a Beatle! McCartney asked if it was OK to play tonight and of course I said yes but I would have to sort out the Great Hall porters. Sid and Mick were busy getting 900 chairs out of the cellar. Don't you just love architects? Employ ex-forces, fifty-plus year olds? Well let's put the chair store under the stage. Provide a Lift? No, just steps. Light plastic chairs? Nope, just big heavy wooden ones. Eventually after some ten years the University did put in some strange kind of Stannah stair lift contraption – in response to the half a dozen or so heart attacks I suppose.

Well Sid and Mick had put out around 300 chairs, complete with cast iron securing rods, when I burst in. "Stop! Sorry you two but there's a rock show on tonight." They were setting up for a classical music concert the next night so I received a very short response. "Piss off."

"No honestly, in a few minutes Paul McCartney will walk through those doors, he wants to play here tonight."

"Piss off, it's Rag Week," was the considered response.

"Look, honest …" I was interrupted by the appearance of Mr Paul McCartney.

"Hi, are you two the guys I'm giving heart attacks to?"

They were like putty in his hands. "What kind of music do you usually have on here?" Paul asked.

"Proper music, we have classical on tomorrow. Not your pop rubbish," replied Sid. So after a short discussion we decided to leave the seats that were up out but the rest of the hall would be empty. Now all I had to do was get an audience – five hours. OK. The thing that really upset me was that my regular audience, the ones that attended religiously week-in week-out, some 1000 plus, were scattered from Blackburn to Barrow. How could I let them know so that they could have a share in the reward that they deserved?

I phoned all the nine ticket agencies I had in the NW and asked them to stick up notices in their windows. I then borrowed a megaphone and proceeded to walk round campus announcing that tonight, for 50p, you can see Paul McCartney and Wings in the Great Hall. I was told on numerous occasions to "Piss off." I ended up pleading with people to believe me – honestly, it really was harder than you would think!

Now I had to sort out Bill Taylor, the Students' Union Executive member who had an event booked that evening in Bowland Refectory. I am indebted to Bill, now Sir William, who takes up the story:

"We had organised a disco with a semi-pro band, the lads came from Preston, one took the day off work and hired a van etc. We were paying them £40. I was 'avin' me tea in the refec. When you came through with a loud hailer and said, "Are you all coming to see Wings tonight, only 50p?" I told you to eff off. What the hell was going to happen to our gig?"

The next problem was Gray Austerberry, the Secretary of the Students' Union. He was from Normanton, a Yorkshire mining community, and this was the height of the miners' strike. Gray and I were good friends; he persuaded me, a couple of years later, to come out of retirement and take up rugby league again for the university team. He had helped organise the show in Bowland refectory, to raise money for the Miners' Strike Fund. "Who the bloody hell is going to come to Bowland refectory tonight with the fucking Beatles 100 yards away?" he moaned at me and then demanded to go down to the Great Hall and meet Mr McCartney. "Leave it with me, you'll get a crowd," Paul assured a rather skeptical miner's son.

I was talking to the leader of the band who played in the refectory that night and he told me a story …

Re-wind a few hours earlier. He had taken the afternoon off work to drive up to the university and set up the PA for the evening. In his words, "I arrived on the campus with no idea where I was going, where on earth Bowland refectory was. I parked up next to the Great Hall and saw some blokes playing football. I went to them and asked them if they knew where Bowland refectory was. They said that they weren't students and had no idea. I said that I needed to find the Social Secretary as I had a band and we were playing in Bowland that night. This Scouser said that they were also in a band, looking for a gig that night as well. So I said to him that if he wanted I would have a word with the Social Secretary and ask if they could support my band. Then the Scouser, in the big, baggy suit looked at me, smiled and said, "Thanks, that's really kind of you". I looked around at them. Suddenly I realized that Paul McCartney, Denny Laine and Henry McCullough etc. were grinning at me and Linda, with babe in arms, just winked. I felt about a foot high but they all thought it was hilarious."

Back to the main story now. Come the evening, my stewards had turned up; they didn't believe the rumours either and admired my attention to detail in bringing in a PA to complete the Rag stunt. "What do we do charge them, 50p to get in and £1 to get out?" they asked. "For fuck's sake it's Paul McCartney and Wings. Look at the PA."

"Struth, that's an elaborate stunt," they all agreed.

"Oh, bloody hell, never mind just man the doors!"

Well, 1100 not too hopeful people turned up, but unfortunately not, as I had planned, to see the first ever date on Wings because the band had played a couple of dates on the way up to us. It was a really memorable night, although the band didn't have a full set to play; they repeated 'Hippy Hippy Shake' and 'Roll Over Beethoven' three times I think.

At the end of the show, Paul McCartney explained to the audience that they had to finish as they had no more numbers to play. However, there was a great band, friends of theirs, playing in Bowland refectory after the show and he and the rest of the band would be going down. Well that meant Bill and Gray had to cope with approximately 1000 descending on them – serves 'em right for moaning!

Paul and the guys didn't go down as they were leaving in their minibus straight away. Rachel, Alan and I went to their bus with a brown paper bag full of £550, mostly coins, from the door. Except for some petrol money, Paul gave the rest back, telling us to put it in the miners' strike fund.

My outstanding memories of that crazy day? Just what a nice guy Paul McCartney was, and I also thought Linda was a terrific, a friendly person as well, totally unrecognisable from the picture painted at the time of a hard, driven business woman.

Band on the run indeed!

Barry Lucas

Paul Young and The Royal Family

14 October 1983 — Support: The Passion Puppets

Paul Young, from Luton Bedfordshire, was a former member of the band Q-Tips who dissolved in early 1982, allowing Young to pursue a solo career.

Before joining Q-Tips, Paul Young was the vocalist in an outfit called Streetband, who had a hit with the quirky song 'Toast' which peaked in the UK Singles Chart at No. 18 in November 1978.

Young is famous for his solo hit singles such as 'Love of the Common People', the 1983 No. 1 'Wherever I Lay My Hat', 'Come Back and Stay' and 'Every Time You Go Away' which all reached the top 10 in the UK Singles Chart.

The band came to Lancaster promoting the July 1983 release of his debut album *No Parlez*, the UK number one album that turned him into a household name.

Paul's backing band on the right comprised Ian Kewley, Laurie Latham, Mark Pinder and Pino Palladino, known as The Royal Family, along with two female backing singers, Kim Lesley and Maz Roberts, otherwise known as The Fabulous Wealthy Tarts.

In July 1985, Young appeared at Live Aid held at Wembley Stadium, London, performing the Band Aid hit 'Do They Know It's Christmas?'

Paul Young presently fronts a touring Tex-Mex band called Los Pacominos.

Formed in 1983 in Camden, London, **Passion Puppets** were a British new wave band that caught radio listeners with one clever single, 'Like Dust', on the Stiff label, before abruptly vanishing. Seemingly an ode to Italian Western films, 'Like Dust' was a cult hit on Canadian radio in 1984 and is better remembered than the group that actually performed it.

Paul Young had first performed at Lancaster in The Nuffield Theatre as part of that year's Graduation Ball, which in those days utilised the Great Hall, the Nuffield Theatre and Cartmel Refectory. He was lead singer with a band called Q-Tips. I went to watch the first number to see if they were going down OK – remember, there were approximately twelve bands on at a Grad Ball so I was only intending to see one quick number. But oh no I wasn't, I couldn't leave. The band were all right but the singer was something special. I spoke later, at about 3.00 am, to their manager and offered my opinion: "You have something amazing there, ditch the band, concentrate on the singer". Well …

In the summer of 1983 Paul Loasby had left Harvey Goldsmith's and set up his own, very successful (at that stage) promotions company, but Harvey was still putting the occasional act into Lancaster. He had phoned, wanting to do Wham! for Freshers' Week. Did I want it? Wham! were massive at that time and were playing Wembley among other arena dates on this tour. Of course I wanted it. So, Freshers' sorted, off I went on holiday to Guernsey.

I was just laying out my suitcase on the hotel bed when the room phone rang. It was Paul Loasby. Don't ask me how he knew I was there, I have no idea to this day. He wanted to put Paul Young into Lancaster … For Freshers'. "Sorry Paul, no can do, Harvey has just put in Wham!." Paul pulled every trick in the book; best mates, favours done, in a hole, promised date, everything he could think of. I had to blow Harvey out and give him the date, his very company depended upon it! Well mates are mates. Eventually persuaded, I called Harvey to say I couldn't get the hall that night and I put Paul Young on instead, hoping that Harvey wouldn't notice the tour schedule. To this day I'm not sure I did the right thing – Paul Young is a better singer but to have had George Michael (so to speak) …

On the night Loasby couldn't make it up for the show but he rang me to say that he had a great idea. 'Wherever I Lay My Hat' was No. 1, would I get a top hat, fill it with ice and a bottle of champagne and take it into Mr Young's dressing room? Ok Paul, but you're paying.

Barry Lucas

Pentangle

13 November 1970 Support: Amazing Blondel
1 December 1972 Supports: Wizz I C.O.B.

Pentangle are an electric folk band, first active from 1967 to 1973 with a lineup of Jacqui McShee (vocals), John Renbourn (vocals and guitar), Bert Jansch (vocals and guitar), Danny Thompson (double bass), and Terry Cox on drums.

Pentangle rapidly established itself as one of the earliest exponents of the British folk rock movement and became very successful, touring North America in 1968, playing at Carnegie Hall and the Newport Folk Festival. However, in addition to attracting fans of traditional British folk, they also drew audiences from the rock, pop and psychedelic folk worlds.

On New Year's Day 1973, Bert Jansch decided to leave the band. "Pentangle Split" was the front page headline of the first issue of *Melody Maker* of that year.

In 1994, McShee formed a new band named Jacqui McShee's Pentangle which, with a few personnel changes, is still performing today.

Support on the evening were **Amazing Blondel**, making their second visit to Lancaster following their gig with The Who earlier in the year.

Pentangle's second Great Hall concert featured **Wizz** Jones the English acoustic guitarist, singer and songwriter still performing today.

C.O.B. or Clive's Original Band featured Clive Palmer, former founder member of The Incredible String Band. Clive was an old friend of Wizz Jones, the pair having busked in Paris together in the mid '60s. COB split up in early 1973.

Clive Palmer's death on 23 November 2014 in Penzance, after a long illness, was announced by Wizz Jones, who referred to him as …

> "One of the finest musicians I have ever known … an inspiration and a well loved friend."

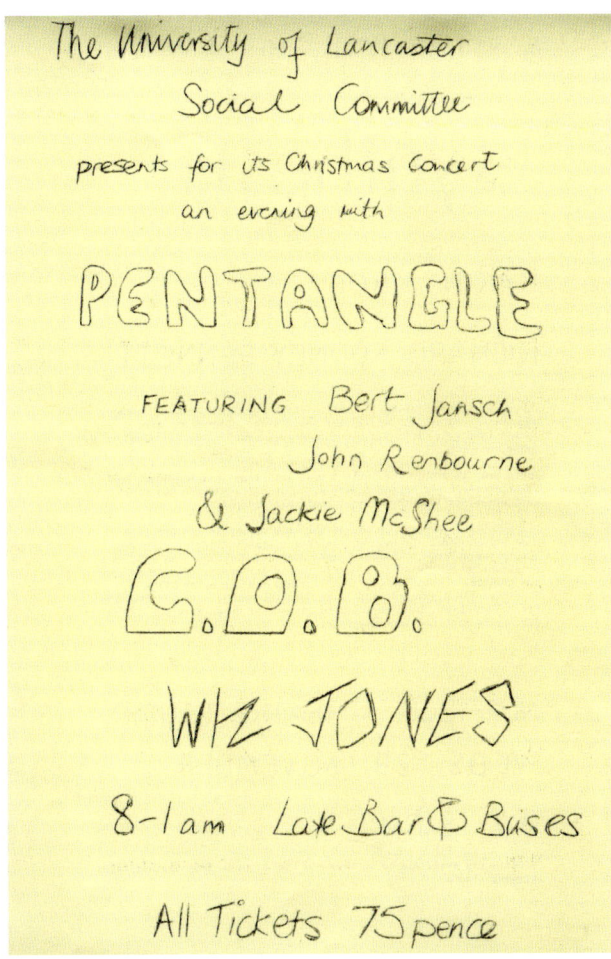

Peter Gabriel

25 August 1978	No support

Peter Brian Gabriel was the original lead singer and flautist of the progressive rock band Genesis. Following his departure in 1975 Gabriel went on to forge a successful solo career with the 1977 release of 'Solsbury Hill', his first single, which went to No. 13 in the UK Singles Chart.

Other notable singles from Gabriel included 'Games Without Frontiers' 'Sledgehammer' and the 1986 chart hit with Kate Bush 'Don't Give Up'.

His 1978 Great Hall concert promoted the release of his second eponymously titled solo album in June 1978, otherwise known as *Scratch*, which referred to the Hipgnosis album cover (Hipgnosis was an English art design group based in London that specialised in creating cover art for the albums of rock musicians and bands). The album was produced by Robert Fripp.

Lancaster setlist: 'On The Air', 'Moribund The Burgermeister', 'Modern Love', 'Flotsam And Jetsam', 'White Shadow', 'A Wonderful Day In A One-Way World', 'Humdrum', 'Waiting For The Big One', 'Band Intro/D.I.Y', 'Home Sweet Home', 'A Whiter Shade Of Pale', 'Here Comes The Flood', 'Slowburn', 'Mother Of Violence', 'I Don't Remember', 'Solsbury Hill', 'Perspective', 'The Lamb Lies Down On Broadway'.

University of Lancaster Student Union and Harvey Goldsmith Entertainments by arrangement with Tony Smith and Hit & Run

Present

Peter Gabriel in concert

FRIDAY, 25 AUGUST 1978 at 7.30 p.m.

in THE GREAT HALL

No 1485	Ticket £3

Once again I was offered a world superstar at an inconvenient time – the summer vacation. Since leaving Genesis, he had built a very successful solo career and been instrumental in setting up the highly acclaimed Womad Festival. He had such stature in the music world that I simply could not turn the date down, despite the fact that there would be no Lancaster University students around. It was a no-guarantee, door-percentage, so no money was at risk, so there was a certain profit for the Students' Union coffers. Anyway, I rationalised, there were plenty of students about – local schools and colleges as well as students returning for their own summer vacation from colleges around the country.

I'm not a great fan of Peter Gabriel so I can't really comment about the show. It wasn't a massive audience but that was just as well because I do definitely remember the first number. Mr Gabriel, in full theatrical dress, decided to enter, singing, with a radio microphone, from the back of the Great Hall at the foyer doors. He had to make his way through the audience to the stage. It wasn't as easy as it sounds, as people were continually refusing to let this guy through because they assumed he was just a punter trying to get to the front to get a closer view of Peter Gabriel. I eventually had to send stewards in to protect him and clear the way. As a way of arriving on stage for an opening number it isn't really recommended – put it this way, I can think of better.

Barry Lucas

Pink Floyd

7 May 1971 Support: Ron Geesin

The Pink Floyd, as they were billed, were formed in 1965 by students Nick Mason, Syd Barrett, Roger Waters and Richard Wright. David Gilmour joined the band in 1967 as the fifth member. They went on to be one of the biggest bands on the planet and one of the most commercially successful and influential groups in the history of popular music. The early Pink Floyd were very much the creation of Syd Barrett, the band's frontman on lead guitar and vocals. Barrett departed the band in 1968 due to mental health problems from excessive drug taking and died in 2006. In October 1970 Pink Floyd released the album *Atom Heart Mother*, which was orchestrated by their guest support act on the evening, Ron Geesin (note the misspelling in the concert ad).

Ronald Frederick Geesin is a Scottish musician and composer, noted for his quirky creations and novel applications of sound. In 1970 Geesin released *Music from The Body*, the soundtrack album to Roy Battersby's 1970 documentary film *The Body*, about human biology and narrated by Vanessa Redgrave and Frank Finlay. The music was composed in collaboration between Ron and his friend and golfing partner, Roger Waters.

I received this email from Ron Geesin in reply to a request for his memories around the gig:

Hello Paul.

No, I don't recall much of any gigs! The point is that they were designed as sub-conscious eruptions, so I left that part of my brain to deal with the situation when out on the stage. Obviously I had a palette [store] of modules that could be organised in many different ways on the spot. I do remember that Lancaster University was a particular appreciator of my cavortings, so I must have visited several times. My diary has no mention of PF for that day, but I played golf with Roger Waters the day before.

Best waves,

Ron Geesin

Copy of cashed cheque for the services of Pink Floyd

It was Friday 7 May 1971 and I was wandering down the Spine to the Great Hall, early afternoon. I was going with some trepidation, not because my finals were starting in three days time and I should have been revising, but because I was going to meet one of the biggest names in rock music.

Pink Floyd – even then a legend (probably even more so today) – were going to play the Great Hall that night. I was paying the unprecedented sum of £1500, a fee I was not to exceed as a guarantee for about seven years. I had been summoned by Sid Cooper, the Great Hall porter, to come to the hall because they had arrived and there seemed to be a problem.

The perfectionist nature of the band was already well known and for some reason they had arrived at the venue early for those days. It was only later in the '80s that roadies and artics used to arrive at 8.00 am, or even occasionally 7.00 am. This doesn't look good. Damn, I should be revising Anglo Saxon – actually there was no point really, I was never going to pass that one!

But what was wrong? I walked in the back of the hall and the guys were on the stage, arguing. What the hell was the problem? The stage was too small? The sloping roof over the stage was going to cause difficulties? The acoustics in the hall? Yes, that must be it – Floyd were all about their sound, the attention to detail, after all.

It was a sell-out, obviously. Would it go ahead? Would they cancel? Who would be blamed? I walked, with dread, up to the stage. What on earth could I do about the acoustics – rebuild the back wall before 7.30 pm, fly some acoustic mushrooms from the roof, like they had put up in The Royal Albert Hall to sort out their sound problems – where am I going to get mushrooms from on a Friday afternoon, Stanley's Fruit and Veg. stall in Lancaster Market? Don't think so.

"What's the problem?" I asked nervously, not really wanting to hear the answer.

"Oh, are you the Social Sec? Sorry, but we are having a slight disagreement. Two of us want to go back to London tonight to watch the FA Cup Final at home, but two of us want to stay in The Royal King's Arms tonight, have a few beers and watch the match in the hotel tomorrow afternoon."

Remember, in those days the Great Hall concerts, for some reason beyond my recall, went on until 1.00 or 2.00 am.

Bloody hell, they're human after all, arguing about watching the Cup Final! Brilliant, I could cope with that!

The PA was set up in a way I had never seen before or since in the Great Hall, whereby speakers were placed all around the floor of the hall, encasing the audience in the sound.

A fantastic night – I've still got the drum stick Nick Mason broke on the gigantic gong at the back of the stage. Of course the whole concert was made by our own in-house Pink Custard Light Show – exploding blobs of coloured ink, projected onto a backcloth of Lonsdale College's white bed sheets, borrowed for the evening. By now, the previously mentioned Maurice Hubbard (ex-Lonsdale College President) was a convert to the concept of the Great Hall concerts and was running a light show with Duncan.

As I'm writing this I'm playing 'Piper at the Gates of Dawn', part of a fourteen disc set of Floyd's that Paul Loasby (who will appear in several parts of this book) gave me for my sixtieth birthday. Little did I know that my best mate from the business and Leeds University Social Secretary for two years, main man at Harvey Goldsmith's and the most imaginative, innovative promoter ever, was to become Dave Gilmour's manager and later Dave Gilmour's son was to become a student at Lancaster Uni. Jane Silvester, of the Alumni Department, was showing them around the university and asked Dave if he could remember his gig in '71. He replied that he couldn't remember anything from those years.

Barry Lucas

Quite a fascinating little addendum to the Floyd occurred a couple of years ago. Paul and I were at Carnegie Publishing in the very early days of planning the book, my phone rang – naughty I hear you sigh, phone on in a meeting – but … it was Jane Sylvester from the University Alumni Office. 'You'll never guess who's sat in my office at this very moment?' It was a statement rather than a question, of course I couldn't even if I wanted to. 'Who?' I asked, trying to sound interested. 'Dave Gilmour and his wife. They are thinking of Dave's son coming to Lancaster University as a student next year and are here to look round.'

She said later that as she was taking them on a conducted tour of the Uni they were passing the Great Hall and so she said Floyd had played there in '71 and did he have any memories of the gig. '1970s? Can't remember anything that happened on the road in that decade,' he answered. Well the past was a foreign country…

Dave's son did choose Lancaster University…

John Angus

The Pirates

13 October 1978   Support: Blazer Blazer

Formed in 1959 and originally known as Johnny Kidd and The Pirates, the band scored numerous hit songs from the late 1950s to the early 1960s, including 'Shakin' All Over' and 'Please Don't Touch'.

Their stage act was theatrical and included full pirate costumes, complete with eye-patches and cutlasses.

'Shakin' All Over' reached No. 1 on the UK Singles Chart in August 1960 and has been covered by numerous bands, including Suzi Quattro, Cliff Richard and The Who, who would cover it on their 1970 album *Live at Leeds*.

Tragically Johnny Kidd died aged thirty in 1966, in a motor car accident on the A58 Bury New Road, Breightmet, Bolton, Lancashire.

Many years later in 1976, three former members of the band re-formed: drummer Frank Farley, bassist/singer Johnny Spence and guitarist Mick Green. Mick Green was famous for his unique "choppy-style" guitar playing (lead and rhythm at the same time) which influenced such great musicians as Wilko Johnson of Dr. Feelgood and Pete Townshend of The Who.

The band eventually split in 1983.

Rock band **Blazer Blazer** were formed in 1975 by two Canadians who came to the UK; guitarist Derek O'Neil, who had previously worked with the Pat Travers Band and vocalist Jeb Millington.

Completing Blazer Blazer's lineup up on the night were, Steve Barnacle, bass and Nicko McBrain on drums. McBrain joined Iron Maiden in 1982 to become their long serving drummer. Immediately following this Lancaster concert with The Pirates, the band embarked on a UK tour with AC/DC. They released the one single in 1979 on the Logo label, 'Cecil B Devine'.

The Pirates swashbuckling on the Great Hall stage © Geoff Campbell

Planxty

21 February 1975   Support: Steve Ashley

Formed in 1972, Irish folk rock band Planxty were one of the most influential bands in the history of Irish traditional music.

The original lineup consisted of Christy Moore (vocals, acoustic guitar, bodhrán) Andy Irvine (vocals, mandolin, mandola, bouzouki, hurdy-gurdy, harmonica), Dónal Lunny (bouzouki, guitars) and Liam O'Flynn (uilleann pipes, tin whistle). They quickly revolutionised and popularised Irish folk music, touring and recording to great acclaim.

Steve Ashley is a British singer-songwriter, recording artist, multi-instrumentalist, writer and graphic designer. Ashley is best known as a song writer and first gained public recognition for his work with his debut solo album *Stroll On.* He was a member of the short-lived Albion Country Band in the early 1970s. Steve Ashley the graphic designer was most probably responsible for the striking concert advert reproduced here. Steve Ashley still tours and performs, having released his tenth solo album in 2015.

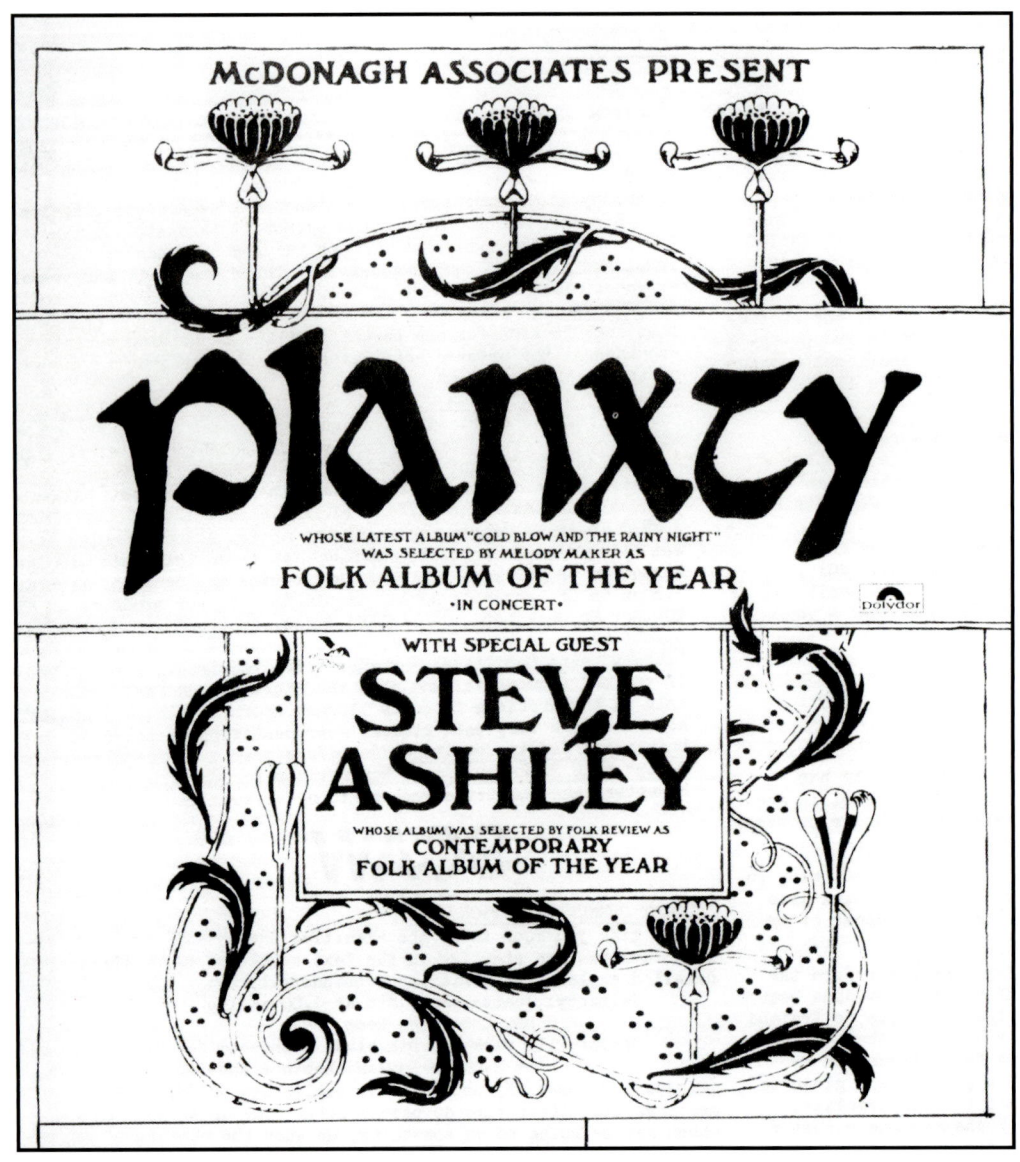

Prefab Sprout

4 May 1984   Support: Hurrah!

Prefab Sprout are an English pop band formed in 1976 in Witton Gilbert, County Durham, which rose to fame during the 1980s. Though critically acclaimed and considered by many to have released some of the best pop albums of the decade, the band never matched this acclaim with commercial success. Their biggest success came with the 1990 album *Jordan: The Comeback* (one of two albums produced by Thomas Dolby), which reached No. 7 in the UK album chart and was nominated for a BRIT award. The band also had a UK Top 10 hit with their 1988 song 'The King of Rock 'n' Roll'.

The band's best-known lineup comprised Paddy McAloon (vocals, guitar, keyboards), Wendy Smith (vocals, guitar, keyboard), Martin McAloon (bass) and Neil Conti (drums).

Hurrah! also hailing from the North East of England were a British jangle pop band, previously known as The Green Eyed Children. They were formed in the early 1980s and remained active until 1991.

They were a solid band from the '80s, without any major chart success, but they nevertheless attracted reasonable attention and audiences.

Paul Loasby, promoting on his own as PLP, had bought either the whole tour, or most of it, but he assured me that he wasn't too bothered about not getting the, usually most lucrative, London date because he had Newcastle, near to their home town, which he was obviously confident would do excellent business.

Well, Lancaster didn't, and when he arrived with the band he was unusually subdued.

"What's the matter, other than the fact you're losing money tonight?" I enquired.

"You bloody well wouldn't believe it," he explained, unwittingly doing his best Victor Meldrew impersonation, "I had the home town date but it wasn't selling tickets as well I had expected. I asked the local ticket agencies why not? They pointed out, rather pityingly, that the gig night was also Kevin Keegan's last appearance in a Newcastle United shirt. A god, saying farewell to his loyal followers … Who'd go to a rock 'n' roll gig on a night like that?"

The details you have to be aware of to be a music promoter.

Barry Lucas

The Pretenders

14 October 1980 Support: Moondogs

The Pretenders were formed in 1978 in Hereford and fronted by American singer songwriter, Chrissie Hynde. The band first came to prominence in 1979 with the release of their first single 'Stop Your Sobbing' during the punk and new wave movement of the late 1970s. Completing the lineup of the original band were Pete Farndon (bass), James Honeyman-Scott (guitars) and Martin Chambers (drums).

January 1980 saw the hit single 'Brass in Pocket' reach No. 1 in the UK Singles Chart. Tragically the band broke apart in 1983 as a result of the drug-related deaths of James Honeyman-Scott and Pete Farndon. Since then, numerous subsequent personnel changes have taken place over the years, with Hynde as the sole constant member.

In September 2012, as part of the entertainment lineup for the 2012 Singapore Grand Prix, The Pretenders re-grouped, with Hynde and Chambers from the original lineup, along with Nick Wilkinson, James Walbourne and Eric Heywood. Glastonbury 2017 saw the band appear on The Other Stage.

The Moondogs (alternatively known as just 'Moondogs') were a power pop trio from Derry in Northern Ireland that had some success in the late '70s and early '80s. They were made up of Gerry McCandless (guitar, vocals), Jackie Hamilton (bass) and Austin Barett (drums).

UNIVERSITY OF LANCASTER
Box office enquiries
Tel.: Lancaster 63352
TUESDAY OCTOBER 14
at 7.30 p.m. (Bar)
STRAIGHT MUSIC presents
PRETENDERS
№ 286
This portion to be retained
(PTO)

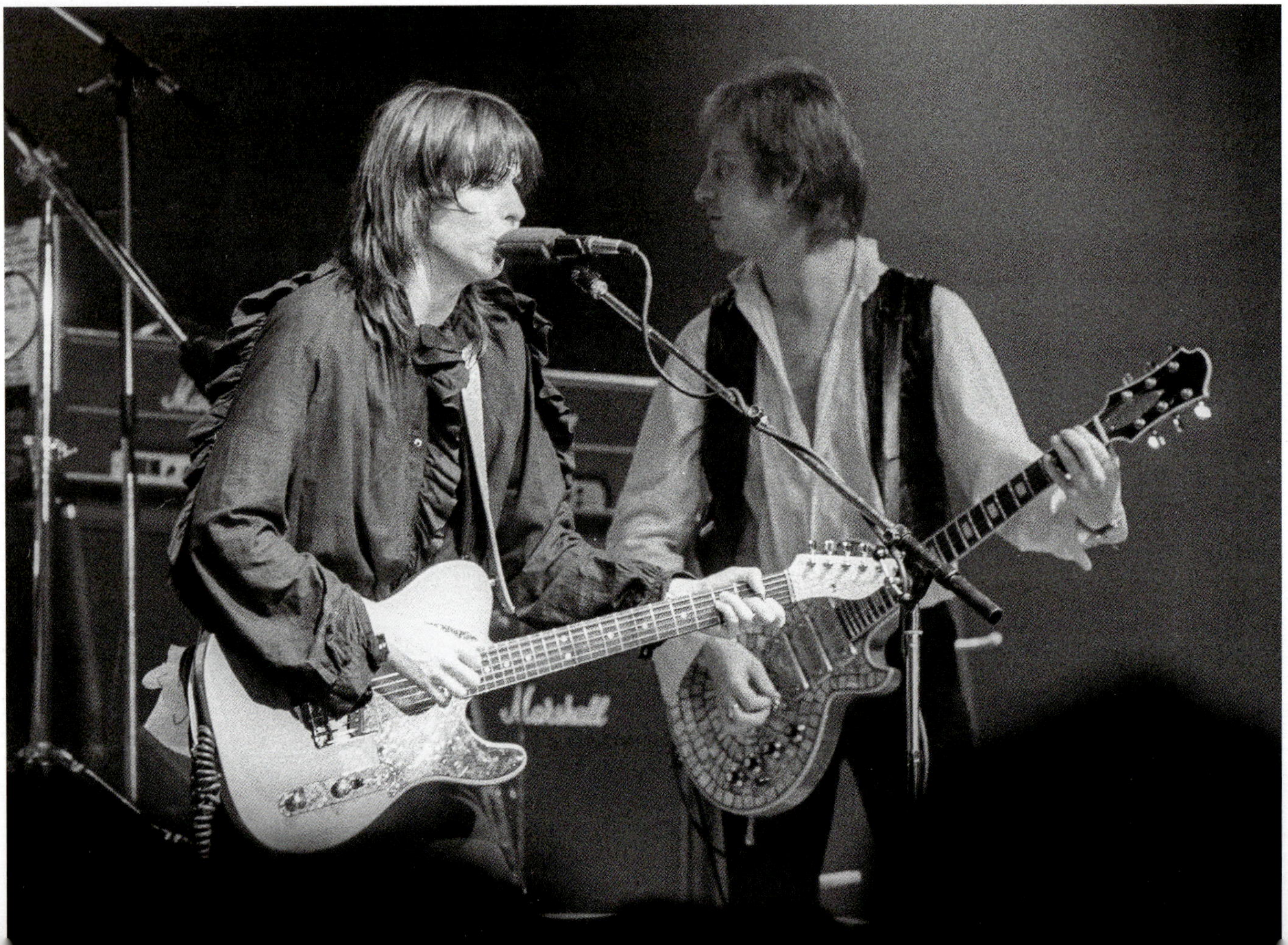

Chrissie Hynde and James Honeyman-Scott © Geoff Campbell

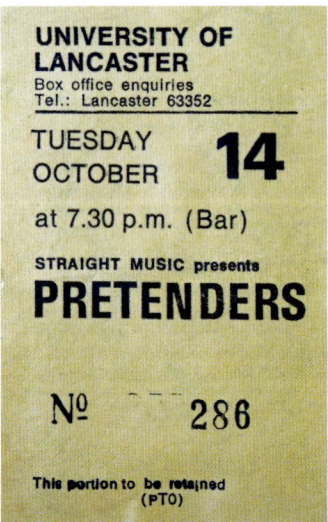

I was very disappointed when I saw The Pretenders' tour schedule for the Autumn of 1980. They were to play Blackpool Opera House on 14 October, a day that would have opened that year's Lancaster concert season after the Freshers' Ball. Phil McIntyre was promoting the show and, as a Preston lad and ex-Preston Polytechnic Social Secretary, he knew the area well. I was doing several shows with Phil so I phoned him to ask him how the Blackpool date was doing. "Bloody crap, on the floor," was his answer.

Chrissie and the band, crap sales, I couldn't believe it. Well I had no students, it was the end of August I think, so I said pull it and put it into Lancaster. I guarantee it will fly. 14 October; no real selling time but, I believed, no real problem either. I told him I could sell it out in a week. I like Phil, no nonsense, quick decisions. He agreed, it was done and it certainly flew when I put it on sale, remembering to keep some tickets back for the returning students this time (n.b. Free).

The band's tour manager (he might actually have been the manager) was very insistent that Chrissie would not tolerate any photography. If she saw anybody taking shots she would walk off the stage, simple as that. So I had to double up on the security into the hall and confiscate any cameras. Of course in the days before mobile phones it was an easier, but by no means straightforward, procedure.

Some of you will remember that occasionally we put the front lighting truss' legs on the floor at the corner of the stage, in order to create a larger, freer stage area. When we did this we put three 6ft tables, inverted, around them and a steward in each to stop the audience rocking the rig. We had to do this for this show. Geoff Campbell was my head of humpers by this point. Geoff is an outstanding photographer, as can be seen throughout this book. He started working for me on the concerts as part of the humping team, soon graduating to running the get-in and get-out. He was always taking photos of the shows and they were much admired and sought after in the music business. He became a member of the Students' Union staff, as my assistant, in '81 when we were in the process of expanding the entertainments by opening The Sugar House, a 1200-capacity nightclub in Lancaster. We were both extremely upset that we wouldn't have any shots of Chrissie Hynde but then I had a thought. I suggested to Geoff that if he went down to the stage left exit, and got in via the steward, he could get into the area around the lighting truss' legs and take some shots before anybody saw him. A plan! Geoff did just that. Chrissie saw him. Bollocks! She'll walk off the stage! But no, she smiled and acted up to the camera, posing, pouting, licking the fret of her bass guitar, brilliant photos! But the manager also saw Geoff. He couldn't cross the stage with the show in full swing so he tried to get across the front of the audience. Some hope – it was as full as only the Great Hall could be. The legendary 10ft golden shoe horns had been used that night. Geoff left it as long as he could, getting as many shots as possible. It was like a slow motion Hollywood thriller but it probably needed the band to break into The Keystone Cops music. Geoff made his escape in the nick of time. I denied any knowledge of his existence when I was quizzed later by the manager.

all © Geoff Campbell

After I left the University at the end of December 1984 Geoff continued to run the shows and The Sugar House. At least he did until July 1985, when he left to become the first professional Entertainments Manager at Exeter University, very much their gain and Lancaster's loss. He became a very successful promoter in that area and stayed until he retired in 2014. He had many years of success in Exeter, bringing major artists, using the experience he had accrued at Lancaster. Yet another Lancaster concerts success, taught him everything he knew, you know (!).

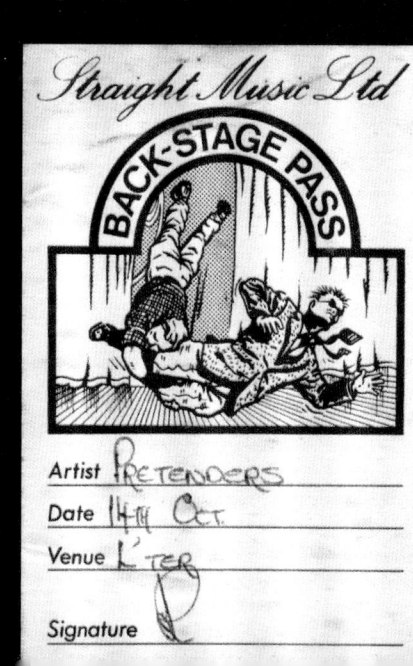

Barry Lucas

Procol Harum

24 April 1970 Supports: Skin Alley I Farm
19 March 1976 Support: John Miles

The English rock band Procol Harum were created in 1966 following the break-up of an Essex band called The Paramounts, that included singer and songwriter Gary Brooker and guitarist Robin Trower. Trower left the band in 1971 to pursue his solo career.

Procol Harum are best known for their chart topping hit of June 1967 'A Whiter Shade of Pale' which spent six weeks at the No. 1 slot in the UK charts. The band's name was created by Guy Stevens, their original manager, who named the band after a friend's Burmese cat. The cat's pedigree name was Procol Harun, Procol being the breeder's prefix. Stevens was also responsible for naming the Great Hall veterans, Mott The Hoople. Their name came from the title of a book Stevens read by the American novelist Willard Manus, whilst in jail serving time for a drugs offence.

Skin Alley were a British progressive rock band that existed from 1968 to 1974 and were founded by Thomas Crimble, who went on to have brief career as a bassist for Hawkwind. Skin Alley released four studio albums and also featured Nick Graham, an original member of Atomic Rooster with Vincent Crane and Carl Palmer.

The second of three 1970 support slot appearances for the band **Farm**, the others being three months earlier as guests of Deep Purple, and later in November of 1970 as support to Argent.

Geordie **John Miles** provided the support, on the back of UK chart success with his singles 'Highfly' (1975) and 'Music' (1976). John returned to Lancaster for two headlining concerts in the late 1970s.

Note the incorrect spelling above!

Courtesy of Ray Wilkinson Music Research Archive

Public Image Ltd

9 December 1983   Support: First Priority

Following the break up of the Sex Pistols in 1978 John Lydon formed PIL along with guitarist Keith Levene, bassist Jah Wobble and drummer Jim Walker.

As the years progressed, the PIL lineup would change, adding renowned drummer Martin Atkins in 1979.

PIL kept going as a Lydon project until 1992, when Lydon disbanded the group. Their final lineup consisted of Lydon, Ted Chau (guitar, keyboards), Mike Joyce of The Smiths (drums), John McGeoch of Magazine and Siouxsie and the Banshees (guitar) and Russell Webb (bass).

Notable UK charting singles from the band included 'Public Image', reaching No. 9 in 1978, and 'This Is Not a Love Song', achieving the No. 5 slot in 1983.

In September of 2009 Lydon re-formed PIL, seventeen years after the band's break up in 1992.

2015 saw the band release their 10th studio album, *What The World Needs Now*. They are still active today.

Support on the night was provided by Edinburgh punk outfit **First Priority**, who later went on to become The Crows.

"This photo, taken at a Public Image Ltd gig in December 1983, is one of those Cartier-Bresson 'decisive moments' for me. Definitely one of my better shots. I'd arrived late to the concert and had to rely on a long lens to shoot over the crowd, from the back of The Great Hall, but nevertheless managed to capture a menacingly angelic John Lydon."

© Dean Weston

Queen

9 November 1974   **Sheer Heart Attack Tour**   Support: Hustler

Following Queens' sensational 1973 support appearance for Mott The Hoople, the band were back in town, this time as headliners.

Earlier in May 1974 Queen were forced to cancel remaining dates on their Queen II tour as a result of guitarist Brian May contracting hepatitis in New York.

The band were soon back on the road and commenced their second tour as a headlining act, with nineteen concerts at eighteen different venues around the UK, including a date in Lancaster.

Queen's setlist contained much of the material from the soon to be released album *Sheer Heart Attack*.

Hustler were a London rock band that existed from 1974 to 1977, consisting of Steve Haynes (lead vocals), Mickey Llewely (guitar, backing vocals), Kenny Daughters (keyboards), Kenny "Tigger" Lyons (bass, backing vocals), Tony Beard (drums, 1974–76), and Henry Spinetti (drums, 1975–77).

They released two albums, *High Street* and *Play Loud*.

A *SCAN* newspaper concert review from 18 November 1974.

15 tons and what do you get?

Walking into the Great Hall last Friday night one couldn't help but notice the way the stage seemed to sag under the weight of Queen's fifteen tons of equipment. From the back of the hall, row upon row of lights looked down on a stage overflowing with speakers and amplifiers. Queen were certainly going to make themselves noticed. Sometime after 10 O'clock, they walked on to a darkened stage and began to play. As the volume increased and the lights began to flash, the audience prepared themselves for an amazing concert. What Queen lack in subtlety they more than make up for in sheer power. Unfortunately they seem unable to sustain and build on this power. As the evening wore on it became obvious that Queen were not going to live up to their early promise. Although they play well together, they seem to lack an ingredient essential to any good show. Instead of building up the excitement to a climax, the music becomes repetitive and the concert monotonous. Even the excellent lighting failed to prevent boredom from setting in. Despite the most impressive display of equipment ever seen in Lancaster the concert was a drag. Queen did demonstrate yet again that a band can only be as good as the people in it.

Steve Williams

OOPS STEVE!

This is the second gig that Queen played at Lancaster but they were paid rather more than the £40 they received the last time. By now Queen were BIG: a major tour, massive venues and … a university? Well, it was THE university. Mel Bush had put the date into Lancaster, as he was to do with Bad Company a month later. Paul Loasby was the Leeds University Social Secretary and he pleaded with me to speak to Mel and get him a date. I did try, honest I did, Paul, but Mel was having none of it. He had had a bad Leeds experience with David Bowie, so despite my entreaties, no chance. What a shame, another Lancaster triumph!

On the day, the road crew were having real problems with the PA. They had a terrible hum, which was usually caused by laying the sound and the light cables too close together. Easily solved. But nothing would solve this. For about two hours all the crew strove in vain to sort out the problem. It was starting to get critical. Eventually the head roadie just said, "Give up. Let's wait for the lads to get here".

Around 2.00 pm the band arrived. What to do? "No worries," said the lads as they all got their jackets off, tool kits out and got down to work – except for Freddie, too mundane by half for Freddie! I must probably explain here that all the rest of the band were science graduates and Brian May has a PhD in astro-physics. The problem was quickly solved.

Incidently, if I thought the first gig was good …

Barry Lucas

Ralph McTell

1 November 1974 — Support: Jack The Lad
6 March 1976 — Support: Prelude
25 February 1977 — Support: Magna Carta
27 April 1979 — Support: Bob Fox & Stu Luckley

Originally from Kent, folk singer Ralph McTell is best known for his 1974 Christmas hit song 'Streets of London'. First recorded in 1969 for McTell's album *Spiral Staircase*, McTell re-recorded 'Streets of London' with Lindisfarne bassist Rod Clements and backing vocalists Prelude.

The song was a million-seller, which gained him an Ivor Novello songwriting award in 1993.

With Ralph making his debut in 1968 he is now approaching fifty years as singer-songwriter and continues to record and perform.

Jack the Lad were a folk rock/electric folk group from northeast England, formed in 1973 and consisting of three former members of Lindisfarne.

Formed in 1970 from Gateshead, Tyne and Wear, **Prelude** are a vocal harmony folk band, with Brian Hume (vocals, guitar), his wife Irene Hume (vocals) and Ian Vardy (guitars, vocals). Prelude are best known for their a cappella version of the Neil Young song 'After the Gold Rush' which had a nine week stay in the UK Singles Chart of 1974, peaking at No. 21. The band returned to Lancaster in 1977 for a concert as guests of John Martyn. Prelude continues to tour today.

Magna Carta are a progressive rock group originally formed in London in April 1969 and still in existence today. The original lineup of the band was Chris Simpson (guitar, vocals), Lyell Tranter (guitar, vocals) and Glen Stuart (vocals). In the early '70s Tranter left the band, being replaced for a year by Davey Johnstone, Elton John's current long serving guitarist.

Bob Fox & Stu Luckley were a British folk duo. The pair recorded an album called *Nowt So Good'll Pass*. This album was enthusiastically greeted by the music press and won Folk Album of The Year in 1978. It still remains one of the most respected recordings in the genre. Bob, originally from Seaham in County Durham, has had a long solo career since 1982, specialising in traditional and contemporary songs of the North East.

Recently I met up with Tom Levitt, who had been Students' Union Secretary in 1973 and Labour MP for High Peak from 1997–2010. He told me of a rather unusual event at a Ralph McTell concert. He was employed as a steward in the Great Hall at the time and at one particular McTell show two 'Satan's Slaves', Lancaster's very own Hell's Angels chapter, decided to ensconce themselves on stage, either side of the mic stand. Not a pretty sight at any time, but at a folk concert?

Tom bravely decided that this was going to spoil the ambience of the evening somewhat and undertook to sort the situation on his own. He approached the two bikers, saying that Mr McTell would like them to vacate the stage before he came on. No response. So Tom decided to tell them that Barry Lucas wanted them to move. No response. Running out of options, Tom had to play his trump card, telling them that Edge (the Angels' leader) demanded that they move. They looked at each other and decided that discretion was indeed the better part of valour. To Tom's immense relief, they left the stage and went with him out of the hall. Who was the first person they met in the corridor? Edge, of course! Tom gulped. "Did you want us to get off the stage?" they asked Edge. Edge caught Tom's pleading look: "Yes, and stay off!" he said. Passing Tom, Edge whispered, "That's a pint you owe me".

Barry Lucas

The Ramones

2 February 1980   Support: The Boys

New York punk band The Ramones visited Lancaster six years after their formation in 1974.

All leather and winklepickers, the band had a major influence on the 1970s punk movement in both the United States and United Kingdom. With all of the band members adopting pseudonyms ending with the surname "Ramone", although none of them were actually related. Members Johnny, Joey, Dee Dee and Marky Ramone formed the lineup on the night, punching out numbers from the 1980 Phil Spector-produced album *End of The Century*.

They are best remembered for the singles 'Sheena Is a Punk Rocker', 'Rock n Roll High School' and 'Baby, I Love You'.

The Ramones finally disbanded in 1996.

The Boys are an English punk rock/power pop band formed in London in 1976. After recording four studio albums and eight singles, as well as recording under the name The Yobs, they disbanded in the summer of 1982. The band re-formed in 1999 and released a new album in 2014.

© Doug Price

© Geoff Campbell

February 1980 saw two shows in six days put into Lancaster by the legendary promoter, John Curd. I say legendary because, although not greatly known by the general public, in the music business he has seen it all, done it all. Starting as a school boy promoter in the early '60s with bands such as The High Numbers (later to be called The Who), he has been at the forefront of most rock genres, introducing many of the world's legends to the great British public. And more importantly he is a proper promoter, more of which I will tell you later.

The Ramones, the legendary American punk band, played Lancaster on 2 February. Believe it or not, even in these early days, bands were beginning to take massive entourages on tour. Instead of knocking up some sarnies, or getting a meal in one of the university's private dining rooms, off one of the refectories, now some bands were taking catering companies on the road with them. This was one of those early occasions. The tour manager asked if I could provide a dining room near to the Great Hall dressing rooms. I asked the porters for ideas.

"There's only the Music Department's rehearsal room," said Jack Nicholson.

"That'll do," I replied.

"But it's full of equipment and in use in the morning."

"No problem, these are musicians, they're not going to trash a music room, are they?"

Privately, I wasn't as sure as I sounded. But I elicited promises of good behaviour from the band's tour manager. The show went ahead, and a great one it was; one to say, "I was there when …"

So, John Curd, proper promoter. At the end of the night, as the audience was spilling out of the main entrance doors, I spotted two guys handing out flyers. Suspicious, I went out to challenge them. I didn't want rival promoters getting to my audience as the university roads were not public domain. I asked who they were, what were they doing? "Oh hi, I'm John Curd, are you Barry Lucas? I drove up here to leaflet for my date with Dave Edmund's Rockpile next weekend. Could be a cross-over audience".

So, he's driven up from London to Lancaster, a 500-mile round trip, to hand out flyers to all the exiting customers. Now that's proper promoting. Mike Lloyd, promoter/agent from Stoke, used to tell me, Harvey Goldsmith wasn't a real promoter, his bin man could sell out a Rolling Stones' tour, promoting was making 400 tickets into 600 for Budgie on a wet November Tuesday night in Hanley. Curd knows how to promote.

Next morning I was woken up by a phone call from Jack in the Great Hall. "You had better get down here quick, the Vice Chancellor is on the warpath!" I arrived to find The VC, Dennis McCaldin (head of the Music Department), and a couple of University House security men, congregated in the music rehearsal room, backstage near the Great Hall dressing rooms. Yes, you all know the one! Inside was not a pretty sight. "What on Earth was going on last night? Who gave you permission to use these facilities?" demanded the VC. Not wanting to drop Jack in it, I assumed responsibility; after all, as I explained, I had to have somewhere for the caterers, all major venues have this kind of space, it was expected etc. etc. "But look …" Dr McCaldin pointed to an seventeenth- or eighteenth-century harpsichord into which a powder fire extinguisher had been emptied. I couldn't think of an excuse, only bluff it out. "But how do you know this was anything to do with the band …?" I started to say. Then I looked up to the wall behind the VC. Plastered the length of it was the graffiti "Melodies are for puffs. Riffs are for men!" Oops, fair cop guv. "Sorry, send me the bill," was all I could meekly respond.

To be fair to John Curd, he was equally disgusted when I phoned him later. He told me to stop the cheque and deduct the damages. No argument. Can't say fairer etc.

Well, punk was about upsetting people, wasn't it?

Barry Lucas

I now have to make a very grovelling apology to The Ramones. For 30 plus years I have been telling that harpsichord story. Well …
On the night of the book launch in the Great Hall, Geoff Campbell and his wife, Ren (who also did 'the door' for several years), came up to me at the end of the evening. 'That story about the Ramones and the music room – it didn't happen,' Geoff announced as a bombshell.
'What do you mean, I've been telling that story for 30 years. I've told it on T.V. radio, in magazines, in newspapers, in pubs, at dinner parties … even on Radio 6 Music, though they did censor it!' I blustered.
'Well Ren pointed it out to me and I immediately recalled the night you were talking about. The Ramones were so nice, polite, courteous – they even emptied their own ashtrays so that they didn't create extra work for the cleaners. It was The Clash – Topper Headon, the drummer, what did it. I was backstage organising the get out when the band asked me to get Topper out – he'd trashed the room. Even The Clash were embarrassed by it. They told me to throw him on the bus. He was totally out of it and smaller than me so I obliged.' The Ramones and Clash gigs were only 9 days apart and age can play funny games with your memory but really … I know all four of the original band have sadly died but I hope if they are in that great rock 'n' roll super group in the sky, they can forgive me.
As for The Clash, it probably fits their image at the time better, so re-read the above story amending names as appropriate.

Ravi Shankar with Allah Rakah

31 October 1972

Ravi Shankar was an Indian musician, composer and master of the sitar, an instrument with between eighteen and twenty-one strings used in Indian classical music.

Ravi was George Harrison's sitar teacher, and a big influence on the Beatles and countless other bands while performing at the great '60s festivals such as Woodstock and Monterey.

In August 1971 George Harrison organised The Concert for Bangladesh at Madison Square Garden in New York City, in which Ravi Shankar participated. After his musicians had tuned up on stage for over a minute the crowd broke into applause, to which the amused Shankar responded: "If you like our tuning so much, I hope you will enjoy the playing more."

This Lancaster concert was billed as the only European university appearance; it was also the only UK appearance outside London during that European tour.

Ravi as always, was accompanied on stage by Alla Rahkar, his trusty tabla player. Alla, an exponent of Hindustani Classical music was an electric showman with his frenzied displays of percussive wizardry.

Ravi Shankar is the father of both Grammy Award-winning singer Norah Jones, and Anoushka Shankar, also a noted sitarist. He passed away in 2012 at the age of ninety-two.

Refugee

3 February 1973   Support: Darien Spirit

The band Refugee was assembled by former The Nice members bassist Lee Jackson and drummer Brian "Blinky" Davison, with the addition of Swiss ace virtuoso keyboardist Patrick Moraz, who later went on to join Yes from 1974 to 1976 and The Moody Blues from 1978 to 1990. The band played epic classically based rock music.

Refugee released the one self titled album on Charisma Records in 1974.

Darien Spirit were a three-piece folk rock band that included former Bonzo Dog Doo-Dah Band bassist, Dennis Cowan. They released only one album, *Elegy for Marilyn*, in 1973.

Ravi Shankar

The only university date in the UK for Ravi, which I thought was a real coup. Ravi Shankar had become the darling of the popular music world by this time, thanks to The Beatles and the darling of the liberal middle classes, thanks to The Concert for Bangladesh with George Harrison and a vast collection of concerned superstars. That box set sold in phenomenal numbers around the world and featured the brilliant, never-to-be-forgotten, moment when the whole American audience gave Mr Shankar a standing ovation, only to be interrupted by the legendary sitar player explaining that he had only been tuning up! Well at least nothing quite so embarrassing happened at Lancaster.

I had to find him a good hotel in the area – not an inconsiderable feat in the 1970s. The only place around here at the time was The Midland Hotel in Morecambe. Although not as good a hotel as it is now after its restoration, it was at least a proper hotel with a history and an imposing architecture. Alan Murray and I picked Ravi Shankar up from Lancaster railway station and took him in Alan's old Ford Consul to Morecambe. In his room Ravi was impressed, looking out of the window he said that it was just like Cannes. Alan and I looked at each other, suppressed giggles and agreed. But I know we were both wondering what kind of "cans" he meant. We left and arranged to pick him up at 6.00 pm.

Driving down Morecambe promenade, Mr Shankar was waxing lyrical about the beauty of Morecambe Bay while periodically winding down the window to spit large amounts of phlegm out. I could see that Alan was nervously watching to make sure that the window was wound fully down each time. By now Ravi couldn't decide whether it was Cannes or St Tropez that Morecambe most reminded him of. I could see Alan looking in the car mirror. "Just come back in bleeding February mate and let's see," we were both thinking.

Now to the concert. I must confess that the sitar leaves me a bit cold. I can appreciate the musicianship and the technical brilliance but one 'tune' – you know about twenty-five minutes – is usually enough for me, although I would later promote Ali Akbar Khan (known as Ustad – master), who was allegedly a better sitar player, in The Nuffield Theatre. In those days, for that type of show, the audience sat cross-legged, or more often, given the nature of the tobacco smoked, laid full-length on the Great Hall floor. Not for Ravi Shankar you didn't. The first thing he did after walking onto the stage was to tell the audience to sit up straight. Next, he proceeded to lecture them on posture. He then demanded they put out their cigarettes, tobacco was bad for them he insisted. I remember wondering how well that had gone down with Messrs Lennon and Harrison.

Life lesson given, on with the show.

Now, given the world status of Ravi Shankar at that time, and the fact that it was the only university date in Europe, it was obviously a sell-out wasn't it? Well, no it wasn't, for we only sold about 600 tickets. Why? Answers on a postcard to me please because I haven't the faintest idea; perhaps the audience was in Morecambe Bay watching the millionaires' yachts pull in from St Tropez to visit the £1 shops.

Barry Lucas

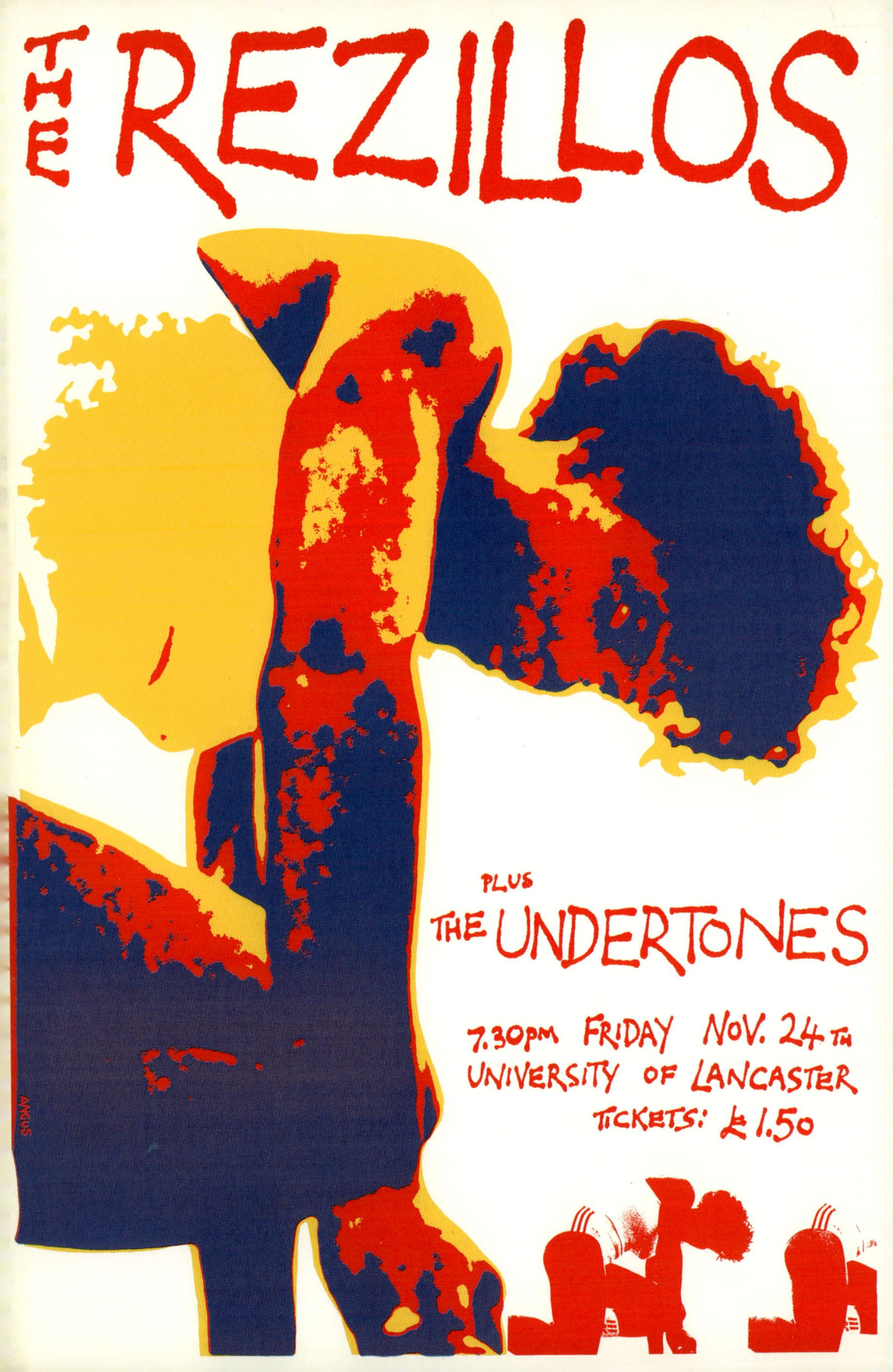
THE
REZILLOS
PLUS
THE UNDERTONES
7.30pm FRIDAY NOV. 24TH
UNIVERSITY OF LANCASTER
TICKETS: £1.50
ANGUS

The Rezillos

24 November 1978   Support: The Undertones

The Rezillos are a punk/new wave band, formed in Edinburgh in 1976 and are best known for their 1978 UK Top 20 hit 'Top of the Pops'.

The Rezillos originally consisted of Eugene Reynolds (vocals), Fay Fife (vocals), Jo Callis (guitar), William Mysterious (saxophone), Angel Patterson (drums), Hi-Fi Harris (guitar) and Dr D. K. Smythe on bass guitar.

This visit to the university promoted their 1978 album *Can't Stand the Rezillos*, released in July and reaching No. 16 in the UK Albums Chart.

Following the split of The Rezillos in 1979, the band morphed into The Revillos until 1996, then back again to be re-formed as The Rezillos. They continue to play live and record to the present day.

Another tremendous Lancaster support act on the evening was the Northern Irish band **The Undertones,** fresh from the release of their debut single 'Teenage Kicks' in June '78.

The Undertones returned to play the Great Hall in December 1980 as headliners.

The Rich Kids

3 February 1978   Support: Circus

Formed in 1977 by Glen Matlock, following his departure from the Sex Pistols, The Rich Kids also featured Midge Ure and Rusty Egan. Rusty later founded the band Visage, along with Mick Jones of The Clash, who featured as a live session player. The Rich Kids released the one album, *Ghosts of Princes in Towers*, and three singles during their short existence from March 1977 to December 1978.

Support on the night was provided by **Circus**, an American power pop band active in the early and mid '70s.

Richard and Linda Thompson

26 October 1974   Support unknown
24 October 1979   Support unknown

Following his departure from Fairport Convention in 1971, Richard Thompson teamed up with Linda Pettifer in 1972, forming their folk rock duo, and making two visits to Lancaster University as headliners, plus a visit providing support to Traffic, in April of 1974. The concert featured former Fairport Convention members Dave Pegg and Simon Nicol.

Richard and Linda were married in 1972 and together went on to release six albums between 1974s, *I Want to See the Bright Lights Tonight* and 1982s *Shoot Out the Lights*.

Following their divorce in 1982, both pursued solo careers.

© Geoff Campbell

John Angus

Robin Trower

7 February 1975   Support: Mandalaband

From 1967 to 1971 Robin Trower was the lead guitarist with Gary Brooker's Procol Harum.

Before launching his own eponymous band, he joined singer Frankie Miller, ex-Stone the Crows bassist/singer James Dewar, and former Jethro Tull drummer Clive Bunker to form the short-lived combo Jude. This outfit did not record and soon split up.

However, for his solo project Trower retained Dewar as his bassist, who took on lead vocals as well, and Trower then recruited drummer Reg Isidore (later replaced by Bill Lordan) to form the Robin Trower Band in 1973. Robin Trower's most famous album is *Bridge of Sighs* (1974).

Mandalaband were the 1970s creation of composer and producer David Rohl. The original band (Mandalaband I) was short-lived and produced only the one eponymous album.

The theme of the album was centered around the Tibetan resistance movement against Chinese occupation; however, Rohl, while chief engineer at Strawberry Recording Studios in Manchester, went on to record a second album, *The Eye of Wendor* (Mandalaband II), using the talents of many well-known musicians and vocalists, including Justin Hayward, Maddy Prior, Paul Young, all of 10cc and Barclay James Harvest.

Following a thirty-year break from music composition and production, Rohl reformed a new incarnation of Mandalaband and released the first album of a two-part progressive rock concept work, *BC – Ancestors*, in 2009, followed by its partner album, *AD – Sangreal*, in 2011.

For this visit to Lancaster Mandalaband consisted of David Rohl (piano), Vic Emerson (Hammond, Moog and Claviolines), Ashley Mulford (guitar), John Stimpson (bass), Tony Cresswell (drums) and Dave Durant (lead vocals).

I used to love Robin Trower – my kind of rock – but it was the threat of cancellation that made this gig stand out. Roadies are a peculiar breed; in the '70s they were mainly young guys on the road, different town every night, plenty of booze, drugs and girls. The associated glamour of rock 'n' roll meant that they basked in the reflected glory of the stars they were working for. When they hit the hall they were the show, at least for the five or six hours before the actual stars turned up, and then they, like Cinders, disappeared, no longer belles of the ball, just humpers and bumpers! But for those few hours, how they loved it and how they lorded it – perhaps not all of them, but in my experience the vast majority.

The day I had Robin Trower in the Great Hall (he had played the Lower Ashton Hall, with Nazareth, some years before) I knew we were going to lose money, a rare event for the Students' Union in those years. I think we were paying £750 but I had only sold about £500 worth of tickets, so add on the promotion costs and you can see I was about to lose a great deal; the 'walk-up' would never cover it. There I was in the porters' lodge of the Great Hall, trying to guesstimate how much that loss would be, so I was not in a good mood. In walked the band's head roadie, "Where's our beer?" he demanded. Now, there was nothing in the band's rider about beer for the road crew, just teas, coffees and sarnies. I pointed this out to him but to no avail. "We want two cases of lager and a case of beer or the show doesn't go on!"

Oh music to my ears on that particular day! I got up, reached down half a dozen Trower gig posters, turned them over and with my big, red marker pen started to write "Gig Cancelled". "What are you doing?" the now confused roadie asked.

"Well, you said no beers, no show, so, as I'm not providing any beers, I take it you're calling off the show. No problem. I'm just going to put these up around the hall's doors".

I reckoned that I would lose less with a cancelled show, especially if they cancelled it (no artist's fee), than if the show went ahead – so quids in! I wouldn't have wanted to cancel, too many people had travelled long distances for me to let that happen if I could possibly avoid it. But …

I could just see the realisation beginning to spread across the roadie's face. How was he going to tell Robin Trower when he arrived that a roadie had cancelled the show and the band wouldn't be paid that night – all because he didn't get any beer!

After a couple of minutes he slunk out of the office and the crew began unloading the van – sober!

Barry Lucas

Rockpile

8 February 1980   Support: The Fabulous Thunderbirds
17 October 1980   Support: Gary Myrick and The Figures

Making two visits in the same year, Rockpile were a short-lived yet influential British rock group that were founded in 1976. Rockpile were Dave Edmunds (vocals, guitar), Nick Lowe (vocals, bass guitar), Billy Bremner (vocals, guitar) and Terry Williams (drums).

Formed around the partnership of Lowe and Edmunds, the band took its name from the title of a 1972 album by Edmunds. Whilst Rockpile were primarily known as a backup group to those two artists' solo projects, Rockpile did release one official album titled *Seconds of Pleasure* in 1980, spawning the minor hit 'Teacher Teacher'. Rockpile broke up in 1981.

The Fabulous Thunderbirds are an American blues rock outfit from Austin Texas who are still performing today. Best known for their 1986 hit single 'Tuff Enuff' the band featured guitarist Jimmie Vaughan, the older brother of the late Texas blues guitar legend Stevie Ray Vaughan. The Fabulous Thunderbirds are still fronted by their original lead singer and harmonica player, Kim Wilson.

Texan blues rocker Gary Myrick formed his band **Gary Myrick and The Figures** in Los Angeles in 1980 and they are still touring and playing Texas blues at its best.

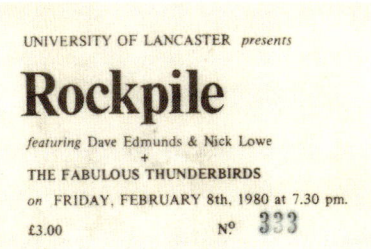

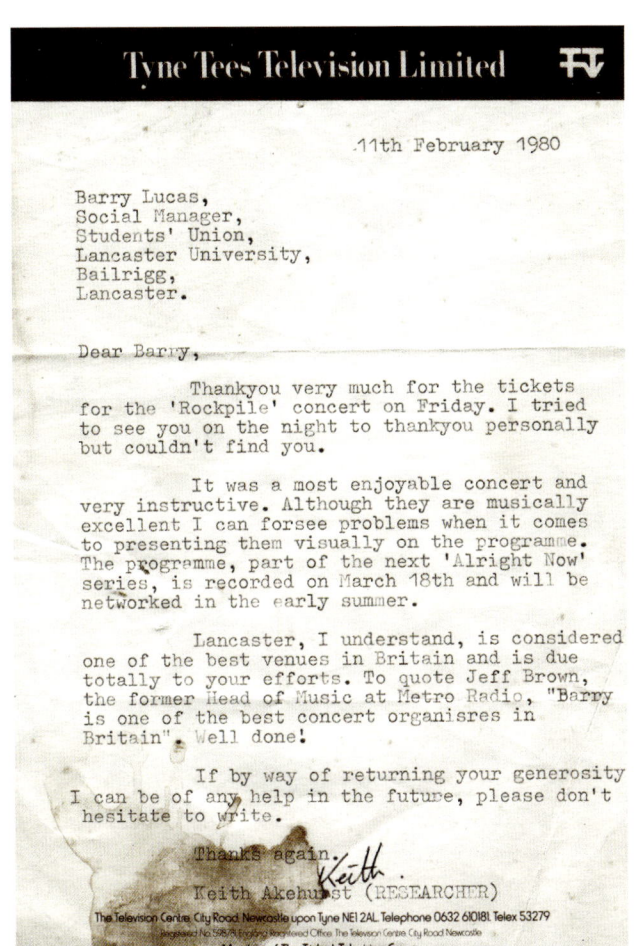

Rory Gallagher

3 December 1971	Support: Mick Abrahams Band
24 April 1975	Support: Jackie Lynton Band
28 January 1977	Support: Joe O'Donnell Band
29 November 1981	Support: Rage

Rory Gallagher graced the Great Hall stage with his famous battered sunburst-finish Fender Stratocaster for four classic Lancaster University concerts.

Born in Ballyshannon, County Donegal, Rory originally featured centre stage, with his blues band Taste, from 1966 to 1970, the band releasing a total of four albums (two studio and two live).

One classic performance from Taste came in 1970 as part of the Isle of Wight Festival, alongside Jimi Hendrix and The Who.

Taste were hailed as one of the best power rock blues bands of the day and supported Cream at their 1968 farewell concert in The Royal Albert Hall.

1971 saw Rory Gallagher start a band under his own name and assemble the musicians, with Wilgar Campbell on drums and his long-serving bassist Gerry McAvoy.

This was the lineup for Rory's first Lancaster gig in 1971, as ever dressed in his check shirt and blue jeans performing tracks from the recently released album *Deuce*.

Subsequently Campbell was replaced by Rod d'Ath on drums, and keyboardist Lou Martin was added to the outfit, forming the lineup for the next two concerts.

Prior to the 1981 concert, drummer d'Ath had been replaced by Brendan O'Neill and the keyboards had been dispensed with, effectively trimming the band back down to the original Taste three-piece power trio.

The 1970s were Gallagher's most prolific period. He produced ten albums in that decade, including two of them live: *Live in Europe* and *Irish Tour '74*.

Many modern guitarists such as The Edge, Johnny Marr of The Smiths and Joe Bonamassa have cited Rory Gallagher as an influence on their careers.

Tragically, Rory Gallagher died in June 1995 from complications following a liver transplant. In 2010 a bronze statue of Rory was unveiled in his birthplace of Ballyshannon.

Mick Abrahams is an English guitarist and was the original guitarist in Jethro Tull, performing on their 1968 album *This Was* before leaving the band. He went on to found the bands Blodwyn Pig and the Mick Abrahams Band.

The **Jackie Lynton Band** provided support for the 1975 concert. Jackie has been in the rock and blues business since the 1950s and continues to tour today.

The **Joe O'Donnell Band** is a Celtic rock outfit from Limerick, Eire. Joe is a classically trained violinist. He is still active with his current project, Joe O'Donnell's Shkayla.

Rage were a British heavy metal band active in the early eighties that emerged from the ashes of a band called Nutz. They recorded three studio albums before disbanding in 1984. Not to be confused with the German heavy metal band Rage who appeared as support to Marillion in 1984.

Simply the nicest guy I have ever met in rock 'n' roll. With his brother, Donal, who was his manager, head roadie and personal assistant all rolled into one, they made a great team and were so grounded. Donal would set the PA up and then take a chair into the middle of the hall and listen to Tchaikovsky full blast through it.

One of the greatest blues guitarists in UK history, in his two-hour sets he would send his band off for a well-earned rest while he did a half hour solo, acoustic numbers. He simply had no idea how to act out the superstar role.

Barry Lucas

above all © Geoff Campbell

© Geoff Campbell

Roxy Music

24 November 1972 Supports: Graphite I Slo' Dive Dancer

Formed in 1971 by lead vocalist and chief songwriter Bryan Ferry, Roxy Music made their first TV appearance on The Old Grey Whistle Test in June of 1972, quickly followed by the release of their first album, *Roxy Music.* The band visited Lancaster University in late 1972. Roxy Music were highly influential as pioneers of the more experimental, musically sophisticated elements of glam rock and significantly influenced early English punk music. The band attained popular and critical success in Europe and Australia during the 1970s and early 1980s.

Lancaster band lineup:
Bryan Ferry – vocals
Brian Eno – synthesizers
Andy Mackay – sax, oboe, keyboards
Phil Manzanera – guitars
Paul Thompson – drums

Possible Lancaster setlist: '2HB', 'Would You Believe?', 'Sea Breezes', 'Ladytron', 'If There Is Something', 'Re-make/Re-model', 'The Bob' (Medley), 'Virginia Plain'.

The band **Graphite** had previously appeared in the Great Hall as guests of Mott The Hoople in 1971.

All that is known about **Slo' Dive Dancer** is that they were a Lancaster band active in the early 1970s.

Roy Harper

12 November 1969 Support: Bridgit St John

An early concert by Mancunian Roy Harper, the English folk rock singer-songwriter and guitarist who has been a professional musician since 1964. Over his career Roy has released twenty-two studio albums and ten live albums.

His influence upon other musicians has been widely acknowledged by musicians such as Jimmy Page, Robert Plant, Pete Townshend, Kate Bush, Pink Floyd and Ian Anderson of Jethro Tull.

Bridget St John is an English folk singer-songwriter best known for three albums she recorded between 1969 and 1972 for John Peel's Dandelion record label.

Her second album, *Songs for the Gentle Man,* was produced by Ron Geesin who appeared as support to Pink Floyd's Great Hall performance of 1971.

Roy Harper

I've told my wife that I want a Roy Harper song at my funeral which might surprise those who know me and my love of heavy rock, but when I'm sitting in that pavilion in the sky I'd love to hear his, 'When an Old Cricketer Leaves the Crease'. Mind you she knows I then want The Doors, 'When The Music's Over.' Roy Harper appeared later at The Sugar House. It was a Sunday and he arrived early afternoon with his bicycle. He then spent about 2 hours riding round and round the club's main room singing away. That was his sound check. A strange man, brilliant but strange. But I can forgive him everything for that one song.

Barry Lucas

Roxy Music

Island Artists contacted me one day in June 1972. It was Alec Leslie, one of the directors of Island, asking me if I had a specific day in November free. I had but who was it for? There followed an intriguing and very revealing conversation. Read on if you want to know how the music industry really works …

They couldn't tell me the name of the band yet because that hadn't been finalised. I said that I couldn't give up a prime, early year date (remember the university term starts in October) for a band I hadn't heard of. I was told not to worry as the band didn't exist at the moment but all I needed to know was that the following was going to happen:

They would be a revolutionary band, playing a form of music not really heard before. They would have a fantastic frontman/singer. They would have an amazing first album before the tour began. The album would have great reviews. There would be articles in the music and national press. He then went on to name the papers, sometimes the actual journalists, and virtually told me what the articles would say – that's two or three months before they were written! TV would follow and the shows named. Record company reps would flood the local area's music stores with full window displays. All this before they had even performed a set. And a few weeks later I was told what the band's name was to be: Roxy Music.

It all came true, every promise, every word. It was a truly remarkable piece of marketing, from a standing start, unknown to super stardom, in four months.

The show was brilliant – of course it was written in the script. The band's manager was raving about the venue and the crowd. I said, "Thanks, but I know we'll never see you again, you're already too big".

"Oh no," he insisted, "we will always remember our early days, our roots, we'll always play Lancaster and Leeds".

I said thanks but I didn't believe him … and I was right, they never returned to Lancaster.

But as an interesting footnote, a few years later they did play Leeds after Paul Loasby, the then social secretary, gave them a staggering amount of money for two nights in Freshers' Week. It was, in some ways, a deal that was responsible for moving bands' fees to a new level. It was money that I couldn't have matched but I certainly wouldn't have paid it if I could. Paul and I had a few arguments about it but, at the end of the proverbial day, he was probably right. The shows would sell out, the prestige for Leeds was tremendous, his students were deliriously happy and he made a couple of 'bob', so where was the problem? But a problem had been created for nearly every other provincial promoter.

Barry Lucas

John Angus

Sad Café

20 January 1978   Support: China Street
24 January 1982   Support: Rocking Horse

Manchester band Sad Café visited Lancaster on two occasions, the first being prior to the September 1979 release of the bands best known single 'Every Day Hurts' which reached No. 3 in the UK Singles Chart.

The original lineup of Sad Café included Wythenshawe vocalist Paul Young, guitarists Ian Wilson and Ashley Mulford, bassist John Stimpson, Vic Emerson (keyboards), Tony Creswell (drums) and Lenni (saxophone).

Frontman Paul Young went on to achieve greater chart success as the co-lead singer (with Paul Carrack) of Mike + The Mechanics.

Lancaster band **China Street** provided support for their 1978 gig.

Little is known about the 1982 support act **Rocking Horse**.

Sammy Hagar

6 February 1982   Support: Grand Prix

Rock vocalist and guitarist Samuel Roy "Sammy" Hagar, also known as "The Red Rocker", hails from California and first came to prominence as the lead singer and guitarist of the 1970s band Montrose. He subsequently went on to pursue a solo career, scoring a hit in 1984 with the single 'I Can't Drive 55', a reference to the US road speed limit.

He also went on to enjoy huge commercial success when he replaced David Lee Roth as the lead singer of Van Halen in 1985, but left the band in 1996.

His present musical project is as lead singer of a band called Chickenfoot.

Grand Prix were a new wave of british heavy metal band that released three albums during the 1980s, the best being the 1983 album *Samurai,* on the Chrysalis label. Their softer approach to heavy metal earned them comparisons to the American band Journey.

This was in the early days of the fitness 'fads' – there were certainly very few rock 'n' roll icons pumping iron in the gym, or rather there were none who admitted to it! Sammy Hagar was different; his stage show was so dynamic, his lycra-clad body thrown around the stage so enthusiastically, that he had to be extremely fit. And he was. I had heard the rumours of his five-mile dawn runs every day but I didn't really believe it. I should have done because that is what he did. However, not many of the band joined him running in the morning after the show the night before.

Barry Lucas

Lancaster University Student Union in Association with Kiltorch
Presents
Sammy Hagar
+ GUESTS
SATURDAY FEBRUARY 6th 1982   7.30 p.m.
No. 025   £4.00

Scorpions

12 October 1980 — Support: Blackfoot

Best known for their 1984 anthem 'Rock You Like a Hurricane' and the 1991 ballad 'Wind of Change', German rockers Scorpions were formed in Hanover Germany by Rudolf Schenker in 1965. They are one of the most successful rock bands to come out of continental Europe, with sales of over 200 million records worldwide. The band's debut album *Lonesome Crow* was recorded and released in 1972. The band also included Rudolf's younger guitarist brother Michael, who eventually left Scorpions in 1973 to join up with UFO. Their 1991 single 'Wind of Change' was taken from the band's eleventh studio album *Crazy World* and was an anthem for the political changes in the late 1980s and early 1990s and the fall of the Berlin Wall. It was a worldwide hit reaching No. 4 in the US Singles Chart and No. 2 in the UK charts. According to accounts, the volume level on the night severely tested the structural integrity of the Great Hall's foundations. The band are still very active today with lead singer Klaus Meine still up front and Rudolf Schenker on guitar. 2015 saw Scorpions release their eighteenth studio album, *Return To Forever*.

Lancaster band lineup:
Klaus Meine – vocals
Rudolf Schenker – rhythm guitar
Matthias Jabs – lead guitar
Francis Buchholz – bass guitar
Herman Rarebell – drums

Blackfoot are a southern rock band from Jacksonville, Florida. They were formed in 1972 and were contemporaries of Lynyrd Skynyrd, but with a harder rock sound, and are still active today.

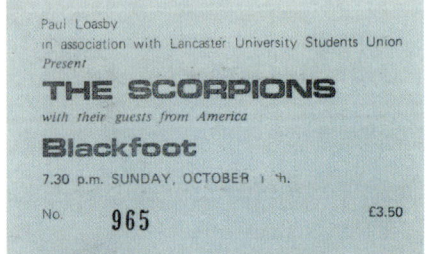

Scorpions do not travel lightly © Geoff Campbell

Klaus Meine of Scorpions © Geoff Campbell

This is one of my favourite photos from the Great Hall shows. My poor Scottish head of stewards, Gordon Findley, pinned in front of the stage apron. It captures the glory and atmosphere of the concerts at Lancaster University's Great Hall.

Four articulated lorries arrived at 8.00 am on the morning of the show – we had only been able to unload three as we just couldn't get any more gear into the hall. The PA was stacked on the floor of the hall, not the stage and it reached up to the goldfish bowl lights on the balcony! Wow, was it loud.

Barry Lucas

Scorpions both © Geoff Campbell

The Selecter

23 February 1980
30 January 1981 — **Celebrate The Bullet Tour**

Supports: Holly and The Italians I The Bodysnatchers
Support: The Pharaohs

The Selecter are a 2 Tone British ska revival band from Coventry, formed in the late 1970s, and were one of the essential bands of the British ska movement, fronted by the enigmatic "Rude Girl" Pauline Black, adding her unique voice to the band's edgy, politically themed sound.

The band's name refers to the Jamaican word for a disc jockey. The band were one of the most successful ska bands of the 2 Tone era, notching up several top forty singles in the British charts, including 'Three Minute Hero' and 'On My Radio' which peaked at No. 8 in the UK Singles Chart.

Their first Great Hall appearance as a headline band saw The Selecter perform tracks from the upcoming February 1980 release of their debut album *Too Much Pressure* on the 2 Tone/Chrysalis label. The album achieved a No 5 slot in the UK Album Chart.

Late 1980 had seen the departure of two Selecter band members, Desmond Brown (keyboards) and Charley Anderson (bass guitar). Their replacements were former Pharaoh keyboard player James Mackie and ex-China Street bassist Adam Williams. James and Adam featured on stage in the Great Hall with The Selecter for this 1981 Celebrate The Bullet Tour concert.

Following the 1982 split of The Selecter, James went on to join Madness for a year as their touring keyboard player. Although not directly involved in the recording studio, during his spell with the band James toured extensively as a live musician and made many TV appearances with Madness including NBC's prime time US show Saturday Night Live; with an audience of 60 million people.

Madness performed live, their 1982 hit single 'Our House'.

Holly and the Italians were a short-lived American new wave band that were formed in Los Angeles, California, in 1978 by Chicago-born singer and guitarist Holly Beth Vincent, bassist Mark Sidgwick and drummer Steve Young. The band gained popularity during regular opening slots for fellow Americans Blondie.

The Bodysnatchers were an all-female, seven-piece British 2 Tone ska revival band of the late 1970s and early 1980s. The Bodysnatchers released two singles on the 2 Tone label, playing together for less than two years, before the group disbanded in 1981, not having released an album.

The Pharaohs, were a ska band from the Morecambe and Lancaster area, formed by ex-China Street bassist Adam Williams in April 1979. The original lineup was; Tommy Smurthwaite (vocals), Adam Williams (bass), Neil Gowland (guitar), James Mackie (tenor Sax/keyboards), Paul Boardman (trombone), Phil Boardman (trumpet), Dusty Hall (alto sax) and Bernie Kelly (drums). The Pharaohs released two singles on the El Topo label recorded at Boss Studios in Lancaster and were produced by Adam Williams. 'J'ai Beacoups De Vous', B side 'Pharaohs' Stomp' and a second single; a cover version of Wilson Pickett's 'In The Midnight Hour'. In 1980 James Mackie and Adam, moved on to join The Selecter.

James Mackie on stage with The Selecter in 1981 © Geoff Campbell

Pauline Black and Arthur 'Gaps' Hendrickson of The Selecter in 1980 © Geoff Campbell

Pauline Black and
Adam Williams of
The Selecter in 1981
© Geoff Campbell

The Sensational Alex Harvey Band

11 October 1974   Support: Slack Alice
5 February 1977   Support: Bandit

The Sensational Alex Harvey Band were formed in 1972 by Alexander James "Alex" Harvey.

In 1972 Alex joined forces with a Scottish band of up and coming rockers called Tear Gas. This new band, with Alex at the helm, changed their name to The Sensational Alex Harvey Band. The band's shows were noted for their theatrical content and idiosyncratic style of delivery.

The band consisted of guitarist Zal Cleminson, bassist Chris Glen and cousins Hugh and Ted McKenna on keyboards and drums respectively.

The Sensational Alex Harvey Band had Top 40 hits in Britain with the single 'Delilah', a cover version of the Tom Jones hit, which was a UK No. 7 in 1975, and also with 'The Boston Tea Party' in June 1976.

As SAHB the band released a total of seven studio albums, plus their tremendous 1975 Live album.

Possible Lancaster setlist: 'Faith Healer', 'Action Strasse', 'Tomahawk Kid', 'Give My Compliments To The Chef', 'Delilah', 'The Tale Of The Giant Stone Eater', 'Vambo', 'Midnight Moses', 'Dance To The Music', 'Tomorrow Belongs To Me', 'Gang Bang', 'Framed'.

The second visit to Lancaster saw the band billed as SAHB, without Alex due to Harvey's retirement in late 1976 with back problems. This concert featured tracks mainly from the album Fourplay, released in January 1977 and the first to be recorded without Alex Harvey.

Lancaster setlist: 'Smoldering', 'Chase It Into The Night', 'Jungle Rub Out', 'Big Boy', 'Outer Boogie', 'Love You For a Lifetime', 'Young and Rich', 'Stay', 'Pick It Up and Kick It', 'Too Much American Pie', 'Theme From King Kong'. Encore: 'Zal's Riff'.

The band were later to join up with Alex once again, releasing the album Rock Drill, but alas splitting for good shortly afterwards.

Alex Harvey passed away in 1982 following a massive heart attack while waiting for a ferry at the Belgian port of Zeebrugge.

Slack Alice are a British blues band formed in 1973 by singer-songwriter Cliff Stocker and are still active on the blues scene today.

Bandit were a British rock band that existed from 1976 to 1979. Bandit returned to Lancaster to provide support for John Miles in April 1979.

Shakin' Stevens and The Sunsets

8 December 1970   Supports: The Kaycee Jazz Men | George Matthews Allstars Steel Band

Shakin' Stevens, otherwise known as Michael Barratt, or just plain "Shaky" is a platinum-selling Welsh rock 'n' roll singer and songwriter who was the UK's biggest-selling singles artist of the 1980s.

In the UK alone, Stevens has charted 33 Top 40 hit singles, including four chart topping hits with 'This Ole House', 'Green Door', 'Oh Julie' and 'Merry Christmas Everyone', which has re-entered the UK Top 40 each December since 2007.

February 1971 saw him make a return visit to Lancaster, to do his stuff for a Rag Ball, with The Kinks headlining the concert.

Little is known about the undercard entertainment on the evening.

Sharks

9 February 1973   Supports: Mike Absalom | Jo Anne Kelly's Spare Rib

Sharks were assembled in September 1972 by Andy Fraser following his departure from Free and were immediately signed to Island Records.

The band played Lancaster in support of the upcoming release of their debut album, *First Water*.

The lineup was:
Andy Fraser – bass, piano
Mr Snips (real name Steve Parsons) – vocals
Chris Spedding – guitars
Marty Simon (an American) – drums

Lead singer Snips had previously fronted the Hull band Nothineverappens and landed the Sharks job following auditions that also saw Leo Sayer and Robert Palmer applying for the gig.

Interestingly, Chris Spedding, who was probably best known for his only charting 1975 single 'Motor Bikin', was a member of Mike Batt's novelty band, The Wombles, from 1972 to 1976. Spedding appeared in live Wombles concerts costumed as the character Wellington, playing his Gibson Flying V.

Sharks released one more album, *Jab It In Your Eye*, in March 1974 before folding in October that same year.

Mike Absalom is an English pop, folk and Celtic music singer, guitarist, songwriter, harpist, poet, artist and children's entertainer who is still active today.

Jo Ann Kelly the legendary English blues singer and sister of Dave Kelly who currently performs with the Paul Jones Blues Band, made her first Great Hall appearance. She returned to Lancaster three years later as a guest of the Climax Blues Band.

Courtesy Alan Leak

Siouxsie and The Banshees

8 August 1981   **Juju Tour**   Support unknown

Siouxsie and The Banshees were formed in 1976 by John McKay (guitar), Kenny Morris (drums), Siouxsie Sioux, real name Susan Janet Ballion (vocals) and Steve Severin (bass).

During their active years from 1978 to 1989 other band members included Peter "Budgie" Clark from The Slits (drums), John McGeoch, formerly of the band Magazine (guitars), John Valentine Carruthers (guitar) and The Cure frontman Robert Smith (guitars and vocals).

The band played Lancaster in support of the album *Juju*, later peaking at No. 7 in the UK Album Chart and becoming one of their biggest sellers

By all accounts this was a legendary Great Hall concert for those lucky enough to have witnessed it.

Siouxsie and the Banshees released eleven studio albums and several UK Top 20 singles, including 'Hong Kong Garden', 'Happy House' and 'Peek-a-Boo', plus a US Billboard Top 25 hit 'Kiss Them for Me'.

Lancaster setlist: 'Israel', 'Halloween', 'Paradise Place', 'Spellbound', 'Placebo Effect', 'Tenant', 'Night Shift', 'Sin In My Heart, 'Voodoo Dolly', 'The Staircase (Mystery)', 'Head Cut', 'Arabian Knights', 'Eve White/Eve Black', 'Happy House', 'Helter Skelter', 'Skin', 'Love In A Void'.

© Geoff Campbell

Siouxsie and The Banshees

Punk was at its height when I was offered Siouxsie and The Banshees, and at the time she was arguably the hottest punk act. The only problem was that it was in August when there were no students on campus, but by then the concerts were seen as an income-generating business for the SU so I had no difficulty justifying the event.

I'd had some problems with violence at the smaller punk shows, where you could still swing a punch or a boot, but I felt quite confident that a gig this big would go off without any such incidents.

On that August day, however, I saw 1800 or so punks queued up outside and I had a feeling of slight disquiet. Just then the heavens opened – I told the porters I was going to hold the doors for about half an hour and they were to put on the hall's heating at full blast.

"But it's August, about sixty degrees, what do you want the heating on for?"

"Trust me, just do it."

The audience streamed in, punks wringing out their Mohicans like paint brushes. Once inside the heat did its work – it was like a sauna, steam filling the hall. Ever tried fighting in a sauna? No? No one tried it on this occasion either, and it was a great show and a quiet night.

PS. A further little story about Siouxsie happened in the late '80s when I was running, for three months, a large 6000-capacity tent in Finsbury Park. One of the shows in there that summer was Siouxsie and The Banshees. The promoter rang me the week before the show to say that Siouxsie was very anxious that she had a clean, upmarket toilet near her dressing room, for her exclusive use. Not an unreasonable request for the headline act, I thought. So I duly ordered one. It came on the Tuesday for the Saturday show – big mistake.

The site crew had been using the designated staff Portaloos for about six weeks and by then there was evidence of life forms unknown to the scientific world appearing out of various cracks and orifices in those strange, plastic sentry boxes. Worried about the possible effects of these alien organisms on the more delicate areas of the human body, the crew managed to discover a way of entering the executive loo and using it for five days. I was unaware of this, but on Saturday afternoon I was to discover the horrendous truth.

Siouxsie's manager came running up to me: "What the bloody hell are you doing? We had to have a toilet for Siouxsie's exclusive use. A top of the range facility!" he screamed.

"But you have, it's there," I, rather smugly, pointed out. However he then opened the toilet door. "She can't use this, she's going ballistic, and she says it's a shit house!"

I tried to keep a straight face as I replied, "Well actually that's …"

"I know, I know, that's what it is," he said breaking into a grin, even he could see the joke, although I did have to bring in, at considerable expense, an emergency cleaning company.

Barry Lucas   all © Geoff Campbell

The Sisters of Mercy

7 October 1984　　**First and Last and Always Tour**　　Support: Skeletal Family

Formed in Leeds in 1980 by Andrew Eldritch (vocals, drums) and Gary Marx (guitar), The Sisters of Mercy are one of England's leading Goth bands of the 1980s and took their name from a Leonard Cohen song.

The band soon released their debut single, 'The Damage Done' in 1980 on their own independent record label, Merciful Release, going on to release three studio albums and sixteen singles; the best known being 'The Temple of Love' reaching No.3 in the UK singles chart of 1992.

The band visited Lancaster in March 1985 in support of the release of their debut studio album, *First and Last and Always*.

The Sisters of Mercy continue to perform live.

Skeletal Family were an English gothic rock band formed in Keighley, West Yorkshire, in December 1982. The group signed with Chrysalis Records and released two 1986 singles, 'Restless' and 'Just a Minute'.

Slade

6 March 1981　　Support: Export
15 December 1983　　Support: Raid The North!

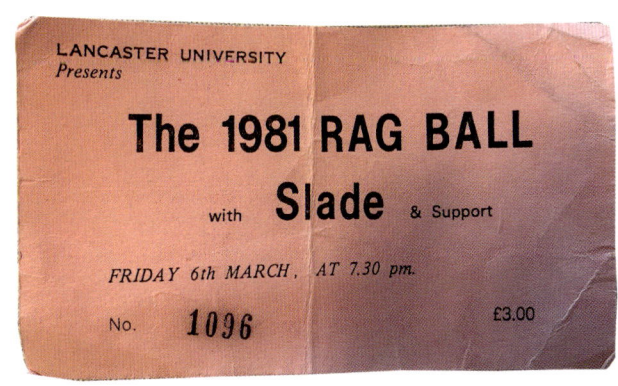

Originally known as Ambrose Slade, Slade are an English glam rock band from the Black Country in the West Midlands. They rose to prominence during the early 1970s with seventeen consecutive Top 20 hits and six No. 1s. *British Hit Singles & Albums* names them as the most successful British group of the 1970s based on sales of singles. They were the first act to have three singles entering at No. 1. All six of the band's chart-toppers were penned by Noddy Holder and Jim Lea. Total UK sales stand at 6,520,171 and their bestselling single, 'Merry Xmas Everybody', has sold in excess of one million copies.

Slade have released over thirty albums, three of which reached No. 1 in the UK Albums Chart. Their releases have spent 315 weeks in the UK charts and they had earned twenty-four Top 30 UK hits as of 2016.

Their 1983 Great Hall appearance was a fabulous Christmas concert. Three days later Slade played their last ever UK live gig in Liverpool on 18 December 1983.

The band **Export** were formed in 1980 by erstwhile Hard Stuff vocalist Harry Shaw. Following a self-financed album *Export*, the band achieved a major American deal with Epic Records, releasing an album in 1984, *Contraband*, and in 1986 the critically acclaimed Lance Quinn produced *Living In Fear Of The Private Eye*.

Raid The North! were a Middlesbrough rock band, originally known as Taurus; a NWOBHM band reminiscent of Whitesnake.

Christmas concert 1983 photo courtesy of Ian Edmundson @ www.slayed.com

Dave Hill of Slade photo courtesy of Ian Edmundson @ www.slayed.com

After their initial explosion onto the UK's music charts, Slade suffered a downturn in their recording fortunes. They were always a popular and exciting live act but their records mysteriously ceased to sell for a period. It was during this time that I went to drop off some more concert tickets at 'Ear 'Ere Records because they had sold out of that week's show. I went upstairs to see Nigel, only to find him entertaining Noddy Holder from Slade. He was being taken around the chart returns shops (a handful of record shops whose sales figures were collected nationally to determine that week's record charts) to enthuse them and their customers about Slade's latest single. Something worked, although I'm not sure it can all be attributed to 'Ear 'Ere's influence, and Slade's record sales recovered over the next few years. Having said that I still found it surrealistically absurd to hear 'Merry Christmas Everybody!' ringing out in March!

While Noddy was a really funny and engaging guy, it was nothing compared to another occasion when I went upstairs at 'Ear 'Ere to find Nigel and the gorgeous Kim Wilde eating fish and chips out of newspaper. She was making a tour of chart shops to push her new single. However, the sight of Kim with Lancaster chip fat slowly running from her lips down her chin was a northern lad's fantasy and a memory which will live with me forever …

'Ear 'Ere Records was a quite remarkable record shop. This had little to do with me (except it was my idea and my suggestion to drag Nigel back from the wilds of Lowestoft) but everything to do with the staff, especially Nigel and his carefully hand-picked lieutenants: Eric, Roger and Malcolm in particular. Everybody employed in that enterprise was intelligent and musically motivated, and they each knew and cared about specific music genres. Somebody in that shop could answer any query and generally obtain any recording, even some illegal bootlegs!

'Ear 'Ere is the only record shop in music history to be awarded a platinum disc when we sold the one millionth copy of Boney M's 'Rivers of Babylon'. I went down to WEA Records headquarters in London with Nigel and Malcolm from the shop. We were ferried around the capital in a chauffeur driven Rolls Royce, and wine and dined, before being awarded the disc at a press conference. A platinum disc had never been awarded before, or since, to a record shop.

A couple of years ago Roger sent me a link to website devoted to great record shops of the world – the 'Ear 'Ere entry was sandwiched between a record shop in New York and one in San Francisco. A small market stall in Lancaster indeed!

'Ear 'Ere Records – the greatest record shop ever.

19 April 2014.
Courtesy of:
Michael Taylor
www.themarpleleaf.co.uk

Today is Record Store Day. It's brought back a flood of nostalgia for the greatest record store that ever existed.

Anyone who remembers 'Ear 'Ere in Lancaster knows what I mean. It was a cosier and friendlier version of the record shop in Nick Hornby's High Fidelity. It was also where you could get tickets for gigs at all kinds of places around the North of England. But from my early forays in there after school, to look meaningfully at prog album covers from the likes of Genesis and King Crimson, to the more serious record buyer I became, it was the centre of my world.

I remember going in as a young teen one Saturday and looking through the racks. Some lad approached me and asked me what music I liked. He was probably just being friendly, but it seemed at the time to be the equivalent of the "got the time, mate?" question at a concert or football match. So I bolted and caught up with my mum on Lancaster market. Back then there was a ferocious mob called the Marsh Mods who had lined up outside punk gigs and battered anyone in sight. Then there were the Morecambe Punks, who would use belts and chains to mash anyone who crossed them. We developed myths and scare stories about the violence these gangs would inflict on you, most of it wildly exaggerated, but it hung over you and was a caution not to stray too far from safety.

But in reality 'Ear 'Ere was safe neutral ground. As I became more confident (cocky?) I became a regular in there. You could listen on the headphones by the counter, get recommendations from the staff, especially one character who worked there called Malcolm. The manager was Roger, or to most of us "Beardie". A nostalgic Facebook post elicited the comment from an old mate that these guys had as big a stamp on his musical DNA as John Peel.

You could put your name down to pre-order records and it was the first time I'd used a nickname rather than my surname with adults. I remember a few of us sneaking out at lunch break from school to buy 'Going Underground' by The Jam in 1980, then swaggering back in possession of the fastest-selling single of that era.

I used to be in awe of people who would ask for rare records that they didn't have in stock, but would get the staff working hard looking through books and old stock lists and seeing if they could try to order it for you. They'd also sell fanzines, a few t-shirts and badges, some they'd even give away, but mostly it was shifting units in the golden age of pop music.

And their plastic bags were such a status symbol around school. You'd cart your school books to lessons in an 'Ear 'Ere bag, the height of cool, but woefully impractical for such a purpose.

I don't buy much music these days, but I fervently stick to the principle that the local record store is a totem of a civilised culturally advanced society. So when I want a new album by a band I still follow slightly slavishly – Elbow, Manics, etc. – then Piccadilly Records in Oldham Street, Manchester, get my custom. I also love their devotion to new music and always sample something from their Top 100 of the year. It's hit and miss, but those moments of serendipity are what makes life interesting. It's what has always made life interesting – so on this day of all days, I raise a glass to the greatest record shop ever: 'Ear 'Ere in Lancaster. May perpetual light shine upon your memory.

But its real claim to fame came with another celeb. superstar visit. This time we knew in advance and could publicise it in plenty of time, so that on the day vast crowds gathered to welcome David Bellamy to promote his legendary single 'Brontosaurus Will You Wait For Me', with the unforgettable flip side, 'Oh Stegasaurus'. And don't snigger – in 1983 it made No. 88 in the UK Singles Chart.

Barry Lucas

The Smiths

9 March 1984   Support: Red Guitars

Formed in Manchester in 1982 The Smiths consisted of vocalist Morrissey, guitarist Johnny Marr, bassist Andy Rourke and drummer Mike Joyce. The Smiths were the definitive British indie rock band of the '80s, marking the end of synth-driven new wave and the beginning of the guitar rock that dominated English rock into the '90s.

The Smiths released four studio albums, one live album, ten compilation albums, twenty singles, one video album, plus fourteen music videos on the Rough Trade, Sire and WEA record labels. Following emerging tensions and the exhaustion of Johnny Marr, the band dissolved in 1987 around the time of the release of the album *Strangeways, Here We Come*, which reached No. 2 in the UK Albums Chart.

The **Red Guitars** were an English indie rock band active from 1982 to 1986. Based in Hull, the Red Guitars' first single, 'Good Technology', was a minor hit, selling 60,000 copies. Their singles 'Marimba Jive' and 'Be With Me' both reached No. 1 on the UK Indie Singles Chart.

The tour was promoted by a relatively new kid on the block, Phil McIntyre from Preston, who by then had already become a major player. He was also refreshingly innovative compared to the big-name promoting dinosaurs. His younger brother, Nigel, had his finger on the pulse of the North West music revolution and had secured The Smith's major UK tour.

We had a massive sell-out on our hands but it was 7.30 pm and no sign of the band. I was worried. I asked Phil if there was a problem. No, he reassured me, they won't be here until about 8.50! Why, I wanted to know, what about sound checks etc.? He told me that all the guys in the band wanted to watch *Coronation Street* with their various mums, with Nigel having to drive to each one and pick them up after it was finished. Annie and Jack Walker would have been proud of them.

Barry Lucas

Sparks

25 June 1974 — Support: Beverley Martyn
16 November 1974 — Support: Pilot

Originally called Halfnelson, brothers Ron and Russell Mael from Los Angeles exploded onto the UK music scene with their band Sparks in 1974 with the single 'This Town Ain't Big Enough for Both of Us'.

Taken from the album *Kimono My House,* the single peaked at No. 2 in the UK Singles Chart and the album at No. 4.

When *Kimono My House* was released, UK's Sounds wrote, "Sparks have got the musical extravagance of Wizzard, the sophisticated feel of Roxy Music and the menacing power of the Third Reich."

The band are noted for Russell Mael's falsetto voice and Ron Mael's scowling face behind the keyboard.

Following a great reception in the Great Hall, the band returned six months later for a follow-up concert in promotion of the band's recently released fourth album *Propaganda*.

In 2015 Sparks announced a collaboration with the band Franz Ferdinand, appearing at the 2015 Glastonbury Festival.

English folk rock singer, songwriter, guitarist and former husband of John Martyn, **Beverley Martyn,** provided the June support act.

Pilot were a Scottish rock band, formed during 1973 in Edinburgh by former Bay City Rollers members David Paton and Billy Lyall. They are best known for their 1974 hit song 'Magic'. Another single, 'January', gave them their greatest success in the UK, securing the No. 1 spot in the UK Singles Chart in February 1975 and staying at the top of the charts for three weeks.

Two concerts by a quite unique band. They managed to crossover, their audience ranging from teenie boppers on *TOTPs* to underground musos.

The brothers, Ron and Russell Mael, were the embodiment of that broad appeal: one the handsome singer and one the strange keyboard man; one full of bouncy energy, one stone-faced, expressionless. It was a fascinating, captivating combination. And the music was equally appealing. The single 'This Town Ain't Big Enough For Both Of Us' reached No. 2 and their albums enjoyed similar success in their charts.

That first tour was a riot for all concerned, musicians, road crew, management and record company reps. It hit Lancaster big style. At the end of the show the dressing rooms were full of groupies – and I mean full to bursting. I told the band's manager that I had to clear them out, they were blocking the roadies' attempts to get the PA out of the hall and the porters were getting frustrated and annoyed, they had been here since 8.00 am this morning and they had to be back in at 8.00 am the next morning.

"What do you want to do?" he asked, looking quite bemused himself.

I came up with a plan. "Look, you've got two tour coaches with you, get the band and odds an' sods on one and I'll get the stewards to fill the other with the fans. Then all back to your hotel. OK?"

He agreed and we set about the task, but it was not as easy as it had seemed when I first suggested it. We could have done with a couple of Lakeland sheep farmers and their dogs to help round them up – they just kept escaping in giggling screams. But finally it was done.

The band were staying at the Royal King's Arms in Lancaster. I was meeting Phil Long there, who was the Island Records rep, a great guy who had become a good friend through the shows and the record shop. Now, the Royal King's Arms was certainly not a funky, trendy hotel in those days – but then has it ever been? When Nigel and I arrived the hotel manager, resplendent in full dinner suit, was looking aghast as what seemed like hundreds of groupies flooded into his small hotel foyer and bar, along with various band members and management. He couldn't believe what was happening to his genteel and outdated hotel lobby. The handful of resident guests soon fled the bar for the imagined relative safety of their hotel bedrooms. Then the place was crashed by the returning road crew and the party really began!

The band's road manager stood by the hotel manager and pushed £10 notes into his top pocket as he gasped and started to protest as yet another Bacchanalian scene unfolded. The crew told a couple of tables full of girls that they were having a competition for the best breasts on tour. Out came a Polaroid camera, out came several pairs of breasts – that meant 2 x £10 notes for the top pocket! Blue Nun, that disgusting, sickly, German white wine, had suddenly become the rock 'n' roll drink and the bar was unable to cope as rounds of six or eight bottles of the stuff were ordered repeatedly. That seemed to somewhat appease the hotel manager as his tills became so full of notes that they had to be continually emptied. At about 1.30 am a naked girl came running down the stairs, giggling "They want to …" Her words were lost in laughter as three naked roadies carried her back up. I know, I know but this is now, that was the '70s and rock 'n' roll touring. More £10 notes appeared and disappeared into pocket.

Anyway, the next morning I went back to the hotel to say goodbye to Phil. The foyer was full of girls working out their alibis.

"I'll say I was staying at yours, you say you were staying at mine."

"Dad will kill me if he ever finds out."

"I know, but it was fun wasn't it!"

The support act featured on that date was Beverley Martyn. I know it seems a peculiar choice of bill but by then major acts had learnt the lesson of taking similar artists out with them. Some could be too close to their audience's taste for comfort (see Mott the Hoople and Free shows).

Beverley was a lovely folk singer and acoustic guitarist. She would have been highly successful ten years earlier and indeed nearly cracked it on the Island label. I had had her on several dates over the previous few years and I was pleased to see her. But when I went over to talk to her, as she arrived in the afternoon for her sound check, she revealed a grotesque black eye. "What the hell happened, Beverley?" I asked, actually quite concerned.

"Well," she said, "John [John Martyn, the legendary folk rock/jazz guitarist and her estranged husband] was staying with me and he came home after a heavy day in the pub". John was a fearsome Scottish drinker with all the clichéd national characteristics that involved. "He decided to have a bath while I cooked tea. After about twenty minutes or so I heard a strange sound from the bathroom and went to investigate. John had passed out and was slowly sliding under the water. I grabbed his hair and yanked him up. Unfortunately I forgot I was still holding a large kitchen chopping knife and the first thing John saw as he came to was me yanking his head up by the hair, brandishing a large knife. Glaswegian instinct kicked in and he thumped me. My fault, should have guessed that would happen".

You couldn't make it up.

The second Sparks show was a memorable one for me but for a very different reason. By now it was known in the business that I looked after the Students' Union coffers very carefully. I managed to make sure that the SU made money on nearly every show by one means or another, unless I made a booking mistake – and sometimes I did make a right booking mistake! After the early days when you could, as a promoter, make a killing, the bands virtually always insisted on a percentage clause to make sure that they made more money if the show sold out. However, percentage deals were always open to argy bargy over the numbers attending in those pre-computer, box office days.

Mick Cater was the leading booker at Island Artists. He was later to leave with the company director, Alec Leslie, to set up as a major promoter, and he then became manager of UB40 at their height. That year he knew I had a show on a certain night and the next morning he got into the office early to ring me at 8.45 am. The phone was downstairs in the hall, it was winter, I was freezing my nuts off, hung over and tired. I would have, and did, agree to anything to get back to my warm pit. Mick proposed a 95% of gross ticket sales deal (which meant I would almost certainly lose money). I agreed. Obviously, it really was bloody cold.

On the night of the concert, Alan Murray and I had collaborated on putting together an amazing collection of expenses, unforeseen costs etc. It had taken us hours but we had to get a fair deal for the SU. Mick just sat in the office we had prepared in the music rooms. He listened to us for a few minutes as we went through our carefully prepared routine. Then he stopped us.

"Just give me what you think we should have."

"But what the hell do you mean? You're on 95%."

"Look, Barry, I just wanted your name on a contract with an outrageous deal in the band's favour. I know you'll find some way of giving me what you wanted to. I just want the contract to show around London. So I phoned you that early that morning, I knew you'd agree to anything."

Barry Lucas

The Specials

2 November 1979   Supports: The Selecter I Madness

2Tone Tour 79

The Specials are an English 2 Tone ska revival band formed in 1977 in Coventry, by songwriter and 2Tone label founder, Jerry Dammers. The band arrived in Lancaster for a date on the 2Tone Tour heading up a fabulous triple bill with The Selecter and Madness in support. The Specials are best known for their 1980 hit, 'Too Much Too Young', which reached number 1 in the UK singles chart the 1981 unemployment-themed single 'Ghost Town' which also achieved a number 1 slot in the UK Singles Chart for the band. After seven consecutive UK Top 10 singles between 1979 and 1981, three members of the group, including lead singer Terry Hall, abruptly left to form Fun Boy Three.

The remaining members of the band continued on as The Special AKA through to 1984, achieving further chart success with the UK Top 10 single 'Free Nelson Mandela'. Soon afterwards Jerry Dammers dissolved the band completely and went on to pursue political activism.

The Specials re-formed in 1993 and have continued to perform and record with varying lineups (but without Dammers).

The Selecter made the first of their three university performances, providing support to The Specials.

Completing the night's fabulous triple bill were **Madness**, making their only visit to Lancaster, early in the band's career. October 1979 had seen the release of the band's debut album *One Step Beyond*, with the single of the same name, written by Jamaican ska singer Prince Buster, reaching No. 7 in the UK Singles Chart.

One of the most successful bands of the early '80s and led by Graham "Suggs" McPherson, Madness have had fifteen singles reach the UK Top 10 and a No. 1 single, 'House of Fun'.

Madness are still going strong, forty years after they formed, releasing an album in 2016 called *Can't Touch Us Now*.

Top: Terry Hall and The Specials © Geoff Campbell

Centre: Pauline Black and Compton Amanor of Selecter © Doug Price

Right: Suggs and Madness © Geoff Campbell

The Specials on the Great Hall stage November 1979 © Doug Price

The 'nutty boys' on the Great Hall stage 1979 © Doug Price

Spirit

21 June 1981   Support: Inner City Unit

Spirit were an American band who went through many splits and re-formations over the years of their existence. Following the band's formation in 1967, Ed Cassidy and his stepson Randy California (aka Randy Woolfe) were on stage together again, visiting the university for a concert supporting the release of the album *The Adventures of Kaptain Kopter & Commander Cassidy in Potato Land,* a skit on George Orwell's 1984. Their most commercially successful single in the United States was 'I Got a Line on You', but they were also known for the albums *The Family That Plays Together, Clear* and *Twelve Dreams of Dr Sardonicus*. In 2014 a lawsuit was commenced by the band Spirit against Led Zeppelin, claiming that the iconic guitar arpeggio opening of 'Stairway to Heaven' infringed the copyright of their instrumental track 'Taurus' written by Randy California in 1968. A US judge ruled that a jury must decide and in 2016 subsequently cleared Robert Plant and Jimmy Page of plagiarism.

Inner City Unit are a punkadelic outfit still touring today. The band were created by former Hawkwind member Nik Turner following his departure from the band in 1977. Nik Turner still occasionally performs under the name Inner City Unit, but most of the time leads the band Space Ritual, which is made up of former members of Hawkwind.

Squeeze

31 October 1982   Support: OK Jive

The songwriting partnership of Chris Difford and Glen Tilbrook formed Squeeze in Deptford, London, in 1974. Other original members recruited to form the first lineup were keyboard player Jools Holland, bass guitarist Harry Kakoulli and drummer Paul Gunn.

Shortly prior to the Lancaster gig, Kakoulli and Gunn had been replaced by John Bentley and Gilson Lavis respectively.

Keyboardist Jools Holland left the band for a solo career in 1980, being replaced by highly rated singer-keyboardist Paul Carrack, a former member of British soul-pop band Ace.

The band are best known in the UK for their hit singles 'Cool for Cats', 'Up the Junction', 'Labelled with Love', 'Another Nail in My Heart' and 'Pulling Mussels (from the Shell)'.

Writing in *SCAN* newspaper, reviewer Batters said:

> "Squeeze, on their final tour of the UK before a visit to Jamaica, were a completely different kettle of fish compared to the evenings warm-up act. They made an impressive wham-bam start with 'Mussels', 'Another Nail In My Heart' and 'Up The Junction' which really woke the crowd up".

OK Jive were a quintet of Ruby Jive, Lee Partis, Datsun Cherry, Bavon Wayne and 'Chopper'. OK Jive made a brave attempt to conquer the charts in the early '80s with their brand of 'Congo' pop'.

Squeeze

This story has little to do with the band and nothing to do with the Great Hall but it's worth telling anyway and will strike a chord with those Lancastrians lucky enough to have experienced it.

About ten years or so after I had left the university I was approached by John Allan, that legend from Lonsdale bar. The college was celebrating an anniversary year – I think it was 30 years – and wondered whether I would like to help my old college? I went to a meeting, in Lonsdale bar of course, and told the assembled academics of the good old days (only John and one other Merton Atkins could remember) before the Great Hall existed. Events like the Graduation Ball of 1969 were held in Lonsdale. There was a circus tent erected over the quadrangle and all the rooms around, JCR, SCR, coffee bar, offices etc. were used as bars and food outlets. I saw Family headline there that year. So I offered to re-create that, and as a climax to the weekend persuaded Jools Holland to bring his Rhythm and Blues Orchestra, Ruby Turner, Sam Brown *et al*. During the show one of my stewards introduced me to the new(ish) landlady of my old local, The Ring o' Bells. She told me she was a great fan of Jools and asked if she could be introduced. I don't like doing that but for old times' sake I agreed. But I did ask Paul Loasby, who by this time was Jools' manager. He agreed so I took her in and we introduced her. Jools was delightful and when she asked him where he was staying, he replied The Royal King's Arms. She said that she had a pub just down the road from the hotel and she invited him for a late drink (there were many of those down at the Bells then!). Jools said he'd think about it but Paul looked at me and shook his head as if to say 'no chance'.

I'd just finished a long day and Mary and I went home rather than the Bells for yet more beer. The next day I found out that we had missed a magic night. Around midnight Jools had turned up at the pub. After a couple of drinks he joined Bill Roberts who was playing a rather battered upright piano in the corner. Bill's a local famed jazz/blues artist but that night he had to share his stage with an up and coming piano player. Apparently it was an amazing night as they jammed together until the early hours. Oh to have been there …

Barry Lucas

Glen Tilbrook of Squeeze on the Great Hall stage © Andy Docherty

Status Quo

1 December 1973	**Hello Tour**	Support unknown
8 March 1975	**On The Level Tour**	Support: Snafu

In 1962 two schoolboys, Francis Rossi and Alan Lancaster, formed a band called The Spectres. After a number of lineup changes, the band became The Status Quo in 1967 and Status Quo in 1969.

They are one of the most successful bands of all time in the UK.

They have had over sixty chart hits in the UK, starting with 1967's 'Pictures of Matchstick Men' and the most recent being in 2010. This is more than any other rock band and twenty-two of the sixty reaching the Top 10 in the UK Singles Chart. They have produced thirty-one studio albums, with a further 6 live albums.

Amazingly their only No. 1 UK Singles Chart hit, and probably their best known, was 'Down Down', released shortly prior to the 1975 Great Hall gig and no doubt performed on the night.

In April of 1994 the Quo did achieve a second No. 1 slot with a song called 'Come On You Reds', which was billed as being released by "Manchester United FC featuring Status Quo".

In 2015, the band passed a milestone achieved by only a handful of musicians, by spending a total of 500 weeks in the UK Albums Chart.

All the Lancaster concerts featured the classic Quo lineup:
Francis Rossi – guitar, vocals
Rick Parfitt – guitar, vocals
Alan Lancaster – bass, vocals
John Coghlan – drums

These days they've transformed their heads down rock, playing many of their legendary songs – from 'Pictures of Matchstick Men' and 'Down Down', to 'Whatever You Want' and 'Rockin' All Over The World' – in a stripped-down acoustic style. Guitarist Rick Parfitt sadly passed away in late 2016.

Snafu were a British rhythm and blues rock band of the 1970s featuring vocalist Bobby Harrison and the talented slide guitarist Micky Moody. Snafu were notable for combining a British rhythm and blues tradition with US inspired elements of funk and country music. Soon after the band's formation they embarked on European tours as support to The Doobie Brothers and The Eagles. Snafu released three albums: *SNAFU* in 1973, *Situation Normal* in 1974 and *All Funked Up* from 1975. A year earlier in March 1974, the band had visited Lancaster providing the support to The Kinks. Snafu were in existence from 1972–1975.

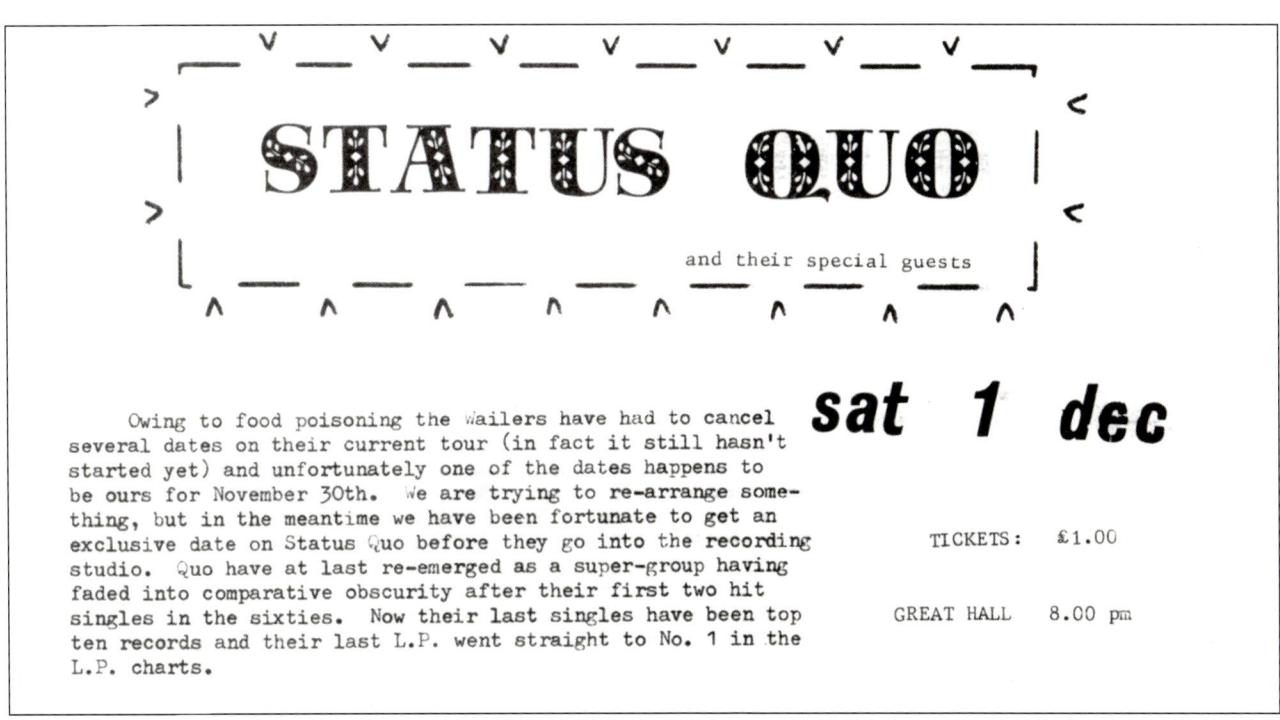

Status Quo

I had Status Quo on a couple of times, but one date, possibly around October 1978, isn't featured in this official history. One Monday morning Mike Lloyd from Hanley, Stoke, phoned me. I have mentioned him several times in this book; he helped me in the early days and taught me a great deal about commercial promoting. Mike was friendly with Status Quo and put them on numerous times at Hanley's Victoria Hall and other venues in the area. The band had just returned from an Australian tour and had asked Mike if he could find them a cash gig that weekend. Apparently they had met and befriended a few fans in Sydney and wanted to fly them over to see one of their shows in the UK. Mike wanted to know if I could do a date at Lancaster, leaving me only five days to organise, promote it and sell tickets. I have said elsewhere in this book that I love sorting promotion problems out and here was a beaut!

No Internet, no Twitter, no Facebook. Five days; book the hall, print the posters, flyers, tickets etc. Get them out and get the word out, sort some staff out and sell two thousand tickets, no problem …

Well the gig happened and I even got one of my security staff, an ex-student who was renting a bungalow in Westgate, to put the Aussie friends up for a night or two. Mind you, I did have several volunteers offering spare beds for four Bondi Beach beauties.

Status Quo's 1975 Lancaster concert was alas memorable for something other than the music. You might remember the Birmingham pub bombings of 1974, the six suspects of which had been arrested at Heysham Port and initially interrogated at Morecambe Police Station. In 1975 they were to stand trial at Lancaster Castle in one of the most famous court cases in the world at that time. There was a very tense atmosphere in the surrounding area. Before the show, I received a phone call from Lancaster Police. Apparently they had received a bomb threat/warning for an explosion at that night's Great Hall concert. The Police said that they would normally be fairly relaxed about this kind of call but a) the Birmingham six were on trial in Lancaster, and b) the caller had used a certain IRA code word, so they had to take it very seriously. They asked me if I could begin a check with my staff whilst they sent up some officers. Bloody hell, this was 6.30 pm and I was due to open the doors for a sell-out in an hour – how bloody inconvenient and annoying!

Well, I asked some staff to begin looking around the venue. I went down the side corridor and into the glass store/washing room. "Bloody annoying nuisance," I thought as I began to look around the area. I started kicking empty cardboard boxes. "No bomb here," I declared to myself. Suddenly I stopped, what the hell was I doing, kicking boxes to see if there was a bomb hidden inside? Hey, intelligent or what? You could tell I had a degree! Nothing went bang. Except the concert was a banging success. Phew!

Barry Lucas

Steel Pulse

4 February 1978 — Supports: China Street I The Venus Boys
27 October 1978 — **Handsworth Revolution Tour** — Support: China Street
9 May 1982 — Support: Handsworth Reggae Sound System

From the Handsworth area of Birmingham, Steel Pulse are one of the UK's most highly regarded roots reggae outfits being rivalled only by Aswad in terms of creative and commercial success. The band were formed in 1975 by rhythm guitarist and lead vocalist David "Dread" Hinds and guitarist Basil Gabbidon. In early 1978, following a successful tour as a supporting act to the Jamaican musician Burning Spear (aka Winston Rodney), Steel Pulse were quickly signed up to the Island Records label. In July 1978, their first highly acclaimed studio album, *Handsworth Revolution* went straight to number nine in the UK album charts, just ten days after its release.

Steel Pulse arrived in Lancaster for their October 78 Great Hall concert straight after returning from a twelve date European tour supporting Bob Marley and The Wailers.

Allying themselves closely with the Rock Against Racism movement, Steel Pulse chose to tour with sympathetic elements of the punk movement, including The Stranglers, The Clash, XTC etc.

The band once stated that: "Punks had a way of enjoying themselves – throw hordes at you, beer, spit at you, that kind of thing".

Steel Pulse were the first non-Jamaican act to win the Grammy Award for Best Reggae Album in 1987 for their sixth studio album *Babylon the Bandit.*

Over forty years after their formation, Steel Pulse are still busy touring and recording with founder member David Hinds and his long serving keyboard player Selwyn Brown.

Rock Against Racism was a campaign set up in the United Kingdom in 1976 as a response to an increase in racial conflict and the growth of white nationalist groups such as the National Front. The campaign involved pop, rock, punk and reggae musicians staging concerts with an anti-racist theme, in order to discourage young people from embracing racism. The campaign was founded, in part, as a response to statements and activities by well-known rock musicians that were widely regarded as racist.

China Street October 1978 supporting Steel Pulse © Geoff Campbell

John Angus

Steel Pulse were an excellent reggae band and the mainstay of the Rock Against Racism movement, but with this show it is the support band I wish to remember. China Street were a local Lancaster band – as you can probably guess from their name – and were as good as it gets.

With a little bit of luck, good management and record company support money – any one of those, or a combination of the above – they could have been superstars. Over the years I have been asked many times to manage local bands and I can say that I have never really been tempted. I was never hungry enough to sit outside office doors in London awaiting an answer and making a nuisance of myself until I was heard and noticed. But with China Street … maybe I might have made a difference, rolled the dice in their favour … we'll never know.

Go back to this time and you'll find a band that was truly innovative, unique and special. They blended rock and reggae, something common now but unheard of in the early months of 1978. They had attracted record company interest and were in a southern studio, putting down some tracks for a promo EP (older readers please translate). The studio next door had a newly formed band rehearsing and recording: the singer Sting, the band The Police. They came in to listen to the new arrangements being played by China Street in the adjoining studio. Something different, something new, something unique. Well, the band with millions behind them were impressed with this new sound and the rest, as they say, is history.

Barry Lucas

John Angus

Lancaster band **China Street** made four guest appearances in the Great Hall over the space of a year.

Formed in 1976 the band consisted of Martin Pilkington (guitars and vocals), Dusty Hall (saxophones and vocals), Adam Williams (bass guitar) and David Willan (drums), later adding Chris Sugden on keyboards, more specifically a Fender Rhodes piano.

China Street took their name from the Lancaster Street where some of the band members shared a flat in the mid '70s. Their first university gig was as guests of The Jam in December 1977, which resulted in an invitation to support the band for the whole of their first major UK tour. Their next appearance was as support band to Sad Café a month later in January 1978, before two dates in quick succession supporting Steel Pulse. China Street's first UK tour proper was to support Steel Pulse on the whole of their Handsworth Revolution Tour.

Rock Against Racism single cover

October 1978 supporting Steel Pulse
© Geoff Campbell

The band are remembered as pioneers of the independent record label Criminal Records, one of the very first and established in 1977. Their first 7" single – A side 'You're A Ruin'/ B side '(I Wanna Be) Your MP' – was released on their new label and soon attracted music press attention, with a special feature about the new independent label and a "how to do it yourself" article appearing in *Melody Maker*.

The subsequent press exposure eventually led to interest from the major record companies and in January 1978 China Street entered Surrey Sound Studios, after signing a deal with EMI, and recorded the single 'Rock Against Racism'.

China Street disbanded in early 1979 with Adam Williams going on to form local band The Pharaohs with James Mackie and Dusty Hall. Following Adam's spell with The Selecter he progressed on to production work with Annie Lennox and Dave Stewart of The Eurythmics and Bronski Beat. Moving into the 1990s he then became a producer and director, working on assorted video projects with artists such as Norman Cook, Adamski and Seal and produced the video for their 1990 hit single 'Killer'. Adam currently works in London and is involved in the development of 3D augmented reality and Telepresence systems in sound and vision.

More local entertainment came in the shape of former members of Lancaster punk band The Kassels. Jeff Hurst along with Ian and Andy Holmes teamed up with Kenny Matthews on vocals, to form **The Venus Boys**, later known as The Venus Mob.

The **Handsworth Reggae Sound System** provided the pre-concert 'blues party' dub disco, but information is scant regarding the other billing that night **The Lou's**.

Steeleye Span

11 February 1972   Supports: Keith Christmas Band I Morgan
26 October 1973   Support: Horslips

Steeleye Span the English folk rock band formed in 1969 and still active to this day, have a valid claim to be one of the longest-lived and perhaps the most commercially successful of all the folk rock bands of their era due to their unique fusion of both British folk with electric rock music.

Their first visit to Lancaster in February 1972 would have seen the band, no doubt, feature tracks from their recently released, extraordinarily titled third album *Ten Man Mop or Mr. Reservoir Butler Rides Again*.

Fronted by folk singer and Blackpool girl Maddy Prior, they went on to achieve major chart success with two UK single releases, 'Gaudete' in 1973, and their best known 'All Around My Hat', produced by Mike Batt, which went to no. 5 in the UK Singles Chart of 1975. The band also has over twenty studio albums to their credit.

Keith Christmas (born Keith Peter Christmas) is a British folk rock singer and songwriter from Essex. He released his first album *Stimulus* in 1969. Through the 1970s he released four more albums and played support roles for a number of illustrious acts including The Who, Frank Zappa and Captain Beefheart. Christmas also played acoustic guitar on David Bowie's *Space Oddity* album and appeared at the first Glastonbury Festival in 1970.

The band **Morgan** were an English progressive rock band that existed from 1971 to 1973. An interesting member of the band was bass guitarist and vocalist Tim Staffell. Tim, along with Brian May, was a founder member of the band Smile, which eventually evolved into Queen, Staffell being replaced by one Farrokh Bulsara. Following the breakup of Morgan, Staffell went on to craft models for the Thomas the Tank Engine children's TV series.

Horslips returned to the Great Hall in 1974 as a headlining band.

Steve Forbert

12 March 1980   **Rock Goes to College Concert (BBC)** No support

Steve Forbert is an American singer songwriter from Mississippi, best known for his song 'Romeo's Tune', which reached No. 11 on the Billboard Hot 100 Chart in 1980.

On the release of his first album in 1978, *Alive on Arrival*, critics hailed Forbert as the new Bob Dylan due to the timbre of his voice and thoughtful songwriting, although arguably being called the new Dylan is not something any artist would like to have hanging round their neck!

Global success evaded Forbert but he continues to write and record, with recent albums including *Strange Names & New Sensations* (2007), *The Place And The Time* (2009) and *Over With You* (2012).

Forbert also landed a cameo appearance in Cyndi Lauper's 'Girls Just Wanna Have Fun' video, playing her boyfriend.

Rock Goes to College was a BBC series that ran between 1978 and 1981 on British television. A variety of upcoming rock-oriented bands were showcased live from small venues and broadcast simultaneously on television and radio during a 40–50 minute recorded live performance. The venues were small university, polytechnic or college halls which held a few thousand people; often tickets were given to the Students' Union to distribute for free. The bands chosen were also, in some cases, ones that did not have a mainstream following at that time, although many went on to be very successful.

A BBC DJ would also be present to introduce the band for the television audience and on this night it was Pete Drummond.

The concert was broadcast on the evening of the 31 March 1980.

Lancaster setlist: 'Going Down to Laurel', 'Romeo's Tune', 'Complications', 'Down by the Sally Gardens', 'What Kinda Guy', 'Steve Forbert's Midsummer night's Toast', 'Thinking', 'The Sweet Love That You Give (Sure Goes a Long Long Way), 'Say Goodbye to Little Joe', medley: 'Nadin, Pokeseller Danny, You Can Not Win If You Do Not Play'.

BBC's 'Rock Goes to College' came to Lancaster and I've got to be brutally honest here, it was a bit of a disappointment. The audiences at Lancaster were, by now, used to seeing the world's superstars but the college circuit in general enjoyed the TV show and saw acts of a higher calibre than they were used to. It was their only way of seeing 'major' names in their venues. Lancaster audiences were, by now, spoilt.

Steve Forbert was an excellent artist and a really nice guy but not exactly a household name. Tickets were free and yet I could still only get about 350 there. I apologised to the BBC producer and director but they told me not to worry, the TV audience would think it had been a sell-out.

Don't ask me how he did it but when I watched it on TV I thought there were 1500 crowded into the hall – and they say the camera doesn't lie!

Barry Lucas

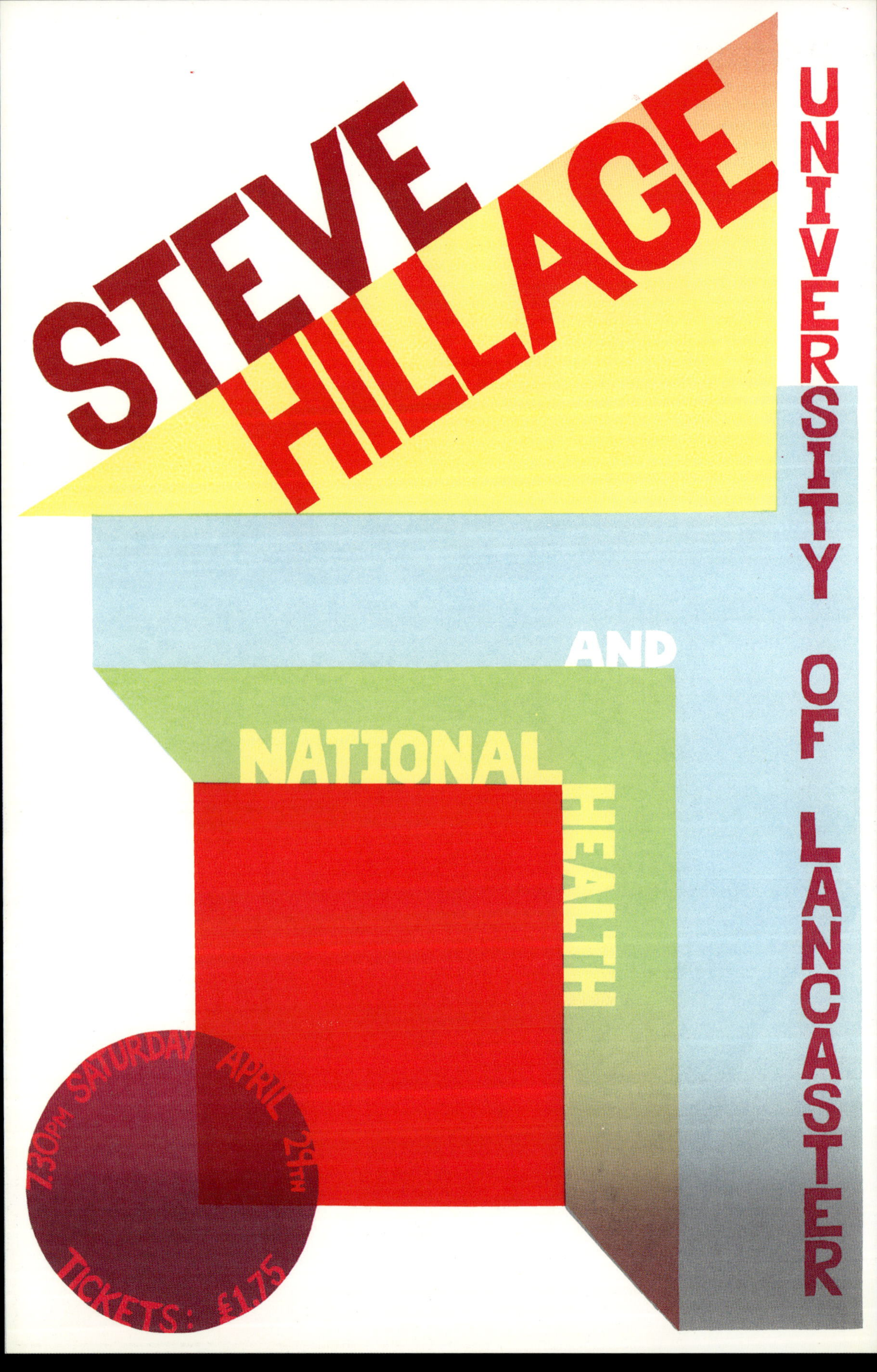
STEVE
HILLAGE
UNIVERSITY OF LANCASTER
AND
NATIONAL
HEALTH
7.30PM SATURDAY APRIL 29TH
TICKETS: £1.75

John Angus

Steve Hillage

29 April 1978 — Support: National Health
7 November 1979 — Support: Trevor Rabin

Steve Hillage, "the hippie from outer space", will be remembered as one of the main inventors of space rock.

The former Gong member (1972 to 1975), Steve Hillage visited Lancaster twice with his own solo project.

In 1975 Hillage released his first acclaimed solo album, *Fish Rising,* soon after he had left Gong and went on to release a series of studio LPs between *L* in 1976 and *And Or Not* from 1983, with two live-albums entitled *Live Herald* (1978) and *BBC Radio 1* (1992).

His first Great Hall appearance coincided with the release of his fourth studio album, *Green* in April 1978 followed by another concert in November 1979 promoting his fifth studio album *Rainbow Dome Musick.*

Hillage currently works with his former Gong colleague Miquette Giraudy, together forming the underground ambient dance outfit, System 7, making full use of Hillage's electric guitars prowess.

National Health were an English progressive rock band associated with the Canterbury Scene. Founded in 1975, the band included former members of the band Hatfield and the North. With a frequently changing lineup, they toured extensively and released their first album, *National Health*, in 1978.

Trevor Rabin is a South African-American musician best known as a guitarist and songwriter for the British progressive rock band Yes from 1983–1995, and since then as a film composer.

Please note; the 7th of November was a Saturday night, not a Friday as billed

Steve Winwood

15 July 1983 — No support

This was the third appearance on the Great Hall stage for the legendary Steve Winwood, following his two visits with Traffic in the early 1970s.

Born in Handsworth, Birmingham, he was a former member of The Spencer Davis Group, Traffic, Blind Faith and Ginger Baker's Air Force. Winwood launched his solo career in 1977 and visited Lancaster for a three-hour concert, with no supporting act, on his first full solo tour.

The tour was in support of his third solo album *Talking Back To The Night*. Winwood had recently had success with his first two albums, *Winwood* and *Arc of a Diver*, and chart hits with 'While You See a Chance' and 'Valerie'. The albums were recorded at his home in Gloucestershire with Winwood playing all the instruments himself. This was the first time that he had toured and performed the songs live in concert with a band.

The Great Hall audience that night were treated to three hours of his new material mixed in with some classic Traffic and Spencer Davis numbers.

Lancaster band lineup:
Steve Winwood – vocals
James Hooker – piano
Bobby Messano – guitar
Eric Parker – drums
Carole Steele – percussion
Fernando Sanders – bass, vocals
Godfrey Wang – keyboards

Possible Lancaster setlist: 'Roadrunner', 'Help Me Angel', 'Arc of a Diver', 'Valerie', 'It Was Happiness', 'Second-Hand Woman', 'Vacant Chair', 'Talking Back to the Night', 'Slowdown Sundown', 'Dust', 'Night Train', 'Somebody Help Me' (Spencer Davis Group), 'Low Spark of High Heeled Boys' (Traffic), 'Dear Mr Fantasy' (Traffic), 'I'm a Man' (Spencer Davis Group), 'Big Girls Walk Away and I Go', 'Your Silence Is Your Song', 'While You See a Chance'. Encore: 'Keep On Running' (Spencer Davis Group), 'Still in the Game', 'Gimme Some Lovin' (Spencer Davis Group).

Stiff Little Fingers

19 February 1979 — Rough Trade Tour

Supports: Robert Rental and The Normal | Essential Logic

Stiff Little Fingers are a punk rock band from Belfast, Northern Ireland, that started out as a schoolboy band in 1977 at the height of the troubles. The band were originally called Highway Star (after the Deep Purple song) and performed doing rock covers, until they discovered punk. This Lancaster concert was in support of the Rock Against Racism movement.

They split up after six years and four albums, although they re-formed four years later, in 1987. Despite major personnel changes they are still touring and recording, with Jake Burns, their lead singer, the only member to have been with the band during all its incarnations.

Reviewing the concert in *SCAN* newspaper Peter May wrote: "From the outset of their set it became evident that they are an angry band, a situation that is doubtlessly inevitable in Belfast, where violence and death are reality rather than merely subjects which make good songs and fit the current vogue"

Robert Rental was the stage name of Robert Donnachie (1952–2000), a British pioneer of the post-punk DIY industrial electronic music scene in the United Kingdom. He worked alongside Daniel Miller, aka **The Normal**. Together they produced the one single, 'Double Heart', and one album, *Live At West Runton Pavilion, 6-3-79*, on the Rough Trade label.

Essential Logic are an English post-punk band formed in 1978 by saxophonist Lora Logic after she left the punk band X-Ray Spex. The band split in 1981 and re-formed in 2001, continuing to tour today.

Live Stiffs Tour 1977

5 November 1977
Elvis Costello and The Attractions
Ian Dury and The Blockheads
Nick Lowe's Last Chicken in the Shop
Wreckless Eric and The New Rockets
Lary Wallis's Psychedelic Rowdies

Lancaster was the final date on the first of two legendary Stiff tours. With Stiff Records having signed all the named artists as individuals, bands had to be formed in order to tour; these were largely based on the session musicians used for the artists' solo records. There were a total of eighteen musicians on the tour, several doubling up; for example, Ian Dury playing drums for Wreckless Eric while the last two "bands" had the same lineup of Nick Lowe, Larry Wallis, Dave Edmunds, Terry Williams, Pete Thomas and Penny Tobin. The gig ended with everyone on stage performing Dury's 'Sex & Drugs & Rock & Roll'.

Live Stiffs Tour 1977 L-R Wreckless Eric, Ian Dury, Davey Payne, Elvis Costello. © Lawson Wakefield

Stiffs grand finale © David Stewart

Ian Dury was a part of that amazing Stiff Records package. There were two Stiff tours and the second was an inspired idea to commission their own train to take them on a trip around the UK. Whilst both had some highlights, it was the first which possessed the magic. A lineup of Elvis Costello, Ian Dury and the Blockheads, Wreckless Eric, Nick Lowe with Dave Edmonds and Larry Wallis, was a really historic package – a true night to remember.

It is here that I must apologise to the memory of Ian Dury. I had always been a fan but for many years now I have listed him as one of the most unpleasant artists I have had to deal with, and indeed on that night he was, to me, to the stewards, the humpers and the porters. On several occasions I had to intervene to prevent him getting a "slap". However, a couple of years ago I read about Ian Dury's medical condition and how this brought on massive highs and creative brilliance, but also deep, dark moods and angry, aggressive behaviour. This gig must have been one of those and I have since taken Ian Dury off my list of nasty acts.

Since writing the above I have heard a story which goes some way to explaining the atmosphere of that night. At an Alumni reunion recently I was talking to a couple of ex-Students' Union presidents and Mark Lane. He was my head of stewards for a couple of years in the mid '70s. On the night in question Mark was backstage in the corridor talking to a couple of stewards. Ian Dury came along and tripped over Mark's foot. It was obviously a total accident but unfortunately Elvis Costello saw it differently. He believed that Mark had done it deliberately. He launched himself at Mark, joined by several members of the various bands. More of our stewards joined in in defence of Mark and a backstage battle took place, all centred around Ian Dury, who was unable to get up but could deliver very creative abuse from his prone position. No wonder I was to get many complaints from my stewards about the attitude of the stars that night.

Barry Lucas

Be Stiff

17 October 1978
Wreckless Eric
Jona Lewie
Rachel Sweet
Lene Lovich
Mickey Jupp

Route 78 Tour

The second Stiff Records UK package tour 'Be Stiff '78' kicked off its two-week run on 10 October 1978 and was undertaken by a specially chartered train that arrived at Lancaster Railway Station on the 17 October.

The troupe then continued on to the USA, with Mickey Jupp being left behind for the US leg, due to his fear of flying.

This '78 Stiff event was designed to build on the excitement of the 1977 Stiff promotional tour that had featured Nick Lowe and Ian Dury etc.

Although the lineup wasn't as strong as 1977, it was still a great night's entertainment and tremendous value for money.

The bands lined up as follows:
Lene Lovich & The Musicians Union
Mickey Jupp & The Cable Layers
Wreckless Eric & The Four Rough Men
Rachel Sweet & The Records
Jona Lewie & Two's Company

As in the 1977 Live Stiffs concert, all band members were on stage together for a finale, performing a rendition of the Devo single 'Be Stiff'.

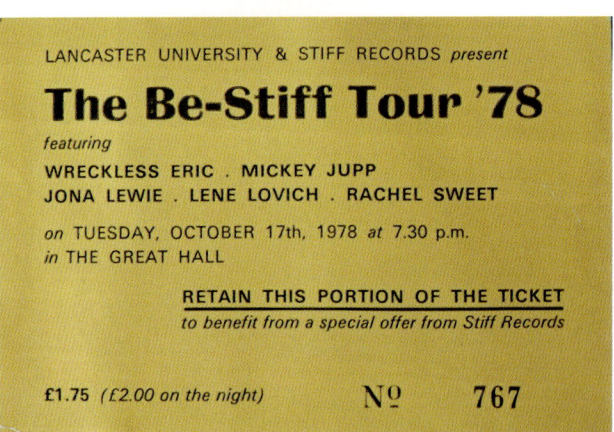

Stomu Yamash'ta

27 November 1972

Stomu Yamash'ta is a Japanese percussionist, keyboardist, composer and experimental artist. He is probably best known for his work leading the jazz-rock fusion group Go, which released three albums from 1976–77. The band featured Steve Winwood, guitarist Al Di Mieola, and drummer Michael Shrieve.

Beginning in 1972 Yamash'ta started recording jazz rock fusion albums blended with traditional Japanese influences.

He released *Floating Music* in 1972 and visited Lancaster to promote the album, with his short-lived band called Come To The Edge featuring drummer Morris Pert, bass guitarist Phil Plant and keyboards and saxophonist Robin Thompson.

In 1973 he then formed Stomu Yamash'ta's East Wind, a band which included keyboardist Brian Gascoigne, guitarist Gary Boyle and bassist Hugh Hopper. This group released two albums, *Freedom Is Frightening* (1973) and the soundtrack *One By One* (1974). Gascoigne and Boyle also played on his next album, *Raindog* (1975), with vocals by Murray Head and Maxine Nightingale.

In the latter part of the 1970s, he then formed and led his super group Go, featuring Steve Winwood, Al Di Meola, Klaus Schulze and Michael Shrieve. Leaving Europe in 1980, Stomu Yamash'ta retired to a Buddhist temple in Kyoto. His retirement was brief and he later went on to release a number of recordings employing synthesizers, pre-recorded taped sounds, orchestral instruments and percussion. Of these recordings his so-called 'space music' of the 1983 album *Sea and Sky* is still available on CD. Stomu continues to occasionally release albums in his electronica/ambient genre. His 'Space Theme' was used by the BBC on *The Hitchhiker's Guide to the Galaxy* (the radio series).

Stomu was a genius and when he appeared in the Great Hall a unique concert occurred. However, he was also one of those favours to Island that I had to honour, to repay them for all the great Island superstars that appeared at Lancaster.

Robb Winn phoned me to ask if I would promote Stomu Yamash'ta on a Wednesday in the Great Hall. "Stomu who?" was my immediate reply.

"Don't worry, straight percentage to you so you can't lose money but I need to put a tour together for him – it's a bit political here (with a small p)."

"OK, we can't lose, but who is he? What does he do?"

Well, he bangs lots of drums; there must have been about forty on stage that night. He is also quite an important musical figure who wrote the score for Ken Russell's *The Devils* and several Kurosawa films, including the legendary *Seven Samurai*.

Anyway the date happened, the three men turned up but not the dog! I think the 90% of the ticket receipts that Stomu took, as payment, were £48.10p. Didn't even pay his train fare.

Barry Lucas

The Stranglers

14 September 1978 — **The Black and White Tour** — Support: Skids
12 October 1979 — **The Raven Tour** — Support unknown
27 February 1981 — **The Meninblack Tour** — Support: Modern Eon

The Stranglers began life as the Guildford Stranglers in September 1974 in Guildford, Surrey, and made three visits to Lancaster University.

The original founding members were singer/guitarist Hugh Cornwell (from Kentish Town, London), keyboardist/guitarist Hans Wärmling (from Sweden, replaced within two years by Brighton-born keyboardist Dave Greenfield), London-born bass guitarist Jean-Jacques Burnel, and drummer Jet Black (real name Brian Duffy), a native of Ilford, Essex.

In total the band achieved twenty-three Top 40 singles, including 'Golden Brown', 'No More Heroes' and 'Peaches'. The Stranglers' first visit to Lancaster in 1978 saw the band playing a short set, only an hour long, resulting in a stage invasion (see picture).

In August 1990, Hugh Cornwell left the band to pursue his solo career.

SCAN newspaper concert reviewer Steve Rogerson wrote: "As the first forty minutes drew to an end (that was the set minus encore) the capacity audience had started to overflow onto the stage and by the end of the encore, it had become so crowded that the punks were even holding the microphone in position. The roadies looked on in horror. Those, anyway, will have gone home happy, no doubt most of them with souvenirs pilfered from the stage."

The 1979 Raven Tour was notable for the use of its innovative pyrotechnics during the show. BBC television's *Tomorrow's World* arrived on campus to film part of the Lancaster University concert, for an article on pyrotechnics. Footage of the The Stranglers performing their final song, 'Toiler on The Sea', in the Great Hall, complete with fireworks, can be found on the internet.

Skids were a Scottish punk rock and new wave band, formed in Dunfermline, Fife, in 1977 by the late Stuart Adamson (guitar, keyboards, percussion and backing vocals), William Simpson (bass guitar and backing vocals), Thomas Kellichan (drums) and Richard Jobson (vocals, guitar and keyboards). Their biggest success was the 1978 single 'Into the Valley' and their 1980 album *The Absolute Game*. Richard Jobson is now a filmmaker and television presenter.

Modern Eon were a British post-punk new wave band, formed in Liverpool in 1978. They released one album, *Fiction Tales*, on the independent UK label Dindisc in 1981. They disbanded in 1982.

both © Geoff Campbell

The Black and White Tour 1978 © John Angus

The Stranglers played Lancaster on three occassions. Punk accelerated the acclaim afforded to several bands, but many of whom would have made it without the 'leg up' that punk's notoriety gave them. The Stranglers were one such band.

The October 1979 gig was filmed by the BBC's groundbreaking science show *Tomorrow's World*. This was because the Stranglers were employing a company to create an incredible indoor firework display – it would be fun getting it past Health and Safety today but hey, surprise, surprise, nobody died – launched by a revolutionary computer controlled, firing system. With rockets blazing trails from the back of the balcony, over the heads of the audience and band, it was a fairly spectacular show.

But outside there was to be another awesome display, again set off by a computer-led system. However, the Southern softies from the BBC hadn't reckoned with the Lancashire weather. It poured down, soaking everybody and everything. So much so that the state-of-the-art computerised firing mechanism wouldn't work. It coughed, sneezed, spluttered and died. So *Tomorrow's World* filmed the boffins at the computer desk calmly pressing buttons while in the real world a rather wet technician risked life and limb with a box of matches, crawling around in the mud, setting off the display. It really amounted to a series of rockets but it sounded and looked like a major blitzkrieg.

It was the next morning that I had to stand with the Vice Chancellor, surveying what looked like a disaster zone. The beautiful University lawns were now a perfect replica of the Somme. I was not a popular person that day but we did get Lancaster University on the telly!

Barry Lucas

Hey Paul,

I've been waiting for this book to happen for years!

I was fifteen when I saw my first concert at the Great Hall. It was the Stranglers 1979 Raven Tour. The noise was deafening and the atmosphere was electric. Just to see hundreds and hundreds of people in one area so enraptured and caught up in the moment will live with me forever. I saw many concerts after that including The Stranglers again and The Clash. In the early eighties I saw Hawkwind (where the highlight was being allowed backstage to meet Dave Brock and the legend that is Ginger Baker), Slade (amazing night) and, dare I say it, Haircut 100! Nothing will ever compare to my first concert though. So much so I wrote an essay at school about my experience which was read out by the teacher to all the class. Please let me know when the book will be coming out. It will be great to reminisce.

Steve Buchanan.

HARVEY GOLDSMITH ENTERTAINMENTS
and ALBION MANAGEMENT in association with
LANCASTER UNIVERSITY

Present

The Stranglers

THURSDAY, SEPTEMBER 14th, 1978
THE GREAT HALL . 7.30 p.m.

Nº 1166   Ticket £2.50

The Raven Tour 1979
© Doug Price

Stray Cats

8 March 1981   Support: The Barracudas

Stray Cats are an American rockabilly band formed in 1979 by guitarist and vocalist Brian Setzer, double bassist Lee Rocker and drummer Slim Jim Phantom, in the Long Island town of Massapequa, New York.

They achieved a Top 10 chart success with the single 'Runaway Boys' in 1981.

The group, whose style was based upon the sounds of Sun Records artists from the 1950s, were heavily influenced by Eddie Cochran, Carl Perkins, Gene Vincent and Bill Haley & His Comets.

Over three decades since the band's formation, Stray Cats have gone through numerous breakups and reformations. In 2007 they reunited for a successful and long-awaited US tour, with ZZ Top and The Pretenders. This was their first North American tour in over fifteen years.

The Barracudas were an English surf rock band that formed in the late 1970s.

The band's original lineup consisted of Jeremy Gluck (vocals), Robin Wills (guitar and vocals), David Buckley (bass and vocals) and Nick Turner (drums).

They are notable for their summer 1980 hit 'Summer Fun', which started with an excerpt from a spoof 1960s advertisement for the Plymouth Barracuda, in which one of the announcers has difficulty pronouncing the word barracuda. The single reached No. 37 in the UK Singles Chart.

Supertramp

14 November 1975   Support: Joan Armatrading

Supertramp (known as Daddy from 1969–1970) were an English rock band formed in London in 1969. Though their music was initially categorised as progressive rock, they later incorporated a combination of traditional rock, pop and art rock into their music. The band's work is marked by the songwriting of founders Rick Davies and Roger Hodgson, and by the prominent use of Wurlitzer electric piano and saxophone.

Though their albums were generally far more successful than their singles, Supertramp did enjoy a number of major hits throughout the 1970s and 1980s, including Hodgson's songs 'Give a Little Bit', 'Take the Long Way Home', 'Dreamer', and 'It's Raining Again', and Davies' songs 'Bloody Well Right' and 'Goodbye Stranger'. Supertramp reached their commercial peak with their 1979 album, *Breakfast in America*, which has sold more than twenty million copies worldwide. The album also produced their highest charting UK single 'The Logical Song'.

This classic 1975 Great Hall concert featured many of the songs from their 1974 album *Crime of The Century*, which peaked at No. 4 in the UK Albums Chart, along with new material from their 1975 album *Crisis, What Crisis*.

A special mention must be made here of Supertramp's saxophonist, John Helliwell, who also served as an MC during the band's concerts, talking to and making jokes to the audience between songs. During the writing of this book I spoke with John and he was kind enough to recount his memories to me of a great reception from the Lancaster University audience.

Lancaster band lineup:
Roger Hodgson – vocals, keyboards, guitars
John Helliwell – woodwinds, keyboards, backing vocals
Bob Siebenberg – drums, percussion
Dougie Thomson – bass
Rick Davies – vocals, keyboards, harmonica, composition, melodica

Supertramp continue to tour with original members Rick Davies, Bob Siebenberg and John Helliwell.

Joan Armatrading's first Great Hall performance, as Supertramp's support act on the night.

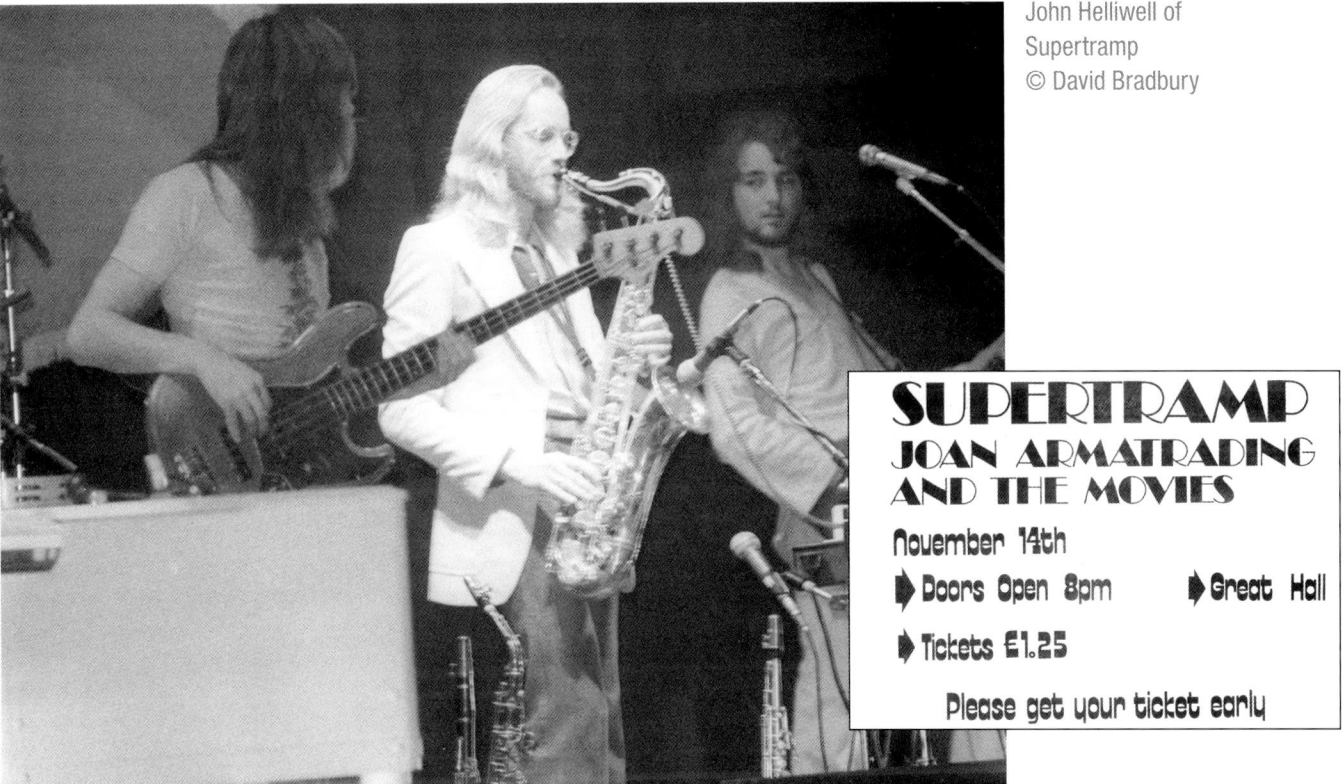

John Helliwell of Supertramp
© David Bradbury

SUPERTRAMP
JOAN ARMATRADING
AND THE MOVIES

November 14th

Doors Open 8pm — Great Hall

Tickets £1.25

Please get your ticket early

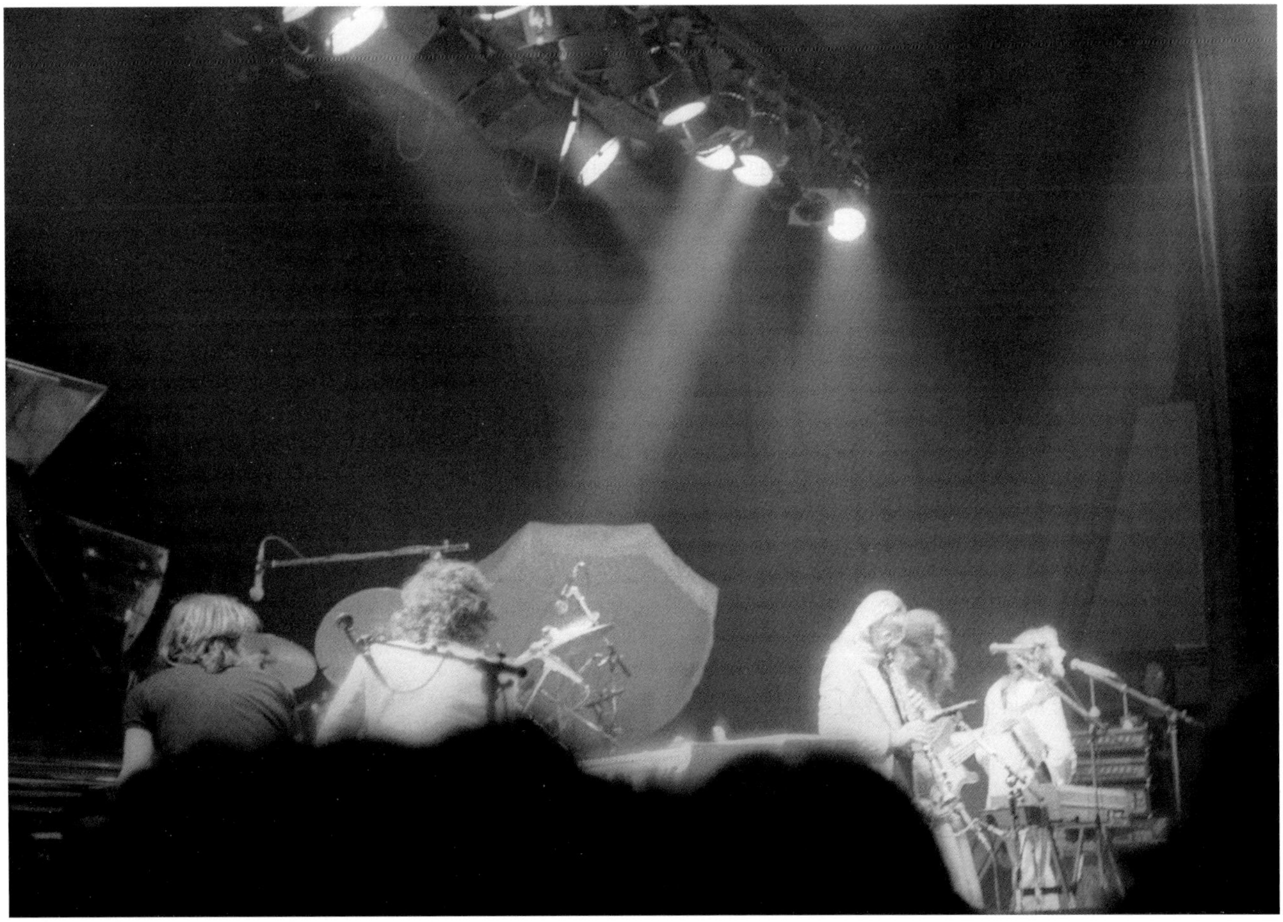

© David Bradbury

Sutherland Brothers and Quiver

16 February 1972 — Supports: John Martyn I Bronco I Claire Hamill
27 January 1974 — Support unknown
20 June 1975 — Support unknown
7 October 1977 — Support: City Boy

Aberdeenshire brothers Iain and Gavin Sutherland began performing as a folk rock duo in the early 1970s. Their first Lancaster concert featured the brothers, billed as 'The Sutherland Brothers Band', performing tracks from their self-titled 1972 Island Records album. In the same year The Sutherland Brothers released their second album *Lifeboat*, which included a single entitled 'Sailing'. Upon release the single failed to achieve commercial success for the brothers but would in time become a major hit for Rod Stewart, reaching No. 1 in the UK in September 1975 for four weeks.

From 1973–1978, in an effort to diversify and expand their folk-based sound, the Sutherland Brothers joined forces with a rock band known as Quiver, to become Sutherland Brothers and Quiver, appearing for a further three concerts in the Great Hall.

Under this combined moniker, the group recorded several albums and had a significant international hit single with the song 'Arms of Mary' in 1976, which reached No. 5 in the UK Singles Chart.

The band were just at their peak as the punk music explosion happened and they ended up being ousted from their residency at London's Marquee Club to make way for the likes of The Damned and X-Ray Spex. The group quickly found that its cheerful, folk rock style had fallen out of fashion and disbanded after recording a final album in 1979.

Claire Hamill from County Durham in northern England, is a British singer-songwriter. During her career she has been compared by several commentators to Joni Mitchell. Claire Hamill began singing professionally in 1971 when she was offered a recording contract with Island Records. As well as her solo career, she has collaborated with Wishbone Ash, appearing on stage with them on their visit to Lancaster for their 1981 *Number The Brave* concert.

A 1972 support slot for university veteran **John Martyn.**

Completing a great night's entertainment for this 1972 Sutherland Brothers concert were the band **Bronco**. The previous year, in April 1971, Lancaster had seen Bronco as a headline band; returning in November 1971 alongside John Martyn, as guests of Amazing Blondel.

A possible support band, for either the 1974 or 1975 date, may have been folk rock duo **Gallagher and Lyle**, best known for their 1976 hit single 'I Wanna Stay With You'.

1977 support act **City Boy** were a moderately successful English rock band of the late 1970s, characterised by complex vocal arrangements and heavy guitars. Their most popular songs were '5.7.0.5.' and 'The Day the Earth Caught Fire'. The band split in 1982.

The Sweet

19 March 1981　　　　Support: Bashful Alley

Glam rockers The Sweet came to play Lancaster at the beginning of the 1980s, having achieved notable success in the UK charts with thirteen Top 20 hits during the 1970s. The single 'Block Buster!' topped the charts in 1973, followed by three consecutive No. 2 hits in 'Hell Raiser (1973), 'The Ballroom Blitz' (1973) and 'Teenage Rampage' (1974).

Their first self-written and produced single, 'Fox on the Run', reached No. 2 in the UK Singles Chart in 1975.

The Sweet had their last UK Top 10 hit in 1978 with 'Love Is Like Oxygen'.

The original band comprised Steve Priest (bass), Brian Connolly (vocals), Mick Tucker (drums) and Andy Scott (guitars). A somewhat different lineup appeared at Lancaster for this 1981 concert. Brian Connolly had departed in 1979 due to personal problems, The Sweet adding guest keyboard player Gary Moberley and guitarist Ray McRiner.

The Sweet were due to perform at the university in May 1974 but a large portion of the tour was cancelled. In early 1974, Brian Connolly was attacked in London and was badly beaten, sustaining a kick to his throat that resulted in damaged vocal chords. It is said that as well as damaging his vocal cords, it shattered his confidence and he began drinking heavily. Brian Connolly died at the age of fifty-one on 9 February 1997 from liver failure and repeated heart attacks, attributed to chronic alcoholism through the 1970s and early 1980s.

Two versions of The Sweet continue to perform at present: Steve Priest's Sweet and Andy Scott's Sweet.

Scott's is based in England and Priest's in Los Angeles.

Billed to appear as support on the night with The Sweet were an outfit called The Steve Lynton Band, but stepping into the breach at the last moment when Lynton failed to turn up, were actually local Lancaster band **Bashful Alley**. They were early proponents of the NWOBHM (New Wave Of British Heavy Metal) which later spawned the likes of Iron Maiden, Def Leppard and Saxon.

Formed in 1980 and comprising Rob Tidd (Guitar), Ian 'Truff' Threlfall (Bass), Dave Slamin (Vocals) and Ian 'Donkey' Brown (Drums), all the members were at the time, Lancaster University students. Bashful Alley released a self-financed 7" single called 'Running Blind'

They were to disband in 1984.

It was great to hear from guitarist Rod Tidd about his memories of the night.

'For our gig with The Sweet, someone from the Ents office contacted us because the support band couldn't perform for some reason, and asked if we could step in. Naturally we jumped at it, thinking it could be our 'big break'. Alas, it wasn't.

On the night the show was pretty sparsely attended, and The Sweet themselves were basically a bunch of divas, all turning up in identical, over-the-top fur coats and a 'don't talk to me – don't even look at me' attitude. I like to think we blew 'em off stage'.

Rob Tidd and 'Truff' Threfall of Bashful Alley opening for The Sweet. Courtesy of Rob Tidd

T Rex

12 March 1971   Support: Red Dirt

Originally called Tyrannosaurus Rex, T Rex were formed in 1967 by singer-songwriter and guitarist Marc Bolan, real name Marc Feld.

The band enjoyed major UK successes with glam rock hits like 'Jeepster', 'Ride a White Swan', '20th Century Boy', 'Children of the Revolution', 'Telegram Sam' and 'Metal Guru'.

Over in America, the group had only the one major hit – the Top 10 'Bang a Gong (Get It On)' – before disappearing from the US charts in 1973.

T Rex produced a total of 13 studio albums and shortly following the release of what was to become their final album, *Dandy in the Underworld*, tragedy struck. While driving home early in the morning of 16 September 1977 after a night out at a nightclub, Gloria Jones, Bolan's girlfriend at the time and with Marc Bolan as a passenger, crashed his purple Mini 1275GT into a tree on Queen's Ride Barnes, in south London. Jones was severely injured and Marc Bolan was killed in the crash, two weeks before his thirtieth birthday.

After learning about Marc Bolan dying in a car crash, The Damned Guitarist Captain Sensible wrote the song 'Smash It Up (Part 1)'.

This was a second appearance in the Great Hall for T Rex with the band being billed in a support slot for a Rag Ball event. Top of the bill were to be The Faces, who failed to turn up on the night.

Red Dirt were a blues band formed in East Yorkshire around 1968 and comprising Dave Richardson (vocals), Steve Howden (guitar), Kenny Giles (bass) and Steve Jackson (drums). They built an impressive live reputation in clubs and venues in the North of England.

Hi Paul,

I knew Barry Lucas in the 1970s.

My name is Barbara Macari, née Moorhouse. My Dad was the head porter in the Great Hall. His name was Mick Moorhouse. I am sure Barry will remember him. I saw a lot of bands in the Great Hall as I used to get in for free!

I remember seeing:
T Rex
Tina Turner
Slade and many more.

My dad always tried to let me meet the bands.

I met Marc Bolan and he gave me a kiss and laughed at me because I said I liked his little red shoes.

I also used to help in the minor hall upstairs in the cloak room when orchestras were performing. I used to get paid whatever was in the dish on the table at the end of the night. One night I took £51 which was a lot of money in those days.

Later on in life I ended up working at the uni as a cleaning supervisor. In the past I have shopped for toiletries for Princess Alexandra when she came for degree ceremonies.

Also my daughter used to go to school with Barry's daughter and they were very good friends.

Small world isn't it.

PS give my regards to Barry

Regards

Barbara Macari

Whenever I watch *The Antiques Roadshow* or *Flog It* and they feature rock memorabilia, I break out in a cold sweat. I have given, or thrown away, all the posters, flyers, tickets etc. I had from the Great Hall concerts, and I never ever asked for autographs. If only I had known then what I know now …

We had had Tyrannosaurus Rex on at the Graduation Ball in 1970 but it was the time of their return as T Rex that still gives me nightmares to this day – nightmares of regret that is.

For each show you promote you have a legal responsibility to complete a form for the Performing Rights Society which details the songs performed, who wrote them, arranged and published them. It was very necessary in earlier times when acts performed songs written by others, but by the late '60s most bands were performing their own material. Monies were subtracted from the fee at a percentage rate and returned to the writer etc. As the bands did their own writing and arrangement they got their own money back minus a large administration fee deducted by PRS. You can imagine most artists were not amused, very resentful in fact.

On this night I gave Mark Bolan the form and he returned it a few minutes later. The sheet read: "'Get It On' – written by Mickey Mouse, arranged by Donald Duck, published by Walt Disney" – on and on, for the whole set, with every cartoon character you can name and signed by Mark Bolan. I looked at the form; I couldn't send that in! So I ripped it up and made one out myself with what I remembered of the set.

Now every time I watch those antiques programmes I think that if only I had kept that PRS form it would indeed have been a totally unique piece if rock 'n' roll memorabilia, and my pension!

Barry Lucas

The Teardrop Explodes

31 January 1982 — Support: The Ravishing Beauties
10 October 1982 — Support: Screen 3

The Teardrop Explodes were a British post-punk/neo-psychedelic band formed in Liverpool in 1978. The band were formed by Julian Cope who had previously been in the short-lived yet locally renowned band Crucial Three along with Pete Wylie (who went on to form Wah!) and Ian McCulloch, later of Echo and the Bunnymen.

In 1981, the group were at the height of their popularity, achieving the No. 6 slot in the UK Singles Chart with the single 'Reward', and in April a Top 20 hit with 'Treason'.

The Teardrop Explodes released a total of three studio albums, promoting the release of the album *Wilder* on their first visit to Lancaster in January.

Following the band's dissolution in December 1982, Julian Cope began a career as a solo artist, appearing at The Sugarhouse in Lancaster in March 1984.

He later went on to pursue a career as a writer and cultural commentator which continues to this day.

Screen 3 were a British post-punk new wave band from Norwich, active from 1980–1984 and again from 1990–1992. Heavily influenced by The Cure's first album, *Three Imaginary Boys*, the original Screen 3 lineup formed in 1980 and consisted of Neil Dyer, Richard Kett and Brett Cooper. Trumpet players Peter Jay and Jason Votier were added in late 1981.

The Ravishing Beauties were a three piece all girl punk pop band, comprising Virginia Astley, Kate St John and Nicky Holland. Virginia's father was Edwin Astley, a composer responsible for the theme music to TV shows such as *The Saint*, *Randall and Hopkirk (Deceased)* and *Dangerman*.

You might get an inkling of the Teardrop show from the photo but you really cannot understand the sheer size of the stage set and the problems it generated.

My mate, Paul Darwin, was tour managing the show and I think we were the second date. Obviously the band had sat in the pub over the summer with some theatre set designer luvvie and dreamed up this stage set. As the drink flowed they took to designing a rock show on the back of numerous beer mats.

Paul was at his wits end that morning as he phoned me at 8.00 am and asked me to get to the Great Hall. When I got there he explained that the previous night they had taken the hall's side doors off and then the windows in the roof. But still they couldn't get the whole structure, with the solid stage risers, into the venue. Well, we tried every which way, even taking off the Great Hall doors in the foyer but neither could we. So what you see is a fraction of that ridiculous stage set. As far as I know the vast majority of the set stayed on the artics for a scenic tour of the UK and never saw the light of day.

Barry Lucas

January 1982

Both images on this page October 1982 © Geoff Campbell

Tears For Fears

26 March 1983   Support: Verba Verba

Formed in 1981 in Bath, by Roland Orzabal and Curt Smith, Tears For Fears took their name from a phrase found in Arthur Janov's book *Prisoners of Pain* published in 1980.

Tears For Fears arrived in Lancaster on the back of the release, two weeks earlier, of their debut album *The Hurting,* which focused specifically on the emotional angst of adolescence. The album went on to reach No. 1 in the UK Albums Chart of 1983 and spawned three UK Top 5 singles, 'Mad World', 'Change' and 'Pale Shelter'. Orzabal and Smith then made their major international breakthrough with the 1985 album *Songs from the Big Chair*, which sold over 10 million copies worldwide and topped the US Albums Chart for five weeks. It peaked at No. 2 in the UK and spent six months in the Top 10. Five singles from the album reached the UK Top 30, with 'Shout' reaching No. 4, and their highest-charting hit, 'Everybody Wants to Rule the World', reaching No. 2. Smith and Orzabal parted company in 1991, after the release of their third platinum-selling album *The Seeds of Love* (1989), though Orzabal retained the Tears for Fears name throughout the remainder of the 1990s.

The duo re-formed in 2000 and released an album of new material, *Everybody Loves a Happy Ending* in 2004.

In July 2016, the band played their first live dates in the UK in over ten years.

To date, Tears for Fears have sold over 30 million albums worldwide, including more than eight million in the US.

Information on **Verba Verba** is scant, but they were from Newton Aycliffe in the North East of England and featured a brother and sister in the lineup.

Ten Years After

15 January 1972   Support: The National Head Band
12 October 1973   Support: Yakety Yak

Ten Years After were a blues rock band founded in the mid '60s in Nottinghamshire, by guitarist Alvin Lee and bassist Leo Lyons. Between 1968 and 1973 Ten Years After scored eight Top 40 albums in the UK Albums Chart and were best known for tracks such as 'I'm Going Home', 'Hear Me Calling', 'I'd Love to Change the World' and 'Love Like a Man'. 'Love Like a Man' was the group's only hit in the UK Singles Chart, where it reached No. 10 in 1970. Interestingly it was the first record ever issued with a different playing speed on each side; a three-minute edit at 45rpm and a nearly eight-minute live version at 33rpm on the flip side. The band dissolved in 1975, being reunited in 1988 to continue through to the present day, sadly without legendary guitarist Alvin Lee who passed away in 2013.

The National Head Band were a hard progressive rock outfit formed in 1969 comprising Rusty Ford (guitar, vocals), Lee Kerslake (drums, keyboards, vocals), Dave Paul (bass, keyboards, guitar, vocals) and Jan Schelhaas (keyboards). They split in November 1971. Jan Schelhaas was later to become a member of The Gary Moore Band and Caravan, whilst Lee Kerslake later went on to join up with Uriah Heep.

Yakety Yak were a fifties-style rock 'n' roll band, formed in 1969 with the emphasis being very much on doo-wop. The seven-piece band recorded an album on Dart Records in 1974. Previously, in March 1973, Yakety Yak had been on stage in the Great Hall providing support to Vinegar Joe for a Rag Ball event.

Featuring the legendary Alvin Lee, fresh from stealing the show at Woodstock, Ten Years After were one of the greatest blues rock bands in the UK to play the Great Hall. But the concert was also personally significant, not for the music but for the introduction of a valuable – no invaluable – member of my team who was to play a very important part in the Lancaster story.

In the week of the show a young first year student came into my office. His name was Alan Murray and he had come to offer his services. He said that he had been looking at my autumn programme and especially the ticket prices and believed that I was running the concerts as a commercial operation to make money for the students' union. Was that right he wondered? I told him that it was. He said that in that case he would really like to help on the shows. Normally I would have just said, "Thanks, but no thanks." But there was something that prevented me doing that – I don't know why but I asked him about his background. He was a working class kid from Liverpool, the only one in his family to go to university. In the sixth form, he and some of his mates had decided to promote bands in Liverpool, mainly at The Stadium, I believe. It was an impressive list of bands with Ten Years After and Elton John (and he did turn up!) among many others. I said, "OK, start this weekend."

Alan was reading economics so I soon asked him to take charge of the door. He did so successfully and quickly graduated to helping sort out the deals, the percentages etc., with bands and their tour managers. Alan became the most important part of the concert team, a valuable sounding board, advisor and financier. When we were earning the Students' Union extra funds through 'massaging' the percentage deals he was invaluable in confounding the tour representatives and money men.

Alan worked on all the shows throughout his three year degree, then continued while he did an MA followed by a PhD. He then went to work for BOC in Manchester but, for petrol money, came back to help on each show. He continued to do this for several years … before moving on to work in various finance roles for Chloride Group and The Burton Group. Alan then joined Hanson plc working for them between 1988 and 2007 and progressing to become Group CEO between 2002 and 2007.

He has made a great success of his life – I taught him everything he knows! But seriously he became a great friend and a lot of the Lancaster story I am telling here is down to him. Thanks, Alan, I will always be in your debt.

Barry Lucas

Alan Murray and Barry Lucas

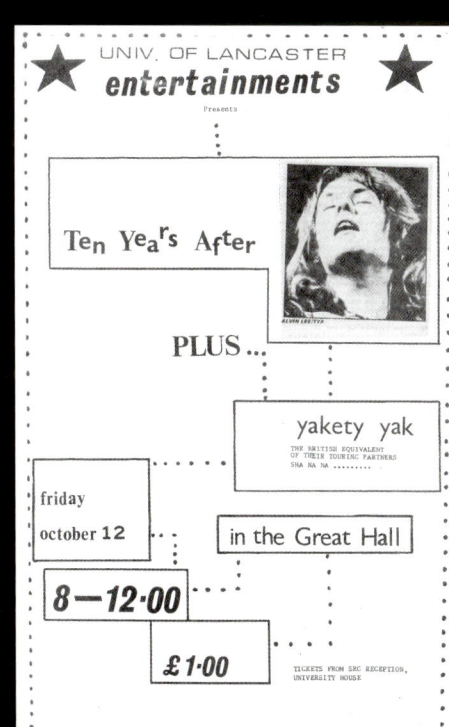

Thin Lizzy

5 November 1976 **Johnny The Fox UK Tour** Support: Clover

Thin Lizzy were an Irish hard rock band who formed in Dublin in 1969 and were best known for their singles 'Whiskey in the Jar', 'Jailbreak' and 'The Boys Are Back in Town'.

Two of the founding members, drummer Brian Downey and bass guitarist/ vocalist Phil Lynott, met while still in school, with Lynott assuming the role of frontman and leading them throughout their twelve studio album-recording career.

Fresh from an October tour of Europe in support of Robin Trower, Thin Lizzy embarked on a sell-out twenty-five-date tour of the UK, including Lancaster and Leeds, which were the only two university venues on the schedule.

The Great Hall lineup on the night was:
Phil Lynott – bass guitar, lead vocals
Brian Downey– drums
Scott Gorham – guitar
Brian Robertson – guitar

The tour was in support of Thin Lizzy's seventh studio album, *Johnny The Fox,* which peaked at No. 11 in the 1976 UK Albums Chart. The album produced the hit single 'Don't Believe a Word'.

From 1974, Thin Lizzy decided to switch from using one lead guitarist to two. Though others had earlier used similar techniques, Thin Lizzy are widely recognised as one of the first hard rock bands to employ a double lead guitar harmony – a technique pioneered by Wishbone Ash in the UK, and independently in the USA by Lynyrd Skynyrd and The Allman Brothers Band. This style was later refined and popularised in the mid-'70s by bands like Judas Priest, and later by the emerging new wave of British heavy metal groups such as Iron Maiden and Def Leppard. Iron Maiden in particular have praised Thin Lizzy extensively and covered their song 'Massacre' from Thin Lizzy's *Johnny the Fox* album.

After Lynott's death in 1986 at the age of thirty-six, various incarnations of the band have emerged over the years, based initially around guitarists Scott Gorham and John Sykes, though Sykes left the band in 2009. Gorham later continued with a new project including Downey. The Thin Lizzy that tours today are led by alumni Scott Gorham, Brian Downey and Darren Wharton (all of whom played in Thin Lizzy with Phil Lynott), the lineup being completed by Damon Johnson (guitar), bassist Marco Mendoza (Whitesnake, Ted Nugent) and The Almighty's Ricky Warwick on vocals and guitar.

This concert featured the first supporting role at Lancaster for Huey Lewis's **Clover**.

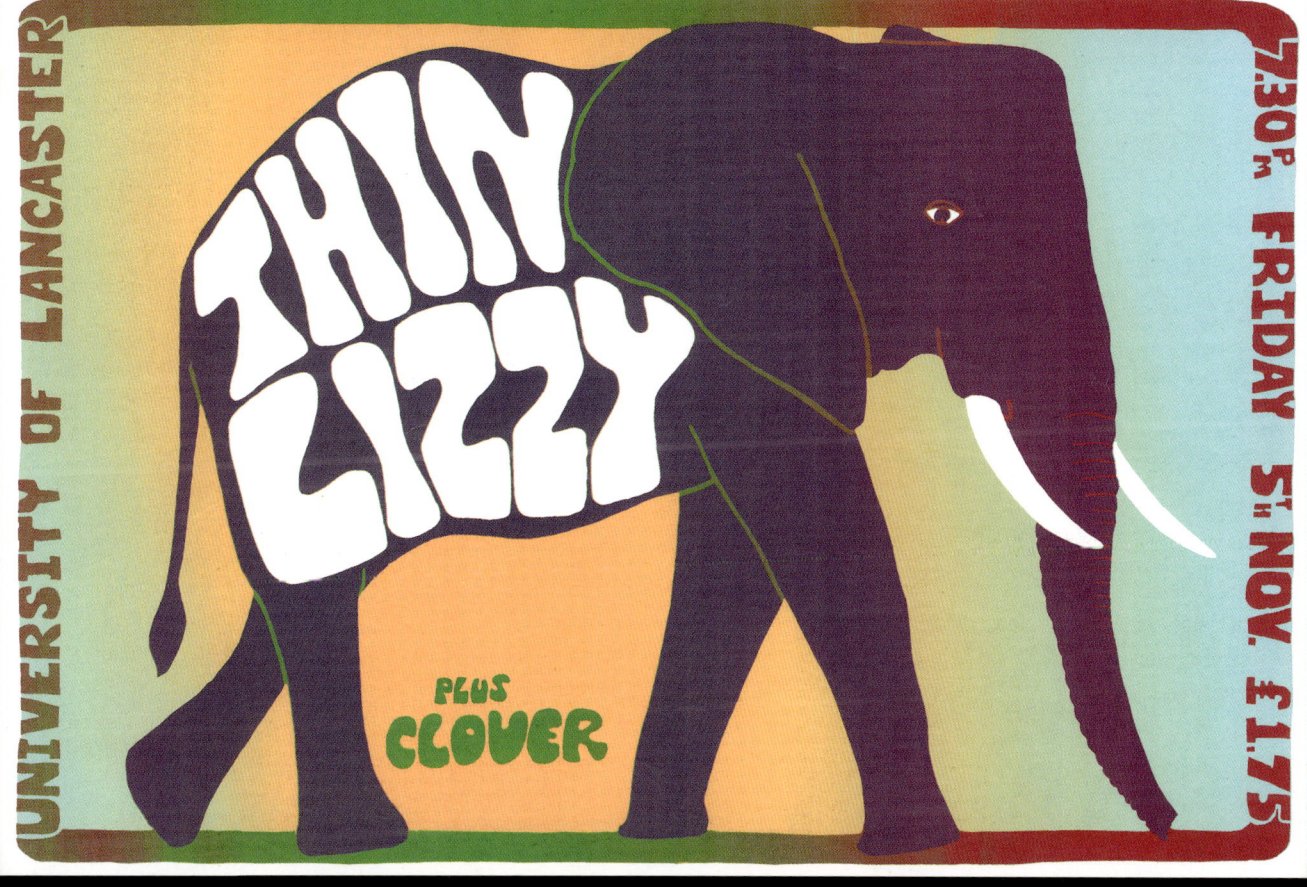

Thin Lizzy

The legend that is Phil Lynott. I can still see him today, centre stage, using the follow spotlight on him and reflecting it off the scratch plate on his guitar to pick out the pretty girls on the balcony.

By this time Thin Lizzy had hit super stardom and their contract and rider reflected this. One demand was that the mixer desk had to be centre stage, a specified distance back – remember, by now the band were usually only playing festivals or stadiums. I signed the contract but explained, in writing, that this particular clause would mean that the mixer desk would be situated in the next building. Apparently this so amused the band's management that they carried it around with them to show others in the music business for months.

I must mention an interesting anecdote which occurred many years later. I was going to see Limehouse Lizzy, a Thin Lizzy tribute, at The Platform in Morecambe (at the time a very successful local authority venue managed by my wife, Mary). They are an excellent band and well worth checking out. I was going with a couple of friends and asked my son, Simon, if he wanted to come along. He did. He is a Professional Golf Association coach and his first job as an eighteen year old was at Malahide, just outside Dublin (the relevance of this will soon be revealed). About three numbers into the show I saw him texting. I absolutely hate the obsession with mobiles so I asked him to leave it alone for just ninety minutes. He said, "But I'm just texting Steve."

"Why? Who the hell is Steve?"

"I was telling him I was watching a tribute to his dad."

"Who's his dad?"

"Phil Lynott. I met Steve when I was in Ireland and we became good mates."

"Let you off."

A few minutes later he was holding up his phone. "What are you doing now?" I wanted to know.

"He wanted to watch some of the show."

Now, how cool is that from your son?

Barry Lucas

The unmistakable figure of Phil Lynott on the Great Hall Stage
© David Bradbury

John Angus

Third World

19 November 1978   Supports: John Cooper Clarke I The South African Drongoes

Third World are a Jamaican reggae band formed in 1973 by keyboardist Michael "Ibo" Cooper and guitarist and cellist Steven "Cat" Coore. They are best known for the single 'Now That We've Found Love' released in 1978 and reaching No. 10 in the UK Singles Chart.

To date, the prolific Third World have recorded twenty-one studio albums, five live albums and over thirty singles.

This was another Great Hall concert in support of the Rock Against Racism movement.

The band continues to perform with six members, including three of the original core members at the forefront.

The "Bard of Salford" **Dr John Cooper Clarke,** as he is now known, was the tremendous supporting act on the night.

First up on stage that night was a band billed as **The South African Drongoes** of which little is known, although a special mention must be made here of a local Lancaster outfit who existed around the early 1980s similarly called, The Drongos.

The Drongos were part of a Lancaster Musicians Collective with three saxophonists in the lineup along with former China Street guitarist Martin Pilkington, Pharaoh drummer Bernie Kelly and Lancaster bass guitarist Geoff Dade.

The Thompson Twins

8 May 1983 — Support unknown
20 March 1984 — **Into The Gap Tour** — Support: Savage Progress

The Thompson Twins were an English new wave band from Sheffield formed in 1977 and finally disbanding in 1993. Massively popular in the mid '80s, the band scored a string of hits in the UK and broke into the US and Canada, enjoying huge popularity around the globe. The band were named after the two bumbling detectives Thomson and Thompson from Hergé's comic strip, *The Adventures of Tintin*.

Originally a four-piece band, they expanded to a seven-piece outfit then downsized in 1982 to the classic three-piece Thompson Twins that visited Lancaster University on two occasions.

The band were best known for hits such as 'Hold Me Now', 'Doctor! Doctor!' and 'Love On Your Side'.

Quick Step and Side Kick was the third album for The Thompson Twins, going to the No. 2 spot in the UK Albums Chart. It was released in February 1983 and was their first album as a trio. The single 'We Are Detective' from the album was released in April 1983, reaching No. 7 in the UK Singles Chart and for the first time featuring the vocals of Alannah Currie.

The tour to support *Quick Step and Side Kick* brought the band to Lancaster in May 1983.

Their second visit to Lancaster was in support of the album *Into The Gap* which produced their best charting single 'You Take Me Up', which reached No. 2 in the UK Singles Chart April 1984.

Lancaster lineup for both concerts:
Tom Bailey – keyboards, lead vocals, guitars
Joe Leeway – percussion, backing vocals, keyboards
Alannah Currie – percussion, backing vocals, drums
Andrew Bodnar – bass guitar

1984 support act **Savage Progress** were an English pop group in the 1980s that had European success with hits in Germany, Austria and Switzerland.

They were a mixed-race group of musicians who used traditional pop styles as well as reggae, Caribbean dance rhythms and African rhythms. The band included former Thompson Twins drummer Andrew Edge.

By this time Lancaster was firmly established as a major prestigious venue that all the acts wanted to play as part of any UK tour, large or small. This Thompson Twins tour featured only the country's main venues and, of course, Lancaster was on it. The set was illuminated by the first totally computerised light show, a massive lighting desk filling half the back wall of the hall, under the balcony. It was certainly a first for Lancaster and, if I remember correctly, a first on a tour in this country.

Barry Lucas

After the show Paul Loasby, who was promoting this tour, invited me back to the band's hotel for a couple of drinks. Never one to refuse free alcohol, I enthusiastically accepted. The band were staying at The Post House (J 34) so off we went, to one of the most embarrassing rock 'n' roll moments of my life. I was sitting at the bar with Paul when the band joined us. Suddenly from across the room I saw a figure frantically trying to get my attention. I froze. It was a well-known guy from Lancaster at the time. He had opened a big nightclub in the town and was our own version of Peter Stringfellow. Despite my best efforts to avoid eye contact, he marched, well staggered, over to join us. 'I'm your biggest fan,' he opened with. It's a line I'm sure they had never heard before! Well it didn't get any better and after a few minutes, or was it hours, he said that he wanted his kids to be rock 'n' roll stars and wondered what advice they'd give him. I just had to leave. I never really forgave him – I had to leave all that free booze!

Tina Turner

25 February 1984   **UK Tour 1984**   No Support

Anna Mae Bullock, better known as Tina Turner, could arguably have been one of the biggest stars, at the height of their career, to have performed in the Great Hall.

Tina Turner rose to fame in the 1960s singing and performing with then-husband Ike Turner, and later went on to enjoy a highly successful solo career.

Born in Tennessee in 1939, Tina Turner began performing with musician Ike in the 1950s. They became known as the Ike and Tina Turner Revue, achieving popular acclaim for their live performances and recordings, until Tina left in the 1970s after years of abuse. Following a slow start to her solo career, Turner achieved massive success with her 1984 album *Private Dancer*. She later went on to deliver more chart-topping albums and was elected into the Rock and Roll Hall of Fame in 1991.

After success with the single 'Let's Stay Together', which charted at No. 6 at the end of 1983 in the UK, she started a sell-out tour in England. Her single 'Help' was also released just in time for this tour. The Lancaster setlist included some new songs and was much more rock orientated than all her concerts before.

Lancaster setlist: 'Cat People', 'Acid Queen', 'Lets Pretend We're Married', 'Hot Legs', 'Get Back', 'Nutbush City Limits', 'Givin It Up For Your Love', 'Night Life', 'River Deep-Mountain High', 'Let's Stay Together', 'Help', 'Proud Mary', 'Hollywood Nights', 'Out Of Time'.

Band members:
Kenny Moore – pianist, lead vocals
James Ralston – lead guitar
Jack Bruno – drums
Bob Feit – bass guitar
Chuck O'Steen – keyboards, vocals
Lejeune Richardson – backing vocals, dancer
Annie Behringer – backing vocals, dancer

Left to right: Annie Behringer, Tina Turner and Lejeune Richardson © Geoff Campbell

opened the book by describing the journey back to Lancaster with Tina Turner's promoter, Barry Marshall. Of all the acts to appear at Lancaster, Tina, in some ways, was the most remarkable and summed up what had happened to that small, new university in a mad fourteen years.

At the beginning of 1984 Geoff Campbell and I were getting worried. By now the audiences at Lancaster were spoilt and used to a steady procession of the world's superstars. But, as of January, we had no major star in place for the rest of the academic year. So, Geoff and I went to London to chat up a few agents and promoters as we simply had to find something outstanding. We ended up in Liverpool Street, Islington, at Paul Loasby's offices, in a bit of a desperate state – still no major act. We retired to Paul's favourite pub for lunch – favourite because it was fifteen yards outside his office door – and lunch was to be several pints followed by bottles of Chardonnay back at the office. Paul has dramatically changed since those days, as back then he was one of rock 'n' roll's legendary party animals. After about thirty minutes of listening to us bemoaning our/Lancaster's fate Paul left the table and borrowed the pub's phone (no mobiles then). He returned to the table: "Do you want Tina Turner?" he enquired matter of factly.

Do we want Tina Turner? To me she was a true music business legend who, from the early days of the '60s with Ike, had bestrode rock like an Amazonian colossus. Nobody who saw her perform in Monterrey will ever forget it. Do we want Tina Turner? Are you 'aving a laff?

The journey back to Lancaster was a joyous one for Geoff and I.

The tour was a massive success and re-established Tina, giving her a status she would never relinquish. The tour posters were those massive ones for building bill boards which were hopeless for our small, agency shop windows. It didn't matter though, the show sold out in a few hours. A couple of days later I was walking down the Spine when a mature student stopped me and went ballistic. He didn't know Tina Turner was playing the University and now it was sold out. Why hadn't I advertised it, he wanted to know. "Look, mate, of course I didn't advertise it, or rather I didn't come round to your room to tell you, but 2000 people did know it was on … somehow."

The interest and demand generated was immense. Mick Byron of Byron's Hair in Lancaster had six hair industry bigwigs (sorry) driving up from London. Could I do ANYTHING? He would pay ANYTHING. A senior police officer rang me: "I know it's a sell out, but could you get a couple of CID in the projection box at the back of the hall?"

"Oh, OK I suppose so, anything for the Old Bill."

"Great. There's fourteen of us coming up. Thanks!"

© Geoff Campbell

The show was brilliant, but, dear reader, do you remember my musings on Eric Clapton? Well Tina needed several changes of costume so we built a small changing area at the back of the stage. However, we found we couldn't use it because the balcony was packed and overlooked it, so she would have to dash back to the dressing room. It would all be a bit frantic. I was sitting in the porters' lodge with Barry Marshall when the tour manager came in, going berserk. Apparently my stewards (yes, the same ones I foolishly didn't sack over Mr Clapton's Southern Comfort incident) had burst into Tina Turner's dressing room as she was changing. Can it get any more embarrassing, or any worse? We went down to the backstage. I demanded to know what they were playing at. Would you believe the answer? No, you wouldn't. In front of the tour manager, tour promoter and me, they said, with totally straight faces, that they thought they heard her call out for some stewards to help her out of her dress!!

Only now, thirty odd years later can I see the funny side – I think.

Barry Lucas

Tom Paxton

14 May 1971 — Support unknown
2 February 1973 — Support: Bridgit St John
28 February 1975 — Support: Bryn Haworth

Tom Paxton is an American folk singer-songwriter who has had a music career spanning more than fifty years.

Paxton's songs have been widely covered over the years by musicians such as Bob Dylan, Joan Baez, John Denver and Dolly Parton.

He has performed thousands of concerts around the world.

His biggest successes as a songwriter were the songs that became hits for others. These were covered many times over and turned out to be Tom's most valuable copyrights. 'The Last Thing on My Mind', 'Bottle of Wine' and 'The Marvelous Toy' were his most popular works. But other artists were also attracted to such socially conscious compositions as 'What Did You Learn in School Today?' and 'Whose Garden Was This?', as well as his reflective, melancholy songs such as 'Ramblin' Boy' and 'I Can't Help But Wonder Where I'm Bound'.

In March 2015, Paxton released his new studio album, *Redemption Road*, his sixty-first album to date. Tom continues to perform yearly tours of the United States and UK.

Bridgit St John was back once more in the Great Hall, having previously provided support to Roy Harper in November 1969.

From Blackburn, Lancashire, acclaimed slide guitarist **Bryn Haworth** is a singer-songwriter who has been performing his own unique brand of rock, country and gospel blues for over thirty years. Over his career he has recorded, as a session guitar player, with top musicians including Chris de Burgh, Joan Armatrading, Cliff Richard and Gerry Rafferty. Bryn also writes his own songs and has had several of his compositions recorded by other artists, including Lulu, Sandy Denny and Mary Black.

What a lovely bloke – a true gentleman. A great folk legend who gave three fantastic concerts at Lancaster. But it was the first one that was really memorable for me, for the wrong reasons. In those days I still played sport in The Roses weekend, football for the Students' Union and cricket for the University First X1. So I was required for combat in York that year, the weekend Tom was due to play in the Great Hall. I was in an unprecedented run of twenty-eight consecutive profit-making shows, something of legendary proportions. I was leaving the show in my staff's hands, even my trusty right-hand man, Alan Murray, was over in York on football duty. But it was hardly an onerous deal, an international folk superstar, solo artist and one of the nicest people in music to deal with. I phoned on Sunday morning, before taking the field of battle, to ask how it went. To my dismay we had fallen seventeen people short of break even, eighteen short of another profit – we had lost £16.75, but a loss is a loss, the first for twenty-nine shows. I was devastated, so it was to the bar to revive my spirits for the footie match.

Barry Lucas

Toyah

10 December 1982 **Mini Tour UK** Support unknown

Toyah Ann Willcox is an English singer and actress with a career spanning more than thirty years. Willcox has had eight UK Top 40 singles and released over twenty albums, written two books, appeared in over forty stage plays and in ten feature films.

She is married to former King Crimson guitarist Robert Fripp.

Between 1977 and 1983 she fronted her band Toyah, before embarking on a solo career in the mid '80s. Her biggest hits include 'It's a Mystery', 'Thunder in the Mountains' and 'I Want to Be Free'.

Lancaster band lineup, 1982 Mini Tour UK:
Toyah Willcox – vocals
Joel Bogen – guitar & backing vocals
Phil Spalding – bass & backing vocals
Keith Hale – keyboards & backing vocals
Simon Phillips – drums

Simon Phillips had previously appeared in the Great Hall with The Jack Bruce Band in 1977 and later in his career went on to be the long-serving drummer for American band Toto. Keyboardist Keith Hale was a former member of Hawkwind.

Toyah Willcox continues to record and tour.

Traffic

29 January 1971   Support: Amazing Blondel
26 April 1974   Support: Richard and Linda Thompson

Traffic were an English rock band originating from Birmingham. The group was formed in April 1967 by Steve Winwood, Jim Capaldi, Chris Wood and Dave Mason, following Winwood's departure from The Spencer Davis Group. They began as a psychedelic rock group and diversified their sound through the use of instruments such as the Mellotron and harpsichord, sitar and various reed instruments, and by incorporating jazz and improvisational techniques into their music. Their first three successful singles were 'Paper Sun', 'Hole in My Shoe' and 'Here We Go Round the Mulberry Bush'.

Traffic's first three albums combined psychedelic rock and soul with elements of British folk music, giving them a unique, groundbreaking sound. Their most popular single was 'Dear Mr Fantasy' from the album of the same name.

Following the second departure of Dave Mason from Traffic in 1968, Winwood joined up with Eric Clapton, Ginger Baker and future Traffic bassist and sometime Family man, Ric Grech, to form Blind Faith.

The Blind Faith project proved to be short-lived and in 1970, following the split, Winwood set about recording a solo album. After Chris Wood and Jim Capaldi became involved, the decision was taken to release this album (what would eventually become *John Barleycorn Must Die*) under the Traffic name, despite the absence of Dave Mason. Around 1971, Mason left for good (having been in and out of the band from the beginning) and the band experienced a variety of personnel changes. The resulting band added some jazzy elements to their style, pioneering the jazz rock genre, with their compositions tending to stretch out over longer lengths. With their albums *The Low Spark of High Heeled Boys* (1971) and *Shootout at the Fantasy Factory* (1973) their popularity in the US grew. After two more albums, personnel problems resulted in the band calling it quits soon after their 1974 Lancaster concert.

Traffic made two visits to Lancaster to play the Great Hall. Their first, in 1971, was notable for the non-arrival of Elton John, who was billed to appear as one of the support acts alongside Amazing Blondel.

1971 Traffic lineup:
Steve Winwood – guitars and vocals
Jim Capaldi – drums and vocals
Chris Wood – keyboards
Ric Grech – bass
Possibly Dave Mason – guitars, sitar

In September of 1974 Traffic released their seventh album, *When the Eagle Flies.* For this concert two new members had been added to the lineup, Rosko Gee and Rebop Kwaku Baah, the Ghanaian percussionist, who along with Rosko Gee went on to join German band Can, playing with them until their breakup in 1979.

1974 Traffic lineup:
Steve Winwood – keyboards, guitars, vocals
Jim Capaldi – drums and vocals
Chris Wood – sax, flute, keyboards
Rosko Gee – bass
Rebop Kwaku Baah – percussion

Veterans of a total of 6 Great Hall appearances, **Amazing Blondel** did turn up to support Traffic for their 1971 concert.

Richard and Linda Thompson, in their first of two visits to Lancaster University, provide the support for the 1974 concert.

Traffic

What a great concert that must have been, I hear you all say – well it certainly would have been if it had ever happened that way.

Traffic were one of the world's super-groups at the time – the incredible Steve Winwood vocals, Jim Capaldi's driving drumming, Dave Mason's guitar and Chris Wood's keyboards produced great albums and arguably even greater live performances. I had booked them for a Great Hall show and added my old friends and growing Lancaster favourites, Amazing Blondel.

However, out of the blue I was offered Elton John for a date on a British tour his agent was organising for his return from his gigs in the USA. I had just got a copy of Tumbleweed Connection from 'Ear 'Ere Records and was knocked out by it, especially Bernie Taupin's lyrics. I was certain that he was about to become really huge, so at £150 it was worth a gamble. Added to the £125 for Amazing and £750 for Traffic it meant that I had to sell thirteen hundred or so tickets but I had little doubt it would do the business, especially if Tumbleweed Connection got the exposure and reviews it deserved.

Elton John broke big in the USA, probably against all expectations. He went massive and his returning tour now became eagerly anticipated. I received a call from his agent, flushed with reflected success, explaining that he was adding a support to the English tour. I said no thanks as I already had two supports. He naturally wanted to know who they were. He certainly didn't like my response, especially on hearing 'Traffic', when there was a deadly silence at the end of the phone. "Traffic, supporting?" Well, I explained that as Traffic were worldwide superstars of considerable standing and were being paid five times more than Elton John, I therefore expected him to be the support artist! There was a great deal of umming and aarhing but I did explain that I had a signed contract from his office and that I expected it to be honoured.

Fast forward to show time, 8.00 pm. The doors had opened and at 7.30 pm all the bands had sound checked – Elton John's crew had done this for him but that wasn't totally unusual, even then. I was walking across the hall foyer when Elton's head roadie slammed the phone down and stormed out of the porters' lodge, swearing. "Bloody hell, Reg has broken down!" Now here I must own up to not being a massive rock 'n' roll anorak as I answered, "I don't give a fuck about Reg, where is Elton John?" There followed a disbelieving look from the roadie as he proceeded to explain that Elton John was in fact Reg Dwight and he had broken down at Charnock Richard services.

I explained the problem to Traffic's tour manager who said that he thought it was a way of Elton John getting top spot on the bill, as Traffic would have to go on stage immediately after Amazing Blondel. I said, "Surely not!!! Who would stoop to that?"

He offered to drive down to Charnock Richard and pick him up, I just had to delay the show slightly – he had a fast car and the shows went on until after 1.00 am in those days. On arriving at the service station he phoned to say there was no sign of Elton John. "Has he turned up there?" he asked hopefully. Well he hadn't. In fact I never got to know what happened to him, it didn't seem to damage his career too much. Perhaps it would have, if he had still been seen as a support act after all that American success, so luckily it all turned out all right for him in the end!

Steve Winwood and Traffic 1971

The Tremeloes

19 February 1971   Supports: Money I Ashley

The Tremeloes are an English beat group founded in 1958 in Dagenham, East London and originally called Brian Poole and The Tremoloes (sic).

The quintet consisted of lead vocalist Brain Poole, lead guitarist Rick West, rhythm guitarist/keyboardist Alan Blakley, bassist Alan Howard and drummer Dave Munden.

On New Year's Day 1962, Decca Records auditioned two bands at its London studios: Brian Poole and The Tremoloes, a veteran group from Essex and a relatively unknown Liverpool quartet known as The Beatles. Decca chose The Tremoloes over the newcomers because, as a London based outfit they would be more accessible than the Liverpool based Beatles.

To say it was a bad decision is an understatement, but The Tremeloes did produce some hits for Decca, ultimately placing thirteen songs in the British Top 40 with the first in 1963 being a cover of the Isley Brothers' Twist and Shout.

Their best known hits were their 1967 UK No.1 hit 'Silence is Golden' and 'Here Comes my Baby' (written by Cat Stevens) reaching No.4 in the same year.

Following the 1962 audition and subsequent signing to Decca, the band altered the spelling of their name to 'Tremeloes' as the result of a misprint in an East London newspaper.

A version of The Tremeloes are still active today.

Little is known about **Ashley**.

Also on the bill that night were a covers band called **Money** from Manchester. Later the same year Money had stepped into the breach for Barry Lucas to provide entertainment at very short notice when The Moody Blues pulled out of a concert at the last minute (see Blue Jays entry).

This was a Rag Ball featuring one of those legendary bands of the mid '60s. It really is amazing when you go to see one of the acts from that era, it's sixty to ninety minutes of non-stop hits. Your youth comes flooding back, well, it does if you're of a certain age. Of course the Singles Chart dominated music from that period and the top bands regularly released four, five or even six records a year. Most hit the Top 10 and so were played constantly on the radio and television, embedding themselves into your subconscious. It's embarrassing how many numbers you can sing along to!

This show is remarkable for one thing. The band were obviously very '60s in style, that is what the audience wanted after all, but were also dated in their show presentation. A few small PA column stacks, fitting into a transit van, proper '60s pop, was all the equipment on stage. This was, in some ways, very fortunate indeed. Many of the audience probably had a more impressive speaker set-up for their record players in their bedrooms at home. It was at this show, early in 1971, that the University administration started its determined attack on the Great Hall popular music concerts. So by 1985, when I resigned, no wonder I was tired of fighting this continual battle. They began it here by calling in the Audio Visual Aids Department to do an investigation (exposé) into sound levels. They hoped to use this to get the Great Hall shows stopped, curtailed or emasculated. Given the nature of this particular show, the very small PA and what was to follow in later years, their report makes for very amusing reading today.

  Interpretation:

1) The above results are measurement of sound level and are not necessarily the same as noise, since noise can be generally defined as unwanted sound   .

4) At no location other than within the building was the activity in the Great Hall measurable or even detectable.

5) Table 2 comprises measurements made while the dance was being held in the Great Hall. The figures for locations 1, 2 and 3 (Great Hall balcony, and foyer and Nuffield corridor) illustrate the very high level of sound generated by the equipment used by present day groups. It is comparable with the sound levels in the vicinity of a large jet airliner taking off. Close to the stage, levels must be approaching the Threshold of Pain and performers working constantly under these conditions (and possibly some members of the audience who regularly attend) are in some danger of suffering permanent auditory damage.

Conclusion:

There appears to be a majority opinion in favour of limiting in some way the level of sound produced by groups in the Great Hall.

The above results relate, I am told, to a "quiet" night in as much as the dance was not well attended and the groups appearing were "quieter" than many who have performed here in the past.

Good old Mr Glover, if only he'd have known what was to come. But how's that for a paternal attitude to 'young people enjoying themselves'? If he had turned up at The Scorpions he'd have prophesied Armageddon.

Barry Lucas

U2

2 March 1983 **The War Tour** Support: The Nightcaps

U2 visited Lancaster in support of the release of their third album *War*. It was their first tour as a fulltime headlining act, taking over a year to complete and comprising over a hundred dates.

The tour was in three legs, taking in Europe, North America and Japan, and the shows were typically ninety minutes long.

On stage, Bono was emotional and very theatrical, and during songs he would climb lighting rigs and plunge into the audience. When performing 'Sunday Bloody Sunday' Bono waved a huge white flag around him.

Band members:
Bono – lead vocals
The Edge – guitar, keyboards, backing vocals
Adam Clayton – bass guitar
Larry Mullen Jr – drums

Photographer Dean Weston recalls taking these great shots of U2 at Lancaster:

"I was a second-year undergraduate and occasional official concert photographer for the students' union at Lancaster University when U2 played there on 2 March 1983. I have a confession to make: I didn't know who the band were at the time, but took along a single roll of Ilford HP5 black and white film, shot all thirty-six exposures and hurried out halfway through, feeling somewhat unimpressed. Had I realised just how big U2 would become, I might have taken another roll.

I remember a lot of interaction between Bono and the audience – during tracks, between tracks. It seemed to be not so much U2 on stage as Bono's backing band, to me.

How could I have known that they would become such a global phenomenon and that to see them in their early days in a relatively small venue ought to have been something to relish?"

Dean Weston

Lancaster setlist: 'Gloria', 'I Threw A Brick Through A Window', 'A Day Without Me', 'Two Hearts Beat As One', 'New Years Day', 'Sunday Bloody Sunday', 'The Electric Co.', 'Send In The Clowns', 'I Fall Down', 'October', 'Tomorrow', 'Twilight', 'Out Of Control'. Encores: 'Party Girl', 'A Celebration', 'O'clock Tick Tock', 'I Will Follow', '40'.

Little is known about support act **The Nightcaps**.

Great Hall crowd participation with Bono © Dean Weston

The one question I am always asked in the pub, at dinner parties, at shows etc. is "Who are the nicest artists you have put on?" There are about four I mention, that sometimes change depending on the company, my mood or my memory, but U2 are always there.

At this stage of their career U2 were a monster band so it was simply amazing to get them to play a university gig. What a coup! It was a Sunday, people had once again travelled far and wide. By 11.00 am there was a queue of about twenty to thirty people who had already journeyed from Scotland and Newcastle. Bands are very nervous about fans hanging around venues and sneaking into sound checks, and U2's manager approached me and asked about the fans milling around outside. I said that he was not to worry as security would be on from midday and the public would not be allowed to enter the building. "No, that's not what we're concerned about. It's early March, bloody freezing and they've travelled so far. Could you let them in to watch the sound check?" I couldn't believe my ears, too many years dealing with precious superstars had ruined a lot of the music business for me. Here was a band who actually cared about their fans and, believe me, that was depressingly rare. No problem as far as I was concerned, let them in.

Later that evening when we opened the doors and got the sell-out crowd in, the band's manager approached me again. "There's twenty or so outside without tickets and they've come miles to see us. I know it's a sell-out but it is a stand-up, could you sell them tickets and let them in? OK, we are on a percentage of all the tickets sold but you can have all their ticket money for the Students' Union. We don't want it, just let them in." Once again I just couldn't believe it, I was so used to bands arguing about the final breakdown figures, wringing the last £1 out of the deal, yet here was a band who actually valued their fans above money. I really had never come across that in thirteen years of music promotion. They might be multi-millionaires now but they weren't then. I just hope they feel the same today about their fans …

After the show I was doing the settlement backstage but the band weren't interested in the money they were due. They were far more fascinated by the fact that I had recently got married, in a small town in the Republic of Ireland, a Protestant Englishman to an Irish Catholic woman. One of the band was planning to do something similar and they were interested in all the problems we had faced and the hoops we had had to jump through. He was experiencing the same prejudices and hostilities from the Catholic church that we had. I explained that the old, small town priest wouldn't conduct the ceremony and that we had had to draft in a young priest from the west coast. That was more important to all the band than the monetary settlement. I knew I had fiddled them a bit on the overheads to make more money for the Students' Union, so I left their dressing room feeling really guilty for the first time in my promoting life.

Barry Lucas

© Dean Weston

UFO

18 January 1979　　Support: Liar
23 January 1981　　**The Wild, The Willing and The Innocent Tour**　　Support: Fist

UFO are a British hard rock/heavy metal band that were formed in 1969, by lead singer Phil Mogg, guitarist Mick Bolton, bassist Pete Way and drummer Andy Parker. In 1973 the band recruited eighteen year old guitarist Michael Schenker from the band Scorpions. This marked a departure from their space rock sound to a more hard-edged rock sound. They released a string of critically acclaimed rock albums in the '70s that gained them a following in America and made them stars in the UK. In October 1978 Schenker left the band, making a brief return to the Scorpions before going on to form his own Michael Schenker Group. UFO are best known for the single 'Doctor Doctor' written by Michael Schenker and Phil Mogg. It remains a staple of every UFO concert and of The Michael Schenker Group and has been covered on stage and in the recording studios by heavy metal bands, most notably by Iron Maiden, who also used the song as the last one being played over the PA just before their show starts. June 1978 saw the release of the album *Obsession* and the visit to Lancaster in 1979 was in support of this album. 1981 saw them pack the Great Hall again on The Wild, The Willing and The Innocent Tour promoting the album of the same name. In total UFO have released twenty studio albums and many live and compilation albums. Though the lineup has changed many times over the years the core members of the band were:

Phil Mogg – vocals
Pete Way – bass
Andy Parker – drums
Paul Raymond – guitar

The band continues to tour and record.

Guests of UFO for their first visit to Lancaster were a rock band called **Liar** that existed from 1975 to 1979. Formed by Dave Taylor, formerly of Edison Lighthouse, the band released two albums, *Straight from the Hip* and *Set the World on Fire*.

1981 support band **Fist** are an English heavy metal band hailing from South Shields, Tyne and Wear. Fist are one of the original bands that were considered to be part of the new wave of the British heavy metal movement in the late 1970s and early 1980s. The band first formed in April 1978 as Axe, but only recorded one song, 'S.S. Giro', under that name. The group re-formed in late 1979 under the new name of Fist, soon signing with Neat Records and releasing their first single, 'Name, Rank and Serial Number', in April 1980. Fist continue to tour and record.

Hi Paul,

I have just read the article in the *Visitor* newspaper about the concerts at Lancaster University. My story is about going to my first ever gig at the uni and seeing a band called UFO, around 1980/81. I was sixteen and still at school. I'm still gigging today, and going to see some of the biggest bands around, but this is the one that stands out and I still talk about it today. We arrived early so as we could be at the front of the queue. The smell of patchouli oil and the anticipation of my first concert. Then the sound checks started. The atmosphere just in the queue made the hairs on the back of my neck stand up. The doors opened and we ran to the front of the stage. I cannot remember the support band. UFO then came on and the atmosphere just went electric. The band were picking up on this and the place was buzzing. I can remember being that tightly packed with the crowd moving side to side and my feet coming off the ground but still being upright moving with the crowd. I knew if I did fall I wouldn't be able to get back up. The gig was brilliant and at the end of the set the atmosphere was fantastic with the crowd shouting "more more, UFO UFO". They didn't disappoint. Three times we shouted them back on and three encores is what we got. To cap a perfect night, the track 'Doctor Doctor', their anthem. Never seen another band do three encores since!

Another great memory around the same time was Ian Gillan and his band and hearing Gillan sing 'Smoke On The Water' live.

Fond memories of a great venue. Sadly missed but never forgotten.

Dave Holt, Morecambe.

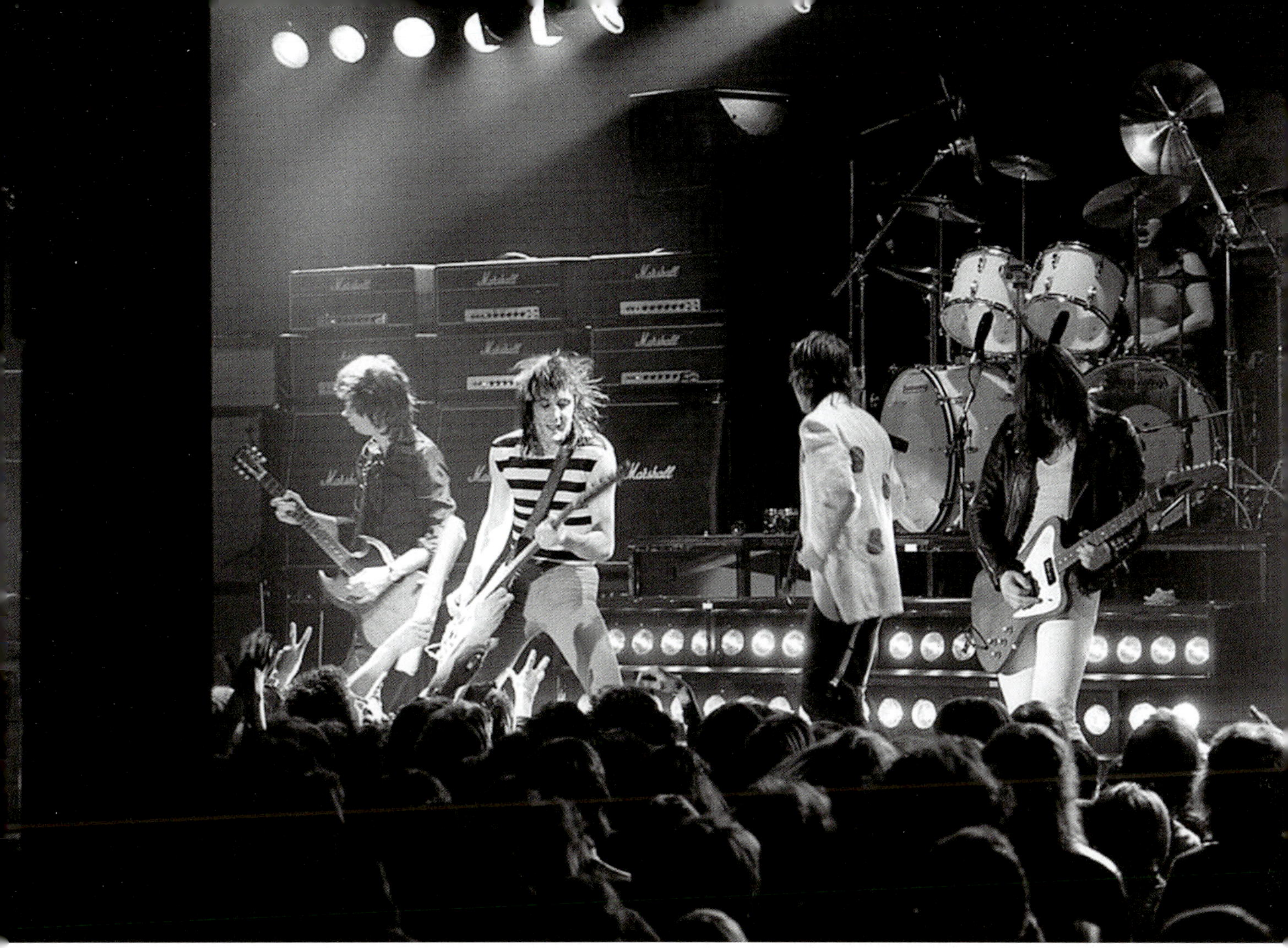
Marshall

Marshall

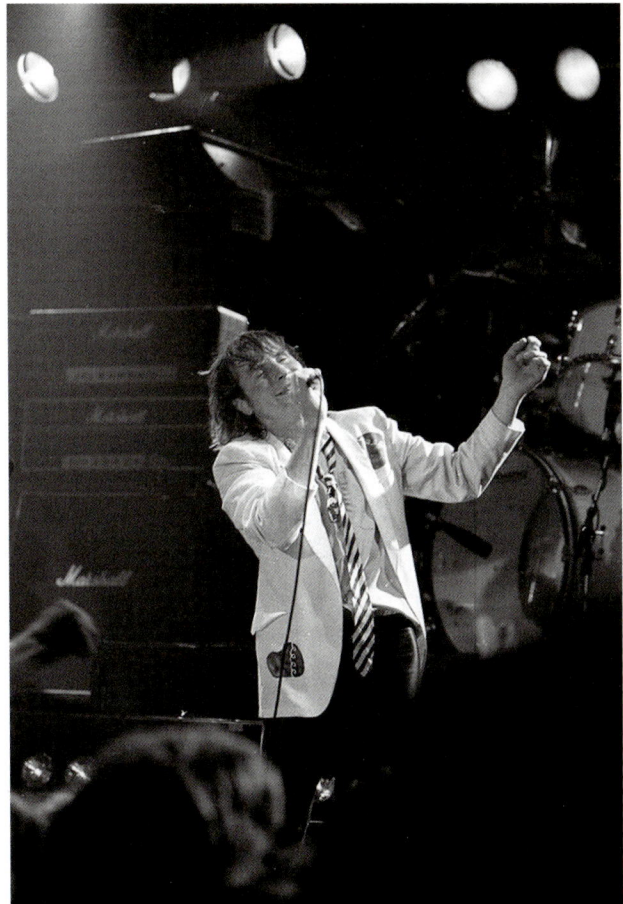

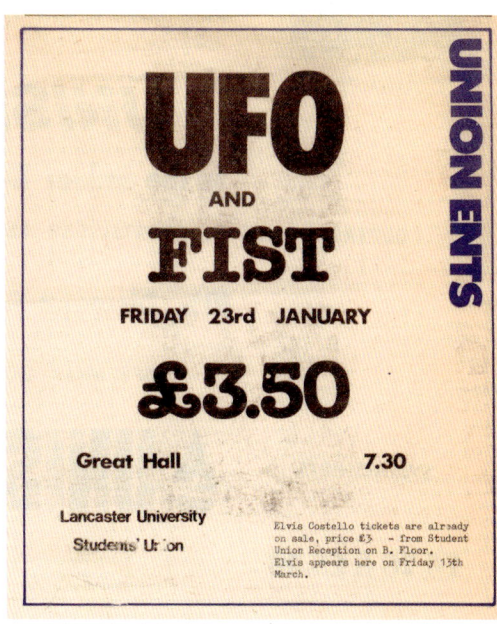

UFO
AND
FIST
FRIDAY 23rd JANUARY
£3.50
Great Hall
7.30
Lancaster University
Students' Union
Elvis Costello tickets are already on sale, price £3 - from Student Union Reception on B. Floor.
Elvis appears here on Friday 13th March.
UNION ENTS

Ultravox

7 December 1980   Support: Fatal Charm

Ultravox are a British new wave band, formed in London in 1974 and originally called Tiger Lily. Between 1980 and 1986, they scored seven Top 10 albums and seventeen Top 40 singles in the UK, the most successful of which was their 1981 hit 'Vienna', notable for spending four consecutive weeks at No. 2 in the UK Singles Chart without ever getting to No. 1. It was kept off the UK No. 1 slot by John Lennon's 'Woman' for a week and then by Joe Dolce's novelty hit 'Shaddap You Face' for a further 3 weeks.

Other successful singles for Ultravox included, 'Dancing with Tears in My Eyes' and 'All Stood Still'.

The band has been led by two different front men who never played together in the band at the same time. From 1974 until 1979, singer John Foxx was the frontman and main driving force behind Ultravox. Foxx left the band in 1980 to embark on a solo career and following his departure, with the three remaining members in hiatus, Midge Ure took over as lead singer, guitarist and frontman.

The band came to Lancaster following the release of their fourth studio album *Vienna* in July 1980. The album had a slow start, but the release in January 1981 of the title track as the third single from the album heralded the band's commercial breakthrough.

Ultravox's eleventh studio album, *Brilliant*, was released on 28 May 2012. Following the album's release, the band, featuring the '80s lineup of Midge Ure, Billy Currie, Chris Cross and Warren Cann, embarked on the Brilliant Tour, performing shows across the UK and Europe in late 2012.

In November 2013 Ultravox performed as special guests on a four date UK arena tour with Simple Minds.

Fatal Charm were a female fronted, new wave/synthpop band from Nottingham.

Remember, I had a special relationship with Island. Island Artists wanted me to join them for several years and 'Ear 'Ere Records had a direct account with Island Records, one of only 120 in the whole of the UK, so we got to hear things …

Island had been at the forefront of the underground/progressive music scene from the mid '60s through the '70s. They had arguably the most innovative and exciting stable of artists. They introduced the public to many new acts and styles of music and they had turned many local bands into superstars.

But Punk had happened and Island were suddenly becalmed, washed up on the beach. A flopping, gasping dinosaur. They needed a new act, a 'punk' band, an act that would once again enable them to speak to the kids. I remember the day when the Island Records rep. came into 'Ear 'Ere to announce that they had found the answer. The new, revolutionary saviour of Island was a band called Ultravox. Today that seems farcical but then they really believed it. Island thought they had their answer to The Pistols, The Stranglers and The Clash!

Obviously it wasn't and they weren't. But they were good and had fairly immediate success. I had a date on their sell-out tour. On the morning of the gig I had a call from their tour manager, Paul Darwin, an old friend from Manchester who had toured many bands into Lancaster over the years. He was enquiring whether we had any flying points at the Great Hall. I said that we hadn't but to wait as I was on my way up to the venue.

When I got there Paul told me that it was vital that they flew the front of stage monitors from the ceiling. I said once again that there were no flying points so it was the end of the conversation as far as I was concerned. Paul explained that there were so many comments going around referring to Midge Ure's height that they didn't want monitors on the stage as they gave the impression that he was even smaller than he actually was. The Great Hall's ceiling was wood and slightly lower than the actual roof so Paul wanted to know if they could just cut out some flying points. I nearly had a heart attack. I had had enough stick from University House about the shows and had spent years trying to out manoeuvre them as they tried to stop the concerts and the nasty riff-raff locals coming and despoiling their academic Camelot on the hill. "No, it can't happen," I told him categorically.

"OK, do they still serve Boddies in County Bar?" Paul asked, changing the subject. Paul was from Manchester, and Boddies was then still a very special local brew, with a distinctive, unique taste, not the anaemic rubbish sold all over the UK that it is now. "Fancy a couple?"

I was always a sucker for a good pint – still am. We went to County Bar. Four or five pints and several games of pool later we returned to the Great Hall. I walked in and nearly shit myself. Above the stage were several rock 'n' roll monitors, hanging from our lovely, wooden ceiling. "Paul …"

"Well, just think of it this way, we've improved your venue, at no extra cost, now you can offer flying points to touring bands."

The porters were sworn to secrecy and I got away with it. At least I thought I had, until that summer's Graduation Ceremony when the VC, slightly bored and dozing, looked around his lovely hall and his eyes scanned the ceiling above his throne only to see a series of black holes, staring like skeletal eye sockets at him. I was summoned to his office, yet again, on the Monday morning to explain …

Fast forward to September 2014, I was speaking at the University 50th Celebrations and I was a guest at the evening dinner in the Great Hall. I couldn't resist it. After the meal and speeches, as final drinks were being drained, I had to sneak up to the stage. Sure enough there were the eyes, still staring down at me … I'm sure one winked!

Barry Lucas

The Undertones

8 December 1980   **The See No More Tour**   Support: Orange Juice

The Undertones were formed in Londonderry, Northern Ireland, in 1974 and from 1975 to 1983 and consisted of Feargal Sharkey (vocals), John O'Neill (rhythm guitar, vocals), Damian O'Neill (lead guitar, vocals), Michael Bradley (bass, vocals) and Billy Doherty (drums).

In November 1978 The Undertones played the university, appearing as a support to The Rezillos at the time of the release of their debut four-song EP *Teenage Kicks* on the Good Vibrations label. It became a hit with support from DJ John Peel, who considered the EP's title song ('Teenage Kicks') his all-time favourite single.

The Undertones released a total of thirteen singles, including 'Jimmy Jimmy' and 'My Perfect Cousin', along with four studio albums between 1978 and 1983 before Sharkey announced his intention to leave the band in May 1983, citing musical differences as the reason for the break up.

The Undertones re-formed in November 1999, initially to play concerts in Derry. For their re-formation, The Undertones replaced Sharkey (who declined to rejoin The Undertones) with singer Paul McLoone.

Since 1999, The Undertones have performed several tours across the UK, Ireland, Continental Europe, Japan, Turkey and North America and continue to perform live.

The Undertones © Geoff Campbell

Orange Juice were a Scottish post-punk band founded in the Glasgow suburb of Bearsden. The band was formed by Edwyn Collins and existed from 1979 to 1985.

They were best known for the band's only UK Top 40 hit 'Rip It Up', which reached No. 8 on the UK Singles Chart in February 1983.

Edwyn Collins went on to pursue a solo career, having a chart hit with his 1994 No. 4 single 'A Girl Like You'.

Edwyn Collins of Orange Juice © Geoff Campbell

Van Der Graaf Generator

2 May 1970   Supports: Martin Lazenby | Grisby Dyke

Van der Graaf Generator are a progressive rock band formed in 1967 in Manchester by singer-songwriters Peter Hammill and Chris Judge Smith, along with bassist Hugh Banton, while they were studying at Manchester University.

They were the first act signed to Charisma Records and achieved considerable success in Italy during the 1970s, earning themselves a cult following as one of the era's preeminent art rock groups.

Lancaster band lineup:
Peter Hammill – guitar, vocals
Hugh Banton – organ, bass pedals, bass
Guy Evans – drums, wind instruments
David Jackson – saxophone, flute

Van der Graaf Generator played the university in support of the release of their second album, in February 1970, entitled *The Least We Can Do Is Wave to Each Other*. The band released a total of twelve studio and five live albums.

The group took its name from a piece of electric equipment designed to produce static electricity, the Van de Graaff generator, which is spelled with an extra f.

In 2005, Hammill, Banton and Guy Evans on drums embarked on a reunion tour with the same Lancaster concert lineup, which continues to the present day. The band released their thirteenth studio album in September 2016 entitled *Do Not Disturb*.

Support on the evening was supplied by Vand Der Graaf's fellow mancunians **Grisby Dyke**.

Lineup:
Derek (Grisby) Foley – Guitar
Lou Stonebridge – vocals
Ron Henshall – saxophone/flute
Dave Buckle – drums
Graham Moores – guitar
John (Dyke) Titley – bass

The band were formed around the same time as VDG, in 1968 and had what could be best described as a psychedelic fluty sound. They supported many groups, including Fleetwood Mac, Deep Purple and Rod Stewart and released the one single 'The Adventures of Miss Rosemary La Page' on the Deram label in 1969. Grisby Dyke disbanded in 1970.

Little is known about **Martin Lazenby**.

Van Morrison

17 March 1979   Support: Earl Okin
13 June 1982   Support: Herbie Armstrong

Van Morrison is an Irish singer-songwriter known for his inventiveness and originality as a solo artist, creating classic albums such as *Astral Weeks* and *Moondance*.

Van Morrison was born on 31 August 1945 in Belfast, Northern Ireland. More than two decades later in 1968 Van Morrison released *Astral Weeks*, an astonishing album that stretched the frontiers of rock music. On his follow-up record, *Moondance* in 1970, he deployed a snappy R&B band behind tautly structured songs.

Morrison has always seemed oblivious to public taste and their reaction to him, and his artistry and later albums such as *Back on Top* (1999) and *What's Wrong With This Picture?* (2003) continue to explore different modes of self-expression.

Morrison made two visits to Lancaster including a memorable St Patrick's Day concert in 1979.

Earl Okin is a London singer-songwriter, musician and comedian.

His first TV appearance was as a child on the show *All Your Own* in 1959, but he then began his career proper as a musician, recording his first single in the 1960s at Abbey Road. During the '70s he opened for such acts as Fairport Convention, Van Morrisson and Wings, and then he moved through the folk circuit, where he encountered the likes of Billy Connolly and Jasper Carrott, who started to introduced comedy to their acts. When this circuit crumbled, Okin moved to the new alternative comedy circuit and was invited to perform at the now legendary Comic Strip. He has been on the circuit ever since.

Okin is also an Edinburgh Fringe veteran, claiming to have performed more shows there than anyone else (502 over eighteen years) and has performed his variety act around the world.

A musician his entire life, Van Morrison's childhood friend and fellow northern Irishman **Herbie Armstrong** provided the warm up for his 1982 visit.

Herbie spent his teens and early twenties touring Ireland and the North of England with Irish show bands, and also worked for six months in late 1967 as the lead guitarist in Screaming Lord Sutch's backing band.

In the late 1970s and early 1980s he toured the world with his mate Van Morrison, and played lead guitar on four of his albums, *Wavelength*, *Into the Music*, *Common One* and *Beautiful Vision*. He eventually embarked on a solo career, which saw him release his first solo album *Back Against the Wall* in 1983.

Van Morrison Great Hall 1982 © Andy Docherty

Van Morrison

Paul Loasby was effectively running the Harvey Goldsmith office at this time, and when Harvey announced that he was to tour the legendary Van Morrison Paul had to set up the dates. Van had not played live for many years so this was an eagerly awaited tour. Paul rang to tell me he would try to secure me a date – I couldn't believe it, Van the Man, Van the legend, adding to the now growing Lancaster legend. But there were just a couple of little problems: Van insisted on no college dates, no stand-up venues … only minor problems then for Lancaster University's Great Hall!

Paul flew to LA to talk to Van Morrison with the sole aim of persuading him to play Lancaster. It wasn't really a college gig as such, it was a professionally run venue and was now established as part of the city hall circuit. The stand-up bit created its own quite unique atmosphere, Paul told him, and it was the best live venue in the UK where he would have an experience he would never forget. Van agreed and he did!

After announcing the date it soon became apparent we would have a monstrous sell-out on our hands. But what a sell-out! Quite simply the biggest, most spectacular one in the history of Lancaster University. In those days before phone and online sales, web sites etc. you had to write off or physically go to a ticket office to buy a ticket. Such was the demand that I had to get the Students' Union receptionists, Betty and Hazel, to come in early and open up at 8.00 am – not exactly an easy task I can assure you (if you remember them, then you know what I am talking about). Students were sleeping out on the two-floor staircase and into Alexandra Square. It was the same at all the ticket outlets and by 9.00 am we were totally sold out – an hour before tickets officially went on sale!

Show day. Van didn't do sound checks, his road crew did them for him. It had led to a tricky problem the night before in Glasgow. There they had an old fashioned orchestra pit and apparently Van, like many of us, doesn't like heights. The set was in place, he walked onto stage, saw the drop and did the whole show next to the grand piano, whilst at the front of the stage stood a lonely mic stand, still lit up by the spots, trying to dramatically emphasise the legendary singer. No such problems at Lancaster. He arrived backstage from his Lake District hotel, walked past the dressing rooms, throwing his jacket in, onto the stage and into his first song. End of set, walked past the dressing room, was handed his jacket, into car and back to hotel. Gig done.

But the man had a great night – I'll prove it later in this book.

A couple of years on and I once again had the opportunity to book Van Morrison, but this time I had to buy the date and pay a fee, as opposed to Harvey Goldsmith's pecentage hall hire. Well, ticket sales last time had been amazing so no problem, I thought. But this time – and as I sit here typing this thirty plus years on I still don't understand how – he died a death. The day before the show I was personally handing out show flyers around Bowland and Lonsdale coffee bars when a student said, "Oh dear, it must be really poor ticket sales!" Too right, we lost a bomb. Why? Answers on a postcard please – who in their right mind would be a promoter?

Barry Lucas

Velvet Underground

29 October 1971 **Loaded Tour** Support: Gravy Train

The Velvet Underground were an American rock band, active between 1964 and 1973, formed in New York City.

The group was briefly managed by Andy Warhol and served as the house band at The Factory in New York City and for Warhol's Exploding Plastic Inevitable events from 1966 to 1967.

The group's music and attitude shaped the work of David Bowie, Patti Smith, Mott the Hoople, Roxy Music, the Sex Pistols, R.E.M. and literally thousands of other bands.

Brian Eno, co-founder of Roxy Music and producer of U2 and others, famously said that "although the Velvet Underground didn't sell many albums, everyone who bought one went on to form a band".

The group's vocalist/guitarist Lou Reed, keyboardist and Welsh-born viola player John Cale, guitarist Sterling Morrison and drummer Maureen "Moe" Tucker played their first show together in 1965.

Their debut album, *The Velvet Underground and Nico*, featured a classic Warhol-designed popart jacket that depicted a big yellow banana. The album consisted of eleven songs that radically revised the rock and roll sensibility – especially two songs about drug addiction, one despondent and sobering ('Heroin') and another a ribald slice of Harlem street life ('I'm Waiting for the Man'). Several songs, notably 'Femme Fatale' and 'All Tomorrow's Parties', featured the heavily accented vocals of cool German chanteuse Nico.

Following the departure of Lou Reed in August 1970 and the release of their fourth album *Loaded,* Doug Yule (guitars and vocals) became the new frontman of The Velvet Underground and was joined by Willie Alexander (keyboard), Walter Powers (bass guitar) and Maureen Tucker (drums). This was the lineup for this Lancaster appearance.

Gravy Train were a progressive rock band from Lancashire, formed by vocalist and guitarist Norman Barratt in 1970. Together with J.D. Hughes (keyboards, vocals and wind instruments), Lester Williams (bass and vocals) and Barry Davenport (drums), they made four studio albums. Gravy Train disbanded in 1975. Later in Norman Barratt's career he performed with Robin Trower's uni support band Mandalaband on their second and final album in 1978.

Vinegar Joe

23 March 1973 **Rag Ball** Supports: The Roy Young Band I Blackfoot Sue I Yakety Yak

A great value for money Rag Ball triple bill with headliners Vinegar Joe, the British R&B band. Formed in 1971, Vinegar Joe issued three albums on the Island Records label and were renowned for their exciting live shows and also launching the solo careers of Elkie Brooks and Robert Palmer.

Vinegar Joe evolved out of a band called Dada, a twelve-piece jazz rock fusion band that previously provided support to Iron Butterfly and Yes for a Great Hall concert two years earlier in 1971. Elkie Brooks was known as the "Wild Woman of Rock" and comparisons were made to Tina Turner and Janis Joplin. Other band members were bassist Steve York, keyboard player Tim Hinkley and Elkie's husband, guitarist Pete Gage who also played piano, with Conrad Isidore on drums.

Vinegar Joe disbanded in the spring of 1974.

The Roy Young Band were back again following their support slot for Chuck Berry's Great Hall concert in March 1972.

Blackfoot Sue were a British glam rock band, formed in 1970 by the twin brothers Tom and David Farmer and Eddie Golga. A single released in August 1972, 'Standing in the Road', reached No. 4 in the UK Singles Chart. The band dissolved in 1977. Not to be confused with Blackfoot, who supported The Scorpions in 1980.

Yakety Yak, the fifties style rock 'n' roll band, completed the evening's entertainment with their unique brand of doo wap, and later returned to Lancaster in October 1973 to provide support for Ten Years After.

The Wild Angels

11 December 1971   Support unknown

Rockabilly band The Wild Angels were formed in the UK in 1967 and took their name from the 1966 Roger Corman film, *The Wild Angels* starring Peter Fonda.

In 1969 the band provided Gene Vincent with his backup band during his comeback tour of the UK. The lineup for this visit to Lancaster comprised, Bill Kingston (piano), John Hawkins (lead guitar), Keith Read (bass guitar) and Geoff Britton (drums). The band became best known for their version of the song 'I Fought The Law' written by Sonny Curtis of The Crickets, with The Wild Angels achieving a number one hit in Sweden in 1973 with the song before it was covered in 1979 by The Clash.

The Wild Angels released a number of studio and live albums in the 1970s. The original 1967 lineup of The Wild Angels was revived in 2012 by founder members, bass guitarist Mitch Mitchell and drummer "Wild" Bob Burgos.

They still record and tour playing to sell-out crowds all over Europe to this day.

I was so pleased Paul found this concert because, although it wasn't one of my bookings, I ran the event and it certainly was a night to remember. I could not recall when the show took place but I will never forget the night.

Bowland College JCR booked a night in the Great Hall for a social event. To this day I will never understand why they booked The Wild Angels for a student dance/social but they did. What makes the booking even more bizarre was that one of the main organisers was Bill Taylor. Bill had been an elected officer of the Students' Union, a member of the executive that appointed me as entertainments manager. His year of office had finished and he had returned to helping run his college JCR. As an executive member of the Students' Union, Bill used to field all the numerous objections from students about the concerts. There was a "noisy" element who resented a "professional" running the entertainments programme. He once told me that he had been bombarded in Bowland College bar by a number of students bemoaning the fact that I didn't put on "student bands". Now Bill wasn't that au fait with the beat combos of the day and wanted to know what "student bands" were. I carefully explained to him: "Student bands are groups that nobody wants to see, nobody buys tickets for and the Students' Union loses lots of money."

"Oh, we don't want them then, do we?" he replied.

"Certainly not, Bill. Don't worry, I'll carry on booking bands that people want to see."

Incidently, besides being a great character and an amusing fun guy, Bill was also an outstanding politician who later became Mayor of Blackburn and, even though he didn't sort out those 4000 holes, he is now Sir William Taylor.

Anyway, Bowland College did book The Wild Angels but realised that they had no experience of running concerts so asked me if I would run it for them with my concert team. I agreed, which was my first silly move.

On the night, surprise surprise, there were hardly any Bowland College students, or any students of any kind for that matter. But there was an audience – and what an audience! Eleven Hells Angels chapters from all over the UK had turned up. Before we opened the doors, I had a meeting with the eleven chapter heads. I explained that I didn't mind them coming to the show (brave of me or what?) but really I had no alternative, without them there would have been no audience at all. However I insisted that any trouble be taken outside. If there were any disagreements or fights it had to be 1:1 outside the hall. They all agreed, no problems. I think they were all relieved that I was letting them in without any "persuasion" necessary on their part.

About forty-five minutes later and with some 400 people in the hall, I saw about five chapter leaders standing next to the small Great Hall bar area. One of them was "playfully" slapping another around the head with a motorbike chain on a stick. Nigel Waller and myself went up to them and politely requested that he refrain. Amazingly, he did! We then got drawn into a discussion about rock 'n' roll, alcohol, violence, pre-Raphaelite art and existentialism etc. You know the score. I have never smoked tobacco in my adult life but when this 6ft 6in twenty stone biker offered his fags around I readily accepted and coughed my way through my first cigarette since I was nine and behind the school bike sheds.

However he didn't offer a fag to one of the other chapter leaders in the group. Big mistake. He rounded on him, "You tight arsed git, you never offered me one of your fags!"

"No, and I'm not going to," was the reply.

"You're so tight you wouldn't offer me the shit off your underpants."

"I would if you'd lick it off."

"Right."

"OK," he said, lowering his jeans, whereupon the offended Angel bent over and licked his underpants. Now to the poor refectory ladies, working behind the bar, this must have been a fine sight. One hairy Angel apparently kissing the rear of another hairy Angel. One lady just stared, mouth agape while the beer pump flooded the pint glass, drip tray and floor.

The next morning I was summoned to the University Secretary's office to meet with Rene Desirens, the University's Controller of Catering, to explain the scenes of sexual depravity in the Great Hall. Can you imagine the conversation – of course there was no sexual antics, it was just one guy licking the shit off another's underpants! Try to imagine the faces on the other side of the desk.

Anyway back to the hall. There was a semi-circle of angels occupying the curved seating of the Great Hall bar. The girlfriend of one of the chapter leaders was having an argument with her man. Suddenly she got up and marched across the circle to another chapter. She sat on the knee of a rival leader and proceeded to kiss him passionately. I could see my life flashing before my eyes. The jilted ex looked over – I caught his eye and shook my head, pointing outside, reminding him of the deal. An Angel's word is his bond. He nodded then he marched across the bar area, grabbed his girl and slapped her across the face. Now, while I'm not advocating that as a solution to a disagreement, I must admit I breathed a great sigh of relief.

From then on, the night passed peacefully but as I approached Bill Taylor at the end of the night he, ever the politician, got his retaliation in first: "Never again, never again," he said shaking his head. As Meatloaf would later say, "You took the words right out of my mouth …"

Barry Lucas

Wire

9 November 1978   Support unknown

Wire are an English rock band, formed in London in October 1976 by Colin Newman (vocals and guitar), Graham Lewis (bass and vocals), Bruce Gilbert (guitar) and Robert Gotobed (drums).

Wire are arguably a definitive art punk or post-punk ensemble, mostly due to their richly detailed atmospheric sound and often obscure lyrical themes. The group exhibited a steady development from an early raucous punk style with 1977's *Pink Flag*, to the more complex, structured sound involving the increased use of guitar effects and synthesizers on 1978's *Chairs Missing* and 1979's *154*.

The band gained a reputation for experimenting with song arrangements throughout its career.

Wire appeared at the university in support of the album *Chairs Missing*, their second studio album. It was released in August 1978 and peaked at No. 48 in the UK Albums Chart

March 2017 saw the release of the band's sixteenth studio album entitled *Silver/Lead*. Colin Newman and Graham continue to tour with their band Wire.

Wishbone Ash

9 November 1976   **New England Tour**   Support: Supercharge
8 October 1978   **No Smoke Without Fire Tour**   No Support
21 May 1981   **Number The Brave Tour**   Support: Nicky Moore

Originating in Torquay, Devon, Wishbone Ash are a British rock band who achieved success in the early and mid '70s. Their best known albums included *Wishbone Ash* (1970), *Pilgrimage* (1971), *Argus* (1972), *There's the Rub* (1974) and *New England* (1976). They were one of the first bands to use twin lead guitars.

Wishbone Ash were formed in October 1969 by bass guitarist Martin Turner and drummer Steve Upton, eventually adding two more guitarists in Ted Turner (no relation) and Andy Powell, and being managed by music mogul and brother of The Police's Stewart Copeland, Miles Copeland III.

This was to be the first "classic" lineup of Wishbone Ash and on 9 October 1970 they made their first of four visits to Lancaster as the opening act for Free.

A year later in 1971 Wishbone Ash were again billed to appear headlining a concert, with Heads Hands & Feet as support. For reasons unknown, Wishbone Ash failed to turn up. The concert went ahead regardless, with Heads Hands & Feet providing the main entertainment of the evening.

Thanks to Lynne Owen for the *Lancaster Guardian* cutting of the concert and her confirmation of Wishbone's 'no show'. Lynne was there!

Following the release of four studio albums including *Argus* and *Wishbone Four*, 1974 saw the departure of Ted Turner, who was replaced by Laurie Wisefield on guitars. This was the Mk II "classic" Wishbone Ash formation that definitely played the Great Hall on two further occasions, in 1976 and 1978.

1976 saw the band arrive in Lancaster in support of their seventh album, *New England*, released in October of that year.

Lancaster setlist based on typical 1976 concerts:

'Jail Bait', from the album *Pilgrimage*, 'Time Was', 'Blowin' Free', 'Warrior', 'The King Will Come', all from the album *Argus*, 'Rest in Peace' from *Locked In*, 'Runaway', '(In all my dreams) You Rescue Me', 'Lorelei', 'Outward Bound', all from *New England*, 'Bad Weather Blues', 'Mother of Pearl', 'Persephone' and 'It Started in Heaven' from *Locked In*.

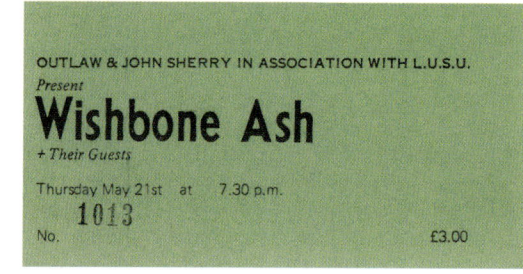

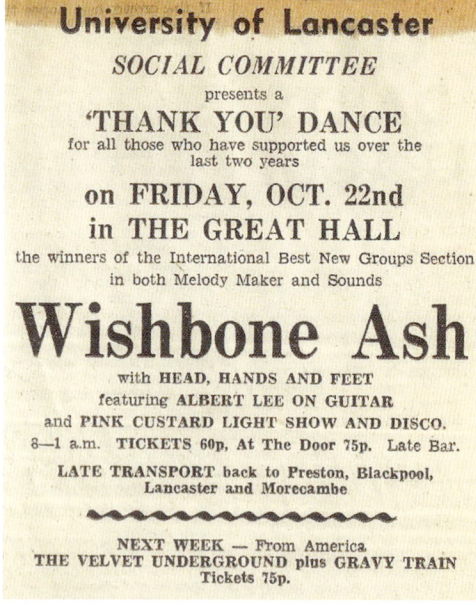

November 1976 © David Bradbury

It's 1978 and Wishbone Ash are in the Great Hall again for a three-hour concert, with no support act, in promotion of their ninth album *No Smoke Without Fire*.

Lancaster setlist, based on a typical setlist for the 1978 tour: 'The King Will Come', 'Warrior', 'Errors of my Way', 'You See Red', 'FUBB', 'Front Page News', 'The Way of the World', 'Phoenix', 'Anger in Harmony', 'Time Was', 'Runaway', 'Lady Whiskey', 'Jailbait', 'Queen of Torture', 'Blowin' Free', 'Bad Weather Blues'.

1981 sees the release of the band's twelfth studio album, *Number The Brave*. Wishbone Ash now feature former Uriah Heap bass guitarist Trevor Bolder, along with Claire Hamill on vocals in the lineup for the 1981 concert.

Lancaster setlist 1981:
'The King Will Come', 'Lady Whiskey', 'Where Is the Love', 'Time Was', 'Living Proof', 'Underground', 'Warrior', 'Throw Down the Sword', 'Loaded', 'Kicks on the Street', 'Phoenix', 'Number the Brave', 'Helpless', 'Jail Bait', 'Blowin' Free', 'Get Ready', 'Bad Weather Blues'.

Over the years Wishbone Ash have released twenty-four studio albums, twelve live albums, ten compilation albums and twenty singles.

Martin Turner regularly performed playing a white Gibson Thunderbird bass guitar, which he bought from Peter Overend Watts of Mott the Hoople.

Currently two versions of the band continue to tour and record: Martin Turner's Wishbone Ash, and Wishbone Ash led by original member Andy Powell.

Supercharge were a 1970s English rock band from Liverpool, founded by singer/saxophonist Albie Donnelly and drummer Dave Irving. They had a No. 3 hit single in Australia with 'You've Gotta Get Up and Dance' in 1977.

They were best known for their 1976 album *Local Lads Make Good* featuring the quirky infamous comedy track 'She Moved The Dishes First', which Donnelly claims they wrote so they could mess about a bit while the band were replacing broken guitar strings.

The Nicky Moore Band were an English heavy metal band fronted by Nicky Moore, who was best known as a former member of the British heavy metal band Samson. He replaced Bruce Dickinson who had left Samson to join Iron Maiden in 1981. Nicky Moore is still active with his band Nicky Moore and his Blues Corporation.

November 1976 support act Supercharge © David Bradbury

Wishful Thinking

14 February 1970   Support: The Committee

An early 'Central Hall' concert by Wishful Thinking who were a British progressive rock band formed in the '60s and successful in 1971 with an album called *Hiroshima*. They were forged from a pop band called The Emeralds, who recorded their debut LP in 1967 and frequently played and toured with contemporary acts of the time such as Pink Floyd.

Wishful Thinking consisted of, John Franklin (lead guitar and vocals), Tony Collier (bass and vocals), Kevin Scott (guitar and vocals) and Brian Allen (drums and vocals).

Besides the eleven songs from *Hiroshima* the band also recorded some other singles including 'Clear White Light' written by Lindisfarne's Alan Hull.

Wishful Thinking is a band prized by obscurantist pop collectors mainly due to their obscurity.

Little is known about support act **The Committee**.

© Ray Wilkinson Northern Lights

The Pink Custard Lightshow

FOUR

Maurice Hubbard and Duncan Laxen

The (Under-assistant) West Coast Promotion Man

For nearly three years my colleague Duncan Laxen and I provided what was effectively the house light show for the bands appearing in Lancaster University's Great Hall.

Barry Lucas was the prime mover in establishing Lancaster University as a premier venue on what became known as the 'college circuit'.

I was delighted when Barry contacted me to ask if I would like to contribute some reminiscences and anecdotes for *When Rock went to College* although these will be few and mere footnotes to his main story. Hopefully they may add a little colour to the tale from a different perspective; specifically that view from up on the Great Hall balcony, half way down.

You didn't realise you were making history, did you, Barry?

The appearance of this book records a time which has passed and chronicles events which will never be repeated. People who weren't there simply cannot believe the legendary bands that played Lancaster almost every Friday or Saturday night. That unique style of promotion and venue access have long gone, so yes, this is a history: a moment in time in the development of rock music into a huge business now operating under a totally different model.

I would like to point out that Barry is fifteen days older than me, and so cannot possibly remember things accurately, especially anything pertaining to myself and my entertainment business acumen!

Let there be more light (technical stuff)

Duncan and I went under the uninspiring name of Pink Custard Light Show and in May 1971 we illuminated Pink Floyd at Lancaster University – probably our crowning achievement!

I have no idea where our name originally came from but obviously pink was popular. Custard? I haven't a clue – thinking about bubbly oil slides perhaps. We eventually went out on the road in a semi-pro capacity with our ageing Transit van. Alas, we didn't last too long, as technology quickly advanced beyond our means and bands were soon touring and arriving for gigs with their own lighting rigs. Even so, many years ago we did provide the lighting for a Genesis gig at the Amethyst Club in Preston. Unfortunately this was a period when the band members all wore black and lighting black attire on a matt black painted stage was not brilliant. Literally.

Our equipment was also a little on the basic side. My boyhood Meccano set was dusted off and I constructed a hexagonal colour wheel by sandwiching off cuts of Strand colour gels between the green strips of Meccano. This assembly was then mounted up with some gear wheels, some axles and a turning handle on a frame made of the red base plates. I placed this in front of a bronze led Rank Aldiss Tutor 1 projector (as seen in 1950s school rooms) and it was spun. It was remarkably effective. We did, though, frequently drop it off the balcony into the audience but thankfully no one was injured.

The Rank Tutor 1, although generally redundant, was much in demand by the likes of us. It accepted two inch glass slides and if the thick glass heat filter between the slide carriage and 1000 watt lamp was removed, the heat would quickly boil whatever mixture of oil oils and food dye that had been placed between the two or three sheets of glass slides. Voilà. Instant psychedelia.

We scoured the country and *Exchange & Mart* and ended up with three units which would be worth a fortune now. Primitive strobe lighting was provided by a similar hexagonal wheel which was blanked out by some card, save for one of the six segments; spun at speed in front of the projector lens it gave a passable effect, but as the light source remained on it was not as dramatic as the electronic strobe we eventually had made. We had a non-modified projector which was used to throw images onto the screen at the back of the stage. Favourite images of the time to use were, Buzz Aldrin on the Moon, the Sun, and various LP covers, most notably King Crimson's first album, *In the Court of the Crimson King*.

The main stage lighting was provided by a miscellaneous collection of secondhand Strand theatre lanterns and PAR cans that were coming into vogue – not focusable but cheap and lighter to rig. We thought ourselves lucky to have four, which pales into insignificance when you see what is used today.

The one particular effects innovation I was particularly pleased with was the making of a small Perspex box, like a narrow fish tank, which was filled with water and placed in front of the Tutor's slide carriage. Liquid food dye was then dropped in and, as these projectors inverted the image, a mushrooming cloud of colour erupted vertically behind the performers. It was very messy though and the heat quickly dispersed the columns of colour. The close proximity of water to a 1000 watt bulb was also not a good move!

After witnessing Traffic's Great Hall performance in 1971, complete with their own lighting, we were particularly impressed with their use of footlights. Duncan then proceeded to build four light boxes with three photoflood bulbs in each and colour gels in front. These were then "played" by a micro switch controller that looked like a small keyboard. Great fun to use and it looked good, and for those reasons they were probably overdone somewhat. Duncan remembers well trying to rein in my enthusiasm for playing the keyboard.

Less successful was our woodchip box lined with cooking foil containing a photoflood lamp switched by a Second World War Bakelite Morse key. The general idea was to create a burst of brilliant illumination, sometimes from the back of the stage behind the drummer and facing the audience. It was the nearest to brown light I ever saw.

Pink Floyd are about to appear on stage.

Making my way up to the balcony a friend stops me and says he hopes that they will perform 'Atom Heart Mother'. I reply that they sadly no longer include this in their set. The band come on stage and launch straight into it!

After the show one of the roadies came over and said how good our strobe lighting had been. The one band we thought would have been most particular about how they were lit turned out to be completely relaxed and let us do what we wanted. I have lived off it ever since.

WHO are you?

One Friday afternoon in the Great Hall and a miscellany of lanterns, projectors and self-made lighting effects have been lugged up onto the balcony and we start setting up.

Tonight it's The Who.

I had seen The Who at The Mothers Club in Birmingham. It was shortly after the rock opera the album *Tommy* had been released and after romping through their earlier hits they had played a reduced version of the album. John Peel had been the warm up DJ that night, and when he appeared in Lancaster some years later I mentioned the Who gig as the last time I'd seen him. I was delighted when his first response was to remark "Oh yes, that was the night Keith Moon did his Judy Garland". Keith Moon had collapsed, falling off his drum stool, resulting in a short interval. It was somehow satisfying knowing it had made as much an impression on John Peel as it had on me.

I digress.

The Who's equipment and crew arrived. We had set up all our equipment ready when Jim Wolff, their tour/production manager bounded up to the balcony, looked about him and demanded "Where is the lighting?" We shuffled uncomfortably pointing to our three projectors and four 500 watt lanterns. "It's here".

He is not best pleased and in no uncertain terms informs us that he doesn't want oil slides, colour wheels, projection or strobes. He wants light and lots of it. Hurriedly some more lanterns are hired from the adjacent theatre studio. We had no controllers so lanterns were connected by yards of extension leads directly into the thirteen amp balcony sockets, the no switch variety. Mr Wolff told us in strong terms to follow his instructions which he would bellow out above The Who's wall of sound (long before the days of headsets and radio communications). The stage is now in darkness: the band enters and our plugs are pushed into sockets. It continues like this for nearly two hours. Plugs in, plugs out, on demand. Duncan was on the follow spot right at the back of the hall and was told to light Pete Townsend, but not when Pete was changing his guitar, which was indicated by frantic waving from Mr Wolff at the other end of the hall. Duncan eventually understood this and moved the spot across onto Keith Moon. It was exhausting stuff but when the house lights went up the formidable Mr Wolff shook hands with us and thanked us for a good show. He was right of course. The day of the underground psychedelic light show had passed.

It's now December 2016 and I am in Manchester doing some shopping. Parking up near the MEN Arena (or whatever it's called this week) I notice huge displays for a band appearing here in April 2017. Nearly fifty years on it's The Who!

Postscript

Not long ago a book was published which detailed every gig The Who had ever played. The entry for Lancaster University listed the support act as 'Pink Custard'. Without playing a note we supported The Who.

Pushing the Boundaries

This chapter contains the artists and events of which I am probably most proud. I have been asked many times over the years to recount stories about all the world famous people that have graced the Great Hall stage. And I have recounted willingly! But it is the shows/concert/lectures in this chapter for which I would really liked to be remembered.

A fundamental change in Students' Union entertainments occurred at Lancaster when it professionalised the social secretary position. At Lancaster, as at every college in the UK, entertainments was run by an elected student given one year to put on his/her favourite bands. The usual scenario was that they lost money – one million pounds a year claimed *The Daily Express* in the early '70s – and Lancaster was no different. By the end of the yearly term of office, having gained experience and learnt how "the Business" ran, the social secretary often got a job with the other side, as a booker in a London agency. Brilliant idea; the students' unions trained up 'apprentices', then released them into the commercial world to rip off the newly elected soc. secs and their students' unions. Great business model!

Lancaster changed all that in 1971 by making the post of social secretary/entertainments officer full time, a member of the Students' Union staff. After all, the Students' Union shops, coffee bars, travel agencies and bars etc. were all run by staff employed by the student body to look after their interests. Frequently the entertainments budget was bigger than those other commercial areas and yet it was run, almost dictatorially, by an elected student. It was lunacy really and it didn't make any commercial sense, but the idea that entertainments be run by professional managers was anathema to students and Students' Union staff. A further complication was that entertainments was treated like the university clubs and societies – it was given a grant, a budget, to spend, to lose, each year. I don't care who you are, if you are told to budget to lose money over a year I can guarantee that you will lose more. It's almost impossible not to. If a show is a disaster you will lose far more than you could ever make on a success – especially as more and more shows were put in with percentage deals attached, a safety net for artists and agents. It was belt and braces for their judgement. Now they could never make a mistake, for if the show bombed the college lost money, paying artists fees and promotion costs; if it succeeded the artists would generally break the percentage and therefore get extra money on top of their negotiated fee. But social life was a massive part of the student experience in the '60s and '70s and the general belief was that only a student could organise that.

Gaz Taylor and I ran the shows at Lancaster from May 1970 until June 1971 – a lot of Great Hall shows and many smaller nights in Bowland and Lonsdale refectories. There were some great nights among the discarded chips and beans, with bands like Pretty Things, Groundhogs and Edgar Broughton belting out blues/rock until the early hours. Gaz was the frontman, he got up on stage and promised the Earth,

Moon and stars – especially the stars – for the next term. I was the backstage organiser. But my role must have been more appreciated than I thought at the time because the Students' Union President, Tim Hamlett, approached me and asked if they made the post a staff position, would I be interested in taking it. I told Tim, who later became a journalist with *The Visitor* in Morecambe and ended up editing the main English language newspaper in Hong Kong, that I didn't believe a Union General Meeting would pass that (see above). Tim said that I should leave the politics up to them, would I do it was all he needed to know. Well, my lady at the time, Rachel Totton, had another year to do, so, although I had a job lined up as a copywriter in Manchester, I said yes. It was passed – I've no idea how – and I was offered the post on the wage of a postgraduate grant (some of you will remember those, grants!). It was the princely sum of six hundred and fifty pounds per year, not enough to get my first Ferrari but I was more interested in delaying joining the real world for at least another year. One really unfortunate, and very sad, by-product of this was the destruction of my friendship with Gaz. Obviously, he thought that he should have had the job as he was the instigator of the whole project, and he certainly knew more about music and the music business than me at the beginning. He went to London and we have never seen each other since, although I did get a quite remarkable letter from him a year or so later, but that is story for another chapter of this book.

It was made explicit that entertainments had to make money and it was no longer to have a grant. That was fine with me. A grant meant you were to lose money on shows and losing money on shows meant that not enough people had bought tickets, which meant that not enough people wanted to see what you were putting on, and why would you book acts that people didn't want to see? To me that was not the job of a promoter; I have always believed your job is to entertain, not to educate. At the very least I had to make enough to cover the costs of employing me and if I wanted to turn what was effectively a sabbatical post into a real job, then I had to make it a commercial success for the Students' Union.

It was then, even in those early days, that I started to think about what "entertainment" actually means. From the '50s, through the '60s, student music was basically jazz, blues, folk and then latterly, mainly rock. But even at a small university like Lancaster, where two, three or four thousand students lived, I realised that they couldn't all count those genres of music as their main form of entertainment. Or, horror of horrors, perhaps they didn't care about music at all! I started to think laterally from quite early on, thanks mainly to guidance from Mike Lloyd from Hanley. What about other forms of entertainment or areas that would interest the student population? So over the next few years, I promoted a wide range of events, some more successful than others, and some with rather hilarious stories.

But initially I wasn't that brave when I decided to venture into other forms of music. One of the first concerts, out of the student norm, was with The Spinners. This legendary Liverpool folk group would have been a staple of the university scene in the '50s and early '60s. But by the '70s their success on mainstream TV family shows with mum and dad appeal meant that they were a not cool for colleges. Many of their songs were still popular in the rugby, football and cricket clubs so I decided that maybe there were enough people in the student body, the staff, the assistant staff and local population who enjoyed their music. It sold out, of course it did – 950 seated in the Great Hall, remember. The band wanted a meal before the show so I booked Cartmel College private dining room. The Spinners insisted I ate with them and the Cartmel refectory staff were ecstatic, not about me being there but about meeting some TV stars in the flesh. They all brought autograph books and wanted signatures – even mine! I tried to explain that I wasn't in the band, but to no avail. I was at the table, that was enough, sign the book. I still watch *Antiques Roadshow* hoping that an autograph book appears and the expert has to explain who this B.A. Lucas was with The Spinners. Other folk artists I promoted in the Great Hall complex who were outside the normal student folk of the time included The Five Penny Piece, The Chieftains, Planxty, Steffan Grossman and the legendary Al Stewart. Some of these were in the main hall, others in the Nuffield Theatre. Of course many other mainstream folk legends featured on the Great Hall stage and they are listed elsewhere in the book.

John Angus

I must also mention here one of the truly great and most influential names in British music history. John Peel was certainly that, as well as being one of the most generous, sincere and basically nicest people I have met. He did a local bands night in the Great Hall during a period when I had a few Radio 1 DJs such as Kid Jenson, Emperor Rosko etc. I also booked John to appear a few times in The Sugar House. Usually top DJs came up, charged £1,000 to £1,500, gave away a few records and t-shirts, and played discs for about an hour in the middle of the evening. John Peel was charging me £650 and he arrived at The Sugar House at 6.30. We sat having a coffee, talking, when around 8.00 pm he noticed there were about fifty people in the venue – remember this was a 2.00 am nightclub. He said that he ought to start but I told him that the majority of people did not come in until after the pubs closed at 11.00. John said that those people had paid to see/listen to him and his choice of music, therefore he should be up on stage. He insisted on starting despite my protestations and played right through until 2.00 am. A later booking saw him cancel due to illness and we tried for several weeks to rearrange the date. It was complicated because he had one golden, unbreakable rule: he wouldn't play on a Saturday because that was when he went to see, or watched on TV, his beloved Liverpool FC. However, after many attempts to reschedule the date he gave in and agreed, for the first time in his life (that's what he insisted to me) to give up a Saturday. But, he said that he was hiring a driver, he might have to give up Liverpool Football Club but he wasn't going to miss out on his pint! On the night he was on the stage I put the big screen on to show *Match of the Day*. John grabbed the mic, Liverpool were to be featured (remember not all the games then were shown on TV as they are today) and he cried, "I think I've died and gone to Heaven. I'm on stage, playing my favourite music, drinking a decent pint, watching Liverpool and I'm getting paid for it!" Fast forward quite a few years and John Peel had tragically died. I was at that Saturday's Morecambe match a few days later. The local DJ legend that is Steve Middlesbrough was doing the usual compering. Steve was a long-time friend of John and at half-time he announced that he was playing 'Teenage Kicks' as a tribute to John. At the end of the record, virtually the whole crowd stood and applauded – it was one of the most moving experiences I have had at a football ground. It also demonstrated what an amazing amount of love and respect John Peel generated. What a great man!

The '40s and '50s saw the great years of jazz on the college circuit, but by the '70s The Commitments line of jazz being "musical masturbation" held sway (I wonder if any advocates of that had listened to Prog Rock?). But I knew there was an audience out there for great jazz artists, a limited audience admittedly, but an audience nevertheless. So I featured artists such as the legendary Ronnie Scott, Humphrey Littleton, The Peddlers and Kenny Ball, among others. George Melly was brilliant and he lived up to all his publicity. It was an outstanding performance at the Summer Ball (AKA Grad Ball, but that's another story) and at 8.00 am the next morning I got a call from Jack in the Great Hall asking if I could come up and sort George Melly out. He was lying in the loading bay, propped up on the Nuffield windows, bottle of champagne in hand, singing. I tell you, if you have to go you want to go like George. I also promoted one of music's greats – in any genre – the legend that is Stephan Grappelli. This man was revered by jazz artists, as he had played with Django Reinhardt, for goodness' sake, and all the legends of The Hot Club of Paris. I saw Yehudi Menuhin playing with him on *Parkinson* and the classical music star was in obvious awe of him. I was given the chance and I felt, for one of only a few times, that I had to promote him whether it would draw or not. I did – I wasn't disappointed. It wasn't a great turn-out but, for once, I can say I believe that says more about the area's awareness than me as a promoter. A fan who was agoraphobic and hadn't been out of his house for thirty years sent me the most amazing plaque he had carved and asked me to present it to Stephan, as he obviously couldn't. It was touchingly memorable and Stephan contacted the guy personally to thank him. The only problem at the gig was the walk from the dressing room to the stage; it was too long and cold in winter so his violin went out of tune on the way!

I must confess to a guilty secret, although I feel less guilty about it today than I did when I was seventeen. I love big band swing music and I have since I was sixteen or so. Sinatra was my all-time favourite, but try arguing that against Stones and Zeppelin fans in the '60s. It's classical music and timeless; listen to Amy Winehouse and Robbie Williams. But in the '70s it was dangerous to admit it – the underground music police would get you. However, I did manage to sneak in Victor Sylvester, Syd Lawrence and Joe Loss. Joe Loss, the favourite of all our mums and grandmothers, gave me the biggest bollocking I have ever had in music. I can still see it today, Joe, in a pair of sky blue boxers, garters and black socks, demanding my presence in his dressing room. He wanted to know why the show hadn't sold out. He said that I must be a totally incompetent promoter as he had never failed to sell out any show since 1940 and that was the fault of the Luftwaffe! He demanded to know what the hell I had been doing. Now, the Joe Loss show was the Saturday night after THE storm had hit Morecambe and Lancaster. The area was devastated, had been for a couple of days (see Graham Parker), so nobody was venturing out and everybody was more concerned about whether their house would still be standing rather than whether their one, two, three slow waltz rise and fall was working. Joe was incandescent and I was, I admit, a bit in awe. My mum and dad had been competition ballroom dancers so Joe Loss was a deity in our house when I was growing up. What would they think of their son being bollocked by a half naked Joe Loss – I could see his baton, for goodness' sake! He wouldn't have any excuses. The explanation was simple. I was an incompetent promoter. I tried to explain but ultimately, for the sake of my mum and dad, I bowed and left.

I have always been a great fan of Glenn Miller too. His music really is timeless. When I was visiting my parents in the early '70s their next door neighbour suggested that I listen to an album by a band I had never heard of, the Syd Lawrence Orchestra. It was basically what you would call today a Glenn Miller tribute. But I was knocked out by how good, how faithful to the great man they were. I decided to book them for a dance in the Great Hall, which would have been easier to justify today with the success of *Strictly Come Dancing*. OK, there wouldn't be many students, but staff, local people? I was, by now, convinced we had a role to play in the local community. Yes the classical music concerts and the Nuffield Theatre did attract a certain audience from the local community, but it was extremely limited and in many ways very similar. I actually believed the large board at the entrance to the University which read 'All Visitors Welcome' – how naive was I? Unfortunately the first show was pretty disastrous. I think most locals thought that the Syd Lawrence Orchestra would be playing Led Zeppelin numbers because they were performing in the Great Hall. But I knew, or rather I thought I knew, that word would get round that those who were there had had a great night. This was proper dance music. Sure enough, tickets for every show after that for several years flew out. The Great Hall was exactly as I wanted it to be; like those films from the war years, crowds of people all moving in the same direction, jammed together, dancing to a great, big band. I sure was "in the mood" on those nights!

However I must point out that, except for punk, the most violent and problematic nights were those Syd Lawrence ones. I remember being in the toilets by the hall bar when one sixty year old said to another, "Great to see you, haven't seen you since the Winter Gardens in 1956. Bloody hell, you nicked my bird then …" and there followed a rolling-around-on-the-toilet-floor brawl. Several twenty or thirty year old scores were settled on those nights. One memorable evening was a very early November date, Syd Lawrence arrived backstage and I met him. I was amazed to see that he was covered in snow, it was 1 November and quite warm. I asked what was going on. He said, "Sorry, just been filming the *Morecambe and Wise Christmas Show*. You've no idea how weird it is to be saying Happy Christmas in October!" Bloody hell! I was shattered because I had actually thought all those famous stars had given up their Christmas Days for our entertainment.

I have even promoted "shows" with some of the most influential poets of the twentieth century. These include C. Day Lewis (who later became Poet Laureate), the Mersey Poets – Roger McGough, Brian Patten, Adrian Henri, Adrian Mitchell – and of course the punk poet Dr John Cooper Clarke.

It was the early days of comedy and not many places were brave enough to headline comics, but I put on several acts in the Great Hall and later The Sugar House: e.g. Billy Connolly, Bernard Manning and Mike Harding. I had Bernard Manning on at a freshers' event in the Lower Ashton Hall (see Climax Blues Band)

and he had had such a rough ride with drunken students that he swore he would never play another student gig in his life. Remember, this was before Mr Manning's later sexist and racist controversies. It took several weeks of careful negotiations before I was able to persuade him to play a Grad Ball many years later. He took the mic onto the Great Hall floor and told three jokes; one clean, one risqué and one just plain blue. He got a riotous laugh from the last and said, "Right, now I know what you lot want!" and proceeded to give a very funny and very blue late night show. Other comics that appeared at The Sugar House included Lenny Henry, The Young Ones and a very nervous, first time out of London, but very funny, Ben Elton.

A fellow Students' Union Manager, Ian King, then at Swansea Polytechnic, befriended the Welsh snooker player Terry Griffith, who then went on to win the World Championships at The Crucible at his first appearance there. Ian phoned me and asked if I would be interested in hosting a snooker exhibition. I was enthusiastic and said that I thought it was a great idea. Terry Griffiths and John Virgo, who had just won the UK Championships at Preston, together with Sue Foster, the women's world champion, and John Williams, the top snooker match referee, would take part in a night of snooker. The idea was that Terry and John would play each other and Sue would play a selection of local snooker league players. They were doing the show at Preston Polytechnic the night before my date so I went down to see if there were any production problems I would need to sort out. In the Preston dressing room I spoke to Terry and John and explained who Sue was playing the next night from the local league. They were horrified. In those days it was very difficult to join the pro circuit, only one or two managed it every year, so the leading pros knew and played regularly against the top amateurs. They both said that on a good day several of those six players could beat them, especially Dave Horner, and remember I was talking to the world and UK champions. So we agreed that they would play the local players and I would find half a dozen decent student players to face Sue. The next morning I had to hurriedly rearrange the night.

On the evening I had arranged the dressing room like a rock 'n' roll show, food and booze laid on. They were knocked out as they had never experienced anything like that in the working men's clubs, or even in the handful of major tournaments available then. This was the early days of the snooker explosion and they were not used to being treated like mainstream entertainers, but that is what I believe sportsmen are. Sue played the students, she won all her games. I was in the dressing room with John Virgo, who was making serious inroads into the Bacardi and coke supply, when he said that he thought he ought to see how Terry's first game was going. We walked into the hall as Terry Griffiths, World Professional Snooker Champion, conceded on the brown – if you don't know snooker that's true humiliation! "Bollocks!" said John. He downed his half pint of Bacardi and coke. He decided this was serious snooker, reputations were at risk. He grabbed his cue and made a 117 break on his first visit to the table – professional excellence re-established. The next day I was told by the hall porters that Terry Griffiths had left his wallet in the dressing room. He was staying at the Crest Hotel in Preston – a two night stay, which made sense if you are not a drinker. So I phoned him to say that I would deliver his wallet to him. What a true gentleman. Here was the world champion but he sat with me over coffee for one and a half hours, talking. He talked of the supposed rivalry between him and the legendary hellraiser, Alex Higgins. The press had typically portrayed the contrast between their characters as a 'hate' rivalry. "Great for business," he assured me. But there was a far more significant difference between the two of them. At an exhibition match with Terry in Wales, Alex had lost to a local player, just as Terry had done that previous night in Lancaster. However, there the similarity ended. Alex immediately challenged his conqueror to another game, this time for a side bet of a grand. Of course an ordinary working class guy couldn't afford to take that bet, Alex knew that, everybody in the hall knew that. But it took away that working guy's "fifteen minutes of fame". Terry said, "That guy in Lancaster last night beat the World Snooker Champion, he will get his picture in the local paper, he can go around the local pubs, play in the local league matches, saying he has beaten Terry Griffiths. But this morning and tomorrow morning I will still be World Champion". I could see that it hadn't damaged him at all, but it had given some unknown a moment of unbelievable glory. "Why on earth would I begrudge him that?" he said, truly mystified that anyone could react in a different way. You know, Terry Griffiths might be the most boring world snooker champion ever but as far as I am concerned he is one of the nicest.

In the mid '70s there was a revival in the interest and appreciation of brass bands. The miners' strikes, the pride of miners marching behind their town's band and the highly successful film, *Brassed Off*, brought the music and the traditional working class culture back into people's awareness. Grimethorpe Colliery Band was a world leader and gave a fabulous show for me in the Great Hall. I also promoted a concert by Sir Harry Mortimer and the City of Coventry Brass Band. They were a champion band but it lead to an unforgettable image which lives with me to this day. Sir Harry approached me with a problem in the afternoon rehearsals. Jack and Mick, the Great Hall porters, had built raised, tiered sections of the stage, as requested by the band. Unfortunately, not being used to this kind of staging arrangement, they had not battened along the back of the top section. Just as Sir Harry was trying to explain the problems this was causing, the trumpet section, fresh from their solos, had sat down on their chairs, only for those seats to push backwards and disappear over the precipice. As we were looking at the stage, a tangle of legs and feet appeared over the heads of the rest of the band. I couldn't suppress a giggle, truth to tell, neither could Sir Harry. But I had to agree, it was dangerous – albeit hilarious.

I kept trying to diversify the range of shows that I promoted. The Arts of India included music, dance, theatre and poetry. There was an appearance by a dancing troupe of Morris Men, admittedly part of a large and very successful beer festival in the Great Hall. I wasn't going to mention this but I've had a drink while writing, so here goes. On the day of the festival there was a particularly unpleasant employee of the university who was a member of CAMRA, an organisation I am eternally grateful for protecting the British pint. But I don't understand why you have to have a beard and a duffle coat to join. Anyway he spent the whole day giving the impression to all the breweries that he had organised the event and passing out his card. A few weeks later and I was amazed as to why I hadn't received any bills from the breweries. Suddenly a very distraught, bearded member of the university's assistant staff appeared in my office. "Why am I receiving all these invoices for thousands of pounds from breweries?" he demanded to know. "Sorry, I presume they thought you were organising the event. I haven't the faintest where they all got that idea from," I said innocently. I have now to confess that I didn't pay the invoices swiftly and I let them run to the final red before I sent the money. Sorry, but I do so hate beards and anoraks. A sort of associated night saw the Lancaster University version of the highly popular ITV show *The Wheel Tappers and Shunters Social Club*. Bands, comics, music, pie, peas 'n' bingo and were provided as the Great Hall became a northern working mens' club for the night. The artists all participated with enthusiasm, and the Irish comic Frank Carson ("It's the way I tell 'em") and Gerry Marsden (as in The Pacemakers) took turns at calling the bingo!

The American blues legends Sonny Terry and Brownie McGhee gave a uniquely memorable evening in the Nuffield Theatre. These artists, both in their seventies, had toured for decades and played with most of the legends of American blues and folk music. Sonny was blind, but didn't in anyway rely on Brownie. In fact when they played in the Nuffield they hadn't spoken to each other for over twenty years and this despite the fact that they had been gigging together for eleven months each year.

Geoff Campbell, besides being a great photographer, was an enthusiastic walker, cyclist and climber. He brought his influence to bear on me in order to get a booking for the mountaineer and explorer Chris Bonington, Doug Scott and some other world famous climbers. Howard Jones, a Students' Union treasurer in the late '70s, was an experienced caver and member of the area's mountain rescue team. It was through him that I managed to book several world-renowned cave divers to tell their amazing stories. However I must mention Chris Bonington again. I had just booked him after he had appeared all over the national media for some amazing feat on Everest. Although he lived in the region, he had no connection at that time with the university and I don't suppose he ever dreamed that one day he would be its Chancellor. But a couple of days before he was due to lecture in the Great Hall I received a request from Mr Bonington: could I please furnish him with a map of the campus and directions to the Great Hall? I could not believe it; he could navigate his way around the Himalayas but get lost on the Spine!

In the '70s it was announced that the hundredth anniversary of the collaboration of Mr Gilbert and Mr Sullivan was to be celebrated. I have never been a G&S fan – in fact I really dislike it – but I knew that their operettas were incredibly popular. I also believed that they were musically significant and deserved to be commemorated. However, professional etiquette meant that I felt that I ought to clear it with Dr Dennis McCaldin, the university's Director of Music and presenter of the classical music concerts. Dr McCaldin was the second person to hold that position. The first one was John Manduell, Sir John now, who left to become Director of the Royal Northern College of Music in Manchester. He was a true entrepreneur, a proper promoter. He managed to attract some quite remarkable world famous names to the Great Hall but he did not just confine himself to classical music giants. In the first year of the Great Hall I attended one of its finest concerts featuring Johnny Dankworth and Cleo Lane. These legendary names of the jazz world gave an unforgettable performance. Although ill with a throat problem, Cleo Lane sang without a mic at times, showing the hall's extraordinary acoustics off to great effect. It certainly was classical music but it wasn't CLASSICAL MUSIC. John knew the difference. However, Dr McCadin's response to my enquiry as to whether he wanted to celebrate the centenary was, "Certainly not, we only present proper music, not mass appeal, populist rubbish." Did he mind if I did? "Not at all. Why would I be interested or concerned?" he said. I did some research and found that D'Oyly Carte were the bees' knees of G&S. But … I just could not afford a D'Oyly Carte production. With hindsight it was obvious, they did theatre productions, seasons, not one-off shows. However, in my research I discovered that one of D'Oyly Carte's major tenors over the previous decade or so was Thomas Round and he had returned to live in Morecambe. He was also a well-respected opera singer. I approached him to ask if he would like to present a tribute. He said that he would be delighted and could get a couple of other leading figures from D'Oyly Carte to perform. He said that I should approach a local lady, Dorothy Hardy, to furnish me with the other singers and a chorus. She was a charming lady and so eager to help put the show together with a G&S legend like Thomas Round. It was a great night but I do think it showed more than any event I produced at Lancaster why the Students' Union Great Hall shows were so important. Why now they are rightly regarded as a significant part of the social history of the area. They were not just for the long-haired head-bangers, they were for all the community, young and slightly older.

I had been telling Paul Loasby, who was the Leeds Social Secretary at the time, about this diversification. Now, I thought that what I was saying was falling on stony ground as Paul was a devoted rock 'n' roller. But one day we were having a conversation about how we were going to drive down the price of a certain act by exerting our power as venues where acts desperately wanted to play. Paul suddenly said that he had to go because he had a show on that evening. It was a Tuesday, I believe, and I couldn't recall any major acts working that week. "Who have you got on?" I asked, curious indeed.

"Eddie Waring," he answered.

"The rugby league commentator?" I asked, absolutely fascinated, "what the hell is he going to do?"

"Haven't the faintest idea," he said, "but 1000 students have paid £1 to find out!"

"My, but yer learnin', son," I thought.

I have here to confess again, this time to a love of film which probably outweighs my love of music. This was more true in the '60s, '70s and '80s than today when the great TV dramas, especially from the USA, seem to be eclipsing Hollywood. One day a circular arrived on my desk. It was offering something slightly different to social secretaries. I immediately rang the agent – he was amazed, I was the first to respond and my enthusiasm took him by surprise. He was writing on behalf of Philip Jenkinson, the BBC and *Sunday Times* film critic and host of *Film Night*, an erudite, witty and relaxed presenter. He was offering lectures about movies involving film clips, stories, anecdotes etc. on the history of various film genres. I could see the immense potential. But during the critical conversations, my rock 'n' roll promoter instincts took over from my film buff enthusiasm. I could see the value, I would buy a ticket but would two or three hundred others? Right, maybe not. So … let's do the first lecture on "The History of Sex and Eroticism in the Cinema". Kerching, thank you! Sold out. Intellectualism versus Sex – what wins every time?

There followed a series of three hour shows, "The History of … Comedy, Westerns, Science Fiction, Fantasy" – all sold out, all tremendous entertainment. Oh, and I must recount one story. By now I was very comfortable in the company of Philip Jenkinson, a kind guy who told a great story. After one particular show he was staying overnight in the Royal King's Arms. I had to apologise that the bathroom/toilet was in the corridor and that he had to share with about twenty others but this was the best hotel in Lancaster at the time. To compensate and avoid him having to spend much time in his hotel, I took him for a meal in the legendary Steak and Kebab. We were accompanied by my close friend and fellow film fan, Jeremy Oppenheim, who was also at the time the sabbatical *SCAN* editor (the SU newspaper). Over the course of the meal Mr Jenkinson asked us what were our favourite films. I was now sufficiently relaxed, socially and wine induced, to be honest. "John Wayne's *The Alamo*," I proudly announced. I felt Jeremy cringe. But Philip, ever the gent, smiled, perhaps sympathetically, and said, "Well, it's a very good film of its genre, but perhaps I'm not sure it's the greatest film ever made." In hindsight perhaps I might agree with him.

Those are some of the different kinds of evenings, sometimes days, that I used to expand the boundaries of Students' Union entertainments. Added to those were off campus socials, The Sugar House and of course, some fourteen or so graduation/summer balls. I actually rescued the Graduation Ball from oblivion because I think people have forgotten that by 1972 or 1973 the Ball was, like the parrot, deceased. The Students' Union could not sell tickets so I held out against calls to sell off cheap tickets to get an audience – there was no way back from that. The formula was a hackneyed one as it had become just an all-night rock concert, but it could not compete with the shows being put on weekly in the Great Hall. It needed to be drastically altered. So I changed the name to Summer Ball, encouraged staff to join the departing students, insisted on black tie or, at the very least, lounge suits, and evening dresses and broadened the genres of the lineups. In came big swing bands, jazz artists, '60s pop acts, comedians, reggae, steel bands, films in the Nuffield. It worked and within two years the Ball started selling out almost on the day tickets became available. It was now something different and had a broader appeal, just what I believed Lancaster University's Students' Union entertainments should become, and should continue to deliver.

"Regrets, I've had a few but …"

SIX

Actually the regrets I've had I AM going to mention, sorry Frank. Maybe not all, but many of the significant ones.

I suppose most are in that first year or so. I was an elected officer doing the job in my final year and a half at university. I am sorry to confess here for the first time in public that I fully intended to 'break the bank' if I needed to, in order to bring Jimi Hendrix to Lancaster on what I thought would be my final glorious year as social secretary. Unfortunately as negotiations were beginning, Jimi died in September of 1970. In some ways I was relieved that I didn't have to betray my avowed principal of running the university's entertainments as a commercial undertaking.

I was employed from July 1971 for a year's contract, almost as a glorified sabbatical officer, and I was once again negotiating to bring one of my all-time favourite heroes to the Great Hall irrespective of cost (and I hate to admit it, irrespective of loss), The Doors. Here I have to remind you what happened that year when the dreaded rock 'n' roll curse, twenty-seven years, intervened and Jim Morrison died in his bath in Paris in July 1971. I was never again tempted to put my own favourites on, irrespective of commercial considerations.

In 1971, I suddenly received a letter, out of the blue, from Gaz Taylor. We had parted on rather bad terms, as I have said, and this was the first I had heard from or of him since we graduated in the June of that year. Apparently he had moved to London and was working in a bar. He had written to say that in the next flat was a musician who was looking for new management. Gaz had, for some unknown reason, mentioned me and the singer was very interested in talking to me about a management deal. I had heard of him but I thought of him as essentially a folk artist with a penchant for mime and poetry. I could not see that working – a lot of hassle for a few folk clubs and pub gigs. It didn't excite me at all so I politely refused, telling Gaz it would be a waste of my time. Oh, I forgot to mention the folk singer's name: David Jones, but he had changed it a couple of years earlier to David Bowie. Oops …

Elsewhere I have mentioned how not paying an atrocious support band £40, cost me a date for the Tom Robinson Band, who were monstrous in the mid '70s. I also talked of the terrible mistake of throwing away Mark Bolan's PRS form, which would now be priceless. Probably the biggest single – or multiple really – regret I have is throwing away, or not keeping, all the posters, programmes, contacts, signatures etc. I have had over the years. In the early '70s the banks also returned all your cashed cheques so I would have had all those payments to The Who, Floyd, Sabbath, Johnny Winter etc. etc. Now that would have been something. *Antiques Roadshow*, eat your heart out.

Abba

Acts I have turned down and now regret are very few. I did rather spectacularly refuse a booking on ABBA for £40 – I mean what rock acts have you heard of from Sweden? In my defence it was before 'Waterloo'. I regret massively not having the confidence to take a booking.

In 1972 I was offered Ella Fitzgerald and The Count Basie Orchestra. I was a fan of big band, swing and blues and thought long and hard over it. If it had been just a few years later, when my booking policy had changed, I would have jumped at it. But, to complicate things further, this was for the Freshers' Week Ball and I could not imagine it going down well with eighteen-year-olds in 1972. Also, in my defence, I was still in my first year of full-time employment, trying to justify my position. I do sometimes, even today, have nightmares over that one – what a night that would have been!

Something which was out of my control, but which I still don't quite understand, was why we never got a "Live at Lancaster" album recorded in Lancaster University's Great Hall. It was THE university venue by the late '70s and early '80s but it still ended up being *The Who Live at Leeds* and *John Martyn Live at Leeds*. It is that last one that really rankles. John Martyn's performances and his unique relationship with his audience at Lancaster was custom built for a live album but it never happened. Although during the research for this book, Paul did find The Blue Jays' *Timeless Flight* album box set and disc seven is the full recording of their 1975 concert at Lancaster University, including the Moody Blues classic 'Nights in White Satin'. Another two big regrets were Leonard Cohen and Lou Reed, who would have been great additions to the list. But I think I might have had kittens over their riders; even Robb Winn, the agent booking Cohen, just wrote on the attached compliment slip, "Have fun!"

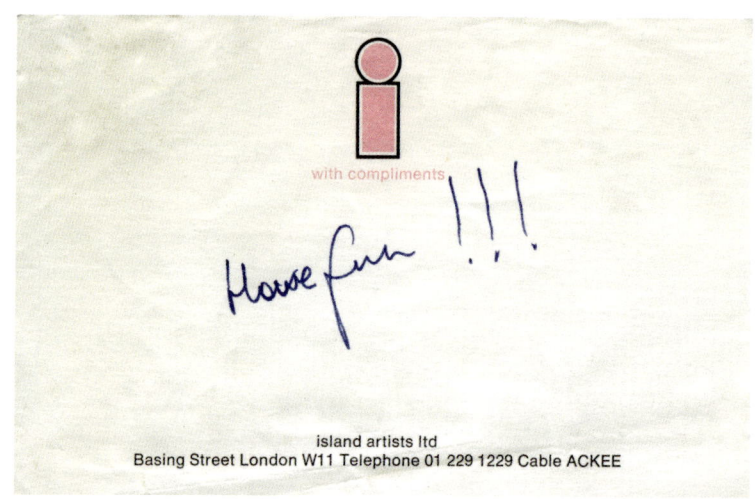

1) It is understood and agreed that the promoter (LUSU) will pay the National Westminster Bank Ltd., Leicester Square, London, W.C.2 Number 2 account .... Two thousand dollars no later than 4th March 1972. The balance to be paid in cash in dollars to the artiste's representative on the night.

2) The promoter will supply, at his own expense, a limousine and a minibus to meet the artistes at the airport and to be at their disposal throughout the day and to take them back to the airport the following morning.

12) The promoter will supply, at his own cost and expense, six (6) bottles of wine of local vintage. (Now I took this to be Mitchell's best bitter).

13) Promoter will provide, at his sole cost and expense, the following: a) A class 'A' sound system, b) Two movable spotlights with operators, c) a Hammond B-3 Organ with 2 Leslie speakers, (with the organ properly tuned), d) a Grand piano tuned to concert pitch. Etc. Etc. And this was in the early days before riders got really silly!

Directors: Anthony A. Williams (Managing) Stephen M. Kenis (USA) Nat Lefkowitz (USA)
Phil Kellogg (USA) Roger H. Davis (USA)

WILLIAM MORRIS AGENCY (U.K.) LTD

147/149 WARDOUR STREET
LONDON, W1V 3TB

Telephone: 01-734 9361   Telex: 27928   Cables: Willmorris, London

March 5, 1975

Mr. Barry Lucas,
Student Council,
University of Lancaster,
University House,
BAILRIGG,
Lancaster.

Dear Barry,

As per our phone conversation to today, enclosed please find copy of the rider for LOU REED.

With regard to Clause 4 it will be necessary for you to supply car-with-driver and one 30-seater luxury coach, London/Lancaster/London. With regard to Clause 8c, the Hammond organ has been dropped but it will be necessary for you to supply two Fender Twin Reverbs for Lou's own use.

Please call me as soon as you have looked over the enclosed rider.

Kindest regards.

Yours sincerely,

NIGEL KERR

Licensed annually by the City of Westminster
NEW YORK · BEVERLY HILLS · CHICAGO · NASHVILLE · LONDON · ROME · PARIS · MUNICH
Registered in England at 9 Clifford Street London W1X 2ED Number 841344

Looking back now, I have one other major regret. From the middle '70s until I left I had to fight a constant battle with the University administration regarding the Students' Union concerts. They hated them. They hated the noise, the disruption, the bars drunk dry, the money generated, the fact that every week hundreds of local people were coming onto their hallowed turf. They hated the school children, the working class teenagers and twenty-year-olds, the coaches of full of the area's FE colleges' students and the publicity the University was generating in the local and national press, radio and TV. The authorities hated it with a passion and tried relentlessly to stop the shows. I was too passionate about the shows to allow that.

Occasionally, the SU Executive, or myself, would come under criticism from students who demanded that I no longer put on mainstream popular artists but instead booked student bands, whatever they were. Here I have reproduced an article from *John O' Gaunt* (the Student newspaper). A letter had been published under the nom de plume "Mrs Phyliss Quottle" complaining about a recent Great Hall show that the writer "had perceived but half a dozen students there". I replied that "the comments raised doubts as to the contents of "Phyliss's" cigarettes!" I presumed by this remark that they meant students of Lancaster University. Now this was basically untrue, i.e. 500 tickets for Free, 400 for Argent, but far more important and, to my mind, dangerous is the assumption that the term "student" applied to those of us lucky enough to squirm through the mess of UCCA and arrive at a university. Every week the school kids of Lancaster, the colleges of Harris, Lancaster and Morecambe, Blackpool, Poulton and Myerscough, sold tickets for us. Several times per term Barrow, Windermere, Blackburn and Chorley colleges of FE, Heversham Grammar School, The Lakes School, Blackpool and Carlisle Sixth Form

```
3. Employer will provide at least two large dressing rooms, one for
Lou Reed and one for the members of his band. The dressing rooms
must be clean and private and each must have an adjoining bathroom.
Employer shall provide one on ice case of Coca Cola (no other soft
drink will be accepted) at time of equipment set-up for crew; an
additional cse of Coca Cola and one case of iced beer plus two
dozen sandwiches for crew and band prior to sound check. In addition
Employer shall supply an adequate number of glasses or cups, ice
cubes in buckets, and sandwiches or buffet for at least 15 people,
and one case of Coca Cola and to cases of cold beer in ice to be
placed in Lou Reed's band's dressing room just prior to show time.
Employer shall also supply a pitcher, water, ice, glasses and two
orange juice to be placed in Lou Reed's dressing room prior to show
time; two bottles Johnnie Walker Black Label and one bottle Jack
Daniels to be delivered to Barbara Fulk in Lou Reed's dressing room
prior to show time. In addition, all dressing rooms supplied by
Employer should include a working door lock with the key supplied
to Lou Reed's road manager at time of sound check.

4. Employer shall provide if requested three (3) cars for Lou Reed
and his group, one limousine with driver for Lou Reed; and two station
wagons for band and staff and luggage, with drivers. The cars and
drivers will pick up Lou Reed and group at airport and take to hotel.
Also the cars will be at hotel for pick up to take to sound check
and return to hotel, from hotel to performance and return to hotel
following engagement. Furthermore, Employer shall provide said cars
and drivers from hotel to airport for departure. In addition, Em-
ployer agrees to provide parking space for 40 foot truck and five
vehicles in nearest proximity to stage door and dressing rooms.

5. Lou Reed will not be available for press receptions, interviews,
or parties of any nature without prior notice and approval by Em-
ployee,
```

My deletions on the Lou Reed rider

Associations and Poulton Le Fylde Sixth Form Society, all sent coaches. Now, I am sorry, but to my mind, they were just as much students (and several of those colleges are officially part of Lancaster University) as those with Lancaster University Students' Union cards. Lancaster University was the social centre for the North West. From our position of privilege it was right that we should cater for all the students of the area and remember, if we got 400 Lancaster University students to an event, we were getting more than any other club or society could manage. Once I received a letter from the Secretary of Barrow-in-Furness College of Further Education's Students' Union:

"Dear Barry, Thank you very much for saving us fifty-two tickets for the Hawkwind concert on 17 November. Please find enclosed a cheque for £39.00 to cover it. We would be very grateful if you could send the tickets to us as soon as possible because the cheque has left our Students' Union without any money and we would like to sell the tickets to our students. Thank you again for your help and would you please let us know if we can run more trips of this kind down to your university as it is the only form of entertainment our Students' Union can afford to provide for our students. Yours sincerely …"

'Nuff said.

The concerts were a vital part of the social life of the fourteen to thirty years olds in the whole area. I had nine ticket outlets from Burnley in the south to Penrith in the north, people regularly travelled from Liverpool, Manchester, Leeds, Newcastle and Scotland. Today, I can recognise that for fifteen years the concerts were a significant part of the social history of the Lancaster area. But, while the University administration at the time was mouthing platitudes about encouraging the local populace to use the University's facilities and about how important it was for the University to integrate with the local area, in reality they were trying desperately to stop this happening. At one stage they even insisted that poor Paula Richardson, who at that time booked the Great Hall, had to ascertain from me what kind of music each band played so that Arthur Gray could censor and prevent any "unsuitable" acts. Consequently, with a straight face, I explained that The Stranglers were a country and western band, and The Undertones played as an Irish folk band – I kid you not, it was recorded in her office and sent upstairs where an august committee pondered over the bookings and then reported to Paula that they considered them suitable to be associated with the University of Lancaster. They then tried a new tactic to get these unruly locals off campus. They arranged for me to go with Arthur Gray, the University Beadle, to see the Winter Gardens in Morecambe. At that time this was a 2,300-seat theatre which was not utilised during the winter months. I was so tired of the running battle with the University that I was prepared to move the shows from the Great Hall and I went to the meeting, with Alan Murray, for a second opinion. But I stated that I would need exclusive use of the Winter Gardens from October until June and then it could return to doing summer holiday shows for five months. It seemed the perfect solution. I certainly thought that it would be a solution which the owners, Moss Empires and Fortes, would jump at. When I came to the university in 1968 there were several events, such as that year's Rag Ball, held in the Winter Gardens ballroom, featuring Spooky Tooth ("Tobacco Road"), Unit Four Plus Two and Geno Washington. So I reasoned that the concept of still larger shows would not be hard to sell, even if it meant bussing students out to Morecambe. The University was offering me all sorts of inducements to get the Great Hall shows off campus so everything looked promising, and with the extra capacity and staging facilities, what kind of bigger names could I get? I thought that the sky was the limit.

However I reckoned without a sub-plot. The companies owning and running the theatre didn't want it to succeed; they wanted it to fail so that they could apply for permission to demolish it and sell off the land for development, probably for more lucrative apartments on the seafront. Therefore they discovered reasons to refuse our offer and tragically the theatre closed. Sadly, they actually managed to get permission for the Winter Gardens Ballroom, a 4,000-capacity venue, to be pulled down. But fortunately the local community rallied and prevented the demolition of the theatre, "the finest example of an Edwardian theatre in Europe" (Director, Theatres' Trust). It has now been given a new lease of life by some brilliant local enthusiasts but has yet to return to its former glory.

In the late '70s the Students' Union commissioned the University's Marketing Department to conduct a survey among the newly arrived first years to establish why they chose to come to Lancaster. As all universities do, Lancaster was forever singing the praises of various departments and the University's national status. The Marketing Department was, at that time, a leading, nationally respected academic department and we awaited its findings with considerable interest. It discovered that approximately 10% of students chose Lancaster for the reputation of the departments/courses they wanted to study. 10% chose it for the collegiate set up, thinking it would be Oxbridge-like, more intimate and friendly than other universities. 10% chose it for its geographifical position, near the Lake District. There were several other insignificant categories but over 60% of students chose Lancaster because of the Great Hall rock shows. The very shows that the University were desperately trying to stop were the reason that these students wanted to come to Lancaster. The Students' Union were very satisfied and very self congratulatory but we never rubbed the administration's nose in it. English, Maths and Sciences – no; The Who, Floyd and Black Sabbath – yes. I rest my case.

Now I have saved the best 'til last, my greatest regret. To put this story into context, my first show was The Who, swiftly followed by Floyd and a couple of years later by Paul McCartney, but there was a notable omission. In the summer of 1982 Geoff Campbell had just been taken on as my entertainments assistant (I was, by now, Union Manager) to help with the Great Hall shows, and more specifically The Sugar House. He was to experience a quite amazing baptism. Returning to the office after lunch, I was asked to return a call to Harvey Goldsmith's office. Of course I was eager to do just that – Harvey was the biggest promoter in the country and he had put several major shows into Lancaster so I was eager to find out what he was offering. He wanted to know if I had Saturday 15 May free. I told him that I doubted it as it was very close to finals starting – they were to begin on the Monday – and there was an embargo on noise for two weeks before. "What do you want it for?" I asked.

"A local bands night," was the reply. That didn't ring true but I enquired about the hall. No, just as I thought, I couldn't have it. I rang Harvey's office and explained. All afternoon I received call after call, begging me to get the date. In the end I said to Harvey that he didn't do local talent nights, what the hell was it all about? Finally, he knew his only hope was to come clean. The Rolling Stones were doing a major European, outdoor, summer tour and had requested Lancaster University as a warm up! I said that was amazing but it didn't alter the facts, I just could not possibly do it. Harvey phoned back almost immediately, "Look you don't understand. Mick Jagger has personally requested Lancaster University for a warm up – this will be a mega outdoor tour. You have to do it." I asked why Lancaster? Harvey said, "He was talking recently to Van Morrison who said it was the best venue in the country to play, so that settled it for him and the rest of the band." Well I had to try again didn't I? Wouldn't you? I even went to see the Vice Chancellor, Professor Reynolds – he looked at me as though I was mad when I asked him to postpone finals for a couple of days so that I could have a rock 'n' roll show on. "Don't be ridiculous", he replied, "students are here to get a degree, not attend pop concerts." I said that of course I understood that but it was not just any rock 'n' roll show, it was THE rock 'n' roll show, and anyway if he could actually ask the students what they would prefer, then … But he just laughed and asked me to leave his office. I tried, honestly I tried. I had started with The Who, I think I would have finished with The Stones. I would have resigned then. It would have been perfect, what a way to go out! Starting with The Who, ending with The Stones, not a bad epitaph.

Leaving the office that evening with Geoff on his first day, he said, "Bloody hell, is it always like this?" Inwardly gently weeping, I assured him that today was indeed a once in a lifetime experience. But if only …

Barry Lucas writing in *SCAN* newspaper, dated 11 October 1974.

'Let all the children boogie'

"Lancaster is the rock venue for miles; from Manchester north to as far as Scotland, schools and colleges send coaches to our concerts. This is something I firmly believe we should allow and even encourage. Perhaps it would be different in a major city with alternative sources of entertainment, but we always maintained that the University should provide this source of entertainment to all young people who wished to hear rock music in the North West".

Barry Lucas writing in *SCAN* newspaper, dated 18 Jan 1977.

"There is one thing I try to ensure, that is the band or artist can play well. The Kursaals, Eddie and the Hot Rods, Ducks Deluxe, Kilburn and the Highroads, all fit that criteria (I also happen to like them all) but so do Ralph McTell, Thin Lizzy, Tom Paxton, Fairport Convention, Procol Harum (all of whom I don't like)"

A favourite band of Barry Lucas – The Frankie Miller Band 1977 © David Stewart

The Off Campus Social Centre AKA The Sugar House

SEVEN

I was going to include a paragraph on The Sugar House as part of my *Regrets* chapter. However, on reflection, I believe that it warrants a whole chapter to itself. The history of the Off Campus Social Centre has never been told in its entirety and its significance to the story of popular entertainment in the area is vitally important. The repercussions of The Sugar House story had a fundamental effect on the Great Hall concerts. I am still, after thirty odd years, consumed with feelings of sadness, disappointment and anger. I sometimes feel that twelve years of my life were wasted on a project that could have been so important to the soul of Lancaster University Students' Union, and indeed to the University and its standing in the local community.

It all began with "The Craig Affair" in the early '70s, when the English Department lecturer, David Craig, and some of his colleagues were accused of left-wing bias in their teaching, and more importantly, in their marking of essays and exam papers. From the outset most could recognise it as a blatantly political manoeuvre, an attempt by a right-wing departmental management to purge its staff. A massive furore developed, students and staff alike were outraged. Strikes were organised, national demonstrations centred on Lancaster, and finally, alternative, parallel university courses were created. Lancaster suddenly had two universities. BBC's *Panorama* did a full one-hour special on the situation. The University administration ground to a halt. University House was occupied by the new student administration. What idealism, what fun!

But eventually, of course, it collapsed. However, the wounds were so deep that an independent commission was set up in order to "cure" the perceived ills. Under Lord Taylor (not the same as the ex SU Secretary who is only a "Sir" today) it produced a long and complex report. One aspect of it was that it stated that students, "up on the hill", were cut off from the town and from young people in the local community. In order to correct this he recommended that there should be a social centre created in the town where young like-minded, people could mix in a relaxed, recreational setting. Lord Taylor's report should be displayed on a blue plaque in The Sugar House today.

It took eight long, often frustrating, years to achieve. At times I was the only person keeping the project going but I suppose the nature of students' unions, lacking senior management for several of those years, led only by one-year student officers, meant that this was inevitable. While I found it very hard going at times, it was something I really believed in. Finally, we found an ideal property, the old City Council Architects Department offices in Sugar House Alley. The department was moving into new offices in Dalton Square and putting the building up for sale. At the end of the "tender" period we were the only ones to make an offer – job done, we thought. But no! Mysteriously, several days after the closing date for offers, the local brewing family, Mitchell's, made a bid to buy the building. Despite our

 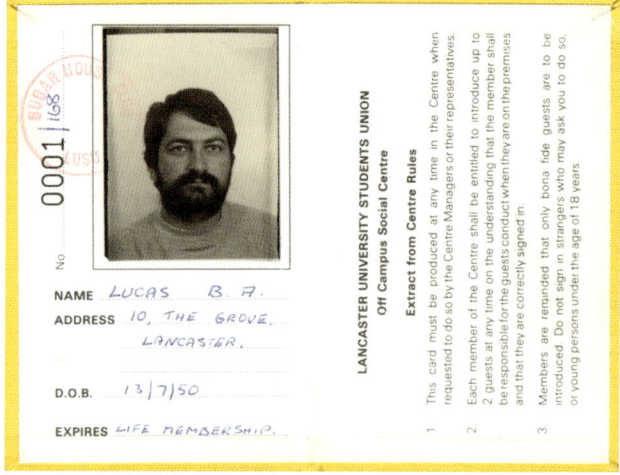

John Angus

protests and that of the minority Labour group city councillors, the council sold the property to them and Mitchell's then said that they intended to open it as a students' centre. Well, as they had just gazumped the University's Students' Union that would be a task and a half! Several meetings followed, with our negotiating team, under President Al Gordon and myself, staging a few dramatic walk-outs, but finally a deal was arrived at. It was by no means ideal as we couldn't take advantage of the national alcohol deals that the student unions were just developing and we were in Mitchell's hands, to a certain extent, on internal layout and decoration.

However, in 1982 The Sugar House (as it had been called after much debate) opened, but it was fundamentally different from what was envisaged by Lord Taylor. When our licence application came up for approval, the local Licensed Victuallers Association objected. I knew the chair very well as he was the landlord of my local, the Ring o' Bells, Arthur Wild. We had many discussions over their stance. Of course, from their viewpoint, I could understand the objection. The concept of the centre, initially, was that it be open seven days a week from 11.00 am until midnight weekdays, 2.00 am Friday and Saturday, with bar, coffee and full restaurant. This would be supported by big screen TV, snooker, pool and darts, and of course be available not only to students, but also to the local population. The LVA saw their trade being devastated, probably correctly. So they objected to that part of the licence which allowed local people to use the venue, even though this was the whole point of the exercise. The magistrates sided with the LVA – surprise, surprise. In their wisdom, they deemed that only fifty local people could become members and that members were only allowed to sign in two guests. Even when admonished by Princess Alexandra, in person, as she officially opened The Sugar House, they would not budge – although I have to admit that they were very red-faced and blustering as they stood like naughty school children listening to a right royal telling off!

However, Geoff and I soon sorted that little problem. Every student had to sign into a book on the front door as a prerequisite of the licence conditions. By the side of the members name were two columns for guests. This was perfectly reasonable management as we had to know who was in the building in case the magistrates demanded proof of our upholding of the licence. Now I know the following was not strictly legal (but what did we care?) but The Off Campus Social Centre was recommended by Lord Taylor to be a place for students and locals to meet and enjoy each others' company. Creatively, we facilitated that. Every local who wanted to come in was written into one of the two guest columns and in that way they were all a member's guest and perfectly legally able to enjoy the facilities.

With hindsight it is obvious to see that the idealistic concept we employed for the running of the centre was never going to work. Students, during the week, wanted – or needed – to be on campus. Financing management, porters, cleaners, chefs, bar staff, heating and lighting costs for seven days a week at least, twelve hours a day, was always going to be impossible. So opening times were rationalised quite early on, but still nightly attendances didn't pick up on bands or disco nights. I have to admit here that the depression associated with sitting in a large venue (one thousand plus) with only fifty to one hundred others started to get to me. By this time I was Students' Union Manager and so had a nine to five weekday office job to undertake, as well as all the entertainments programme, and understandably I began to miss a few nights in The Sugar House. Then one Saturday morning, at the end of October I think it was, Geoff Campbell came to my house. "Guess how many turned up for the reggae band last night."

"Not the faintest, seventy-five?" I replied.

"Not quite, six hundred and fifty," Geoff gleefully offered.

"You're joking!"

"Nope."

From then on The Sugar House took off. For discos the attendances were about a thousand, queues down the alley, one out, one in. Bands started to take off too, though looking at the programme provided (see below) that was not really a surprise.

Only one fly in the ointment now, but it was a nasty great big bluebottle. By this time, 1981, the Great Hall shows were regularly featuring the world's superstars, so if I put on a minor act or an up-and-coming one they died a death. People would not go to see a little-known artist as they would save their money to see Eric, Bono or Tina the next week. Geoff and I wanted to turn The Sugar House into "The Marquee of the North". A venue where new acts could play, where people could see tomorrow's acts, today. An intimate venue, a cheap ticket, that was what we wanted to establish. But the Students' Union Executive at that time could not see it, could not understand it, and were influenced by two of my senior staff. At any time in the previous fifteen years the Executive would have been ideologically behind the project and most would have understood the commercial arguments. The two years of SDLP executives, in 1983 and '84, could not grasp it at all. They were of the "Alan Sugar" brand of management. One president even wanted me to give a written warning to a senior member of the secretarial staff because she wouldn't smile at him in a morning! Geoff and I sat in a meeting in the club with the Executive whilst they berated us over the use of Mark Harris as a DJ. Apparently some of their friends had been telling them, in Bowland bar, that our DJ was crap. I had had enough. "We have 1000 plus every Friday and Saturday night, queues down the road, one-out-one-in policy, for a crap DJ? Tell me we have a crap DJ when we have 150 in and we're losing money!"

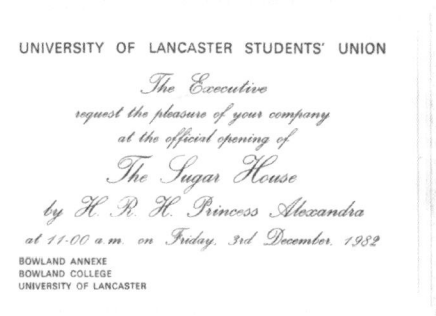

The official opening of The Sugar House from left to right, Lord Taylor of Blackburn, Barry Lucas, Students' Union President Kevan Collins and Princess Alexandra

But it could all be summed up by a conversation I had with the Students' Union Treasurer one Christmas vacation, a Friday night, in the club. Now, I must ask you to remember that we employed people for fifty-two weeks a year, all our heating, lighting, rates etc. costs were for fifty-two weeks a year, students were at the university for thirty-one weeks a year – doesn't take a brain surgeon does it? We needed our local supporters to keep using the venue when the students weren't there. As readers of this book, you will all be aware of my passionate belief in the concerts etc. being available to all of the local community in the North West. This applied equally to The Sugar House. I should not have had to argue this point to students but I did to these two executives in 1983 and 1984. The Treasurer turned to me that night and said, "I can't wait for next week when the students are back and we don't have to put up with this lot any more." He looked around at three hundred and fifty local young people, drinking and dancing, having paid the Students' Union to come in, and he could not join up the dots, morally or commercially. He's probably securely salaried in British management today – say no more. But I was totally sickened.

It was on the overall musical management that we also fell out, probably fatally. The Executive just could not see the way Geoff and I wanted to take the venue forward. They could not see the long game – discos made money, bands are risky. I argued we should be doing both but they insisted live music should go. It was shortsighted and a major factor in my resignation in December 1984.

I need only to list SOME of the acts that graced that tiny stage in The Sugar House to justify my argument. If we had been allowed to continue it would now be a place of legend, a holy grail for young bands desperate to go on that stage where artists such as these had appeared:

Sisters of Mercy	The Mission
Hanoi Rocks	Grandmaster Flash
Bhundu Boys	Lenny Henry
Stone Roses	Alexie Sayle
Happy Mondays	Roy Harper
John Cooper Clarke	Orange Juice
Pop Will Eat Itself	Marillion
Travis	Roger McGough
John Peel	Eurythmics
Balamm & The Angel	Go West
Howard Jones	The Young Ones
Julian Cope	Ben Elton
Simply Red	Alien Sex Fiend
Rik Mayall	Wedding Present
Eric Bristow	Hull Truck Theatre Company
Maureen Flowers	Aswad

Now that's a pretty impressive list for the team of people booking acts into The Sugar House in those first six years. Myself, Geoff Campbell and Mark Harris (yes the very same Mark Harris the Executive were asking me to sack and whom they gave a job to after driving Geoff and myself out).

Sugar House alumni

There are a few stories around about those acts. Firstly, though, to explain Eric and Maureen. Anybody who knows anything about darts knows of Eric Bristow, the Alex Higgins, the George Best of darts. Multiple world champion, character, showman, TV personality, he was a minority sportsman who became a household name. Maureen Flowers was a feisty lady who was a many times world ladies darts champion and also his partner. They gave an amazing night of exhibition darts and a few darts lessons to budding student players!

Phil Mc Intrye, the ex-Preston Poly. Soc. Sec. and now BIG-time promoter, who is mentioned elsewhere in this book, was touring Rik Mayall. I had had The Young Ones show on at The Sugar House and was disappointed to see Phil had put Rik into Southport Floral Hall. I gave him a call asking if he remembered the old days when acts would sometimes do two venues per evening. He said that he sort of remembered it but it was a bit before his time and why was I asking anyway? Well, I said, I have a 2.00 am student venue, only forty minutes from Southport, did he fancy doubling up Rik, twice the money at no extra overheads? Phil's a no-nonsense Northern lad, "That'll do for me. I'll sort Rik," was his immediate reply. On the night they turned up at midnight with a very bemused, and I must confess very nervous, warm-up comic. His name was Ben Elton, a Londoner up North for the first time and not sure how he would go down. No worries, he was brilliant, even the northern lads loved him. Phil must have been impressed because soon after he became his manager; the rest, as they say, is history. Shrewd move, Phil.

Marillion and Fish's love affair with The Sugar House I have mentioned elsewhere in this book!

Alec Leslie was a Director of Island Artists during the period when I was working closely with them and they were constantly trying to persuade me to become a part of their company. He had now set up on his own as a management company and one of the first acts he had in his rota was Go West. He was touring them to gain some live experience and asked me if I would take a date. I knew the problems with the Great Hall and new acts so I said I could take a date in the club but I could only pay expenses. He said that this was not a problem as it was experience he was after for them. I said that I would put them on after a disco as that would guarantee them a crowd. OK by Alec. So those people turning up that night paid for a disco and got Go West thrown in for free!

Roy Harper has been a major folk name for fifty-odd years and my girlfriend in my second year at university (1969) thought he was great. I had had him on as an artist in the Great Hall but he was eccentric to say the least. He spent the Sunday afternoon riding round and round The Sugar House on his push bike. However, I still want his track 'When an Old Cricketer Leaves the Crease' played at my funeral.

The Eurythmics were an early booking in the club. I thought they were a brilliant new band and had heard their single. They were a perfect example of what I wanted to create with The Sugar House because they wouldn't get a sell-out the Great Hall at that moment in time but they would be an 'I was there when' experience for a small audience of aficionados. It was a Sunday and unfortunately the single had charted at No. 7. I say unfortunately because the charts were too late in the week to affect the attendance and there were about sixty people there that night. Annie Lennox went ballistic with me, a pretty scary experience I have to admit. I was a useless promoter, every other date on the tour had sold out, proving I was crap. I took it on the chin but I didn't believe it. I had been around for far too long, longer than Annie or Dave; a tour doesn't sell-out everywhere and die in one town. I wasn't going to argue but the next day I checked with the other venues, where it was the same story as at Lancaster, although the later dates expected a bounce on the new chart position.

The Hull Truck Company are a brilliant, innovative theatre company. They were touring what was then a new play, *Bouncers*. I had read about the play (I had an English degree remember) and thought it would be brilliant in The Sugar House. The play takes place in a disco and the actors wander around the floor, among the punters, performing it. Unfortunately I staged it on a Wednesday, not a usual disco night, thinking students might have heard of/be interested in the play. Not a chance. The total audience was about six. We closed the club and we, the actors and the audience, decanted to a pub and had a great evening.

Aswad played at the club in support of the miners and ended up in the snooker room playing snooker with a load of the Bates Colliery boys – there was an awful lot of peculiar smoke drifting out of there!

I still find it hard to believe, even after all of the acts that have appeared in the Great Hall, that we had Grandmaster Flash in The Sugar House. This is the guy who created hip-hop, the only hip-hop artist ever to be inducted into the Rock and Roll Hall of Fame, and he appeared in Lancaster, in a hall, in an alley! For those of you who remember the now legendary 'Tube' TV show, he left the studio in Newcastle, got on a coach with his band – still in full stage dress – and walked into The Sugar House through the back stage fire doors. Oh, why weren't you there?

Simply Red in Sugar House Alley – it's almost Harry Potter. I had been the external interviewer for Manchester Polytechnic when they decided to make their entertainments position professional – following Lancaster's success, as many colleges were doing. We gave the position to Elliott Rashman and he had a successful couple of years. One day he approached me for some advice. A couple of years previously he had been in a pub and heard a singer that he thought was brilliant, so they chatted, got on, and he became his manager. Over time it had cost Elliott a few bob without return but he had always believed in him. Now he had a band and they had some record company interest. Here was the question, should he give up his job at Manchester Poly. and pursue a dream? I told him that he shouldn't risk it all on a lottery. What are the chances? How many bands make it? You have the beginnings of a successful career in student unions – why take the gamble? A few months later he ignored my sage advice and took the gamble. Silly boy! He put his new band, Simply Red, into The Sugar House as thanks for my advice. Oh, and a year later he phoned me to tell me that I would have difficulty contacting him for a year or so as he had to leave the country as a tax exile. What the hell do I know about the rock and roll business?

And last, but by no means least, John Peel. Elsewhere in this book I have told a couple of Peelie stories, mainly concerning The Sugar House. However, Geoff Campbell told me a few tales of Peel you might be interested in. We had him on a several times because he was a legend, an icon, a really great guy, did a great show … and he didn't charge the earth like other BBC DJs did. There was the time when, for some inexplicable reason, he turned up for a disco booking without any records. He borrowed the house DJ Mark's records, and Geoff and I had to listen to Mark moaning on and on that, when he played this or that track, the dance floor emptied but here it was packed. Over and over again. Then the time when Mark nearly slit his wrists, when Peel played the commentary sound track of Kenny Dalglish's winning goal in the European Cup Final and the dance floor was full with people DANCING! John Peel loved records but his greatest love was for live music. He frequently requested a local band be booked for his gigs, not to give him a rest but because he always believed he might discover someone. One night Geoff booked the local Lancaster band Basking Sharks. For those of you who don't know or remember them, they had an amazing stage show of Heath Robinson proportions. John saw the stage set up and asked if they were using all this paraphernalia. He was assured they were. "I'm not missing any of this," he said and sat on the edge of the stage, in some considerable personal danger, for the whole show. He was so impressed that he arranged for them to go down to London for a performance on his BBC radio show. A few years later Geoff, now in Exeter, was talking to some of his staff who originated in London. He can't exactly remember why but the Basking Sharks came up in conversation. They were absolutely in awe and asked did he really know them and had he actually met them? They had heard the Peel session and were life-long fans!

A few stories, a few artists listed (not all I hasten to add), but oh what might have been. Can you understand, now, why I was originally going to put this in my *Regrets* chapter?

Local bands

Following her first Great Hall appearance in November 1980 for a memorable concert supported by Duran Duran, Hazel O'Connor cancelled a show, scheduled for Sunday night 4th October 1981. I can't remember exactly why now, but I do remember it was fairly last minute and induced a rather hysterical panic; most unusual for me. But October is always a busy month for tours and most bands who were willing to work were booked, so getting a replacement would be a massive problem. Ordinarily it actually wouldn't have been a problem. Oh, so no gig tonight, Lindisfarne are on next week…. But this show was for the Fresher's Concert, I had to have something on.

In the 70s and 80s Lancaster had an exciting and thriving local band scene. I tried to accommodate as many local bands as I could during the 70s, but as national tours became more organised, support slots became rare and the record companies, who largely financed much of the tour, wanted to put their own-label up and coming acts out there. That way they would not only gain experience but would also be able to reach those large live audiences. However, going through the book I have re-discovered many local bands who had their opportunity on the Great Hall stage: Amongst them were The Pharaohs, backing up Selecter, Slo' Dive Dancer supporting Roxy Music, China Street supporting The Jam, Sad Café and Steele Pulse, No Flowers with Bow Wow, Interference supporting The Clash, Natural Scientist as guests of Bauhaus and Urbane Gorilla, who provided support to Deep Purple and Family in the early years.

But now a local outfit was needed pronto for the Sunday night as a replacement for Hazel O'Connor and much more importantly, it was a Freshers' show.

Thankfully, Lancaster band Natural Scientist stepped up to the plate at the last minute and provided me with a headline act for the evening and themselves utilising it as a warm-up for their journey down to London the following day to record a John Peel Session for Radio 1. Over its life, Natural Scientist went through a few lineup changes, but mainly consisted of Boris Forrest, Stuart Baldwin, Iggy, Neil Crossley and Mark Carricker. They were managed by George Jackson from Morecambe who sadly died earlier this year. Their excellent Peel session was thus featured several times over the coming months and eventually went on to tour Scandinavia, Japan and the U.S.A. - and so very, very nearly made it!

The area has had so many 'nearlys' over the years, notably China Street, Ice Factory, DAM and Angelica amongst others. Now the incredible Massive Wagons and The Lovely Eggs - surely it's our turn to spawn a global superstar, just maybe?

Barry Lucas

Lancaster? Where's Lancaster?

EIGHT

"Is it anywhere near Redcar?" Harvey Goldsmith.

It's the end of a journey. Thankfully a lot of my distant memories have not eluded me so far. When I decided to look through Paul's carefully, painstakingly compiled lists of the acts that had played the Great Hall, I was not sure how many stories I was going to remember. 1970 was, after all, forty-seven years ago, but I sat with the list and several blank sheets of paper. Amazingly enough I have stories for over seventy acts; but perhaps it isn't that amazing. From 1985, when I left, until this year I have done many things: Deep Purple at Knebworth, UB40 at Finsbury Park, Paul Weller at Isle of Wight; Terry Marsh's World Championship winning fight, the amazing Nigel Benn vs Michael Watson fight, Walt Disney on ice, Ringland Brothers' Circus; Madness in the Isle of Wight, a series of concerts in Finsbury Park with New Order, Pogues, Hawkwind, Siouxsie and The Banshees, several concerts for the African National Congress, anti-racist festivals in London, Manchester and Cardiff, Jamiroquai in Highbury Fields, Viva South Africa, a celebration of Nelson Mandela's release from prison, among many others. Then the sixteen years as a primary school teacher – I know, the staff room couldn't believe it either that I had swapped rock concerts for numeracy lessons, but actually I really enjoyed that bit. However, the concerts at the University were so significant, so unforgettable, that, quite simply, I didn't forget.

Over the intervening years the local populace hasn't let me forget. They have wanted to talk about, reminisce about, ask about, those years and those shows. They were so important for so many people. There are certain questions which are always asked: "What was your favourite concert?" "Who were the nicest?" "Who were the nastiest?" "What was the most outrageous rider request?" But there are two questions they all end with: "Why Lancaster?" and "Why did they end?" The one I can answer accurately is the first.

It's funny that the music business has gone full circle from the '50s to the present day. In the early days bands toured to make money, gigs gave them an income and if, as a by product, they sold records, all the better. But by the mid to late '60s, the music business was all about record sales. You measured album and singles sales in the millions, not the tens of thousands of today. Record companies would sign bands for hundreds of thousands of pounds in advances, everybody was making money. In order to generate those sales, bands toured and toured extensively; twenty-, thirty-, even forty-date tours were not unusual, rather they were the norm. I once asked Alec Leslie, a director of Island Artists, why Free, at their commercial height, were playing so many twelve to fifteen hundred capacity venues. He told me that of course they all sold out and financially they could have maximised their tour income by playing fewer, larger halls. However, if they sold out a venue, fifteen hundred people would see and hear them, the local newspapers and maybe TV and radio, would preview and review the date, their record company would put displays and deals into all the local record shops, people would be unable to buy tickets for the sold-out show but would instead buy the products, people who hadn't heard of the band would be interested to find out what all the fuss was about – in short, it would generate excitement and interest and that would be translated into record sales. Massive record sales.

As record sales began to decline, artists still needed to perform live to maintain a profile and generate interest in their music. But as productions became ever larger, more intricate and visually impressive, bands simply could not actually get into the smaller venues. It did begin to affect Lancaster. At their height UB40 were interested in playing here. In order to fulfil their staging requirement I would have had to extend the Great Hall stage to over half the length of the hall. "But would it affect capacity?" the band's promoter asked. "Ever so slightly," was my, perhaps ever so slightly sarcastic, response.

So the arena venues were invented – the NEC, Trentham Gardens, Wembley, ice rinks and sports centres were among the first. More were discovered or created and then local authorities began to build them in collaboration with private enterprise. Today we have one in, or around, virtually every major city. So if you live in Lancaster now, sure you can see your favourite band but it will not be in the Great Hall any more; you will have to drive to Manchester, Liverpool, Leeds, Glasgow etc. to see them. Bigger shows, bigger ticket prices, added transport costs, food, drink etc. etc. It is now no longer a night out, it is the equivalent of a foreign holiday, to see a top band today. Or you could always pay a few hundred pounds to see them at a festival.

Bands now make a great deal of money playing live. They don't, in the old sense of the word, tour; they rationalise their costs, they camp in an area for one, two, three nights or more and tell their fans, "Here we are, just come down here to see us." It is only the comedians who now seem to do the old tours of thirty or forty dates. But live performances now make money, for most artists, more than "record" sales and – as has always been the case – it really is all about the money.

"Where's Lancaster?"

I must have been asked that a hundred times by bands' agents, managers and roadies. So if nobody knew where it was, why did everybody come to want to play in the Great Hall at the University of Lancaster?

Well at first it was the geographical location. The University is situated nearly on the slip road of the M6 and it lies almost exactly halfway between Manchester, Liverpool and Scotland. There were potential rival halls but they all had intrinsic problems. Blackburn King George's Hall had some outstanding shows but the old hall was a logistical nightmare for equipment access. Preston at that time only had the old Corn Exchange, with its amazing sprung dance floor. You could see the PA towers bounce alarmingly up and down, as did the audience – to the horror of road crews and promoters. Great fun, but not ideal for the "serious" bands of the '70s. Blackpool had several venues, some iconic, but Blackpool was difficult for audiences to get to, especially before the M55 connection to the M6 was built. Of course it wasn't really that difficult to access but it seemed that it was when travelling any distance from north or west of the area. Lancaster was an ideal "drop off", a good earner between the major city venues of Manchester and Glasgow.

An important part of the attraction was the Great Hall itself. There were problems, especially in the early days, as the shows got more complex, so we made small but significant changes. We put showers in the dressing rooms, a curtain to hide the artists on their journey from dressing room to stage, and a major three phase power supply built directly onto the stage, rather than running temporary cables through the backstage and dressing room areas. The latter did result in a funny story in retrospect. The power supply required for the bands meant that they needed large cables with the necessary connections, so I paid for it to be installed. One day I received a phone call from one of the electricians deployed in the hall: "You'd better come over here and see your new power supply." I went over in eager anticipation. The curtain was drawn back like the launching of some new cruise liner – I could not believe my eyes. Before me was the back wall of the hall with dozens and dozens of thirteen amp plugs, the sort you have in your front room.

"What the fuck!?" was all I could say. The university sparks had by now grown in number and were trying, very unsuccessfully, to suppress their giggles. "How did this happen?" I spluttered. I had been expecting to see a single, large board with a couple of big, impressive tails, not the power supply for somebody's hi-fi. "I've just paid £6,000 for this. What the hell were you doing?"

The electricians shook their heads, trying to look sympathetic, "Don't blame us, nobody asked us."

I could not believe it. "Do you mean that some prat sat behind a desk in Uni. House thought he knew what the bands required even though he had never been down to a show? And he never thought of asking the guys who have to sort it out every week?"

"Got it in one," they replied.

That just about sums up British middle management for me. I must admit, once it was sorted, at great expense to the University, I was able to see the funny side.

The hall was designed for classical music so the acoustics are brilliant. Standing audiences made the problems of sight lines irrelevant. The get-in was so easy for equipment; a loading bay at tailgate level, a straight run down a corridor, no steps and into the hall. Compared to many of the equivalent city hall venues, this was bliss for road crews. Many venues were Victorian civic halls – up stairs, often spiral, parking in city centres, a nightmare. So happy crews and happy nights, it meant the band, the tour manager and the promoter could also enjoy the whole gig.

I suspect most of you reading this were there, maybe not at all the shows but enough. Well it's you, the audience, that I need to thank. The Lancaster audience was, I sincerely believe, the best in the country, and by the mid '70s was educated in the experience of live music. Its response was electric. The music business knew it (see Van Morrison and Mick Jagger, see John Martyn etc. etc.). I can still remember the Lancaster stomp, that incredible, rhythmic clapping and stomping for encores – I've seen and been involved in shows all over the world and I can honestly say I have never experienced anything like it. I can still close my eyes and see it, hear it, feel it, today. Give yourselves a clap.

The final answer as to "Why Lancaster?" has to be the position of Social Manager. Now it isn't false modesty that meant I didn't say Barry Lucas. Of course I brought a combination of 'talents' to the job which worked. But I think that perhaps they were not unique. What was unique at Lancaster was the position of Social Manager. So really the final reason for Lancaster's success was the foresight of the Students' Union Executive in 1971. I have explained elsewhere in this book what a brave, unusual decision it was that created the first professional post for an entertainments officer in a students' union in the UK (actually, as far as I was able to find out, in the world). This had a huge impact on the Lancaster concerts. Not only did I get better as a promoter, learning from mistakes, seeing how I could improve the booking and marketing of concerts, but I kept those skills here in Lancaster to benefit Lancaster University Students' Union and its audience. I didn't, despite numerous offers, take them into the "enemy's camp" and work for the other side, using my inside knowledge to rip off students' unions. Most of my fellow social secretaries, those who became friends and colleagues, went into the "business" and by the mid '70s had become top agents, band managers or promoters. I could therefore open doors that other social secretaries could not, to people who knew of my abilities. Equally, those that didn't know me grew to respect me and understand that this was my job, I was not in it for the glory or the glamour of rock 'n' roll. I gained a reputation as a good promoter who paid attention to detail – the very attributes that, I think, persuaded the Students' Union Executive to offer me the post in the first place. Most students' unions had a social secretary in situ for a year, many did a great job but it was not a career because they were in it for the fun, the buzz. Agents, managers and promoters needed a steady pair of hands at the venues because, if things went wrong on the night the band would turn on those who put the gig in. A poor social secretary could literally lose somebody their job, their house, their family, everything! I was a very safe, experienced pair of hands. I also put together a team of trusted and talented people, although by the very nature of a university environment they had to change, but the quality of people didn't. I can name a few important ones here: Nigel Waller, Jeremy Oppenheim, Veronica Longmire, Mark Lane, Geoff Campbell. But by far the most vital in establishing Lancaster as a professionally managed venue through the '70s was Alan Murray. All together we made a formidable team which was, I believe, unique in the college sector.

When a promoter put a show into Lancaster we were on a percentage of the net ticket sales. In other words, the Students' Union had no financial risks – whatever the audience size, we covered our costs and made money. Not necessarily so for the promoter. But, truth to tell, I worked far harder, cared more, pulled out more stops, for those shows than for my own "bought" ones. I know this was not usual among college dates; many didn't care if their own students' union money was not at risk. I understood that establishing such a good reputation among the country's top promoters was the sound commercial way to run the entertainments programme. Little or no risk, guaranteed profit. OK, we wouldn't make killings, but equally we wouldn't have disasters. As I said previously, one disaster equates to about six highly successful shows. This attitude meant that towards the end of my time at Lancaster about 90% of the shows were external promoters' shows. By then almost all risk had been removed from the students' union. But the Students' Union Executive did not understand; perhaps that was my fault as I never explained fully what I had achieved – it all looked so easy from the outside.

Here we are facing the final question: why have there been no Great Hall shows since 1985? Well, I left on the 31 December 1984 and Geoff Campbell continued, with some success (after all, he did get New Order, which I couldn't). But in the summer of 1985 Geoff took the first professional entertainments post at Exeter University. Lancaster University Students' Union appointed somebody to take over the entertainments programme at the Great Hall and The Sugar House. He/she promoted, I think, three or four shows and lost several thousands of pounds. He/she had to buy all the acts and nobody in the business trusted Lancaster now. Shows with Joan Armatrading and Dire Straits that I had negotiated had been pulled out. The new Students' Union management and executive stopped all "risky" promotions, which for Lancaster now meant all promotions. Even The Sugar House was curtailed – it was all such a shame and do you know, I think I am justified in condemning them for squandering a gold-plated legacy.

Incidently, the official explanation, that licensing laws had changed etc., was simply not true; but they did have to justify the unjustifiable!

The end of a journey. I hope reading this has been rewarding, that it has stirred memories, revealed some stories, amazed and entertained. But most of all, I hope that I have helped confirm that, for a few years, Lancaster was at the centre of the music world, how that happened and why. After all, as Mick Jagger would have said if only he had had the opportunity to be on the Great Hall stage: "It's only rock 'n' roll but I like it."

Leeds? Where's Leeds?

Paul Loasby features frequently in this book, indeed he is a vital part of the story from the late '70s onwards. Paul was social secretary at Leeds University for the best part of 2 years – he was, I believe, the only sabbatical officer they have had in this role – an unbelievable fact, given the role entertainments played at Leeds. He then went to London to be a booker at MAM Agency. He found this so frustrating that he quickly moved to join Harvey Goldsmith – certainly the biggest promoter in the U.K., arguably the world at that time, and swiftly moved up the company ladder. Promoting was his forte; he was brilliant, demonstrating great imagination and creativity. He then ventured out on his own, founding Monsters of Rock at Donnington, football stadium gigs, Barry Manilow at Blenheim Palace – the list is endless. He then moved into management, again with great success, and today his One Fifteen Company manages Jools Holland, Dave Gilmour, Syd Barrett, Deacon Blue, Ruby Turner and Mick Ralphs amongst others. Here he recollects those momentous years at Lancaster …

Reading the chapters of this book occasioned many smiles, laughs and memories of the time I spent with Barry Lucas. For me, the strength of our friendship forms the foundation of the story. Our first meeting was in 1974, at a student union social secretaries conference at Imperial College, London. Barry was dressed in a white suit (what a poser). He told me later that he hadn't wanted to be introduced, but copious quantities of alcohol loosens tongues. All night he constantly took the piss about how Leeds social secretaries were obsessed with cheap ticket prices. It was, he wasn't. We hit it off immediately.

As full-time Students' Entertainment Officer, Barry had an unusual status: the job was unique. By 1974, he was pulling in some big acts to Lancaster University; and at Leeds University I felt we were struggling slightly in comparison. I had chosen to go to Leeds in 1972, purely because of the history of the bands appearing there. I had no idea of what to look for in a degree course (I chose Economics). For me the lure of musical entertainment was the real motivation for going. After arriving, I somehow became Social Secretary at the Students' Union. At the start, I didn't have a clue! But I did have a passion for presenting top artists, as well as a conviction that we should aim for profit (which at that time was not the done-thing in Students' Union circles).

When I met Barry in '74, I knew I'd met somebody who shared my convictions about how things should be done and from then on, we developed a firm and long friendship. The Lancaster to Leeds hotline was an indispensable resource, and I learned a few tricks of the trade that have helped me over the years. Whenever Barry and I were together our conversations were dominated by discussions of ticket sales and deals. We talked endlessly about which acts were considered

hot, warm, tepid, and everything in between. When my turn at Leeds was up we maintained the bond. Barry was always on call as I wended my way through the ultra-competitive, ever-evolving world of the music industry. At Harvey Goldsmith's office, I regularly used Barry to promote gigs on Harvey's tours: Eric Clapton, Peter Gabriel, Bad Company, Billy Connolly, The Boomtown Rats; these are just a few names that come to mind. When I went solo as a promoter, I always suggested Lancaster University on the tour itinerary. The reason it worked was because of Barry. This relatively small but flexible venue, with Barry making sure the promoter's wishes and needs were covered, made it a key venue for any tour. We also had a lot of fun.

Inevitably, the successful era declined as Barry seemed to be edged out by the Students' Union. But reading these pages evokes the highs and lows of a wonderful period: a rock 'n' roll domain in which I thoroughly enjoyed my part.

Paul Loasby

"Another good night for drunkards ..."

NINE

Well if you are reading this chapter the likelihood is that you have bought this 'new' edition of the book. So congratulations and thank you. Since we published the first edition – which sold out fast – so many people have contacted Paul and myself with photos, posters, tickets, memories etc. Then, added to that, my attic discovery of the mysterious Ear Ere Records bag, full of documents and letters which also brought to the surface several, newly remembered, stories I thought you'd like to hear. Hence this 'new' book.

In a few of my stories I mention my battles with University House. It is perhaps hard to imagine today but in the higher echelons of the university administration there was a very real antipathy towards the concerts. Today when I speak to people who worked at the university at the time, there is a very rose-tinted glasses nostalgia in evidence. They talk now in awe and bask in the reflected glory as they list the superstars who graced the Great Hall stage over that period. But perhaps I am being a bit unfair on University House when I put most of the blame on them. In fact nearly all the staff at the university in the '70s and '80s hated the concerts. Security staff, bar staff, cleaners, porters and teaching staff were all constantly criticising the shows, the disruption – the way they brought the real world into the hallowed, academic halls. I feel I am also being unfair to that list – I should mention that many students, especially in the '80s did not want the local population attending, what they saw as, student gigs.

In my 'Ear 'Ere bag was a whole sheaf of papers which clarify the University's position and they make for hilarious reading at times. The invoice for an electrician at the Leonard Skinhead concert was symptomatic of their knowledge and interest. This was a major UK tour by Lynryd Skynyrd that had sold out everywhere, including Lancaster, the last date on the tour. But did anybody in the ivory tower that was University House have any idea what was going on in their Great Hall? No. They thought Leonard Skinhead was a bunch of strange Americans – what a great name for a band though, wish I'd thought of it.

In October 1974, after the Cockney Rebel concert Arthur Gray – the University Beadle – wrote to me (with cc to the University Secretary, second in pecking order to the V.C. at the time), Rod Martindale (Secretary for Student and College Affairs) and the SRC Chairman (my boss) to complain about me exceeding the capacity of the Great Hall. Considering I was to have Queen and Bad Company on later that term, it was perhaps the wrong battle to pick. Luckily this was another example of the 'powers that be' not understanding what was happening. He stated that he had 'good reason' to believe the capacity had been exceeded – it hadn't. These people NEVER EVER, in all the 350 plus concerts, attended a show. Well I refused to put them on between 9.00am and 5.00pm weekdays so what do you expect? I found my memo reply: "the information you stated is absolute rubbish … I was in attendance at that concert, unlike any of the other people you mentioned … I was on the door the whole evening with the band's manager … they were on 90% of the gross ticket sales and came away with approximately £950.00. Tickets were £1 could you try working out the maths?"

In 1975 Jim Dawber (Deputy Beadle) wrote a report about Freshers' weekend. In it he said, "Dr. Feelgood ... by 3.00 a.m. several persons did not live up to his name. A VERY BAD NIGHT – windows kicked in, broken beer bottles and glasses smashed on the Spine and on the roads. Drunks vomiting in the handiest places ... EVERY bar on campus packed ... licensing regulations broken. Persons under age had intoxicating liquor in these bars apart from the fact that they had no legal right to be in these bars. It is impossible for stewards in charge of these bars to control this sort of thing." Except, of course, that is exactly what the law requires of them. But, more significantly, he goes on to talk about the next night, "a 'disco'. Another 'good night' at the hall. Another good night for the 'bars'. Another good night for people wanting to fight. Another good night for drunkards. Not a good night for people on duty OR living on campus. Again, glasses and bottles smashed on the Spine and roads on Campus ... 43 trees, well established saplings, that will cost about £15 to replace, mutilated ... road signs smashed, another cycle stolen, noise of drunks that could be heard all over the campus. The large sign at the entrance to the University states that Visitors are Welcome. Leaving a calling card amounting to about £600 worth of damage makes you wonder."

I can well imagine several of you reading this, given you probably aren't 18 anymore, nodding in agreement. The only problem was, this was a Freshers' Student Disco, not advertised locally, and never attended by local people ... so why did they get the blame. We all know why. And onto PUNK!

From the University Beadle himself: This report is supplied in an effort to ensure that groups of this nature (The Damned) are not booked in the future. There was an audience of approximately 900 of whom extremely few were students. Those attending were dressed either in weird clothing or "Tramp Gear". Not only was clothing painted but also faces were painted in the oddest patterns and the Tramp gear appears to consist of wearing torn clothing tied up with string or secured by safety pins. Several of the audience were wearing safety pins through their ears or nose and certainly in one case through the cheek. I am informed that the "dancing" consisted of the audience jumping up and down as if on Pogo sticks and some were endeavoring to get on to the stage. This was prevented by members of the "Road Gang" associated with the Group and by the student "Bouncers"... I am further informed that a Catering Supervisor hid in the Ladies' toilets for about 15mins because she was afraid of the people who were milling around ... In support of my suggestion that such groups should not be booked in future I point out that the hall was not built as the type of premises to accommodate concerts of this description – even the normal student Pop concert... it is certainly not for students of this University who were minimally represented in the audience. It was very evident that "The Damned" attracted "Weirdos" from the surrounding areas and one bus driver was overheard to say that he would not be involved in driving this "type of person" in the future.

This report was written by a person who had never been in the hall after 5.00pm unless it was for a University function or Classical music concert and to the University Secretary, second in command of Uni House. His response was immediate, "Such concerts constitute, to my mind, so serious a threat to the safety and well-being of University students, members and employees, as well as to the security of University property, that I am NOT prepared to allow the use of the Great Hall in future for concerts of this nature."

What could a poor man do in such a situation? I wrote back by return, "I totally agree with you about the necessity to curtail any events which cause extensive problems to university personnel or property but I am in a very awkward position, as with my hand on

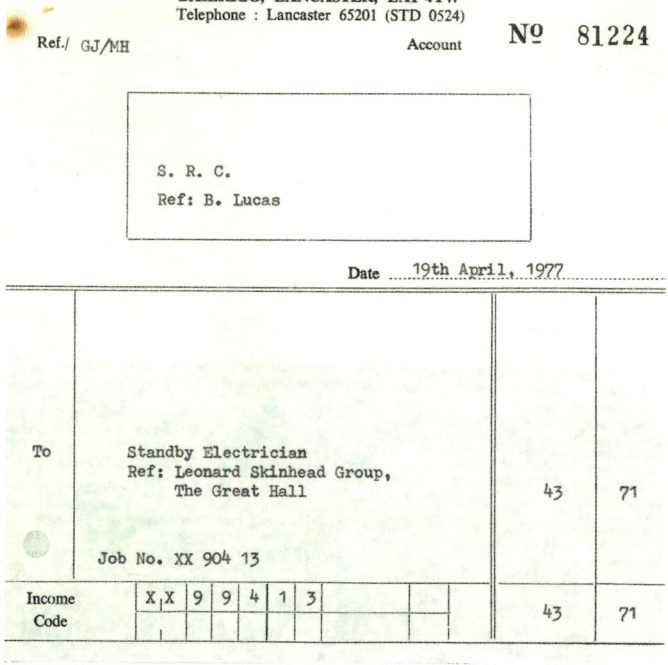

Barry's bill for Lynyrd Skynyrd's electricians

my heart, I cannot possibly define Punk Rock. Of the 3 concerts you named, the first was Power Pop, the second Punk and the 3rd New Wave – these definitions are those supplied not only by the bands themselves, but also by all the British Music Press. Therefore you must see my difficulty in applying a blanket ban of punk rock unless the University is in a position to give me some assistance in classifying artists in their correct category." I followed up with, "I have studied the memo from the University Secretary and cannot but agree with such a detailed and thorough investigation into the events at the Great Hall. However it might have been useful to speak, if only briefly, to either myself, the stewards or staff who were employed to deal with students and members of the public which attend these concerts. A minor point of information might be worth noting is that at the last concert (the only one with real trouble) there were no porters, no security staff (present) and Mr. Robinson (Head of Security) arrived after it had finished and been dealt with … It might also be worth noting that we have more 'trouble' at Syd Lawrence and Joe Loss Big Band dances, and had a rather large fight at the Rag Ball, which was a 90% student attendance – I won't even mention Roses' Weekend with its annual damages bill of several hundred pounds."

His reply, "I have no wish to enter into a 'semantic battle'. If any type of concert persistently poses a real threat to the safety of human beings or to the security of University buildings they will NOT be allowed to use the Great Hall."

Of course those people trying to stop all the concerts were so out of touch, 'semantic battle' is exactly what I dragged them into. In the end they admitted defeat it was all they could do unless they came out and openly stated that they really wanted to stop all the shows. To save face they said I had to detail the type of music each band played. I had to send them to Paula Eastwood (Richardson) who would verify the genre. Hence now The Stranglers were Country and Western etc. I must have been persuasive, look at the list of punk acts we had on. And the University never did manage to close the concerts until 10 months after I had left.

Barry Lucas

Some memories from Mark Lane

In case you've forgotten, Barry, my involvement with the concerts (as a steward) commenced in late 1974 after a few of the lads from Bowland (Rob Wilson, "Big Ged" Hayes, Kev Halloran) who'd been working the gigs previously got me in on the act. Having served my apprenticeship on the doors, in late 1975 I became your "main enforcer" aka "head bouncer" for the next four years whilst I completed undergrad and postgrad degrees. During this four-five year period I probably worked at more than 90%+ of all the events right up to when I'd completed my postgrad degree and departed from Lancaster in October '79.

We didn't ever, in my recollections, refer to ourselves as "stewards"; it was somewhat more ego-preening to label ourselves "bouncers". In reality, for the vast majority of concerts, counselling skills were all that was needed rather than bone-crunching thuggery.

The rewards package was considered excellent: as a steward we earnt £2 or £3 per concert, saw some great bands for free and could, on occasions, bring in a guest. To put the remuneration, which sounds meagre now, into perspective, £2 or £3 would have roughly equated to a dozen pints of best bitter. As your main enforcer, I received a premium rate of £5 per concert, which given the volume of concerts probably netted out at around £100 a year and at the prevailing rate of exchange that would have been around 500 pints.

The team of stewards was a mixed bunch: we needed some real muscle and so the Praetorian Guard was largely recruited through the Rugby Club and supplemented with a couple of mature students with mildly psychopathic disorders (one of whom worshipped Bruce Lee and claimed to be ex-SAS). The rest of the squad were "normal" students who'd run at the first sight of bloodshed but could use counselling skills to talk their way out of trouble. The Praetorian Guard would usually be deployed in the hottest spot which was the stage area; the "counsellor-types" would provide security for the fire doors. As the main enforcer my role was to cover when one of the lads wanted to go for a pint or pee, to troubleshoot if an incident kicked-off and dish out the cash at the end of the evening. Despite undergoing deep hypnosis and regression treatment, my memories do not include any of the many, many gigs which ran perfectly smoothly with little trouble. When asked by you for my anecdotes, I can only recall when things didn't end quite so happily. Inevitably, this means taking my regression back to the Punk era with its anti-establishment violence. So, I've tried to put the things which spring to mind in some form of chronological order as it may help you.

Bad Company
One of the first gigs I worked as a steward involved Bad Company in late '74. We'd always station a couple of stewards in the backstage corridor where we'd often share a bit of good-humoured banter with the bands' roadies who were frequently/always stoned. As the main act commenced, a blitzed roadie approached one of the stewards with an unbelievably good deal, to purchase a "bag of bones" which after translation meant a large bag of shredded cannabis leaves. A quick whip-round amongst the stewards left them a few pounds short, perhaps £10, so a plea was sent urgently to the treasurer of one of the college JCRs requesting a personal cheque be cashed. The obliging treasurer's petty cash box only contained that week's takings from the juke box and two pinball machines, so the entire £10 was sent up to the Great Hall in a large bag containing old sixpence, shilling and florin (two bob) coins. Despite the roadie being disagreeable about the trove of silver, the deal was transacted. Unbeknown to the roadie, the bag was despatched immediately to Bowland College for inspection and certification by an authority in the genus of flowering plants called Cannabaceae whose assessment was damning – it was the wrong genus (more like tea leaves)! After the concert finished, the roadie was escorted discreetly to one of the darker corners of the backstage area by several of the more fearsome stewards who, with a little persuasion, secured a refund in full in notes. The roadie had taken the bag bulging with silver coins to one of the campus bars where it had been exchanged for notes which were then duly returned to the grateful JCR treasurer.

Leo Sayer
During the time I worked at the concerts, there were two occasions where there were attempted assaults upon the lead-performers which involved knives. Strangely, both involved bands which, on the face of it, you'd imagine would have been least likely to attract violence: Errol Brown of Hot Chocolate and Leo Sayer. The Leo Sayer incident was particularly bizarre: a totally inoffensive and polite artist, small in stature (a little over 5' including platform shoes and several inches of afro hair) dressed in hippy-ish clothing. There was no reason to believe this would be anything other than a quiet gig. The attacker, who made his move as Leo was coming onto the stage, was grabbed by myself and two other stewards and frogmarched out of the concert to get an early bus home. Unlike Errol Browne, who didn't even say thanks after a similar incident, I recall the gratitude Leo Sayer showed by finding us after the concert, having a chat with the team and giving us a bottle of vodka to share. A really nice man.

Hot Chocolate
The Hot Chocolate incident, involving Edge, is well-covered in the book. Just a couple of additional comments: First, despite preventing Errol Brown from receiving a serious injury, he didn't have the decency to say thanks to the team or reward us with a bottle of vodka as Leo Sayer had – most disappointing! I remember when his next hit, "I'll Put You Together Again", was released, thinking its what we should have sung him that evening. Secondly, upon attending the court in Lancaster where Edge pleaded guilty and was sentenced, I was asked to submit my expense claim to the court which resulted in a cheque for 12.5p arriving in the post to cover my return bus fare from Campus to Lancaster. I never did bother to cash it.

Elvis Costello Live Stiffs Tour
Again, this incident is well-covered in the book but just a few comments: Ian Drury tripped over as he was coming onto the stage (not backstage) i.e. in full view of the audience. His walk was more like a shuffle given the calliper on his left leg which meant he didn't lift this foot far off the ground and almost slid it along. As he shuffled into the Great Hall and headed onto the stage, this was where his left foot just brushed my foot which was enough to send him headlong onto the deck. Elvis Costello, upon seeing this, then started the skirmish with the stewards by trying to land one on me to which we retaliated. In the meantime, poor Ian Drury was vainly trying to get up as nobody helped him whilst the roadies and stewards were too busy exchanging blows. A story I've dined-out on over the years.

The Damned
There was collective sigh of relief amongst the stewards when we didn't host the Sex Pistols, however this relief turned to dismay when we got The Damned instead. The Punk era ushered in two unwelcome developments for the stewards: the dramatic uptick in violent behaviour meant we resourced the squad with more muscle and the punk's proclivity to show appreciation to the bands by "gobbing" – spitting! This meant any of the team providing security around the stage would get plastered in saliva. The first concert I recall where gobbing really got into full flow was The Damned gig which took place just after my undergrad finals in '77. I remember watching the performance from the stage door and as the pulsating strobe lights picked out the volleys of saliva flying at the band it looked it looked like a snow blizzard. Captain Sensible, David Vanian, who had an arm in a sling as he'd slipped off the stage at the previous gig (you can guess what he slipped on), simply gave up trying to brush off the slobber from himself with his one good hand. A mate had asked me to get Rat Scabies' autograph which he kindly gave me as he came off stage and headed towards the dressing room wearing a thick coat of sputum. Yuck!!!

Blondie
The punks' gobbing phase at Lancaster was ended by an incident at the Blondie concert. Debbie Harry looked stunning as she took to the stage that night and kicked off the performance with one of her early hits. Halfway through this number the punks in front of the stage launched an initial volley of spit at the band. Debbie immediately stopped singing, the band went quiet and she just stood still staring stern-faced into the audience for several seconds. Then, in the most dignified of voices, in a slow deliberate tone which seemed to emphasis every single word she said, "Last year it was considered cool to spit - now it isn't; so will those wanting to gob just F*CK OFF". The Great Hall erupted in a huge cheer and the rest of the evening went smoothly without any further gobbing. Having been admonished by Blondie, I can't recall gobbing ever being an issue at any concerts thereafter.

Buzzcocks
The violence at the Buzzcocks concert is already mentioned in the book. From my viewpoint as your main enforcer, it was the only gig where we totally lost control and I genuinely feared for the safety of my team. There had been a simmering undertone of trouble all night which had been manifest by rival groups of punks pushing and taunting each other. The real trouble started when two of these rival groups started a fight which several of the stewards moved to break-up, upon which both groups and other punks united and turned on the stewards. I recall Rob Wilson and I running for our lives by fleeing through a side fire door with a posse of angry punks in hot pursuit and then seeking refuge in the porters' lodge by the main entrance to the Hall insisting we needed police protection.

The Stranglers
My final gig! This isn't directly relevant to your book, but I'll share the anecdote with you all the same.

Having recently completed my postgrad degree, it was with sadness that I ran the security for the final time in October 1979. A great concert, by my then favourite band, but little did I know how apposite the Stranglers name would become later that night.

Three months previously, I'd been at a departmental cheese & wine do (cheese & wine parties were the then in thing) in the Business School at Gillow House when two drunken members of the Rugby Club picked a fight with an overseas student on my course whom we kept an eye on as he was a haemophiliac. Despite our entreaties for them to leave him alone, they persisted and in the ensuing skirmish I'd broken the nose of one and knocked-out the other. As far as I was concerned, that was the end of the matter, but it wasn't to be.

I was one of the very last to leave the Great Hall after the Stranglers concert and as I walked in the unlit area between the Great Hall towards the Chaplaincy Centre where my car was parked I was grabbed around the neck from behind and pulled backwards into the shadows. With one arm round my neck strangling me and a knife in the other hand, my assailant started describing how he intended to exact revenge for the broken nose I'd given several months previously.

With no hope of fighting my way free, I talked as best I could, and explained the danger he'd caused to a vulnerable classmate whose haemophilia could easily be fatal. After a couple of minutes talking, he relaxed his grip, let me go, sat down on a low wall and just started crying. We sat there together for perhaps 15 minutes chatting and eventually shook hands and went our separate ways. A few weeks later I received a letter thanking me for not reporting his assault.

In many ways it was a fitting ending to my final gig with its theme of strangulation and counselling/talking being successful in defusing a potentially violent situation.

Mark Lane

Mark Lane studied at Lancaster University, completing a joint honours degree in Economics & Sociology and a masters in Marketing. In between degrees (whilst continuing to work at the Great Hall concerts) he was to spend a year in Manchester as a graduate marketing trainee for Golden Wonder, where he helped unhinge any possibility of the UK ever enjoying a balanced diet, by being part of the team which launched Pot Noodle! A 40 year career in the technology sector was to follow which included heading Honeywell's strategic marketing, followed by strategy consultancy before moving into the software industry where he was Vice International Marketing for California headquartered business software giant PeopleSoft. After the dot-com bubble burst, he became marketing and advertising director for UK software group COA. Eventually after several unsuccessful attempts at retirement, Mark retired from retiring and now works in London as an marketing and advertising advisor to tech sector businesses.

Some memories from John (Jerry) Drew CBE

Shakin' Stevens
I only once received a direct instruction from Party HQ in King Street, London (now a NatWest bank) despite the Party's reputation as a tightly centralised organisation with its ruling principle of democratic centralism. Anyway, the instruction in question was 'Book Shaky Stevens' who was, as you may know, a CP member. So, rather shamefacedly I went to you (Barry) and said some version of 'Please, pretty please …' to which I have you saying, "Great idea, exactly my plan". When I relayed the information to King Street I was briefly 'Comrade of the Week'. At the Grad Ball in '74 when you had also booked him, Michael Barratt (Shaky) and I had a very brief conversation about Dialectical Materialism but neither of us were great intellectuals and we ended up talking about other things. You may remember he was a keen drinker at that stage of his life! While President I was once or twice called in after concerns about numbers and fire regulations etc. and I took the approach that the best way to handle it was to look serious and promise to 'sort it' and then do nothing at all. I don't think I even bothered you with the details. We both had more important things to do.

John (Jerry) Drew CBE

John (Jerry) Drew CBE, Lancaster University Students' Union President 1972–1973, later Chief Executive Youth Justice Board Chair Safeguarding Programme Group, producing the Drew Review into South Yorkshire Police's handling of child sexual exploitation.

© Geoff Campbell

Robb Winn

I spoke to Robb Winn for several years before I met him but he was, from the beginning an essential part of the Lancaster Concerts Story. When I first got elected to the position of social secretary in Lonsdale College in 1970 Gas Taylor and I soon had to plan our first major show – we had practised with several low key gigs in Bowland refectory – Groundhogs, Edgar Broughton, Pretty Things etc. We, even then, played around with the concept of rock gigs, having a blues/rock band playing in the refectory and a folk singer Dave Kelly, Jo Anne Kelly, Al Stewart, etc, even poets such as Roger McGough, Adrian Henry, or Cecil Day-Lewis in the adjacent coffee bar. But it was a show in the Great Hall in early May that we were leading up to.

Gas was from Hull (my birth town also, although I left at 2 so it hardly shaped my personality!) and he suggested an agency, McLeod Holden in Hull, as a contact. Robb Winn had just stated there as an entertainment agent…

The story about that first booking The Who is elsewhere in the book, so I won't repeat it. Robb soon was offered a job in London – and what a job!

Chris Blackwell had re-located Island Records from Jamaica to London in 1962, ostensibly to bring reggae from the island of his birth to the UK. They had their first major hit with Millie's 'My Boy Lollipop' in 1964. But the label was young and fresh in contrast to the old dinosaurs of the vinyl world Decca, Pye, EMI, Phillips etc. the exciting new British talent jumped at the offer of a recording deal with them. The rosta was iconic. The label quickly acquired a Who's Who of British rock and folk. Incidentally, in the early 70s Island created direct record shop accounts with a very select number of shops who were able to order directly through them and not their distributing agents. There were only 120 such shops in the UK and Lancaster had one of them, Ear Ere Records.

But having signed this talent, often unknown and raw, developed and launched new and exciting careers, Blackwell wondered why not act as agents and management? So Island Artistes was formed. Robb was asked to join that exciting adventure. In the next few years we booked into Lancaster:

Free, Incredible String Band, Mott the Hoople, Amazing Blondel, Bronco, Traffic, King Crimson, Roxy Music, Stomu Yamashta, Bob Marley and the Wailers, Fairport Convention, John Martyn, Sparks. Not bad eh?

Robb Winn is an important part of the Lancaster story. We became firm friends, a friendship that has lasted 53 years and counting. That is why I have asked him to tell the story of Island Artistes in those days it is a fascinating insight into an unique aspect of the 70s music scene in the UK. Over to you Rob…

Barry Lucas

Some memories from Robb Winn

It was February 1971, and I am on a train heading from Hull to London. I had been invited down to meet Alec Leslie and John Glover, the two gents who ran Island Artists. They wanted to take me on the town, as a "thank you" for looking after the bookings for their artists for the past six weeks. They had both been out of the country on tours of Europe and America and there was no one else in the company to cover… so they asked me if I could help them while they were away. At the time, I was working as an agent for McLeod Entertainment Agency in Hull.

So, here I am in London. Walking down Portobello Rd in Notting Hill Gate, mouth agape, in total awe at the atmosphere that engulfed me for the next twenty minutes. Market stalls are selling their wares, music is blasting out from every stand, and people from all walks of life are singing, selling, laughing, making trade. The scene is so vibrant and so captivating. Eventually I turned the corner into Basing St and there stands before me a renovated church turned office building, I guess? So here I am, in a new three-piece suit, new shirt, new tie, ready to play. As I am sitting, waiting to be greeted, people are dashing everywhere in t-shirts, jeans, and flips. Oops! Alec and Johnny come out to greet me snickering, but only for about an hour! Once composed they thanked me for my effort. They were somewhat amazed that the bands had so many gigs on their calendars that they questioned their validities. Then they offered me an opportunity to join them as the fourth member of the agency team (the third person being Denise Mills, the real person that ran the agency). I couldn't believe it. Everything felt so right, jeans, flip flops, Portobello Rd market, music! I thought I must be dreaming… and so it began.

The building was referred to as Island Records, but the actual "corporate" Island Records was in another part of town. This building should have been called Island Artists because that's what it was dedicated to. It had two recording studios and a large room on the ground floor with four desks, which was the agency (with no individual offices). There was large room upstairs that I called "Camelot" and above that was Chris Blackwells apartment. The whole building was just constantly alive, just alive! People have asked me a million times what was so special about Island Records and Island Artists and my answer is Chris Blackwell. His demeanour, his eloquence, his vision, his incredible eye for talent from a diamond in the rough, and the freedom he gave to everyone to follow their instincts and be creative. This attitude applied whether they be artists, agents, or admin, asserting to just go do it, have fun, be creative, prudent and let's see how we pull it all together.

"Camelot" upstairs was the environment that separated Island from every other record company of its time. It was not just a label, and it was not just about demanding hit records. It was about crafting an experience. Here was forged the company's commitment to artistic integrity that allowed musicians to explore their deepest passions without the constraints of commercial demands. Here was where it all began. The perimeter of the room was nothing but seating, couches, cushions, comfort, and headphones (lots of headphones). This was where each creative department, in-house agents, producers, publishers, were invited to listen to the short list of potential signings. If the music sounded promising, we would then take in a gig to see their "on stage" presence. Then it was decision time. We would all congregate back at Camelot around a huge round table and final opinions would be given to Chris.

The legacy of Island Records still endures, as a testament to a time when passion, creativity and authenticity reigned supreme in the world of music. Barry, your words hold a mirror to an era that forever altered the musical landscape. The genesis of the Lancaster Concerts is steeped in passion and innovation and is a testament to the power of a shared vision and the relentless pursuit of musical excellence.

Robb Winn

More memories

The Boomtown Rats

I have a good friend who passed away a couple of years ago, Mal Thompson. He worked the doors for the concerts, and he once told me a story about how people regularly tried sneak in the side door, hoping a mate would let them in. One night, The Boomtown Rats wee playing, and suddenly there's a hammering on the door, and one of the doormen opens up. "Let me in, let me in!" was the cry, met with "No ticket, go away". "I'm playing" he says, "I'm Bob Geldoff"! The doorman slams the door shut and shouts to Mal, "There's a guy trying to get in, says he's Bob Geldoff. I don't give a **** who he is, he's not coming in". Needless to say, he eventually did get in.

Graeme Hall

The Stranglers

I was fifteen when I saw my first concert at the Great Hall, The Stranglers 1979 Raven Tour. The noise was deafening, and the atmosphere was electric. Just to see hundreds and hundreds of people in one arena so enraptured and caught up in the moment will live with me forever. I saw many concerts after that, including The Stranglers again and The Clash. In the early 80s I saw Hawkwind (where the highlight was being allowed backstage to meet Dave Brock and, the legend that is, Ginger Baker), Slade (amazing night), and, dare I say it, Haircut 100. Nothing will compare to that first concert though. So much so I wrote an essay at school about my experience which was read out by the teacher to all the class.

Steve Buchanan

Some memories from Mark Hagen, executive producer at the BBC

The first thing you have to think about is that there were always a lot of firsts. I would say that – through the combination of being a University venue located in a medium sized city just slightly too far away from Leeds, Liverpool or Manchester – virtually every show at the Great Hall would have been *somebody's* first show. That might have been a new student away from home for the first time, a teenager from the town, or a new convert to the joys of rock'n'roll. And the excitement generated by that made Lancaster a fantastic place to see a gig. It didn't hurt that it was a brilliantly designed venue as well: great sight lines, low stage, dancing on the floor, seating around the three sides of the balcony – perfect.

I went to my first show – Mott The Hoople, supported by Queen – on November 16th, 1973, and my last – The Clash – on January 23rd 1980. In between I must have been to dozens of concerts; you just did back then, regardless of whether you were actually a fan of the band or not. That Mott The Hoople show cost 60p a ticket and so you *could*, even though for a 15-year-old the 20-mile round trip from Bentham was a logistical challenge not universally successfully met.

But it was worth it, it was *always* worth it. Without it, and without the Ear-Ere record shop in town, my life would have immeasurably poorer, and I dare say very different indeed. I've been in bars with Bruce Springsteen, on Tube trains with Taylor Swift, kissed by Paul McCartney, slapped by Dolly Parton and blessed by Little Richard and none of it would have happened without so many of those nights in the Great Hall where – in the words of the late Lester Bangs – we found "the revivifying flames when for once, if only then in (y)our life you were blasted outside of yourself and the monotony which defines most life anywhere at any time, when you felt supra-alive, when you supped on lightning and nothing else in the realms of the living or the dead mattered at all".

Mott The Hoople and Queen

That first time, I'd never heard of Queen, but it's not a bad start to my concert going life! They didn't really have the budget for flamboyance, but they sounded great. Freddie wore boots with a wooden stack heel and sole – you remember those! – and at one particularly dramatic moment leapt into the air and crashed to the stage in complete silence. I can still hear it now. Ian Hunter made jokes about being on *Top of The Pops* that week and play-fought with Ariel Bender. It was the most exciting thing I'd ever seen. Unlike Queen when they came back for 'Sheer Heart Attack'. Based on this performance, much anticipated but very disappointing on the night, drowned in clouds of choking dry ice and Brian May's endless guitar twaddle. I remember hearing 'Bohemian Rhapsody' for the first time in Ear-Ere; oh, how we laughed.

Hawkwind

Hawkwind were intoxicatingly weird and a little bit frightening to a 15-year-old me. We got free badges on the way in and a proper (what we'd now call) multimedia experience throughout. Clouds of dubious smoke, enveloping back projections, exotic dancers and a driving deep bass throb pushing the music forward. I especially remember one projected sequence depicting the life of a tree which was a great deal better seen that it appears written down!

Sensational Alex Harvey Band

Still one of the peak concert experiences of my life a full 50 years on. Alex came on in pitch darkness to the strains of Faith Healer, wielding a portable spotlight shaped like a rifle which strafed the audience with beams of light, and proceeded to deliver an incredible performance. Pirate uniforms, books of lore, show tunes 'Delilah', and the 'Framed' finale with a stocking masked Alex bursting through a polystytrene brick wall. Vambo Sill Rules, OK?

Traffic

Another concert high, one of only two times I was in the balcony. Didn't know any of the material but the whole Great Hall seemed to levitate as one during '40,000 Headmen' and stayed floating for the whole show. First time I'd seen Richard Thompson as well!

Dr Feelgood

On the tour that became the *Stupidity* live album and very much a sign of things to come. My friend Richard Parry taped it on his little cassette recorder and for months we marvelled at Wilko's bragging during 'I'm A Man' – "I ain't never been to Lancaster Uni-ver-sity, but I been to school". He did, of course, go to Newcastle University where he studied Icelandic literature but that's not the point…

Rich Kids

The only time I ever saw the headliner in the bar – I was standing behind Glen Matlock right at the back of the queue and it parted like the Red Sea to let him through. Did I take advantage? Of course.

Blondie

Right on the cusp of greatness, the second band I ever interviewed, and the first backstage. I left my cassette player in the dressing room and playback found Chris Stein and Debbie Harry blaming each other for the fact that the coke had run out. I think they were joking.

Sparks

This one was proper teen mayhem on the day I finished my O levels. We're pretty familiar with Ron Mael now but in 1974? *Weird…*

Supertramp

Supercilious twats with no regard for the audience whatsoever. Bring on the punk rockas…

The Jags

Memory may play me false here, but my recollection is that this was a special gig to celebrate an Ear-Ere anniversary. I do remember coming down from Scotland especially for it and spending the evening with Nigel, Eric, Roger Moorhouse and my closest comrade in arms the (presumably) late Malcolm Redpath. Impossible to overstate how important that shop was to me, starting in the market and culminating in me being the Scottish outlet for several Springsteen bootlegs. Everybody needs a place like that in their lives: inspirational on so many levels.

John Martyn

I'm pretty sure I had a head when I went in, but once he switched that Echoplex on I have no idea where it went.

The Jam

Second time on the balcony, on the *Setting Sons* tour. In my experience, The Jam actually got slightly worse every time I saw them live – I gave up after this one!

Buzzcocks/Penetration? Or was it the Slits? Or both?

Running battles between Blackpool & Preston NE supporters. On leaving I tuned round to see one of my friends being propelled over the bonnet of a parked car primarily for being from Stirling.

10cc

Biiiig fuck off glitter ball. We were easily impressed.

Mark Hagen

Geoff Campbell

As I have mentioned elsewhere in the book, Geoff played an important part in the Lancaster gigs story. I first met Geoff when he was part of my 'team of humpers' in the Great Hall. A sometimes-motley crew who were responsible for lifting heavy objects vital to the show production. By the early 70s bands required teams of local crew to help with the bands, on the tour roadies get the PA and Lights out of the artics, into the hall and on the stage. These varied from around the usual six up to 10 or 12 for the massive shows. Geoff proved a reliable and intelligent member of that crew so when the position became vacant, of organising and leading the crew, he was an obvious candidate.

Geoff quickly assumed that role and took on the organisation of a stage crew which was becoming increasingly expected from major venues of which we had now become. I can safely say that, without Geoff's organisational skills or man management, then Lancaster would not have had the great reputation it had in the music business. Having opened The Sugarhouse and assumed the role of Students' Union General Manager, it was obvious that if I was to continue running the entertainments side of the organisation with its 30 plus staff and expanding commercial activities, I would need help. Walter Townsend, our ex-forces, Finance Officer, suggested that Geoff would be a perfect fit. I agreed immediately as it is what I would have wanted and so...

Geoff got respectable. He initially worked on the Great Hall shows but this time from an office and then when we opened The Sugarhouse he took over the entertainments programme. What a success that was after a bit of a rocky 3 months start. Geoff's contribution to that period of Lancaster's concert story was invaluable. He became a close friend as well as working colleague and I think he might have some stories to tell.

Barry Lucas

Some memories from Geoff Campbell

I first became involved with the Lancaster concerts very early one morning in August 1978. Barry Lucas' Crew Boss dragged me from my bed offering large sums of cash for a bit of work on campus. He was obviously fairly desperate and exaggerating about the cash. All we had to do was unload three forty-foot articulated lorries, help build a stage set and then reverse the exercise! It was a Peter Gabriel concert, and I was there for about eighteen hours. I think the money was £10 and a free gig.

At the time I was living in a student house in Galgate near the campus. Having returned from six months driving to the Himalayas through Iran and Afghanistan I was in need of cash. I did have a proper camera from the trip, an Olympus OM1 as used or at least advertised by David Bailey. So, I thought let's work more concerts and take some pictures. How hard could it be? Well, quite tricky really, using a fully manual camera and only available light. I had no knowledge of stage photography, my previous experience being travel and portrait photography. Darkroom lessons were provided by the Lancaster caver Richard Ellwood (not a lot of available light down a pothole), whilst tea and the darkroom itself were courtesy of Jackie Hall. I used Ilford HP5 film and pushed the development in the darkroom. The first concert I photographed was The Stranglers and their monitor engineer let me work from the side of the stage, but of course there was a stage invasion, so that was interesting for a first gig. Next up, Siouxsie and the Banshees, and I quickly learned how to clean sweat and spit from the front of a lens and press the shutter while my feet were off the ground in the middle of a punk mosh pit. Many more shows followed, as this was Barry Lucas booking bands in a golden period for concerts at Lancaster. I worked every show and took photos whenever I could. The original negatives are still fine after over 40 years, and I digitised and archived them in the early 2000s.

I worked the Lancaster concerts from 1978 until 1985 with a regular group of men and women – the Lancaster Stage Crew ('humpers'). It was always a laugh even though the work was hard and the money poor. We did get to see a lot of great shows, and many of the acts would give us a case of beer after the gig which helped with the breakdown of the gear – although that probably wouldn't pass health and safety now. I progressed from humper to Crew Boss and then Entertainment Manager, learning how the music business worked sat opposite Barry Lucas while still taking pictures at the concerts. I provided daffodils for The Smiths, ate fish and chips with Joan Jett, drank beer with The Clash, and had Mark Knopfler play me Sultans of Swing while I sat on a flight case. I was married one day in the Lancaster Registry Office and the next day worked the Tina Turner concert. Tina wished me luck and I now tell people Tina Turner did my 'Wedding Reception'.

The Selecter, 1980 © Geoff Campbell

The Clash, 1980 © Geoff Campbell

Japan, 1981 © Geoff Campbell

Tina Turner, 1984 © Geoff Campbell

New Order, 1985 © Geoff Campbell

Blondie

Mid-afternoon I suddenly lost about six of my 'humpers' for about an hour, and for nearly 40 years I had no idea what had happened to them. Apparently, the crew were chatting to Debbie Harry and the conversation got around to drugs. I know you are amazed that would happen, Debbie Harry discussing illegal substances! Anyway, the topic of magic mushrooms came up and Ms Harry said that she had never experienced them. Some of the crew lived in Galgate and said there was a field full of them just down the road. She was desperate to try them so off trooped six enthusiastic mushroom gatherers. Now I suppose they were faced with the dilemma of either working for me or doing the bidding of the absolutely gorgeous Debbie … it's a no-brainer isn't it?

Geoff Campbell

More memories

Eric Clapton

When Paul Loasby (frequently mentioned throughout the book) joined Harvey Goldsmith's office, his first tour was with Eric Clapton. Part of the tour was to Ireland and one night the tour was in Cork. Like every act that involves a piano, his contract stated he needed a grand piano tuned to A440 (concert pitch). Paul, nervous on his first tour for the world's leading promoter, went to the hall early in the morning to make sure everything was okay before the crew arrived. The city hall's duty porter opened the hall and showed Paul in. Paul looked around and everything seemed fine, then he walked up to the stage. Sat in the centre was a battered old pub 'jo-anna'. Paul asked desperately, "Where's the grand piano?". "There", came the reply from the porter. "But it's in the rider, he has to have a grand piano!" screamed a desperate Paul. "Oh, to be sure it's a grand wee piano, the best in Cork" said a mystified, but proud, porter. Paul just sank to his knees and wept. He was unable to see the funny side.

Barry Lucas

Thin Lizzy, 1976

I lived in Galgate for 28 years, never a student at Lancaster University, but I had friends who were and spent a large amount of time between 1979 and 1985 in the bars up there, seeing great bands in the Great Hall. My abiding memory of concerts at the Great Hall was how I felt at the end of the night: exhausted, no voice, shirt dripping with sweat but having had an awesome night!

First concert I ever saw was there was Thin Lizzy supported by Clover in November 1976 (I found out later that Huey Lewis was in the band at that time). I can recall it being a freezing cold night, so (as a concert novice) I wore my parka. The parka was no problem when we all sat on the floor to watch Clover, but a big problem when Lizzy hit the stage (I recall an explosion of sound and a blue flashing light as they launched into 'Jailbreak'). I found myself jammed up to the front of the stage, thinking I was going to pass out because I was so hot in that bloody parka! Had to fight my way towards the back to have enough space just to take it off and tie it round my waist, before struggling back to rejoin my mate. After that experience, I only ever went to the concerts in t-shirts and jeans, even if it meant freezing outside waiting for the doors to open.

Peter Griffiths

Joan Armatrading and Ian Drury

I worked with Barry during the 70s when I was a mature student at Bailrigg and (ever mindful of getting over heavy ground easily) Barry decided that it would be a good idea to have some women working alongside his stewards at the gigs in the Great Hall. There are times when a small, determined woman can talk down an overexcited, sixteen stone rugby player fuelled by beer and "stiff little fingers" with more ease than an exasperated, sixteen stone male steward. There are also times that required the same brave, small woman to explain to an overexcited eighteen-year-old student that taking her underwear off and throwing it at the band might not look good the next day.

We had regulars at the Great Hall, Joan Armatrading was a favourite, and she tried to be with us for her birthday each year, usually receiving more birthday presents on the stage than she could carry. Have you ever heard five hundred all women singing 'Willow'? Pretty awesome.

I also worked with John on the Lancaster Free Press in the 70s. We printed a few fanzines given over to the bands at the university, and the best memory was of that was when our intrepid reporter, Stevie, staggered out of Ian Drury's dressing room saying, "Now I can die a happy man, Ian Drury just told me to fuck off and die".

Alongside Barry's gift for getting great new bands, he had a habit of helping women and children at the newly opened Women's Centre. Many of the kids got away to Fly Sheet Camp (run by record producer and musician Simon Emerson, then just Si) funded by Barry.

Brenda Lynton Escreet

Shakin Stevens

Shakin Stevens played the Graduate Ball in 1974. By then I was a member of the Communist Party, although I only once received a direct instruction from Party HQ in King Street London, despite their reputation as a tightly centralised organisation with its ruling principle of democratic centralism. Anyway, the instruction in question was to "book Shakin Stevens" who happened to be, as you may know, a CP member. So, rather shamefacedly, I went to Barry and said some version of "Please, pretty please…", to which he replied, "Great idea, exactly my plan". When I relayed the information to King Street I was briefly 'Comrade of the Week'. At the Graduate Ball, Michael Barratt and I had a very brief conversation about Dialectical Materialism, but neither of us were great intellectuals and we ended up talking about other things.

John Drew

Eric Clapton, 1980

I went to both Eric Clapton concerts at Lancaster University's Great Hall, with my girlfriend (now wife) Janice with me at the second one in 1980. We positioned ourselves about halfway in the centre, however Janice wasn't tall enough to see the stage. Fortunately, we had gone up there on my motorbike and had our helmets with us, so she managed to stand on them for most of the show. Chas and Dave were the 'warm up' band and were pretty good, playing quite a few of their tracks that were soon to become chart hits. When Eric and the band came on, he was obviously 'very happy' from something, and it was amusing seeing the faces of his band when he started the set with Charlie Chaplin's 'Smile' before they all eventually joined in. Albert Lee played most of the lead guitar that night, but Eric was still absolutely tremendous with his playing.

Mal Snape

UFO

My story is about going to my first ever gig at the university and seeing a band called UFO around 1980/81, when I was 16 and still at school. I still giggle today, and even after going to see some of the biggest bands around, this is the one that stands out the most. We arrived early so as we could be at the front of the queue. There was the smell of the patchouli oil and the anticipation of my first concert. Then the sound checks started. The atmosphere just in the queue made the hairs on the back of my neck stand up, before eventually the doors opened, and we ran to the front of the stage. I can't even remember the support band. UFO then came on and the atmosphere was buzzing. I can remember being that tightly packed with the crowd moving side to side and my feet coming off the ground but still being upright moving with the crowd. I knew if I did fall, I wouldn't be able to get back up. The gig was brilliant and at the end of the set the atmosphere remained fantastic, with the crowd chanting "more, more, UFO, UFO". The band didn't disappoint. Three times we shouted them back on and three encores is what we got. To cap off a perfect night they played the track 'Doctor Doctor', their anthem. I've never seen a band do three encores since!

David Holt

Queen, 1974

I went to quite a lot of the concerts up there in the Great Hall but the most memorable one for me was seeing Queen headline in 1974. I had seen them on Top of the Pops performing 'Seven Seas of Rhye' and was pretty much blown away, so when I saw that they were on at the university it was a no brainer.

Me and my mate went and managed to get fairly close to the front, probably about five people back. What a concert it was! Freddie in all his pomp strutting around the stage in several costumes belting out the numbers throughout the evening, and of course at this time they all had long hair. Then there was Brian May with his long white pleated sleeves showing incredible skills on lead guitar. The whole band performed magically together, and the concert was incredible.

After the concert my mate and I walked home to the Marsh and to cap the evening off, when we turned the corner at the Kings Arms Hotel Freddie, Brian, John and Roger were all getting off a coach to go into the hotel.

What an evening to remember.

Mal Snape

The Freshers' Disco

The Freshers' Disco, a staple of every college in the country. The event that got so many of the second- and third-year males to give up their last few days of the summer vacation! Once the Great Hall opened, I had the major venue from 1971 to house 1000-1200 students dancing the night away, although the colleges did smaller college-based ones throughout the week. Freshers' Week usually climaxed (sorry) on the Saturday night in the Great Hall. After doing 2 or 3 of the same formats, I must admit I got bored. I know the old adage "if it ain't bust, don't change it", but in entertainment you need to change before your audience realises it needs a change. We all knew what the event was for but now I needed to freshen it up.

Freshers' Disco
Poster © Mike Day

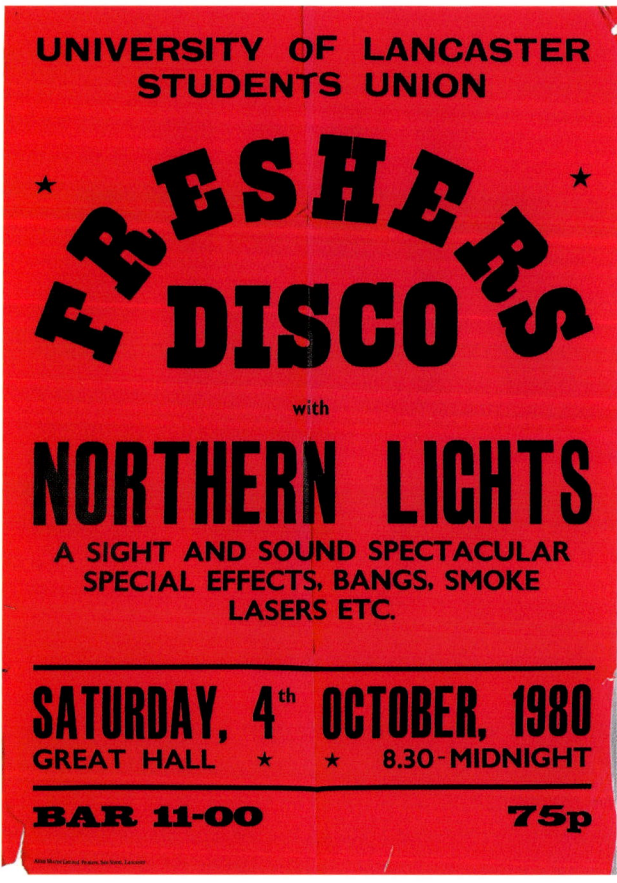

I spoke to Maurice Hubbard and Ray Wilkinson to see what we could come up with. Ray is a fascinating man. I first met him when I was a student social secretary, and he was working for the Audio Visual Aides Department in that strange, round building between the Nuffield Theatre and County College. He often sorted out lights, PAs etc. But I think he, too, saw the restrictions of the university. He left and opened Northern Lights in Scotforth, still going to this day. Ray has the most amazing collection of music archives; I think he has every *Melody Maker* and *New Musical Express* published since the early 60s. He still contacted by film and TV companies for research. So, could we utilise these? Hence Mr. Wizard's Magical Mystery Tour was born.

By some fluke we found that the Great Hall had a power point in the centre of hall roof that could be lowered. God only knows why, but we came up with a plan. Instead of a DJ on stage in front of the crowd, why not have the DJ in the middle of the crowd? This may be common today but was very unusual in 1973. We built a stage in the centre of the hall, had speakers all around and projected memorabilia, photos, adverts, newspaper

images © Ray Wilkinson Music Research Archive

headlines, charts, etc onto the Great Hall stage screen. Star Trek 'Space the Final Frontier' lines opened, before spinning into The Beatles' 'Magical Mystery Tour' started a night of nostalgia. Ray worked the archives with Maurice doing the DJing. And it really, really worked. As the posters around campus used to say, "Who were you dancing with when you last heard this song?".

But like every ents idea, it has a time, a place and a finite life span. One year we realised we were playing music that was recorded before the students were born. So back we went to The Freshers' Disco – hence the poster. But it was never the same, never as good.

Barry Lucas

More memories

Ravi Shankar

In August 1971 George Harrison had organised the Concert for Bangladesh, in which Ravi Shankar participated, so interest was high in him at this time. The concert was in October 1972 and was billed as the 'only European appearance', and I seem to remember it was also the only UK appearance outside London during that European tour.

I had been very involved in committees, student politics and pressure groups in my first year, and probably came into contact with Barry during this time, although I did not know him well. It was a mystery then why I got ticket No. 1 for the Ravi Shankar concert! I do know that I went to the concert on my own (as none of my university friends were as 'hippie-inclined' as I was). I therefore concentrated on the 'tutorial' Ravi gave throughout the concert about the techniques and philosophy of the music they were playing. I found it fascinating and would love to report to you that it changed my life – but it didn't. However, it must have held a special place in my heart as it is the ONLY concert ticket I kept, and I saw many of those great acts that played.

Just to put into perspective the 95p ticket price – during 1971/72 I shared a room in Bowland Tower with my friend, Ali, and we shared a kitty fund for tea, coffee, meals, etc. We only put £1 each per week into this fund and it was more than enough to treat ourselves to a take-away (that meant fish and chips in those days) at least once a week.

The other concerts that I particularly remember were Roxy Music (I've had a soft spot for Bryan Ferry ever since Country Joe and the Fish: "and its 2, 3, 4, what are we fighting for? Don't care, don't give a damn, next stop is Vietnam!") and Hawkwind, where you got stoned just breathing in everyone else's smoke! It turned out my husband also went to that concert (he went to school in Bentham), but I didn't meet him until many years later.

Kirsten Ross

T. Rex, 1970/71

I saw T. Rex in the Great Hall when I was around 15 or 16, either in 1970 or 1971. I was at the front and at one point I actually touched Marc Bolan's foot! I can still remember it vividly and I am now 68.

Linda Craig

More memories from Barry Lucas

Wishbone Ash

When the first edition of the book came out, I took every opportunity to publicise it. Back in the day it would have been so easy to let all the people in Northwest England who had attended the shows know of the book's publication. Every town in the country had some 6 or so record shops and every person interested in music would, at some time in a week, wander into their favourite shop for a browse. So, stick up a couple of posters, some flyers and hey presto the area was covered, the intended audience alerted. But now there are little or no record shops and there weren't even newspapers to advertise in. So, it had virtually to be word of mouth, with a little help from social media.

A good friend of mine and great supporter of live music in Cumbria, Charles Scott was promoting Wishbone Ash in Bootleggers in Kendal. He asked if I wanted to come up, advertise and sell the book at the show. I readily agreed, Ash had been a favourite of mine since I had them as support to Free in 1970. I then had them on as headliners 3 more times.

Andy Powell found out about our plans for me to be the 'support act' and introduce the book before they came on. He looked at the book and said this is not going to work people will just be at the bar drinking and talking. So, he kindly suggested that there would be an acoustic set in the middle section of the show when he would play on his own. He said that he'd wander on, reading the book and then tell the audience what a great read it was and introduce me to the stage where we would have a chat about the history of rock music at the legendary venue that was Lancaster University. It worked really well thanks to Andy and in return I told the story about Wishbones, as a £40 support, blowing Free off the stage. To such an extent that Free couldn't play their massive hit 'All Right Now' they were saving as an encore. Andy was so pleased. He said that recently he was at a party in LA talking to Simon Kirke and saying they'd blown Free off the stage. Simon said that no band ever, anywhere in the world, had ever blown Free off the stage! Charles Scott immediately stepped in and bought a copy of the book off me and presented it to Andy saying that he could take it back to LA as proof. Andy gleefully stuffed it away. I would have just loved to have been at the next LA party and seen Simon Kirke's face.

GBH, Vice Squad and The Insurgents

As can be seen from the *Lancaster Guardian* ad, this show happened on Saturday 20th February 1982. The show was promoted by Phil McIntyre, who is now a major figure in the entertainments world down in London but originally hailed from Preston. His shows and story feature throughout the book. It has been lost in the mists of time, and for an understandable reason.

I have recently downsized from a three-story Victorian house to a bungalow and the guy who owns the Emporium Antiques Centre in Morecambe was buying some furniture off us. Now, bear with me this is going somewhere. The antiquarian, Lee, came to view and saw a sign for The Great Hall. He wanted to know if it was for sale, and I obviously said no. He suddenly put two and two together. "Erm, Barry. Are you Barry Lucas?" When I said yes, he explained he used to be in a punk band, and I'd put him on in The Great Hall. After he'd gone, I looked the show up in the book and there was no mention of that band, so I phoned him to find out more. He'd even bought a copy of the book and was a trifle disappointed to find no recognition of his moment of fame. I wanted to know more so he spent a couple of hours rummaging around in his attic to come up with the advert, tickets and band photo. But what happened?

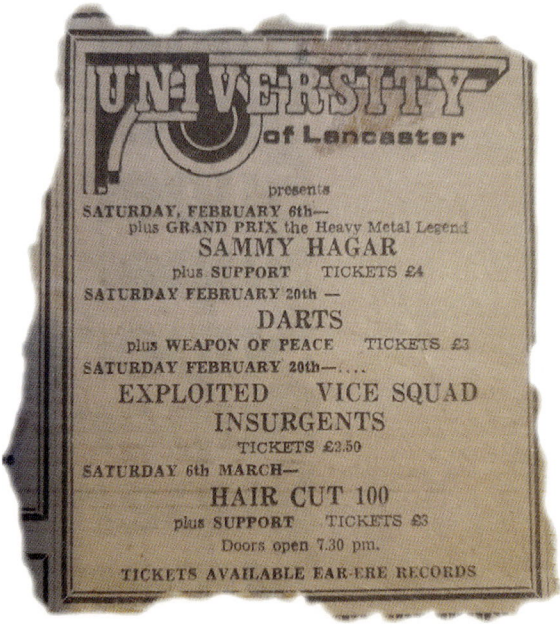

The show was meant to be headlined by The Exploited, but they pulled out because they were offered a Top of the Pops appearance for their single which was starting to sell well. They were replaced by GBH and a local punk band, The Insurgents added. On the night there was a huge row between GBH and Vice Squad, pushing and shoving, handbags job, about who should headline – that is, who should go on last, with maximum exposure, impact, etc. The Insurgents were Lee Clarke (guitar), Waldo (vocals), Ian Wood (bass), Chris Watson (drums). They a popular local band and played all over the country but unfortunately never got a record deal. However, they were only getting paid £60 as support and Vice Squad charged them £20 to use the lights. Then the PA company charged them £20 for the use of the sound. So that left them with £20 between 4 of them and no rider! I wish I'd known, as I'm sure Phil McIntyre would have paid for the production of the show, so they shouldn't have been charged anything.

Barry Lucas

Punk Rock and Fireworks

I have received and studied reports from our security staff following Punk Rock Concerts held in the Great Hall on 3rd February, 17th February and 16th March, 1978. Such concerts constitute, to my mind, so serious a threat to the safety and well-being of University students, members and employees, as well as the security of University property, that I am not prepared to allow the use of the Great Hall in future for concerts of this nature. I expect this instruction to be stricly complied with as from this date. It must be understood by all concerned that the University Secretary is the holder of both the liquor and the music, singing and dancing licences in this case and as such is solely responsible in law for the proper conduct of events held in the Great Hall.

University of Lancaster

University House
Bailrigg, Lancaster, LA1 4YW
Telephone Lancaster 65201 (STD 0524)

From the Office of the University Secretary

KWB/MH   11th October, 1979

Mr. B. Lucas
Union Manager
University of Lancaster.

Dear Mr. Lucas,

I reply to your letter of the 9th October, 1979 regarding a firework display following "The Stranglers" concert on Friday, 12th October.

For a matter with potentially serious consequences it is unfortunate that inadequate time has been given for consideration. For future events of this nature you are required to give ample forewarning. Following the late notification of this event we have made every attempt to contact Martin Blake without success. It is also customary for the B.B.C. to contact me when carrying out activities at this University and I am surprised that they have not done so on this occasion.

I am prepared to permit the firework display to take place providing assurances are given on the following items:-

1. That adequate control of the crowd takes place, not only by means of roping off the area, but in that a sufficient number of marshals are on hand to prevent any break down of control. We are particularly concerned as the display is to occur late in the evening, where there is the possibility of spectators suffering from the effects of alcohol.

2. That the management ensures that there is no danger to spectators or other persons on campus from falling missiles.

3. That there is adequate storage and security of the fireworks before the display commences.

It is also expected that the management of the "Stranglers" will maintain liaison with the University Safety Officer.

Yours sincerely,

A. Stephen Jeffreys,
Secretary of the University.

More memories

Punk Gigs

I just read the article in the *Lancaster Guardian* about the book you are compiling about the 'golden age' of gigs in the Great Hall at the university in the 70s and 80s and it sparked lots of memories. Unfortunately, not enough memories remain useful to you (as we were often 'chemically altered'). I did talk to my friend, and we remembered a lot between us.

The first one we can recall was Fairport Convention with Sandy Denny. We saw John Martin more than once, and I recall the early days we used to sit on the floors (usually rolling joints, which in the case of John Martin were passed to him) and standing up to dance would get you shouted at from the crowd to sit down. That started to change in the mid-70s, where there were two factions: the sitters and the dancers.

We remembered a notable night when Genesis played, and we got in a row with Peter Gabriel after someone called him a "pseud". The concert stopped, with Peter shouting at us from the stage before we walked out. We didn't like him because we thought the over-elaborate costume, etc was all "show" and that he wasn't a true "freak". Some other very memorable ones were Bob Marley and the Wailers (with suits and short hair), Curved Air with Sonja Cristina, the 'fake' Velvet Underground (missing some members replaced with different ones), Rory Gallagher, Edgar Winter Band, an early Roxy Music and Eric Clapton, smacked out whilst the guitarist did all the fancy stuff for him, with Eric just about holding the rhythm.

Then the punk gigs started and things changed a lot. By then I was working as a waitress at the refectory that served the food to the touring bands, so I managed to get into lots of soundchecks. I remember being particularly impressed with Joan Armatrading and her beautiful acapella voice, Echo and the Bunnymen, Orange Juice, and so many more. I remember serving The Undertones their meal in the private dining room, and even though I was only 23, they were obviously really young, ringing their "mammies" before going back on stage. A few years later Fergal Sharkey came back as a solo artist and had transformed from this boy with shirt trousers and an anorak to this sophisticated man in silk and tweeds! Then of course there were the 2tone bands: The Beat, The Selector, The Specials, and the Stiff Records Tour: Elvis Costello, Nic Lowe, Wreckless Eric, etc. All of them as well as the punk bands refused the 'star treatment' of the private dining room and insisted on eating in the refectory. I remember Jean-Jacques Burnell of The Stranglers flirting outrageously with the elderly catering manager who was telling him off for not coming to eat his specially prepared meal. It worked, she was charmed and sat with them drinking!

One gig that stands out is Traffic. They had reformed and it was an extraordinary atmosphere (no chemical enhancement this time), but also incredibly hypnotic and people were passing out! Soon all sorts of rumours were going round about why. That was one of my favourites, I think. Another good memory is the walk home to Lancaster after a good gig, across the fields and jumping a stream!

Lindy

The Adverts and The Damned, 1977/78

So many fond moments, but one the one that remains vivid involves the double headed gig with The Adverts and The Damned.

This was in the time when punk rock mania was at its peak around 1977/78. Most young early punk teenagers had a thing about Gaye Advert, the bassist in the titular band. With some top ten hits behind them, they really warmed up the already raucous crowd, assembled around the front of the stage. So much anticipation in the hall before the headliners The Damned bounced on and continued the fervid ambience.

After a few songs in, Capt. Sensible took offence to some of the antics of the punk crowd at the front, and verbal exchanges were given. A small group of fans sallied off to the toilets, where one of those old-fashioned cotton roll towel dispensers was forced off the wall. The very long cotton towel was removed, and the fans returned to the front of the stage, before there were more verbal taunts between the band members and towel holding punks. Next, we saw this towel launched into the air, over the heads of the performers and it landed directly into Rat Scabies' drum kit. David Vanian, Brian James, Rat and Capt. Sensible grabbed the towel and attempted to chuck it back off stage.

However, the punks had hold of one end of this 30 ft long towel whilst the collective band had grasp of the other end. Then ensued and almighty tug of war when all microphones, instruments, monitors, etc were swept off stage. All the band nearly followed the equipment into the pit. Seeing as the band couldn't hold on to the towel any longer, they let go. Cue more chaos at the gig, until eventually staff and bouncers attempted to calm the situation down.

Some order was restored, but only when David Vanian pleaded with his band and 'fans' for peace and reconciliation. It was a very short gig, typical of the punk ethos. However, it has stayed in the memory for decades.

David Robinson

```
University Beadle.                    The University Secretary.
248
                                      c.c.: The Engineer
28.6.77                                     Mr. R. Diserens
O/T.11                                      Secy., S.R.C.
                                            Mr. B. Lucas


                    GREAT HALL - STUDENT CONCERTS

     A Punk Rock Group named "The Damned" were engaged by the Students' Social
Manager to give a concert in the Great Hall last night. This report is supplied
in an effort to ensure that Groups of this nature are not booked in the future.

     There was an audience of approximately 900 of whom extremely few were students.
Those attending were dressed either in weird clothing or " Tramp Gear". Not only was
clothing painted but also faces were painted in the oddest patterns and the Tramp
gear appears to consist of wearing torn clothing tied up with string or secured by
safety pins. Several of the audience were wearing safety pins through their ears or
nose and certainly in one case through the cheek.

     I am informed that the "dancing" consisted of the audience jumping up and down
as if on Pogo stocks and some were endeavouring to get on to the stage. This was
prevented by members of the "Road Gang" associated with the Group and by student
"bouncers". It would seem that this eventually gave rise to a fight near to the
stage and a man was brought to the foyer suffering from facial injuries. I understand
the actual injuries could not be seen because of the amount of blood. The police and
an ambulance were called (I understand by Jeremy Oppenheim) and the man was conveyed
to hospital. Police officers did arrive but, by this time, the fighting had ceased
and no action was taken.

     I am further informed that the Group left the stage on two occasions because
people were jumping up on to the stage and, round about 11 o'clock, a Catering
Supervisor hid in the Ladies' toilets for about 15 mins. because she was afraid of the
people who were milling around.

     Damage was caused in that a roller towel machine in the Gents' toilet was
pulled from the wall and, later, trees were damaged, no doubt by persons on their
way home from the concert.

     In support of my suggestion that such Groups should not be booked in future I
point out that the Hall was not built as the type of premises to accommodate concerts
of this description - even the normal student Pop concert - and, therefore, it has
been necessary to make improvisations on several points to meet the requirements of
the Public Music, Singing & Dancing licence.

     It is also unfair to expect University staff to endeavour to work when an
audience of this type is on the premises and this is particularly material when, as
in this case, the concert is certainly not one for students of this University who
were minimally represented in the audience. It was very evident that "The Damned"
attracted "Weirdies" from the surrounding areas and one bus driver was overheard to
say that he would not be involved in driving this type of person in future.
```

Philip George

Out of the blue in October I received an email from Tuscany, followed by a WhatsApp phone call (see, not quite a dinosaur – isn't technology brilliant). Philip outlined his life story and what a story it was – I'll just briefly summarise. He was born in Malaysia but moved at an early age to live in India. Then at 17, came on his own, to live in Lancaster (well you just would wouldn't you, in the late 60s). He came here to train as a psychiatric nurse but had a rather chequered employment history!

He worked as a process worker at a linoleum factory, a stevedore at Heysham harbour, at the two psychiatric hospitals in Lancaster, a bookkeeper in a betting shop and a cashier in a gambling den.

He then re-trained to become a solicitor. He worked for several years at Whiteside and Knowles in Morecambe, being taken under the wing of Geoffrey Knowles. A successful career followed as he climbed to be solicitor of the Supreme Court of England and Wales. He also managed time to be an international badminton and county squash player. He lives in a mountain village in Tuscany but is also a member of CAS – the Court of Arbitration in Sport – which sits in Geneva. He now does pro bono work for 'good' causes around the world.

Not bad, eh? He has a fascinating autobiography out, *Racket Boy: What's My Country?* But his call was all about the shows at The Great Hall and how he hardly missed one in around 14 years and he wanted to write about how important those concerts were to him.

Barry Lucas

Memories from a student nurse

In the early 1970s, as a student psychiatrist nurse navigating the hallowed halls of Lancaster Moor Hospital, my weekends morphed into a magnetic dance with the transformative rhythm of Lancaster's vibrant music scene. Wrapped in the warmth of my second-hand navy Army trench coat, I braved winter's chill to partake in the sonic spectacle of the Great Hall concerts at Lancaster University, the heartbeat of a burgeoning musical revolution.

These Saturday extravaganzas were veritable feasts of auditory delight, where legendary rock groups like The Who, Pink Floyd, U2, Black Sabbath, Queen, and others turned Lancaster into a haven for music enthusiasts. The atmosphere crackled with electric energy, and the proximity to these global icons was an immersive experience that imprinted itself on my evolving musical palate.

Post-concert adventures became the canvas on which the night painted its vivid hues. Whether it involved an impromptu nap in a fellow student's bed or a meandering, slightly tipsy journey back through snow-laden streets, each escapade added another layer to the thrill of these unforgettable nights. Lost coats, shared laughter, and the liberating spirit of these midnight escapades became indelible memories, etching a stark contrast to my earlier life in Malaysia.

Transitioning from the restrained culture of Malaysia to the free-spirited environment of Lancaster was akin to stepping into a vivid kaleidoscope. The 1970s marked a cultural awakening in Britain, with influential artists shaping the music landscape. Melody Maker became my compass, guiding me from the simplicity of 'Me and You and a Dog Named Boo' to the profound, intricate compositions of Genesis and Cat Stevens.

Life on the fourth floor was a carnival of laughter, camaraderie, and unconventional indulgences. Soft plants with incense, hedonistic gatherings, and the avant-garde allure of BBC2's 'The Old Grey Whistle Test' painted a dynamic picture of the counterculture spirit that permeated the era.

Amidst this whirlwind of experiences, I maintained my sportsperson's self-discipline, undertaking my daily eight-mile run through the enchanting paths of the Trough of Bowland, finding solace in its desolate beauty. The nurse's quarters transformed into a sanctuary of musical fervour, with each nurse boasting a stereo system, creating a symphony of diverse sounds that resonated through the corridors.

Saunas and showers turned into sanctuaries for uninhibited conversations, eroding inhibitions and fostering genuine connections. Conversations in the sauna meandered from sports to the intoxicating allure of the Great Hall concerts. In this bygone era, the celebrity halo was absent, and music icons were not distant deities but tangible, approachable artists, amplifying the inclusivity and shared joy.

In the heart of this bohemian utopia, my journey through the 70s unfolded as a symphony of liberation. The Great Hall concerts, the revelations in the sauna, and the eclectic sounds reverberating from the stereos coalesced into a unique Lancaster experience. The 1970s became a chapter of my life painted in vibrant colours, leaving me thoroughly immersed in the spirit of the times.

In the spirit of the 70s music scene, the echoes of Woodstock Festival reverberated through every note that graced the Great Hall at Lancaster University. It was an era that embraced the spirit of experimentation, epitomized by the iconic performances of artists like Wishbone Ash and Ten Years After, just to name a few.

As I immersed myself in the concerts, I couldn't escape the feeling of being part of a sonic revolution – a movement that championed authenticity, creativity, and a rebellion against the status quo. The artists who took the stage at Lancaster during 1970 to 1985 weren't just musicians; they were architects of an era-defining sound that transcended boundaries.

The spirit of Woodstock, with its ethos of peace, love, and music, seemed to linger in the air. The music wasn't just a series of notes; it was a powerful narrative that mirrored the socio-cultural shifts of the time. The intricate harmonies of Wishbone Ash, or the searing blues of Ten Years After – all stitched together a sonic quilt that draped the Great Hall in a kaleidoscope of emotions.

The authenticity of that period stood in stark contrast to today's assembly-line music production. It wasn't about ticking boxes or conforming to industry standards; it was about pushing boundaries, challenging norms, and creating a musical experience that transcended the ordinary. Each performance was a journey, an exploration of sound that invited the audience to lose themselves in the magic of live music.

In an age where algorithms shape playlists and auto-tuned perfection dominates the airwaves, the essence of that bygone era feels like a distant memory. Yet, the legacy of these concerts lives on, a testament to a time when music wasn't just heard; it was felt, experienced, and lived.

In that magical era, reminiscent of enchanting Jane Birkin types in the shortest of miniskirts, there emerged a moment – *le taime... moi non plus*. After the hypnotic three-hour spectacle of Alvin Lee and Ten Years After at the Great Hall, the night swirled with a different rhythm. A mischievous detour led me from the third-floor Chatsworth Road bedsit to the captivating embrace of a stranger's flat, where incense waltzed through the air, echoing the romance of Serge Gainsbourg and Brigitte Bardot.

Yet, success wasn't a constant companion! While my athleticism charmed those acquainted from badminton, the pub-crawls with mates highlighted my social shortcomings. Amidst the camaraderie of five or six, I often found myself the lone wanderer, seeking solace in the poetic tunes of Joni Mitchell and the rebellious notes of Bad Company and Bob Dylan and Grateful Dead.

The Great Hall wasn't just a venue; it was a sanctuary where the soul-stirring melodies of Woodstock found a new home. It wasn't about flashy visuals or calculated performances; it was about raw, unbridled talent that left an indelible mark on everyone fortunate enough to be in the audience.

As I reflect on those years when rock went to college, I realize how profoundly different that England was from today's musical landscape. It wasn't just about the music; it was about the experience, the communal energy, and the unfiltered expression that defined an era. The Great Hall at Lancaster University became a time capsule, preserving the spirit of Woodstock and the untamed creativity of musicians who dared to be different.

Philip George

Facts 'n' Stats

Some of the Great Hall greats

Best Guitarists
Eric Clapton
Alvin Lee
Jeff Beck
Albert Lee
Mark Knopffler
Wilko Johnson
Angus Young
Johnny Winter
Brian May
Pete Townshend
Bob Marley
Rory Gallagher
Paul Kossoff

Best bass guitarists
Lemmy
Jack Bruce
Paul McCartney
Phil Lynott
Andy Fraser
Peter Hook
Adam Clayton
Chris Squire
Roger Waters
John Entwistle
John Wetton
Mike Rutherford

Best singers
Tina Turner
Cliff Richard
Roger Chapman
Van Morrisson
Paul Weller
Paul Rodgers
Bono
Paul McCartney
Freddie Mercury
Bryan Ferry
Marc Bolan
Roger Daltrey
Peter Gabriel

Best drummers
Ginger Baker
Phil Collins
Roger Taylor
Keith Moon
Ric Lee
Ian Paice
Simon Kirke
Carmine Appice
Bill Bruford
Jon Hiseman
Phil Rudd
Cozy Powell

Most Great Hall appearances
John Martyn 12
Hawkwind 6
Amazing Blondel 5
Fairport Convention 5
Wishbone Ash 4
Mott The Hoople 4
Boomtown Rats 4
Sutherland Brothers and Quiver 4
Ralph McTell 4
Rory Gallagher 4
Elvis Costello 4
Lindisfarne 4
Climax Blues Band 4

University concert ticket agencies

S.R.C. Reception	Lancaster University
'Ear 'Ere Records	Lancaster
Cobweb Records	Thornton Cleveleys
George Edwardian Boutique	Kendal
Earthquake Records	Barrow
Music Mania	Blackpool
Starpick	Blackpool
Kelly's Records	Barrow
Disc Centre	Lytham
Brady's Records	Preston
Ames Records	Preston
Ames Records	Blackburn

There were also outlets in Windermere and Penrith.

Some of these outlets did not sell tickets over the whole period of the concerts, however, the list does emphasise the area covered by the Great Hall shows and their importance to the region.

More information on the book's featured bands can be found at the following locations

www.thegreatrockbible.com
www.allmusic.com
www.lastfm.com
www.wikipedia.com
www.vintagerock.wordpress.com
www.progarchives.com
www.setlist.fm
www.toppermost.co.uk
www.ultimateclassicrock.com
www.punk77.co.uk
www.discogs.com

A list in memory of the Great Hall greats

Johnny Winter
Andy Fraser – bass player of Free, Bad Company and Sharks
Jack Bruce – Cream
Errol Brown – lead singer of Hot Chocolate
Tommy Ramone
John Lee Hooker
Alvin Lee – lead singer and guitarist of Ten Years After
Chris Squire – bass player of Yes
Lemmy – Hawkwind and Motorhead
Dale Griffin – drummer; Mott The Hoople
Dave Swarbrick – fiddle player with Fairport Convention
Daevid Allen and Gilli Smyth – founder members of Gong
Rick Parfitt – singer, songwriter and guitarist of Status Quo
Pete Burns – singer-songwriter of Dead Or Alive
"Pete" Overend Watts – bass guitarist and founder member of Mott The Hoople.
John Wetton – bass guitarist with Mogul Thrash and Uriah Heep
Chuck Berry

Jackie Lomax
Deke Leonard of Man
Malcolm Young – guitarist; AC/DC
Ray Thomas – flautist; The Moody Blues
'Fast' Eddie Clark – guitarist; Motorhead
Jim Rodford – bass guitarist; Argent
David Holland – drummer; Judas Priest
Mark E Smith – leader singer and founder of The Fall
Jon Hiseman – drummer and founder of Colosseum
Chas Hodges
Pete Shelley – Buzzcocks
Andy Anderson – drummer; The Cure
Ranking Roger – The Beat
Boon Gould – founder member and guitarist; Level 42
Tom Petty
Ted McKenna – drummer; Sensational Alex Harvey Band
Bernie Tormé – guitarist,
Paul Raymond – guitarist; UFO
Martin Pilkington – guitarist, vocals; China Street

Chas Hodges of Chas 'n' Dave providing support for Eric Clapton May 1980 © David Stewart

Martin Pilkington of China Street
© Geoff Campbell

About the authors

Paul Tomlinson

In 1969, a small northern town started to play host to incredible live performances by influential bands of the era. Lancaster University welcomed its first students in 1968 and as soon as 'The Central Hall', as it was first known, was completed in October 1969, rock bands were booked to play in it for Rag Balls, Graduation Balls and Fresher's events.

Over the next fifteen years, conveniently placed just off the A6 and close to the M6 in North Lancashire, the university quickly became a major live rock music venue, going on to stage over 300 concerts and host more than 500 bands in The Great Hall. From folk to prog and glam rock, and from heavy metal to punk, the university quickly became a much sought after stop on the UK tours of many of the biggest bands of the time.

Responsible for staging these concerts at Lancaster University was Barry Lucas, who was to become Britain's first full-time professional university campus impresario. In his first role, as a college social secretary, he began by booking bands to play for the entertainment of students of the university. And boy did he book some bands – his first booking was The Who in May 1970!

Here I'm going to interrupt Paul to give you, the reader an insight into an important part of this book's history. Without Paul Tomlinson you simply would not be reading this, the book would not exist. Some time ago Paul approached me with the idea of a project; a book documenting the history of concerts in the University's Great Hall.

Paul was one of my punters and as a young lad in the mid '70s he saw many of the concerts. He then left the area in the late '70s to live and study in Newcastle upon Tyne and subsequently missed those later concerts from around 1978 onwards, but always remembered those he had seen.

After working abroad and in various parts of the UK for a number of years he returned 'home' to Lancaster. One night at a friend's house some old termly 'Ear 'Ere concert listing cards appeared.

"Do you remember that?"
"Did you go to that?"
"Wow, I didn't know they'd played!"
"Or them."
"How on Earth did they come to play at Lancaster?"

Paul then decided to discover exactly who did play over those 15 or so years. The book has taken him over three and a half years to research and assemble with most of the time taken up by Paul's meticulous work, as he holed up in the bowels of the university library archives, hour after hour going through old copies of *Scan*, *JOG* and the local newspapers. I wouldn't have done it, so the book wouldn't have been written but for Paul and all his hard work. No doubt the research was interesting and occasionally exciting, but I bet it was still a bloody hard slog!

Thank you Paul, from all of us.

Now back to your story …

From AC/DC to U2; Pink Floyd and Roxy Music to Chuck Berry; and from the first known concert, Fairport Convention in 1969, to the last, New Order in 1985, those lucky enough to have been one of an average crowd of around a thousand witnessed some of the greatest rock legends of all time, me included!

The year is 1973 and along with two mates I have a ticket to see a band called Mott the Hoople, who have recently been in the UK singles chart with 'All The Way From Memphis'. What we are treated to is a performance by an unknown support act that was to totally upstage the main act of the night. Their name? Queen.

Anyone who was there will remember it wasn't a great start for Ian Hunter and Mott The Hoople; as they took to the stage, the crowd were still reeling from a heavy dose of Brian May's Vox amplifiers and shouting for more from Queen.

Watching this very early Queen performance was undoubtedly one of those 'I was there moments', such as that experienced at The Cavern Club, Liverpool, in the early 1960s by audiences watching 'you know who' for the first time. We all knew we were watching something special that November night in The Great Hall and it remains a concert I have never forgotten.

And so, armed with this personal memory, *When Rock Went to College* has been written for all of you who were there during Lancaster University's rock heydays.

Barry Lucas

Barry Lucas was born in Yorkshire but somehow found himself in the sixth form at Cheltenham Grammar School. He returned north to Lancaster University in 1968, where in 1970 he was elected social secretary, and this remarkable story began. After fifteen of the most amazing years, he left to help produce Deep Purple at Knebworth, open The Gardens in Morecambe – a renowned rock venue – and work on the production of major outdoor events, including: rock shows in Finsbury Park; UB 40; Siouxsie and the Banshees; New Order; and The Pogues, among others. He also produced two high-profile boxing matches (Terry Marsh's world championship victory in Basildon, and the Benn/Watson tented Commonwealth title fight in Finsbury Park), and organised illuminations switch-ons with Noel Edmonds and Mr Blobby in front of 45,000 people, Womad, and a disco all-nighter in Singapore on Christmas Eve. He has worked for organisations as varied as the ANC, Anti-Racist Alliance, Morning Star, Walt Disney, and Ringland Brothers' Circus! In 1995 he changed direction completely and went into teaching, becoming a successful Year 6 primary school teacher, much to the bafflement of the staffroom. But he still kept his hand in, doing two one-day events on the Isle of Wight, featuring Madness and Paul Weller, and latterly Status Quo and 10cc in Bowness on Windermere. Then, four years ago, he met Paul Tomlinson, an idea was formed and in 2017 a book was born …

Headline band index by year

1969
Blonde on Blonde 53
Bonzo Dog DooDah Band 62
Fairport Convention 105
Roy Harper 236

1970
Argent 31
Arthur Brown The Crazy World of 32
Atomic Rooster 32
Black Sabbath 52
Colosseum 79
Deep Purple 90
Edgar Broughton Band 98
Equals The 100
Family 108
Flying Burrito Brothers 111
Free 114
Gypsy 124
Incredible String Band The 136
Jack Bruce Band The 138
Jackie Lomax's Heavy Jelly 140
Juicy Lucy 168
Marmalade 184
Matthews Southern Comfort 186
Mott The Hoople 191
Pentangle 205
Procol Harum 216
Shakin Stevens and The Sunsets 246
Van der Graaf Generator 314
Who The 17
Wishful Thinking 324

1971
Amazing Blondel 30
Argent 31
Barclay James Harvest 37
Brian Augers Oblivion Express 64
Bronco 65
Groundhogs The 124
Iron Butterfly 136
Johnny Winter Band 164
King Crimson 170
Kinks The 171
Mott The Hoople 191
Mungo Jerry 193
Pink Floyd 208
Rory Gallagher 234
T Rex 284
Tom Paxton 299
Traffic 300
Tremeloes The 204
Velvet Underground 314
Wild Angels The 318
Wishbone Ash 320

1972
Amazing Blondel 30
Argent 31
Chuck Berry 70
Country Joe and The Fish 80
Curved Air 82
Free 114
Gentle Giant 117
Groundhogs The 124
Hawkwind 126
Jeff Beck 150
John Mayall 163
Medicine Head 187
Nothineverappens 198
Paul McCartney and Wings 200
Pentangle 205
Ravi Shankar 224
Roxy Music 236
Steeleye Span 268
Stomu Yamashta 277
Sutherland Brothers and Quiver 282
Ten Years After 288

1974

Fri. Oct. 4th	MAN + BADFINGER + BROWN'S HOME BREW	£1.00	Sat. Nov. 20th	SANDY DENNY & FAIRPORT CONVENTION	£1.00
Sat. Oct. 5th	MR. WIZARD'S MAGICAL MYSTERY TOUR	30p	Sat. Nov. 30th	MOTT THE HOOPLE with MICK RONSON	£1.00
Fri. Oct. 11th	The Sensational ALEX HARVEY BAND + SLACK ALICE	£1.00	Sat. Dec. 7th	BAD COMPANY	£1.00
Sat. Oct. 19th	Steve Harley's COCKNEY REBEL + LIFE	£1.00			
Fri. Oct. 25th	DISCO				
Fri. Nov. 1st	RALPH McTELL with Danny Thompson and Mike Piggott	£1.00			
Sat. Nov. 9th	QUEEN	£1.00			
Sat. Nov. 16th	SPARKS	£1.00			

All Concerts Start 8-00 p.m. in GREAT HALL.

TICKETS:-

S.A.E. SOCIAL MANAGER S.R.C. UNIVERSITY

EAR-ERE RECORDS, LANCASTER

GEORGE EDWARDIAN BOUTIQUE, KENDAL

KELLY'S OF BARROW

P I MEN'S WEAR SOUTH SHORE MARKET BLACKPOOL

DISC CENTRE or RECORD STORE, LYTHAM

1973
Amon Düül II 31
Bob Marley and The Wailers 60
Fairport Convention 105
Fanny 110
Genesis 116
John Martyn 160
Man 182
Manfred Mans Earth Band 184
Mott The Hoople 191
Refugee 224
Sharks 246
Status Quo 261
Steeleye Span 268
Ten Years After 288
Tom Paxton 299
Vinegar Joe 317

1974
Amazing Blondel 30
Bad Company 34
Beck Bogert and Appice 44
Black Oak Arkansas 50
Cockney Rebel 79
Fairport Convention 105
Hawkwind 126
Horslips 130
John Martyn 160
Kinks The 171
Love 176
Man 182
Mott The Hoople 191
Queen 218
Ralph McTell 220
Richard and Linda Thompson 228
Sensational Alex Harvey Band 245
Sparks (x2) 254
Sutherland Brothers and Quiver 282
Traffic 301

1975

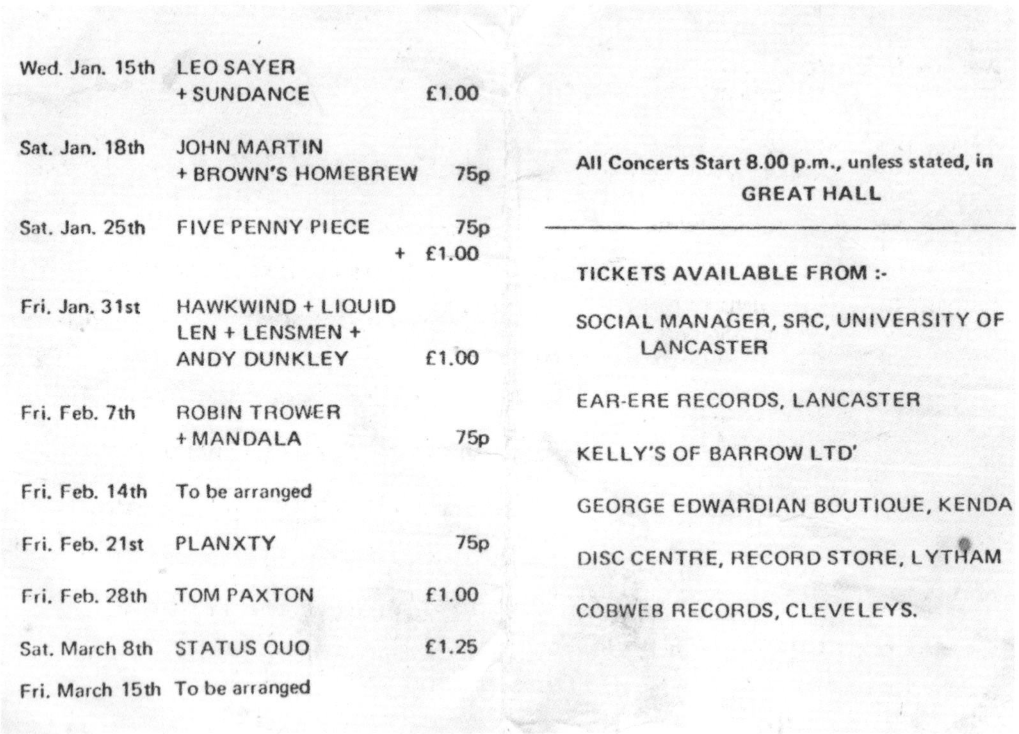

Wed. Jan. 15th	LEO SAYER + SUNDANCE	£1.00
Sat. Jan. 18th	JOHN MARTIN + BROWN'S HOMEBREW	75p
Sat. Jan. 25th	FIVE PENNY PIECE	75p / £1.00
Fri. Jan. 31st	HAWKWIND + LIQUID LEN + LENSMEN + ANDY DUNKLEY	£1.00
Fri. Feb. 7th	ROBIN TROWER + MANDALA	75p
Fri. Feb. 14th	To be arranged	
Fri. Feb. 21st	PLANXTY	75p
Fri. Feb. 28th	TOM PAXTON	£1.00
Sat. March 8th	STATUS QUO	£1.25
Fri. March 15th	To be arranged	

All Concerts Start 8.00 p.m., unless stated, in GREAT HALL

TICKETS AVAILABLE FROM :-

SOCIAL MANAGER, SRC, UNIVERSITY OF LANCASTER

EAR-ERE RECORDS, LANCASTER

KELLY'S OF BARROW LTD'

GEORGE EDWARDIAN BOUTIQUE, KENDA

DISC CENTRE, RECORD STORE, LYTHAM

COBWEB RECORDS, CLEVELEYS.

1975
10cc 20
Baker Gurvitz Army 37
Barclay James Harvest 37
Blue Jays 56
Camel 68
Curved Air 82
Dr Feelgood 92
Fairport Convention 105
Hawkwind 126
Hot Chocolate 132
John Cale 157
John Martyn 160
Kevin Coyne Band The 168
Leo Sayer 176
Planxty 212
Robin Trower 230
Rory Gallagher 234
Status Quo 261
Supertramp 280
Sutherland Brothers and Quiver 282
Tom Paxton 299

1976
AC/DC 22
Budgie 65
Caravan 70
Climax Blues Band 77
Deaf School 88
Eric Clapton 101
Fairport Convention 105
Focus 112
Gong 121
John Martyn 160
Kinks The 171
Kursaal Flyers 172
Man 182
Mike Harding (x2) 187
Nils Lofgren 195
Procol Harum 216
Ralph McTell 220
Thin Lizzy 290
Wishbone Ash 320

1976

Sat. Jan. 24th*	HARRY MORTIMER + CITY OF COVENTRY BRASS BAND 7.30 p.m.	£1.00	Sun. Feb. 22nd*	In association with NUF- FIELD THEATRE
Fri. Jan. 30th	KURSAAL FLYERS + EDDIE AND THE HOT RODS	£1.00	Mon. Feb. 23rd	GRIMMS featuring McGough, Henri, Stanshall, Gorman, Roberts. £1.00
Wed. Feb. 4th*	MIKE HARDING	80p	Sat. Feb. 28th	FOCUS £1.25
Fri. Feb. 6th	In association with the Christian Union from America LIBERATION SUITE + ALEXANDER JOHN	80p	Sat. March 6th	RALPH McTELL + PRELUDE £1.30
			Fri. MARCH 12th	KINKS £1.25
Sat. Feb. 7th*	GILBERT AND SULLIVAN FOR ALL 7.30 p.m.	£1.00	Fri. MARCH 19th	PROCOL HAREM in a two hour concert £1.25
Tues. Feb. 10th*	KICKING MULE TOUR An evening of American guitar + banjo featuring STEFAN GROSSMAN	80p		
Fri. Feb. 13th	MAN	£1.25		
Sat. Feb. 21st	SYD LAWRENCE and his Orchestra	£1.25		

All shows start 8.00 p.m. unless otherwise stated
* seated concert.

1977
AC/DC 22
Be Bop Deluxe 42
Boomtown Rats 62
Damned The 83
Eddie and The Hot Rods 97
Elvis Costello 98
Frankie Miller Band 114
Gilbert O'Sullivan 118
Graham Parker and The Rumour 121
Hawkwind 126
Jack Bruce Band The 138
Jam The 142
Jan Akkerman Band 146
John Martyn 160
Lynyrd Skynyrd 179
Nils Lofgren 195
Ralph McTell 220
Rory Gallagher 234
Sensational Alex Harvey Band 245
Stiff Tour Live Stiffs 274
Sutherland Brothers and Quiver 282

1978

Fri. Oct. 6th	Fresher's Late Night Films (Student Only)	£1.00
Sat. Oct. 7th	MR. WIZARD'S DISCO	50p
Sun. Oct. 8th	WISHBONE ASH (No support on stage 8pm)	£2.00
Mon. Oct. 9th	Off-Campus Students Social Morecambe Pier - 2 Bands + Disco - Late Bar (Student Only)	FREE
Fri. Oct. 13th	THE PIRATES	£1.50
Tues. Oct. 17th	STIFF'S TWO (Adv)	£1.75
	(Door)	£2.00
Fri. Oct 20th	BUDGIE	£1.75
Fri. Oct 27th	STEEL PULSE	£1.75
Sat. Nov. 4th	JUDAS PRIEST	£1.75
Sat. Nov. 11th	LINDISFARNE	£2.00
Fri. Nov. 17th	HAWKWIND	£2.00
Sat. Nov. 18th	CHIEFTAINS	£2.00
Wed. Nov. 22nd	JOHN MARTYN WITH QUADROPHONIC SOUND	£1.50
Fri. Nov. 24th	REZILLOS	£1.50
Thurs. Nov. 30th	MAGAZINE	T.B.A.
Fri. Dec. 8th	BOOMTOWN RATS	T.B.A.

All concerts start 7.30 pm in the Great Hall unless otherwise stated.

1978

Adverts The 26
Bert Jansch 45
Bill Brufords UK 47
Blondie 53
Boomtown Rats 62
Budgie 65
Buzzcocks 67
Chieftains The 70
Climax Blues Band 77
Hawkwind 126
Hot Chocolate 132
John Martyn 160
John Miles Band 164
Judas Priest (x2) 166
Lindisfarne 177
Magazine 181
Mike Harding 187
Peter Gabriel 206
Pirates The 211
Rezzilos The 227
Rich Kids The 227
Sad Café 240
Steel Pulse (x2) 263
Steve Hillage 271
Stiff Tour Be-Stiff 274
Stranglers The 278
Third World 295
Wire 320
Wishbone Ash 320

1979

Average White Band 33
Bad Company 34
Bill Nelsons Red Noise 48
Darts 87
Dr Feelgood 92
Graham Parker and The Rumour 121
Jam The 142
John Cooper Clarke 157
John Miles Band 164
Lindisfarne 177
Motorhead 188
Ralph McTell 218
Richard and Linda Thompson 228
Specials The 257
Steve Hillage 271
Stiff Little Fingers 272
Stranglers The 278
UFO 308
Van Morrison 315

Japan, 1980 © Geoff Campbell

1980
Blues Band The 59
Clash The 72
Cure The 81
Dire Straits 91
Eric Clapton 101
Hawkwind 126
Hazel O'Connor 130
Jags The 141
Joan Armatrading 153
Loudon Wainwright III 178
Mike Oldfield 187
Pretenders The 214
Ramones The 222
Rockpile (x2) 233
Scorpions 240
Selecter The 242
Steve Forbert 269
Ultravox 310
Undertones The 312

1981
Bauhaus 41
Beat The 44
Bow Wow Wow 64
Echo and The Bunnymen 94
Elvis Costello 98
Gillan 119
Human League 134
Iron Maiden 137
Japan 148
Joan Armatrading 153
John Martyn 160
Lindisfarne 177
Orchestral Manoevres in The Dark 198
Rory Gallagher 234
Selecter The 242
Siouxsie and The Banshees 247
Slade 249
Spirit 259
Stranglers The 278
Stray Cats 280
Sweet The 283
UFO 308
Wishbone Ash 320

1982
Altered Images 28
Beat The 44
Boomtown Rats 62
Chieftains The 70
Climax Blues Band 77
Darts 87
Elvis Costello 98
Haircut 100 125
Japan 148
Joan Jett and The Blackhearts 156
John Martyn 160
Judy Tzuke 166
Kid Creole and The Coconuts 169
Level 42 176
Marillion 185
Sammy Hagar 239
Squeeze 259
Steel Pulse 263
Teardrop Explodes The (x2) 286
Toyah 300
Van Morrison 315

1983
A Flock of Seagulls 22
Echo and The Bunnymen 94
Europeans The 105
Joan Armatrading 153
Paul Young and The Royal Family 204
Public Image Ltd 217
Slade 249
Steve Winwood 272
Tears for Fears 288
Thompson Twins 296
U2 306

1984
Alarm The 26
Alison Moyet 29
Big Country 47
Dead or Alive 88
Echo and The Bunnymen 94
Elvis Costello 98
Marillion 185
Prefab Sprout 213
Sisters of Mercy The 249
Smiths The 253
Thompson Twins 296
Tina Turner 297

1985
Bluebells The 59
Boomtown Rats 62
The Fall 108
Marc Almond 184
New Order 195

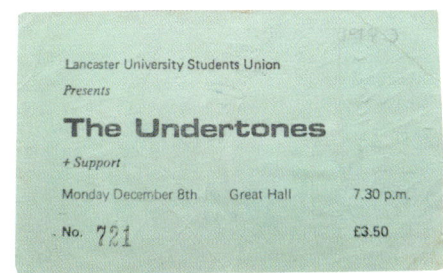

The Undertones, 1980 © Geoff Campbell

Photo index of bands on the Great Hall stage

Aynsley Dunbar 14
10cc 21
Altered Images 28
Bad Company 34, 35
Tom Robinson Band 38
Barclay James Harvest 39
Bill Nelson 48
Billy Connolly 49
Boomtown Rats 63
Buzzcocks 67
Camel 69
Wally 69
The Clash 72, 73, 375
Cliff Richard 74
Climax Blues Band 77
The Cure 81
The Damned 83
Farm 90
Dire Straits 91
Dr Feelgood 92
Echo and The Bunnymen 95
Eddie and The Hotrods 97
Elvis Costello 99
Eric Clapton 103, 104
Fairport Convention 106
David Lewis 107
Gillan 119
Graham Parker and The Rumour 123
Human League 134
The Jam 142, 143, 145
Japan 148, 149, 375, 396
Joan Armatrading 153
John Cooper Clarke 159
John Miles 164
Johnny Winter 165
Judy Tzuke 166
Leo Sayer 176
Lynyrd Skynyrd 179
Clover 180
Magazine 181

Motorhead 189
Saxon 189
New Order 194, 375
Nils Lofgren 196
Orchestral Manoeuvres in the Dark 199
Paul McCartney 200, 201
The Pirates 211
The Pretenders 214
Public Image Ltd 217
The Ramones 222
Richard and Linda Thompson 228
Rockpile 233
Rory Gallagher 235
Scorpions 241
Selecter 242, 243, 257, 375
Siouxsie and The Banshees 247
Slade 250
The Specials 257, 258
Madness 257, 258
Squeeze 260
Steel Pulse 263
China Street 267, 373
Stiff Tour 1977 274, 275
The Stranglers 278, 279
Supertramp 281
Bashful Alley 283
The Teardrop Explodes 286, 287
Thin Lizzy 293
Third World 295
Tina Turner 297, 298, 375
Traffic 303
U2 306, 307
UFO 309
The Undertones 312, 397
Van Morrison 315
Wishbone Ash 322
Supercharge 323
Frankie Miller 347
Chas 'n' Dave 373

Thanks to all the following for their invaluable help

Maurice Hubbard, Pink Custard Lighting
Ray Wilkinson. Northern Lights: Music Research Archive
Rod Williamson on punctuation
Jane Silvester Alumni & Friends Engagement Manager at Lancaster University
Marion McClintock, Honorary Archivist at Lancaster University library
Dave Burridge for saving those ticket stubs
Ian Edmundson for his Slade site and Slade photos
Liz Hartley, Lynne Bell, Diane Scholey, David Summers and all the Lancaster University library staff
Lynne Owen for keeping those *Lancaster Guardian* clippings
The local legend that is James Mackie
Ronnie Rowlands and LUSU
Neil Thompson of the Kassels, F Church, The Permanents
Drummer John Elles
Gary Thistlethwaite, pedal steel and bass guitarist
Paul Robinson for his gig list
Dr John Darwell, photographer, Cumbria
Jeff Walker, UFO fan
Dr George Green and his contemporaries
Phil Wilson
Dave Stocker
Charles Scott of Macbeth Scott & Co. Ltd, Kendal
Greg Lambert
Lauren Holden
Herbert Street
Rob Tidd of Bashful Alley
Malcolm Graham of Farm

Adam Williams of China Street
Kate Henderson
Alan Murray on figures
Paul Loasby on rivalry
Anna Goddard, Lucy Frontani and the team at Carnegie Book Production
Sir William (Bill) Taylor
Andy Kershaw
John Helliwell of Supertramp for performing at our Great Hall book launch

Thankfully, the following people carried a camera:
Geoff Campbell
Dean Weston
Dave Bradbuy
Sheryl Walmsley
Gina Thistlethwaite
David Stewart
Andy Docherty
Neil Yates
Doug Price

John Angus on poster production

And all those who took the time to contact me with their stories.

And of course, Barry Lucas, aided by Marshall Amplification PLC.